D1570724

Divine Enticement

KARMEN MACKENDRICK

Divine Enticement
Theological Seductions

Fordham University Press
New York | 2013

Library of Congress Cataloging-in-Publication Data

MacKendrick, Karmen, 1962–
  Divine enticement : theological seductions / Karmen MacKendrick. — 1st ed.
    p. cm.
  Includes bibliographical references (p.   ) and index.
  ISBN 978-0-8232-4289-4 (cloth : alk. paper) — ISBN 978-0-8232-4290-0 (pbk. : alk. paper)
  1. Philosophical theology.   2. Theology, Doctrinal.   I. Title.
  BT40.M23 2013
  230—dc23

                                                                2012029529

Printed in the United States of America
15 14 13   5 4 3 2 1
First edition

This book is dedicated to my parents, who,
though I doubt it was quite their intention,
taught me all the things a writer needs:
attention to the senses, pleasure in the play of words,
and the importance of good, rich chocolate
and coffee strong enough to stand the spoon upright.

Contents

Acknowledgments

N one of this book has seen print in its current form before, but several speaking and publishing opportunities allowed me to work through earlier versions of the material, to its benefit. David Casey, S.J., the alumni chaplain at Le Moyne College, invited me, along with Ludger Viefhues-Bailey, to give an alumni lecture on faith and new atheism, which drew from Chapter 1. An invitation from Cary Howie to contribute to an issue of *L'Esprit Créateur* (2010) on the topic of sanctity provided an excuse to consider sacramental causality, which reemerges in Chapter 2. For a conference that was part of Boston College's Guestbook project, Richard Kearney asked me to speak about sacramental hospitality; that talk, and the resulting article in the volume *Phenomenologies of the Stranger* (Fordham, 2011), are somewhat differently focused from the ethical discussion of Chapter 3 here, but certainly related. The discussion of prayer in Chapter 4 is the next step in the considerations of prayer that I first undertook in talks given together with Virginia Burrus just prior to the publication of *Seducing Augustine* (Fordham, 2010); for those opportunities, I am grateful to James Wetzel at Villanova University and to the graduate students in religion at Syracuse University. A delightful conference at the University of Bristol, "Desiring the Text, Touching the Past: Toward an Erotics of Reception," proved an odd but fruitful venue for a much shorter version of the chapter here on scripture; my thanks to the organizers, Ika Willis and Anna Wilson. Finally, more extended versions of some of the material that emerges in passing in the Conclusion can be found in two articles, one in an issue of *Postmedieval* (2011) on new critical modes, edited by Cary Howie and Jeffrey Cohen, and another in *Glossator* on the love of commentary (the latter was also the topic of a *Glossator*-sponsored roundtable at the International Conference on Medieval Studies at Kalamazoo, both 2011)—my thanks to Nicola Masciandaro for his invitation to be part of these.

Not least among the riches of my friendships are those that find their way into my work. For their direct and indirect help with the present text, I owe special thanks to a few. Among those with whom I think, and who force me to think better, Virginia Burrus and Bruce Milem continue to be invaluable, not least for the gentle questions and comments by which they constantly save me from intellectual embarrassment. William Robert has endured with grace and good humor far too many obsessive conversations about each chapter. Catherine Keller generously provided me both with conversation and with some of her lovely forthcoming work, which enriched the final chapter here, but also my thinking more generally. Mark Jordan's conversations are always enlivening, and his mention of his own interest in Pierre Klossowski sent me back to some of the texts that have been central to this work. Malek Moazzam-Doulat's mention of Paige Dubois's *Torture and Truth* and Virginia Burrus's citation of that work in her own made Chapter 1 possible. Jordana Greenblatt's fantastic doctoral dissertation, *Words Like That: Reading, Writing, and Sadomasochism* (English, York University, 2010) reminded me of the fabulous Gertrude Stein quotation I use as an epigraph in Chapter 1. Rather than risk missing a name from the many others whose enthusiastic and supportive engagement is the necessary condition of writing, I offer a general but very genuine thanks to all.

The Georg professorship at LeMoyne College has given me for the past two years more time to work, a gift any academic will appreciate. I am likewise appreciative of the chance to work again with Helen Tartar, Fordham's superbly talented and supportive editor, and with the rest of the staff that has made my words into such beautiful books.

Finally, I am grateful, as always, to Alan Griffin, for reasons more extensive and more enticing than I can record here.

Introduction: From the Presence to the Sign

Like a child in its first questions or a lover intoxicated with sharing, the writer grappling with the book does not ask who he is, but whose.

—Edmond Jabès, *El, or The Last Book*

Theology seduced me. I wanted to resist being drawn into its constant uncertainty and intellectual discomfort, but was enticed by its history of gorgeous writing (whether poetically extravagant or mathematically precise) and by the willingness of theological thinkers to take up thought at the limits of thinking, to say at the limits of language, to experience at the limits of the subject. My response has been to try to theorize that seduction—not as a defense, but as a response, as every seduction requires. Theology reaches for our limits, and it opens in our midst, not least in the middle of our saying. "I am interested in language because it wounds or seduces me,"[1] says Roland Barthes, and in theological texts we find the very language of wounding (and a rare source of its celebration) and of infinite seduction. This particular seduction begins in the calling of a name, and continues into ways of reading that name—the strange name of the divine and the strangely reversible, seductive call and response.

To think theology philosophically necessarily creates a certain tension. Much of theology is mythical, by which I do not mean that it is false or make-believe (in the literal sense of making ourselves believe what we otherwise might not).[2] The truths of myth are evasive of other discursive modes, and philosophy, accordingly, has long met them with deep distrust. Jacques Derrida reminds us of G. W. F. Hegel's paraphrase of Aristotle's *Metaphysics*: "Those who philosophize with recourse to myth are not worth treating seriously." Derrida adds: "In a philosophical text, the function of myth is at times a sign of philosophical impotence, the incapacity to accede to the concept as such and to keep to it, at other times the index of a dialectic and above all didactic potency, the pedagogic mastery of the serious philosopher."[3] Hardly an endorsement of the genre, either way, even from one of philosophy's most genre-flexible thinkers.

But this distrust of myth is actually central to the seductiveness of theology for the philosopher, not least where theology emerges as a discipline distinctly elusive of mastery. Seduction does not occur without resistance, a resistance neither denied nor overcome, but sustained in tension with attraction. In the play between philosophy and theology, this tension is best sustained in apophasis, which uses language with such deliberate elusion that it may even speak of the superiority of silence. Barthes situates desire at the seam, the border, of comfortable pleasure and unsettling bliss, which are neither opposed nor identical.[4] The reader of the apophatic text bears no small resemblance to Barthes' "split subject, who simultaneously enjoys, through the text, the consistency of his selfhood and its collapse, its fall."[5] Apophasis says precisely in order to say that (and what) it cannot say. "Pleasure can be expressed in words," Barthes says, while "bliss cannot."[6] Philosophers, where they grant such matters any consideration at all, are better at pleasure, which allows us to clarify its objects from the security of our own subjectivity. But philosophy, accordingly, can be seduced by the subject's blissful dissolution. And that dissolution is most seductive where it is in tension with the pleasure in which our egos are most sturdily secure, in the pleasure of mastering and saying our subject.

My concern with divine enticement—the seductions of theology and of its elusive subject—and particularly with the bodies and words that keep secrets gives somewhat strange form to the fairly familiar concepts taken up in each chapter, concepts that suspend us between consistency and bliss, logical language and stuttering silence. I begin in Chapter 1, following this introduction, with epistemological seduction as a way of thinking the troubled and troubling notion of faith—especially as, to borrow a phrase from both Augustine and Thomas Aquinas, "thinking with assent." This I use to argue against a simple equation of faith with belief, and in favor of a certainty regarding the value of the question. Chapter 2 takes up what are generally understood as signs of the divine, the sacraments. Taking their *sign* quality seriously, this chapter argues that sacraments are a sort of intense sign, signs at their most significant. Sacraments are communal, and take their meaning in communities joined by faith. But the sense of the sacramental may be expanded too: if the world is a sign of God, then any sign could read as sacred—as Augustine in fact held.

If *any* sign can read as sacred, then we must rethink how we read the signifying world and our entanglement with it. In Chapter 3, I focus on the valuative component of this claim by taking up seductive ethics. This has to be done delicately; to mix ethics and theology is, on the basis of rather extensive historical evidence, a dangerous move. I argue for an ethics of responsiveness, and particularly of response to the seductively inquisitive call of beauty—a response, once more, not altogether unlike Augustine's. There is, as I note with the help of Jean-Louis Chrétien, a long Platonic tradition of the ideal of response to the beautiful. This can easily seem simplistic, as if it were ethical to ignore ugliness or suffering, but our response to beauty must include our longing for it in its absence and our pain at its destruction.

Chapter 4 continues the focus on call and response in a consideration of prayer. The question of naming emerges as especially important here; the language of prayer is, at its center, *address.* And as address to the infinite, it calls infinitely to an infinite name. Chapter 5 turns that call around to consider the conversionary power of scriptures, their ability to call on the seducible and to sustain the draw of desire. This they do in some measure, I argue, by performatively promising the story not just of particular meanings, but of how meaning *is*: how signs, including the signs read in those texts, become susceptible of reading at all.

The conclusion returns to a consideration of names, and to the distinction between designation and call central to a theology more seductive than definitive, more enticed and enticing than certain of its ontology. It is not, exactly, conclusive. "Don't be in too much of a hurry to conclude when it is a matter of pleasure," Derrida mischievously warns us.[7] Still less should a seduction rush toward its finish; it is not accidentally appropriate to thinking the infinite.

To begin progressing toward to this non-conclusion, I shall start here with some background in the theory and theorists at work. The theoretical starting point is Augustine of Hippo, whose name has emerged several times already, and in fact my work here first arose out of a frustration with Augustine's own insistence on limiting what seemed to be some of his own most promising (im)possibilities. Not in a traditional sense a negative or apophatic theologian, Augustine in the rigor of his thought nonetheless opens up a great deal of space for just such thinking, not least in the intensity of his desires, both those he embraces and those he fights off. (Apophasis, as Derrida reminds us, can be foreign to desire, such as the desire we have for answers, but it may also "respond to, correspond to, correspond with the most insatiable *desire of God*.")[8]

For many years, I wanted Augustine's vividly described desire to draw his God all the way in; I wanted him to be less committed to maintaining the distinction of creator from creation, to be more of a properly Neoplatonic kind of panentheist. Some of his remarks—for instance, "God is present in the world he is fashioning . . . He makes what he makes by the presence of his majesty"[9]—seem to come so very close to putting the maker in the world, and yet they resist. They resist, even though Augustine has a clear sense of the beauty that permeates the world, of the God who is found—but not *known*—by turning within to one's "true" self,[10] of that truth as Platonic rather than propositional—all of which would seem so much easier with a fully immanent God. In particular, Augustine's views on evil, his insistence that all that exists is good because to be (to emerge from the source of being) is itself good, seem to come tantalizingly close to divine delight in the existence of the world as divine, all-good, itself.[11] I wanted this immanent divine, I have to confess, even as I simultaneously wanted to shift away from the language and the concepts of immanence and transcendence, as I still do. And because Augustine is so engaging and writes so outrageously well, I wanted to find that divine in his work. It always seemed so close.

Yet Augustine is terribly clear in his refusals of the claim that everything is (equally) God and of the easier variants of panentheism, of the world as more or less securely within God, and/or God in the things of the world. Subtler versions of panentheism, though, draw closer to Augustinian thought, and may draw us closer to that thought in turn.[12] But before we can get there, we must acknowledge that the more hostile aspects of his theology—his insistence on human sinfulness, his flirtation with predestinationism—seem to be aligned with his insistence on keeping divine and human separate. So I was drawn to him, but cranky with him too, particularly with him in his own crankier phases. I wondered if I could sort out his loveliness from this irritating *insistence* on distance. I wondered, too, how much I could do work *with* him that wasn't simply work *about* him—that is, whether he offered tools for interesting rethinking or only for something more like an analysis of his own work (fascinating in its own right, of course).

I finally found those tools, and the full force of his thought's attraction, in Augustine's semiotics, as I gradually came to realize that a world that in its beauty calls out the name of its creator (see *Confessions* 10.6, of which much more below) is even more seductive than one in which the creator is simply present, because signs—not least as Augustine reads them—are the very material of seduction, to which that tiny, frustrating, unsurpassable distance turns out to be essential.[13] And when we think that creator as unusually close to the kind of sign that is a name, as named in a tighter and more complex sense than others are named—a strange claim that I shall slowly unfold over the course of this entire text—then we start to get a rather different sense of the divinity "within" and "around" the world: a sense of a call, and a sense of a pull, that do not draw us away from, but inexhaustibly into, what is, not least in its complex entanglement with what is not.

However persuasive, seduction is not rational or logical argument, and, as Barthes points out, the sign is not a syllogism: "Signs are not proofs, since anyone can produce false or ambiguous signs."[14] Augustinian theology is so seductive, not because it argues so solidly, but because it is so significant throughout. Thus reading Augustine began for me a reading of theology's more widely seductive potential, as a reading of its curious semiotics, abstract and carnal at once. This small insight, that signs seduce and that there is in theology a history of reading the world as sign, necessarily blends thinking from either side of the modern.

Readers alert to the relevant conversations will already hear many of the other influences at work. A deeper consideration of Augustinian semiotics demands the inclusion of other thinkers about signs (besides Barthes, these include Umberto Eco and Jean Baudrillard), about distance and proximity and desire (Jean-Luc Nancy, Jean-Louis Chrétien, Maurice Blanchot), about excess (a bit of Georges Bataille, but also Emmanuel Levinas, and traces of Derrida, particularly on the excesses of writing). Pierre Klossowski is primary among those who share a particular fascination with names, a list that includes Blanchot and Derrida as well. I have also made use of a name-obsessed theory of divine signs roughly contemporaneous with Augustine's, that of Valentinian Gnosticism.

I have been more concerned with connections than with canonical status. I suspect, as Patricia Cox Miller writes in her influential consideration of the Valentinian *Gospel of Truth*, "If 'every word unveils another tie,' which requires further words for expression, then the concept of canon as a fixed authority, that is, as a fixed corpus of texts, is mistaken, even delusory."[15] I am interested in an unfixed corpus, as word and body alike—in that which unfixes, unsettles, by the seductive force of its desires. In many ways I take up almost painfully conventional, overworn issues here: sacramentality, prayer, scripture, whether theology has an ethical dimension—but I find that rereading, sometimes through unexpected sources, continues to reveal new pleasures (themselves, often as not, equally unexpected).

Call Me

Desire moves. Eros is a verb.

—Anne Carson, *Eros the Bittersweet*

One thing that all of these sources have in common is precisely seducibility, a willingness to be drawn, though not always to the same things or in the same ways—they all listen to what calls them, and thematize, somehow, that listening. The rigor of their work is itself a response to this seduction, a refusal to settle for an answer because it is easier, an insistence on being pulled further by the enticement of precision itself. I will have much more to say about the question of the draw, or the call, in subsequent chapters, but let me elaborate just a little here, as the image will obviously be a central one. In *Confessions* 10.6, Augustine worries about how he might find God, once he has abandoned the idea of God as a material, spatially locatable being. He claims that he inquired of the beautiful objects of the world as to whether any of them might turn out to be God after all. It is hard to resist the entertaining mental image of the saint-to-be wandering about making serious inquiries of inanimate objects, but in fact his questioning took a different form. "My question was the attention I gave them," he explains. And the answer? "Their beauty [*species*]."[16] They answer in their very form. If I may be forgiven the repetition of the argument I made in an earlier essay,[17] there is a fascinating feedback between call and response here. It is beauty that draws attention, and beauty that answers the very question it draws—but the answer is not at all pregiven. In that beauty, Augustine is not turned away from the world (which would in any case risk a return to his rejected Manicheanism), but is drawn more deeply into it, as a way toward the infinite and elusive "source"—or better, perhaps, the ultimately elusive *sense*—of that beauty. The issue then is not *what* we love so much as it is *how*. (Of course, some whats make for better hows than others.) The best loves have no end to their enticement, and the best love of all is infinite love, which must take the infinite as its object. "In the text, in a way, I *desire* the author,"[18] Barthes claims; Augustine's desire directs itself not out of the world, but all the way into it, in search of the one who has composed its exultant chorus. If the writing of the text is, as Barthes argues, proof of the author's desire for the reader, then the implication of reading the world as written by God is that the world reader is pulled by the reversible draw of divine desire.[19]

R. A. Markus points out that, in Augustinian terms, to love anything less than the divine, the infinite, is to cut desire short:

> To "enjoy" something that is less than the ultimate, infinite satisfaction, that is to say, to allow the will to rest in its possession; or to wish to 'enjoy' it, that is to say, to limit desire to its attainment, without

pointing to a further horizon, is a perversion of the natural and rational order of willing. To allow desire to cease in this way is premature closure of the Christian life, a denial of the restlessness in the depth of the human heart. This is Augustine's way of affirming the necessity of keeping our horizons perpetually open.[20]

That openness is no small part of the seductive character of Augustine's speaking world; seductive desire is not closed off or ended by satisfaction. Augustine on this reading disapproves not of pleasure, but of the separation of pleasure from the unsettling, dispossessive draw of bliss. In a conception that precedes him and will be retained well into medieval thought, Augustine conceives desire as retained in fulfillment, not as satiable or oriented toward its own obliteration.[21] In such desire, seduction is possible.

The strange voice of praise, sung out by the world as beautiful, suggests that Augustine's rejection of an easily intelligible immanentism is more interesting—and vastly more enticing—than I had previously suspected. The whole world *reads* for Augustine as a sign of God; it *says* God to him. This God saying is most marked in the *Confessions*, perhaps, but I find myself in agreement with M. B. Pranger's conviction that Augustine's other works also "contain the basic elements that went into the making of the *Confessions*, in particular, the semantics that prevent them to be read from a merely descriptive point of view."[22] In this thought we hear too Irenaeus, who declares firmly, "in God there is no emptiness, but everything is a sign."[23] This view changes rather sharply in modernity. As Michel Foucault points out, for the modern thinker *only* words are signs, and everything else loses its capacity for significance.[24] We no longer bother to read the world. The world as all signs has just the enchantment that we lose in the later emphases on propositional rationality and production[25]—and not least when we make productive reason philosophically central and forget that there are other ways to read and to reason, other delights to take in other texts.

In most premodern Christian theology, the world is not God. But the traces of God, the signs inscribing the divine name, are everywhere. God "dwells" in the world precisely as the perpetual invitation of and to our questioning, our exploration, our delight. Indeed, every sign becomes a trace, telling of absence and not merely pointing to presence, and this is the sense of sign that allows us to signify the sacred, to read the divine in the ordinary. So too, argues Barthes, the world of the one who loves is saturated with signs,[26] and this coincidence of theology with eros scarcely seems accidental: classically, eros is drawn toward beauty. Derrida is intrigued by the particular sign of the name itself as a trace, all that is left of God in apophasis after its language is emptied of everything that might hold still.[27] This name is a sign of the divine, we might say, but one that fails to provide us with a referent, as the beauty of the world locates its God only as beauty's source, not a thing which is beautiful but a greater beauty that is not *of* something. Nor is this beauty itself a thing. As Denys Turner points out: "In the sense in which atheists ... say God 'does not exist,' the atheist has merely arrived at the theological starting point," from which theologians such as Augustine, Thomas Aquinas, or Meister Eckhart begin.[28]

This deontologization is important against the question that is otherwise raised by a world that is all signs, all significant: if everything points to some God, surely God is the only point—of world and words alike. Surely then the world has value only in its ground, a ground whose security is so extreme that it must leave many of us with an opposing skeptical insecurity. That is, if all signs (and all things) lead us or just point us to a definable God, we rightly say they have no value in themselves. But in a richer and more elusive sense of sign, they don't thus lead us; they are not means to an end but "means" caught up in endlessness; thus from means they become meaning, and every step along the way is a potentially infinite enticement in itself. The world is traced with, and it traces, the elusive sense and sign of a divinity that keeps us from a tidy sacred-profane distinction. All that is is always more: far from reducing the value of the given world, reading it as divine sign multiplies infinitely its interest and worth. In such a significant world, semiotics *could* make sense as an overly secure grounding in the certainty of a creative entity, but it could also (and more interestingly) be read in connection with the negative theologies of God as not a being, theologies that evade the problematic fixity of a divine metaphysical guarantor. They evade, too, a traditional semiotics, in favor of something more mobile and strange.

Semiotics is no longer the deeply theological discipline it was into the early middle ages, but theology retains its semiotic complexity. Even now, we must wonder what, and indeed how, our signs for divinity signify. Jean-Luc Nancy writes, " '*I am God*': it is perhaps impossible to avoid this answer, if the question 'what is God?' presupposes that God is a Subject. And either it does presuppose that—or else it must take the extreme risk . . . of giving no meaning to the word 'God' and taking it as the pure proper name of an unknown."[29] He argues against the presupposition, in favor of the risk: " 'God' signifies: something other than a subject. It is another sort of thought."[30] Derrida wonders, not only of "God," whether the name is even *in* language, and what that could mean.[31] The implicit question here—what kind of name could possibly be proper to the truly unknown; what kind of thought thinks names without subjects and objects—is no small source of enticement in itself, an enticement precisely to thinking, drawing it into the question of its own complex relation to signs and to the limits of its own possibility.

And thought has long been thus drawn. Plato, for important instance, is concerned with—even worried about—the power of words.[32] One might argue as to whether his concern with the inadequacy of verbal signs is properly semiotic, but it does, in any case, carry forward into semiotic theorizing. As Elena Lombardi notes, "Antiquity developed a complete philosophical and grammatical thought on language through the positions of Plato, Aristotle, and the Stoics, the adaptations of the rhetoricians (mainly in the Roman context), and the description and systematization of the School of Alexandria in Greece and of Donatus and Priscian in Rome. . . . This is the grammatical framework Augustine relied upon, and it was solidly maintained throughout the Middle Ages."[33]

This interest in language, and in signs generally, is by no means marginal in premodern thought. In fact, Eugene Vance declares, "The major thread of coherence in medieval culture was its sustained reflection . . . upon language as a semiotic system—more broadly, upon the nature, the functions and the limitations of the verbal sign as a mediator of human understanding."[34] R. Howard Bloch similarly insists, "the place of the language arts is fundamental within the medieval orders of knowledge. Linguistics will lose its centrality at the time of the Renaissance and only since F. de Saussure has it begun to recapture its pride of place."[35]

Language theory is already fairly sophisticated by the time Augustine comes to it, and as a trained rhetorician he would certainly have been aware of earlier theorizing.[36] He adds to earlier theories two crucial elements: the mind of the listener, which interprets the sights or sounds of words; and the theological element in which all signs point somehow to the divine.[37] Augustinian semiotics moves toward divinity—moves, but does not reach.[38]

John Rist writes: "There is no doubt that Augustine's first reflections on signs derive from the older philosophical schools and their more restricted concerns. The Stoics and Epicureans were in sharp disagreement about signs, and Augustine, who took over certain ideas from both parties, offered a very different account of his own, one much influenced by a theory of the nature of a proposition which derived, ultimately, from Porphyry."[39] The emphasis on the centrality of sign to language, obvious though it may seem to us now, begins as almost uniquely Augustinian, as R. A. Markus notes, though it may have its roots in the work of Porphyry's teacher Plotinus.[40]

The Neoplatonic heritage of Augustine's ideas is unsurprising, but here too he develops those ideas well beyond the work of his predecessors. Not all signs are words, he says—smoke is famously a sign of fire, for instance—but all words are signs.[41] As such, they tell us (he'll go on to say that this means that they teach or remind us) of more than they are in themselves.[42] Already we see the seductive potential of signification: *there is more*, signs say, and they draw us in. Words are signs of things, but they do not simply point to things; otherwise, as Augustine notes near the outset of *The Teacher*, a word such as *nothing* would be without meaning altogether, as we cannot quite make sense of the notion of pointing at nothing at all—or, for that matter, at God.[43]

Augustine says that meaningful signification requires at least two stages: "You observe, I think, that everything expressed by an articulated sound accompanied by some significate (i) strikes the ear so that it can be perceived, and (ii) is committed to memory so that it can be known."[44] At work here are sound and memory, then, not seeing and pointing. We must always be alert to the extraordinary complexity of memory for Augustine; words are *committed to* memory, but meaning is *found in* memory, as if it were already there, prior to the commitment of words. There is thus a curious relation between words and the ways in which we learn or teach their meanings. We tend to assume that we learn (about) things when we learn the words for them. But in fact, says Augustine, "a sign is learned when a thing is known, rather than the thing being learned when the sign is given."[45] To use a non-Augustinian example, a child points at a cat and an adult teaches the child to say "kitty"; this does not acquaint the child with felines, but rather teaches it how to indicate their presence (or perhaps its desire for their presence). Thus Augustine declares, "To give them as much credit as possible, words have force only to the extent that they remind us to look for things; they don't display them for us to know,"[46] adding, "when words are spoken we either know what they signify or we don't; if we know, then it's reminding rather than learning; but if we don't, it isn't even reminding, though perhaps we recollect that we should inquire."[47] A word does not teach, nor does a person using words: rather, words and those using them remind us of what we know, or of the absences in our knowing.[48] We find here, as Lewis Mackey says, "a paradox: nothing is taught without signs, but nothing is learned by means of them. Easily recognized as Augustine's version of the Meno paradox, it exploits the duality of sign and significance."[49] The word that gives meaning is created both as an act of memory and as an aid to remembering. Its when is elusive.

Our words in some measure gratify our desire to know, because they "teach" us in the limited sense that they cause us to recall. But they draw out our desire to know, too—ultimately, theologically, to remember what is just out of reach before any memory. They reach toward an infinite meaning, a truth prior to that of any proposition, a meaning they can only and at best approach. And this they do not only when we hear and read them, but when we speak and write them as well, when our words are drawn forth by puzzlement, astonishment, anguish, or delight. Words are drawn by our desire to *be* seductive too, to be worth hearing; not to make the other listen but to make the other want to listen, to want to tell in response to the desire to hear.

The Fall and Redemption of Signs

> If there was only human nature there would be words but they would not be like that.
>
> —Gertrude Stein, *The Geographical History of America*

Words are human conventions, but for Augustine meaning itself is linked to God. That which illuminates, revealing the mysterious connection between signified and sign, is the "inner teacher," Christ, *by whom* we know, yet whom we cannot know fully. This pedagogical interiority functions as a sort of principle allowing us to recognize significance, and to sort it from nonsense as well as from falsehood. Ultimately, all significance has this same teacher not only as its source, but also as its aim or end, "He Who prompts us externally through men by means of signs, so that we are instructed to be inwardly turned toward Him."[50]

This emphasis on Christ as central to signification reads curiously to contemporary semioticians, but it is linked to a widespread late ancient and medieval interest not only in the role of Christian Word, but also in the possible redemption of fallen language. "[T]he Fall," writes Lombardi, ". . . initiates the chaotic dispersion of signs and things, and is 'terminated' by the incarnation, the paradoxical embodiment of the Word that allows for the reconstruction of meaning."[51] This redemptive role is not the institution of some finality, but in fact reinstates infinity, in living things as the release from an ultimate mortality and in signs as the freedom from closed narrative (there is more to say). As sign, Christ is neither some object (or subject) neatly grounding the whole system, nor simply contained within the system as another part. This first and last sign is, rather, what at once grounds and destabilizes signification. The infinite, said Aristotle, cannot be included in any system. For him, this is evidence against an actual infinite; for us, it may well be a troubling of systems instead.[52] What is illuminated by a living sign of infinity is not a space containing meanings, but a path toward the multiple and elusive senses of words. The sign of the infinite keeps semiotics from being a closed system, keeps it in motion,—and this motility is essential to meaningfulness.

In *The Teacher* and *On Christian Teaching*, Augustine's theory of signs is primarily, as Markus notes, a receiver's theory—that is, a theory of how we are able to understand the meaning of what we hear or read (by the inner Teacher's light or guidance). We find a similarly shared-yet-interior sense of meaningfulness in *On the Trinity*, but here language is approached rather more from the perspective of its production.[53] (We should already be wary of too sharp a division.) Here again, the theory of signification invokes Christ, now as an "inner Word" by which meaning is given to language. At first, this inner or mental word seems to be something like a thought or concept, which is subsequently verbalized. Markus cites a key passage:

> The word heard sounding outside is the sign of the word which is luminous within. . . . That word . . . is neither brought forth in sound, nor thought in the likeness of any sound, and need not, therefore, be of any particular language; it precedes all the signs whereby it is signified and is begotten by the knowledge (*scientia*) which remains in the mind, when that knowledge is expressed (*dictur*) as it is.[54]

While the interior Teacher is interpretive, the inner Word is generative: "Where the Teacher interprets the meaning of signs, illumination as here conceived creates the significance with which it endows its objects."[55] Lombardi points out the parallel with Augustinian Christological thinking more broadly. For Augustine, we find the divine at once at a maximum (highest and most distant) and at a minimum (interior) distance: "The meeting between the two is Christ—at the same time the utterance of the Word and the meaning of the interior word of humankind."[56]

We recall that in Christian myth Christ's incarnation is necessitated by humanity's Fall. This too turns out to have a deep semiotic relevance. Augustine's awareness of the seductiveness of words is, like Plato's, often negative, and his concerns with language as something fallen, something that expresses imperfectly and leads us to bad desires, are shared by other thinkers too. This concern is not altogether disconnected from his perhaps better known arguments about original sin. Signs and meanings, like bodies and desires, are fragmented in the originary disobedience of the fall; meaning and will, reading and desire, are shattered together. Will and action are no longer perfectly joined, nor word to meaning; human will is disjoined from divine will, and human language from Word. As Bloch notes, "For Augustine, there can be no distinction between the propagation of men—their increase and dispersion—and the propagation of meaning."[57] The propagation of men (and women) is, of course, the transmission mechanism of original sin: through seminal transmission, Augustine holds, we all participate in the disobedience of Adam and Eve.[58] Meaning propagates in our well-intentioned but inevitably imperfect speech.

So with the Fall of humanity comes the fall of language, and late ancient and medieval semiotics is much concerned with the possibility of a language that speaks again in prelapsarian perfection[59]—a possibility that so lastingly lingers that Barthes can write of "the utopia of language; an entirely original, paradisiac language, the language of Adam," quoting Jakob Boehme to call this speech "natural, free of distortion or illusion, limpid mirror of our sense, a sensual language."[60] The sensory sign and the abstraction of meaning are joined in this mythic perfection. The scene at Genesis 2:19–20 in which Adam gives names is central; some thinkers, such as Philo of Alexandria, even hold that these first names were so exact that they did not differ from the things they named (a sort of ontological onomatopoeia).[61] Here the designation and the call are identical, and the word simply *is* the real presence. Nor is this idea of a perfect original language restricted to Abrahamic thought; Cicero, a great influence on Augustine's conversion to philosophy, believes that things and the words proper to them emerge contemporaneously.[62] Semiotics takes on the function of a search, and once again its aim is its origin: "To signify properly is, within the recuperative, semantically oriented grammar of the period between Donatus [fourth century] and Abelard [twelfth century], to recapture the essence of things before the Fall."[63] All language, it seems, is seeking; the inner Word and Teacher gives it its only chance of meaningfulness, however imperfect and human it must remain.

Here too language and desire are divinely linked. I have argued before that original sin may be read as our distractibility from the fullness and intensity of our desire, our readiness to focus on more fleeting satisfactions.[64] The surprisingly monastic Nietzschean idea that everything worthwhile derives from "obedience over a long period of time and in a single direction"[65] reflects the kind of obedience lost in this lapsing: not to an external authority but to a demanding desire; not contrary to, but a source of, discipline and focus. Where language lapses, desire strays, distracted by short term satisfactions, satisfied by small and partial meanings—something less than the full and proper enjoyment of the divine.

Augustine's hope both for desire and for word is for a return to a proper original fully integrated with reason—though not overcome by it. Despite the deep Augustinian influence on all that follows, my own suspicions of reason and propriety (let alone the idea of a proper and reasonable desire) are too strong for me quite to want to share even that hope.[66] But I do share his concomitant desire for desire, his sense that language makes sense only in the context of desire, his urge for a deeper memory, his sense that semiotics must be incarnationally enfolded, and his ineluctable love of beautiful words, in all of which we must remain aware of the complexity that keeps the idea of return, or of an original, from being a simple repetition.

At the Fall, according to these premodern theories, language is divided from its truth,[67] a truth in some strange sense returned to it by the incarnation. This redemption, however, does not restore a simple unity. Rather, it opens an infinite approach. Within Christianity, the incarnation is the paradigmatic sign of divinity, and the sensuous word is that in which divinity draws and is drawn toward language. This idea is especially developed in some of the less orthodox Christian variants. In comments evocative of the Valentinian *Gospel of Truth* as well, Bloch writes:

> Origen's pupil Denys of Alexandria claims that "the Father, who is divine and universal mind, has primarily the Son for his Word, his revealer and messenger." . . . Eusebius maintains that "the Father murmurs in the ear of man by means of his only son." . . . But even more important, it is Christ, the voice of the Father, who permits a return to pure origin. As the "perfect expression" and source of knowledge of God, Christ the Word restores man to him."[68]

This truth revealed is not a proposition but the strangeness of saying the sacred, the excessiveness called by the name of God. Thus the Fall is understood as the fragmentation of meaning, the incarnation as the rejoining such that meaning and reading are possible again: words are reembodied.

Christ functions as the sign that reminds humanity of significance; more, as the voice that calls back to the divine truth that exceeds its own signing. This truth is not simply a matter of some kind of appropriate correspondence—even as late as Dante, as Bloch notes, we find the theory that "all human language descends from *El*, the name 'which is neither question nor answer.' "[69] Perhaps the postlapsarian division of words is not just their separation from things, but their division from a grammatically provocative *name*. It is not only designation, but still more evocation, that is damaged and in need of redemption.

Few, of course, will be happily willing simply to let lapsed language wander aimlessly in search of its meaning. Augustine's hope in *On Christian Teaching* is that "by following certain traces [the reader] may come to the hidden sense without any error."[70] But what keeps this from simply being a struggle to ground signs in their reference to an absolutely stable metaphysics is Augustine's sense of the richness of semiotic truth-telling, the manifold senses that are hidden in every text. He is a proponent of the concept of "charitable intentionality,"[71] by which signs are to be read with charity—with generous love and in the search for truth. The truths that emerge are many, perhaps inexhaustibly so. The multiplicity of the meanings that we can grasp hints at the ineffability of the meanings that we cannot. From the perspective of knowledge as comprehension, it is a flaw that a given word, and still more a given collection of words in a sentence or longer passage, points in many directions. But if knowledge is more or other than grasping, then it is not only a flaw, or at least not only an unhappy one, that knowing and saying are never comprehensive.

Augustine worries, in fact, about stopping meaning too soon (just as he worries about cutting desire short), about remaining in "captivity" to the sign rather than going on to seek meaning beyond the obvious givenness.[72] Sometimes we refuse to see signs as significant *enough*—we stick with a single, rapidly evident signification, a simple reference. We refuse to be seduced. Ideally, however, a sign continues; by it is set into motion our desire to know the word better—to know its meaning, but perhaps also to know the word itself, its sources, its histories, its sounds. In some simple cases this desire is satisfied by a definition. Sometimes—especially when the words at stake are held not only to refer to, but to come from, the sacred—it is not. Meanings multiply.

Though it sounds rather poststructural, this openness is not the anachronistic imposition it might seem.[73] The importance of maintaining the openness that *silence* is, in particular, has a long history. Though Augustine sometimes warns that it is better to be silent than to speak erroneously or to chatter, the Valentinians make the point more theologically vivid. Patricia Cox Miller explains that in the *Tripartite Tractate*, the *logos* (not quite the Johannine logos-Christ, but an emanation of the divine Father) errs by its well-intentioned effort to *grasp* the incomprehensible divine in words. "From this act of grasping, that is, from the attempt to use language to fix and so limit the disseminative slide of meaning, comes the drama of logos: the 'Father and the Totalities drew away from him, so that the limit which the Father had set might be established (76.30–34).'" That limit is silence, not-saying. The refusal of silence has dramatically undesirable consequences. Miller elaborates:

> What logos created was literalism, a fixing of words to things such that they signify content rather than the search for meaning. . . . The text goes on to show how the creations of this mistaken act on the part of logos are characterized by ambition, desire for control, lust for power, and so on: such are what the desire for fixation unleashes (79.12–32). What logos did not realize, in its refusal of dissemination, was that the infinite deferral of meaning in and by language entails an endless narrativity. Tragically, it was precisely logos' attempt to end the story, an attempt born of the desire to tell the whole story, that produced "little weaklings" . . . (81.1–3).[74]

This insistence on incompletion and multiplicity tells us that we might legitimately think this early semiotics together with apophasis and negation, with the need for silence and not-saying. In so doing, we find a language traced through with reminders of the sacred, never quite fixing the divine, and precisely in that absence continuing in its intense seductiveness and seducibility, aesthetic and intellectual at once. Words may falsely fix meanings, or go forth in search. As Miller continues:

> If full presence—that which the polyvalence of language seems to promise—is perpetually deferred by the disseminative function of words, still the idea of presence functions as a lure—it is what the text desires. Writing is founded in such desire for the other, for the unnameable that words attempt to articulate. If the articulation of this desire yields texts that are only traces of the unnameable, still they are traces.[75]

Language is desirous throughout, and desire is semiotic, and both of them reach toward an infinitely distant, ever proximate divine.[76]

This is not merely an absence, but the *mystery* of the absence that cannot even be represented as such—exceeding the language that is our only access to it.[77] This mystery is not a reductive return to a grounding in being,[78] but language arising out of its own excess, what exceeds and escapes and nonetheless needs it. The rich complexity of this absence and presence, beyond being and nonbeing, offers us a seductive sense of theology that reaches beyond its already intriguing historical roots and into a sense of the exceeding of what is, of what says, of what is said. All knowing is learning, at once novel (we say that we learned something new) and remembered (because the words of our teachers can only remind us). Time too is taken out of a proper order. We find not only a circle of source and *telos*, troubling both terms, but a folding back or a crossing over that returns us to the inner Word and Teacher: that by which we know is that which we are to know. We say in order to tell ourselves what we remember—but sometimes we must also remember to fall silent.

Inside, Outside, and Sliding Always Elsewhere

Who ever desires what is not gone?

—Anne Carson, *Eros the Bittersweet*

Teaching is found within the very act of knowing, which is always learning, always still a search. What we learn inwardly is the very fact of significance, rather than any particular signification.[79] This interior is nonetheless an in-common, as Meister Eckhart (apophaticist par excellence, and much influenced by Augustine) explains: "The word, *Logos* or idea of things exists in such a way and so completely in each of them that it nevertheless exists entire outside each. It is entirely within and entirely without."[80] This Word is at once truth, and that in us by which the truth can be recognized. Such truth is elusive of all saying, yet findable nowhere else but in that saying: it is excessive in a way that defies both immanence and transcendence.[81]

Generation and interpretation cross the same point from different angles—the point at which sign and signified connect, the elusive point at which *meaning* touches. This elusive contact is the seductive power of signs— the power, like that of touch, to awaken us and draw us after it. ("You touched me," says Augustine, "and I am set on fire to attain the peace that is yours.")[82] That by which we know is that which we are to know, and that in turn is that by which we make the words by which knowledge is recollected. We, and words, and the unsayable slide in and around and among one another, crossing and recrossing, enticing.

Both the contact, the slightest lightest passing touch, and the elusion, still reaching, are important. The meaning of the word is never fully grasped. We might think that at least the sensuous sign *is* fully given, that in it, an otherwise evasive abstraction, a concept, is enfleshed in a sound we can hear, a printed word we can read or even touch.[83] But even this is too much; what is given to the senses eludes us by its slip across time—a complaint against the sensory since the pre-Socratic writings of Parmenides, at least. On this argument, we cannot properly grasp any truth through the senses, because by the time we've grasped it, our sensory evidence has changed (even if ever so subtly), and we have to start over again. Perception is not prehension. At first, in *The Teacher* and to some extent in *On Christian Teaching*, material objects appear to be stable, while signs "are granted only the transitive quality of pointing to and reminding of things."[84] But when Augustine interprets the world as all signs, with everything in it saying the divine name in its beauty (saying the divine precisely by what might also tempt us away from that divinity), then stability and intransitivity emerge as illusions. There is an excess to the sensory world too, always more than is graspable or even sayable, always more to draw us on.

If we can't place our hopes for security and stability in the senses, then we might consider the other extreme: that at least the eternal abstract Word is fully (and really) present, even if that presence is imperfectly represented in the sign. But here too we find elusion. The presence of this Word, of the "source" of meaning, is matched by a perpetual distancing, a withdrawal simultaneous or coincident with its approach. Mackey writes (of, interestingly enough, Thomas Aquinas and his famous fivefold proof for divine existence): "The possibility of finite being is the self-restraint of the infinite. Ironically God establishes (the finite in) being by withholding (his own infinite) being."[85] There is not simply some part, not even some aspect, of the divine (being or not) given and some other withheld, but a constant interweaving of what is given and what is withdrawn—such that we cannot, in fact, be certain that they are distinct. The signs of the divine in the world, such as the worldly beauties that draw Augustine's attention, mark this intersection of giving and withdrawing. They are not God, and God is not snugly within them, yet they *tell* somehow; they speak—and that speaking, not least in its demands for attention and question, tells divinity. This telling emanates from and returns to what it tells, yet this is no origin and source. What is told does not remain unchanged by the telling, nor is there some thing sending out and awaiting the return of words. In this complex re-turning beauty can draw us after it; in this, the world seduces us to the divine, not as to a definitive and final goal, but precisely into the in-finite.

We are drawn toward the before of any remembering. Learning by signs, and so knowing by signs, is a drawing into memory, bringing us back to what we "already" know. Memory is where Augustine is sure God dwells ("surely my memory is where you dwell"), even as he notes that "there can be no question of place."[86] We have this knowing only by signs and remembrance; everything tells him of God, but no thing is God. "Language," says Mackey of Augustine, "is properly *commemoration* of the Word."[87] Memory is a continuing draw; the sign is seduced again and further, back before what can be known, into what can only be re-called; which is also to say, what calls us back in turn. The sign is drawn from indication into invitation—into seduction again. It calls us, as Catherine Keller reminds us, always in the flesh: "Theology might be (again?) 'drawn into the mystery of a word that seeks its incarnation . . . in excess of every existing language.'"[88]

What draws is desire too. Desire draws us, and it draws the words that we use and that we find and that we are. "What is . . . important for Augustine," writes Mackey, "—the power that propelled him into language in the first place and, now that he looks back on it, the moving power in all language— is desire. Language is in the service—the converted Augustine would say, in the bondage—of desire."[89] The young Augustine loves the inflammatory power of rhetoric; the older claims to distrust it, but famously, of course, he does so in thoroughly gorgeous prose. That language can willfully evoke desire is fairly obvious. Plato worried about the misleading seductiveness of the poets,[90] and for Aristotle, "rhetoric and logic alike are faculties for providing arguments."[91] Augustine approvingly invokes Cicero's claim that language should teach, delight, and move,[92] but that "movement" part worries him a bit. It still worries us; we speak of twisting words, so that their power to turn us, to move us, works in the wrong direction.

Signs turn and pull us, arouse our desire. The overabundance of signifying gives us always more to wonder and to know. Yet as Miller points out, this overabundance goes hand in hand with an inadequacy: "it would seem that the other side of linguistic plenitude is silence and inadequacy."[93] Words stutter and fall silent, it often seems, just where expressive urgency is greatest. Silence reaches into even the most voluble speech. Language, like thought, is inadequate to the infinite, but in an interesting way: drawn to infinity nonetheless, it is also traced through by what it cannot contain. It does not present the unrepresentable, but it does evoke what can only be called.[94]

What it calls, for those whose semiotics is entangled with theology, is the unsayable divine name, a name that is neither question nor answer, yet both at once: a question without finite answer; an answer to an indefinable query. To be seduced by what is named "God," given the complexities of desire and words, of God and soul, of creator and creation, must mean also to seduce God. In some sense Augustine and the semioticians after him seem to find God everywhere, inside themselves and out in the world. But we do not get any sense that they have found God in a nice, pin-downable sort of way: ah, okay, there it is, now I know. Or: there it is, and not in other places. Rather, we find God as we find what is not there, as neither present nor absent; as a trace, but not simply the trace of a lost presence. This is a presence and an absence indissociable from one another, needing one another, as signs and senses do.

What Do We Call by (Improper) Name?

It is true, I had realized long before this journey that there was much evil and injustice in the world I had now left, but I had believed I could shake the foundations if I called things by their proper names.

—Paul Celan, "Edgar Jené and the Dream about the Dream"

Absence may itself trace the divine name—we find that name too in spaces, and in silence.[95] Such a trace reminds us of a divine distancing, and we are drawn by it into the space of that unfixed distance, a space that can be crossed, but never completely; a space that shifts, made more by dancing than by maps. The divine name does not name a subject, nor an object. Nevertheless, it moves, to call across and toward.

If any sign were wholly given, the divine story would be at an end, the narrative closed as the gift of signification was completed. Instead, words call into the space of language, into the silence that the Valentinian *logos* failed to respect. Silence enters into words as much as words into silence. Michel Foucault writes, "We now know, thanks to Bataille and Blanchot, that language owes its power of transgression to an inverse relationship, that existing between an impure word and a pure silence, and that it is in the indefinitely traveled space of this impurity that the word may address such a silence."[96] The space of the ineffable, the infinite, is in the silence we can only reach toward, only address, with words. Meaning, says Augustine, is gathered in silence after the sentence in which it is found.[97] We do not know what a phrase or sentence means until we have heard it finish—and of course neither finition nor knowing is ever quite completed. The deeply peculiar theological name entwines sounding word and silence together, not in some purification, but in a word that tries to say the silence too, if only by acknowledging how thoroughly it cannot. A name with silence in it is clearly a strange one, and divine names are often associated with a peculiar unsayability that is, once more, not simply an absence (that is, it is not the case that such a name is unsayable because there isn't any such name).

Depending upon our conception of names, we may find fascinating not only the call of the divine name, or its shattering into human words, but arguments against naming divinity at all. There has been a concern in analytic philosophy of religion, for instance, with the question of whether "God" is a proper name, like "Bob," or a title, like "Madame Speaker."[98] The analytic conclusion favors the latter, in a sensible answer that ceases to make sense if we shift calling beyond designation. Philosophy does things with words.[99] Theology does slightly stranger things, not least in the performance of naming, which renders performativity as strange as designation, making both into something curiously evocative. I want to philosophize, theorize, the strangeness without destroying it.

While I will dwell here upon the divine as named, I have to note clearly what has already been implicit: I am using *name* and *naming* in a narrow sense, and a rather improper one too. A proper name in at least one reasonable understanding designates with precision; it is a word that lacks the ambiguity of most words, having only a single referent, and identifying that referent exactly.[100] It is fairly clear that "God" is not a name that designates in the sense in which one could ask, "Where is Bob?" and receive as a legitimate answer "He's sitting on that couch," or "Who is Bob?" and receive as a legitimate answer, "He's the guy on the couch." In this sense, the option "title term" is likely a better one.

From a less analytic perspective, though, "God" *is* a name, but a name in a peculiar and somewhat circumscribed sense, and thus a peculiar sort of sign. It does not exactly *designate* at all; there is no individuated entity to which it might properly refer. It is a name for calling, a name that calls and is called, a name by which we call, but not the name of a thing. Jean-Luc Nancy hints at this in "Of Divine Places": "What is a proper name? Is it part of language? This is not certain, or at least it is not certain that it is a part in the way a common noun is. It does not behave like a sign. Perhaps its nature is that of a *Wink*, of a gesture that invites or calls."[101] *It does not behave like a sign*—except insofar as signs have the happy fault of imperfect always-reaching, not quite referring. The wink is the sign of a distinct yet indirect invitation. Holy names are lacking, says Friedrich Hölderlin; he links this lack to the inadequacy of our joy in divine delightfulness.[102] Nancy plays on this notion: " 'God' is that common noun (that metaphor, proper/ improper by definition) that *becomes* a proper name only when it is *addressed* to that singular existent who lacks a name. It is thus prayer, invocation, supplication or whatever—addressed to the lack of a name."[103] It is the name that calls out to the lack of a name that would fix a designation. It is properly an address, but an address deprived of a designated object becomes rather improper again.

The divine name, then, most commonly for us the word *God*, calls without designation. To clarify: I use "designate," here and throughout, to mean clearly picking out a definite referent; "signify" more broadly to mean functioning as a sign in any sense, including the sense of invocation or evocation. The distinction is idiosyncratic, but I have tried to be consistent in using it (I have undoubtedly failed more than once). The ways in which I use "call" and "address" are drawn from a wider range of sources, and will have to unfold more slowly.

Not precisely a proper name, the divine name (whatever, however, we call it) is perhaps a sort of improper name, a name that does not stay within the constraints of propriety. " '*God*'—what we call 'God,' and not the name Deus/Theos and all its metaphors—is the very name for the impropriety of the name," says Nancy.[104] "God" becomes rather like a nickname, a name by which one is called, but a name that is nonetheless not one's proper name.[105] (The difference, of course, is that people with nicknames have quite proper names too.) We have no proper labels, no fixable meaning or singular sense, but we do not have nothing: we call, and we respond to a calling to which ours is sometimes an answer, sometimes a more complicated question.

Once more incarnation introduces added complexity. Elliot Wolfson notes that, in the *Gospel of Truth*, "The mystery of the incarnation is framed . . . as the declamation of the name of the nameless, the 'great name,' that the Son 'to whom the name belongs' bestows upon the 'sons of the name in whom rested the name of the Father, [who] in turn themselves rested in his name' (38.25–30)."[106] Though it is perhaps most vivid in this line of thought, the intertwining in the name that becomes flesh is widespread in both canonical and noncanonical texts. Again, this incarnation maps meaning. In *On Christian Teaching*, Augustine draws an analogy between speech and incarnation:

> In order that what we are thinking may reach the mind of the listener through the fleshly ears, that which we have in mind is expressed in words and is called speech. But our thought is not transformed into sounds; it remains entire in itself and assumes the form of words by means of which it may reach the ears without suffering any deterioration in itself. In the same way the Word of God was made flesh without change that He might dwell among us.[107]

Without simply identifying body and word, I want to draw on their mutual drawing, their complex and seductive connections. The thought made speech, meaning made sound, like the Word made flesh, does not become something other than itself, nor is it fragmented into its component words or corporeal members. But, as Markus points out, Augustine is surely aware that speaking makes thought, as well: "In expression through language, one gives form to one's thought by words; that is, the saying is also the making of the thought, not just the conveying of a previously existing idea; Augustine's theory of 'word' recognizes some of this."[108] Barthes says that significance "is meaning, *insofar as it is sensually produced.*"[109] On this analogy, then, flesh must be made Word, as much as the W/word made flesh. Only thus can we mean; only thus can we read.

A more difficult analogy between word and Word occurs in *On the Trinity*'s consideration of the luminous inner Word. As Markus explains,

> words are not now thought of as signs of things, or as standing for things; *the verbum quod foris sonat* is the sign of the *verbum quod intus lucet,* but of this latter Augustine never speaks as a sign; and yet, this is, in his view, the "word" most properly so called. Its relation to "words" as normally understood, to the significant sounds uttered when we speak, is left somewhat obscure. Augustine likes to take this relation as an analogy for the union of the divine Word with his human nature assumed in the Incarnation.[110]

The sacred and the sign, the Word and its visibility, draw infinitely toward one another. The letter is spirited not despite, but by its fleshiness. Even the Word becomes sensuous reality without losing any of itself— perhaps even exceeding itself, both as sensuous and as Word.

The sensuous character of signs is one reason to read them as enticing, and to rethink the flesh along with the word. As Wolfson points out, "the body is a complex construct of the imagination rather than a material artifact that can be measured by the dimensions of three dimensional space. The phenomenological parameters of embodiment must be significantly expanded if we are to comprehend the enigma of incarnation, the limitless delimitation of the delimited limitlessness."[111] The Christian incarnation, traditionally understood as a redemption of humanity after the Fall had taken eternity out of human life, is also read as the return of meaning, the ultimate enticement of signs: the divine sign is supposed to call its readers back to both meaning and sense. But here too we must not think that any sign is wholly given.

It is not just the evocative holy names that are deeply strange. Names occupy a peculiar position in sign systems; not only do they call, they may also shift the rules—for Klossowski, for instance, a given name calls out to one that is not simply one (of this, much more in the Conclusion). And names call out not only to, but as bodies when we understand flesh as more than mere matter. This too has its enticements for theology. Wolfson reminds us, "The glory of God . . . inhabits the earthly temple through the agency of the name."[112] Holy names are in divine places (both, says Nancy, now lacking), tantalizingly near to embodiment.

And in fact Wolfson develops several instances in which the association, the almost-identity, of body and name appears in Jewish sources both alongside and prior to its central positioning in Christian thought. He notes, for instance, stories of angels who bear within or incarnate the divine name,[113] and the even more intensely verbal and incarnational Kabbalistic cosmology, wherein "All that is created constitutes one name, which is the name of God formed out of the twenty-two letters that correspond to twenty-two parts of the human body."[114] Though incarnationalism is not canonical in Judaism in the same way as it is in Christianity, and indeed is subject at times to polemical rejections,[115] still, "Just as early Christian exegetes saw in Christ, God made flesh, so the rabbis conceived of the Torah as the incarnation of the image of God."[116] Although the particular versions of incarnationalism differ, there is, Wolfson notes, a kind of incarnational thinking in late ancient Judaism, very possibly in interaction and certainly in interesting resonance with the contemporaneous Christian thought that begins my thinking here.[117] The sense of incarnationalism for these Jewish thinkers is more docetic than realist, but it is not just a term of speech; rather, the very sense of the body is complicated,[118] as it is and must be when we do not begin in separation.[119] Though the world is not conceived in every semiotic understanding as one name, two of the connections made here are recurrent—between names (and, as we shall see in later chapters, between signs more generally) and bodies, and between calling and creation. Understanding the world as divine text means reading the divine name in it, as traced, as belonging somehow to the bodies in which it is always improper, a bit of a scandal.

The enigma of such an address pulls on and eludes language, flesh, knowing. The same words that draw us by their abundantly multiplying meanings draw us as well by their very insufficiency. Frustrating though the sign's imperfection and incompleteness may be, it is also in incompleteness that it allows us to hold open the question by which we seek—and which may indeed be, at the same time, some aspect of the mystery that we are seeking, much as what we seek to know is that by which we are to know. Indeed, as I have suggested, the incomplete, finite nature of words may be something other than a flaw: it may correspond exactly to what words do and even ought to do, which is not merely to show us answers, but also to keep drawing us into questions. If fallen language is language that cannot quite connect, that maintains the space of address, this too would seem to be a happy fault. Desire is sustained in the name called out, even, or perhaps most of all, where that call is a cry of delight.

Seduction

I seek more than the reader's ear. I seek the reader's complicity.

—Marc Augé, *Oblivion*

Desire, crucial to semiotics, is likewise crucial to theological knowledge caught up in the seductive sense of meaning. Such a desire may bring its own delight or a deep dismay in its unfulfillment, or both at once. This doubleness suggests that it might be useful for me finally to clarify the sense of *seduction* that has been (and will be) at work here. We often consider seduction in negative terms, as that which somehow undermines our better faculties (such as reason) to entice us against our own interests. But the term, with its duality of will and resistance, has more positive implications as well—as that which draws for the sake of enticement itself, and not for another goal; as an attraction with the potential for infinity.

Jean Baudrillard opposes the seductive to the pornographic: the elusive, veiled and glimpsed versus the fully presented, obscenely detailed image with nothing to offer that is not already given. The sense of seduction I use here takes from Baudrillard the sense that the seductive is opposed to the pornographic by the latter's finality, which aims at a complete unveiling and equally complete satisfaction, leaving nothing to desire. It tells the whole story, closing the narrative. Of course, nearly any image can seduce or appear pornographic to *someone* (I am not advocating any anti-pornographic position), but some sorts of enticements will, at the least, be more general than others. Seduction draws forth desire with an eye to continuing so to draw, not with some other goal or *telos* in mind.

Seduction is not only incomplete or incompleteable, but inexactly determined. We are not seduced by that which we decide deliberately to pursue—or at least we are not seduced insofar as the pursuit follows from that deliberation. Nor, however, are we seduced by what is imposed upon us against our wills. As I shall note in several chapters, this need for the will's collaboration connects seduction to assent: we say yes to what seduces us. This may well be a complicated yes; the very idea of seduction implies that we would not have gone in that direction on our own, and may even have some reservations. Yet something pulls us onward, and there is something that we enjoy about that pulling.

This possibility that we might have reservations is one ground for regarding seduction as dangerous. Indeed, a reservation unacknowledged is problematic—but not so the fact that some reservation exists. Will is complex, and we do ourselves a nonsensical sort of disservice when we persist in pretending that it is not. Because the will is complex, we may confuse seduction with coercion, but this is indeed a confusion. To play upon the multiplicity of the will (most particularly upon our dual desires for arousal and satisfaction) is not to go against the will as if it did not matter, but to attend to its nuances and its multiplicity with particular care.

Another source of reservations is that seduction has come to be associated with a kind of deception. In fact, nineteenth- and early-twentieth-century American anti-seduction laws (they did exist) were often specifically laws against presenting oneself as intending to marry when one did not.[120] It is true that seduction, even etymologically, leads us where we did not intend to go.[121] But it does not lead us by misleading us. That is: if we are enticed by a lie, then it is the lie, not the enticement, that misleads; we are not wrong about its being seductive but only about its being true. If *only* lies seduced us, that would be a problem, but we lie to be seductive only because the truth is so often boring. I hope to argue for a mode of attention in which we are less often bored without thereby needing to be deceived. For the kinds of thinkers I consider here, nothing is more seductive than truth (which is not only matters of fact).

Perhaps what is bad about bad seduction is actually that it is not seductive *enough*, but rather ends itself by reverting to some aim. That is, it does, on the one hand, seduce us (even "well" in the sense of effectively or strongly) to some particular thing, or place, or position (such as a political position). But, on the other hand, precisely in seducing us *for some end*, it loses its full seductive character, coming to resemble Augustine's "captivity to the sign." The enticement of the infinite is precisely an enticement without end. The signs that draw us entice us because their very nature demands that we go beyond what is given directly; a sign signifies, and what it signifies is not merely itself, nor is it some other thing that is directly presented. The draw of signification connects us to the always-more characteristic of seduction and to the inherence of absence in meaning, of incompletion in overfullness.[122]

The sign may both speak and seek a divine that is a model for a meaning that is infinitely deferred and constantly shifting, even reversing. Foucault points out that, in most cases, a sign "is valid . . . by virtue of this ensemble of all the signifiers which define a language at a given moment."[123] This is basic structuralism, familiar to all of us since Saussure.[124] However, says Foucault,

> In the religious domain one often finds a sign entirely different in structure; what it says, it says by virtue of a profound belonging to an origin, by virtue of a consecration. There is not a single tree in the Scriptures . . . which does not refer back to the tree of the Cross—or to the wood cut from the first tree at the foot of which Adam succumbed. Such a figure . . . [is] bound to the history of a manifestation that is never completed. . . . It presents an image that depends on a forever receding truth.[125]

Words that would speak the divine keep secrets, not least the secret of the source.[126] Precisely in this, as Mahdi Tourage points out, such language emphasizes the eroticism ("a mode of relation predicated on the indefinite deferral of consummation") inherent in all secrecy.[127] The Valentinian *Tripartite Tractate* even suggests that the search for the secret—the search that cannot find—is the divine desire: The unfathomable one "did not wish that they should know him, since he grants that he be conceived in such a way as to be sought for, while keeping to himself his unsearchable being (71.14–19)." Language here "both conceals and reveals meaning," says Miller;[128] language flashes tantalizing not-quite glimpses. "It is this flash itself which seduces," writes Barthes, "or rather: the staging of an appearance-as-disappearance."[129]

The unsayable source nonetheless gives saying—and gives, first of all, naming; he "says nothing; rather, he permits saying."[130] Miller writes here of "the dynamic of desire in language, the desire to name the unnameable that the polyvalence of words animates."[131] Words multiply their meanings, and a divine name ranges strangely, drawing meaning after it, without designating a subject. Seduction keeps in play, wonders toward an infinite meaning, calls an endless name in a voice never quite disembodied.

1

Seductive Epistemology: Thinking with Assent

> Neither a preliminary to reflection, nor a last resort after the exhaustion of
> reflection, but a persistent condition of the possibility of reflection, faith
> inhabits the interim between an origin always already lost and a
> consummation never yet enjoyed. Faith is the first, last, and always word—
> the operative word—of . . . every . . . Augustinian text.
> Faith—that too is not a solution but the name of a problem.
>
> —Lewis Mackey, *Peregrinations of the Word*

There appears to be a curious incompatibility between seduction and any proper sort of epistemology. *Knowledge*, with its firm and enduring grasp of true facts and its carefully maintained distance from opinion, seems clearly opposed both to the reserve, mystery, and elusive play of seduction and to the *un*knowing in the face of the infinite by which even slightly apophatic theology is not inaptly characterized. When we try to think the divine or the sacred, we think that reserve and mystery; perhaps we also think of origin or ground, of joy or ecstasy, or of the world newly revealed as blessed. All of these famously elude any commonsense knowing, even satisfactory expression in words. Yet of course there is a seduction *of* knowing itself. There exists, or more exactly there moves, a powerful will to know, so strong that Aristotle opens his *Metaphysics* by declaring it part of human nature.[1] Philosophical theology, at least, is thoroughly enticed by this desire to know, and theology draws knowledge further without finality, its satisfactions always incomplete, and no less significant for it.

More exactly, the ways of knowing or of thinking appropriate to thinking theologically draw us into a seductive epistemology, a new variant on a definition of faith that Augustine shares with Thomas Aquinas—"thinking with assent" (*cogitare cum assensione*).[2] I do not mean for my considerations of faith here to cover every legitimate sense of the word (in particular, my focus on epistemology differs from the equally legitimate focus on practice and experience).[3] I have most in mind the *thinking*, the cognitive dimension of faith. Yet I also want to note that the element of assent draws such thinking, without losing its intellectual character, close to some other fairly common understandings of religious faith, such as those of trust or fidelity, which can be practical or experiential as well as cognitive.

Thinking with assent is not at all the same as assent without thinking. In his consideration of the Augustinian phrase, Thomas considers the objection that "thinking has no place in the act of faith,"[4] but comes to agree with Augustine's formulation, adding that the kind of belief appropriate to faith "is distinguished from all the other acts of the intellect, which are about the true or the false."[5] Thus, although he uses the term *believe* here, his sense of it is not that of affirming propositional truth-value. For this to make sense, we need first to get past several of the more common perceptions and misperceptions regarding religious faith, most particularly a widespread tendency to identify it entirely with belief, where belief is understood as a weak or ill-supported form of knowledge. "Our" here needs some qualification. Historians and religious scholars have long been aware of other senses of faith, such as the ritual and communal. But philosophers, particularly in the analytic tradition, and the thinkers assembled under the name of "new atheism," do tend to understand faith as a mode of belief—for the latter, in fact, faith can have no other sense at all.

And, of course, there are plenty of religious people who, without being scholarly or academic about it, consider it quite important to *believe*, whether scripture or the proclamations of ecclesial authority, in the manner of facts. At times, this particular understanding has meant, and may still mean, tweaking epistemic rules to allow some unusual things to count as evidence. The insistence that scriptures tell strictly historical stories, for instance, or that they explain the emergence of animal species, would count in this category. Crucial to a seductive sense of faith is the resistance to the often fearful certainty that would make faith into a desperately determined belief: a constant and necessary openness to *question*, a willingness to dwell in questioning, in mystery—and so in a sense of the sacred, as the complication of the world by divinity.

This is an openness with a long history, philosophically as much as religiously. The Socratic elenchus arguably aims not at establishing knowledge, but at the very aporetic wisdom that reminds us that we do not *know*—a wisdom often difficult and painful, but always open. Sean Kirkland writes of Plato's *Apology*:

> Socrates does not say that knowledge or wisdom of any kind concerning virtue is the greatest good for a human being. Rather, this status is reserved for precisely that *daily, repeated, always frustrated, and thus endless discussion of virtue* that we find portrayed throughout Plato's early works. . . . Indeed, it would seem that the constant, elenctic, *aporia*-producing and sustaining questioning of Socratic philosophizing, and thus even a certain self-conscious way of *not possessing knowledge or wisdom of "what virtue is,"* is what is supremely good for human beings.[6]

What draws us into this self-conscious dispossession is not some force applied to us, even through argument, but a non-presence that is compelling precisely in its hiddenness or distance.[7]

It is this dispossessive element, and not the more received Platonism of absolute stability, that makes its way into the more intriguing theological traditions. As we saw in the introduction, Patricia Cox Miller points out that for the Valentinians the attempt to grasp that of which one is necessarily (not just incidentally) ignorant actually intensifies ignorance—ignorance, and not knowledge, is aligned with what is solid and fixed.[8] The very possibility of comprehension, of holding on firmly, belongs to ignorance. The question at issue (the question in question, perhaps), the question of divinity, is not one that lends itself to answers. As Maurice Blanchot says, the "profound question" fascinates and lures us because it "is such that it does not allow one to understand it; one can only repeat it, let it reverberate on a plane where it is not resolved but dissolved, returned to the void from which it arose. This is its solution: it dissipates in the very language that comprehends it."[9] It is, he says, "not extinguished by what answers it."[10] We recognize here on the epistemological plain the echo of divine desire, which is undiminished in fulfillment. Intellectual desire is always entangled in the inextinguishable question.

To this most profound, insistently open question I would add an equally necessary, if perhaps paradoxical, counterpoint: in faith there is also the unquestionable. This does not mean the certain or secure.[11] I mean rather that there is a deep, somehow ineluctable sense of the very importance of mystery, a sense that we cannot avoid the agonies of doubt and the joys of wonder by foreclosing them either as stupidly misconceived (a scientistic response, such as we find in "new" atheisms) or as already answered (a religiously rigid response, such as we find in many fundamentalisms). The faith is in the questioning, but it is grounded in this necessity, this unquestionable sense that the question matters, that there is reason to have trust in it, reason to be faithful to it.[12] In this tension faith emerges as something other than "belief" as we ordinarily consider the term, that is, as a commitment to affirming the truth value of certain propositions regardless of the lack of evidence for them or the presence of evidence against them. Faith emerges, in fact, as a seductive epistemology.

As we have already noted in the Introduction, such faith is so far from confident declaration that it may appear close to an a-theism. Derrida's remarks on apophatic theology are applicable here; apophasis, he says, "is a declaration, an explanation, a response that, taking on the subject of God, a negative or interrogative form (for that is also what *apophasis* means), at times so resembles a profession of atheism as to be mistaken for it."[13] Yet it is precisely not a profession of anything but faith itself; it "suspends every thesis, all belief, all *doxa*."[14] We are drawn into the space of that suspension.

Belief Beyond Justification

Faith means making a virtue out of not thinking. It's nothing to brag about. And those who preach faith and enable and elevate it are intellectual slave holders, keeping mankind in a bondage to fantasy and nonsense.

—Bill Maher, *Religulous*

Religion is nothing but bad concepts held in place of good ones for all time. It is the denial, at once full of hope and full of fear, of the vastitude of human ignorance.

—Sam Harris, *The End of Faith*

"Thinking with assent" is (at best) intellectually problematic if we assent a priori not to *thinking* but to particular *thoughts*—if we have already agreed to believe in a way that actually forestalls full thoughtfulness or open exploration. This version of faith, as belief clung to in the absence of evidence or even the presence of counterevidence, is tenaciously opposed not only to many other beliefs,[15] but to doubt. Doubt becomes less an epistemological state than a sign of sin—or at least of the potential for it. Doubt's openness makes room for the temptations of evil thoughts to enter.

This opposition of faith to doubt, odd though it may seem, is also oddly popular. To take a particularly vivid and fairly contemporary example, late in 2007, a book by the title *Mother Teresa: Come Be My Light* caused something of a stir with its revelations of Teresa's uncertainty, her doubts not only about her work but about the very God to whom that work was dedicated. Evidently these doubts provoked not only astonishment, but concern as to whether the push for her canonization, which had even begun pre-mortem, was appropriate. Could a saint doubt? Articles in the respectable popular press abounded—*Time* magazine, the *New York Times* and the *Washington Post*, among others, published opinionated pieces. At first doubt emerged in these as antithetical to sanctity, because it was likewise perceived as antithetical to faith. If the saints are the most intense among the faithful, mustn't their doubts about an existent (and even interventionist) God lead to our doubts about their saintliness?

Rebuttals from those with a sense of religious history came swiftly. Exemplary among them is the op-ed piece from James Martin, S.J., in the

New York Times Magazine, which appeared just before the book's publication and evoked saints John of the Cross, with his "dark night" of abandonment, and Thérèse of Lisieux, who said of herself that she was "plunged into" darkness.[16] In Martin's response, and indeed widely in thoughtful religiosity, doubt emerges as opposed to faith only in particular ways—it becomes a sort of strengthening test, or a pain by which the faithful identify with passionate suffering.[17] Doubt is not, then, something that destroys faith, but a step on the way to making it stronger, rather as minor illness can lead to a sturdier immune system, or fatiguing exercise to a greater muscular strength. But in this response, "faith" is still identified with certainty, or at any rate with steadiness of belief, belief accompanied by affective security and trust. Doubt is seen not as a necessary part of such faith, but as something that is very likely to emerge within the struggle to maintain belief, and which, when it does, may be turned to faith's purposes. Certainty is still the goal, the point. This is much more apparent, of course, where faith is linked to doctrine more strongly than to rite or practice, as the former offers questions of certainty both more clearly and more often (doubts about the value of rite do emerge, of course, and the next chapter will take them up).

The appeal of certainty and security, whether in belief or in affect, is reasonably self-evident. We don't, mostly, like uncertainty and unsettledness, and so we retreat into comfort even if we have to construct that comfort by strong-willed denial.[18] If we dwell in secure belief, we are spared not only uncertainty, but a lot of mental effort. Stubborn belief offers the security of knowledge without the pesky evidentiary requirements usually attached.

As I briefly remarked above, the idea of faith as belief, knowledge, or some odd in-between version of the two is strong not only in the popular consciousness, but in some, especially analytic, philosophy of religion as well. Here faith is identified with believing in the existence, the identifiable being, of (a) God, and the questions asked about it tend to center on the nature of that belief: What kind of belief is it; does the will enter into it; does it have ethical (or other) implications beyond epistemology and metaphysics; and, for many most importantly, is it *justified*, and if so, how? Alvin Plantinga, for instance, argues that belief in God is "basic," not grounded in other propositions. He is not impressed by dis-proofs of that existence, but neither does it make sense to him to require proof in turn.[19] William Alston defends the evidentiary value of direct religious experience, provided it occurs and is believed in the context of a reliable "doxastic practice."[20] Paul Moser argues for the role of volition in religious epistemology, but his emphasis in that epistemology is still on belief in God's existence.[21] John Bishop's lesser-known but rather elegant *Believing by Faith* argues for a version of fideism as an ethical epistemology, in which we hold religious beliefs (centrally that God exists) to be *morally* justified, rather than insisting upon external evidence or justification for them.[22]

To the modern (and often to the contemporary) mind, and not only in its analytic-philosophical versions, the unlinking of faith from belief seems absurd, and, at a casual first glance, historically improper. After all, theological thinkers have for millennia linked God to truth, and don't we believe what we consider to be true? Further, there are Christian creeds from very early on that seem to provide evidence for the central role of belief: "We believe in one God," begins the fourth century Nicene Creed (*Credo in unum Deum*, says the Latin Church). The more ambiguously dated "Apostles'" creed opens with the declaration "I believe in God the Father" (*Credo in Deum Patrem*), while the slightly later (perhaps sixth century) Athanasian creed declares that if one would be saved, the first requirement is holding to the faith: "Whosoever would be saved, before all things it is necessary that he hold to the catholic faith" ("*Quicunque vult salvus esse, ante omnia opus est, ut teneat catholicam fidem*").

Catherine Keller reminds us to be cautious about credence. To be sure, she writes, "Creeds are a meaningful mode of theological compression. They certainly make 'open statements of the truth.'"[23] In fact, they may be haunted by the open relationality of the flesh of the world and the divine: "it matters whether an imprint of the materiality within God and the God within materiality can still faintly be read from the Nicene origin. And surprisingly, it can."[24] Yet in the very creeds just cited, there is the potential for a worrisome foreclosure:

> The problem comes when that truth becomes absolutized as "the faith": as, for example, in "whoever desires to be saved must above all things hold the catholic faith." Faith here means a set of metaphysical *beliefs* about one God in three persons. . . . Such conciliar statements

often waxed uninhibited in their threats and curses, or "anathemas." . . .
Truth was turned into a belief to which you must assent—or be
cursed, denounced, excluded.[25]

The truly seductive credo, if it is to lead without limit, must do something
other than to compel and foreclose belief, as the creeds have so often done.

Wilfred Cantwell Smith argues for a limitation on this insistence upon
belief as central to credal faith. The senses both of what it is to "believe"
and of what "truth" as the object of belief might be, he argues, have under-
gone considerable historical change. (Recall Thomas Aquinas here: faith
does not have to do with true and false.) The notion that every sense of
"belief," whether or not it has a religious or theological element, must be
a propositional attitude—that is, that it consists in regarding as having
the logical value "true" a particular proposition (generally expressed by a
sentence)—is really a rather new one, taking its firmest hold in the Enlightenment and not much loosening its grip since. The "truth" with which
early Christianity identifies its God is not the truth of a proposition, but
the Platonic truth as such, that from which truth is—much as beauty is,
and goodness. We tend to conflate our modern "true" with this "truth."
The early identification of God with truth takes the latter as the very truth
itself—not something that *is* true, as propositions can be, but as something that is *truth*, from which all other truths of the world derive their
veracity. One believes that a proposition is true, but not a god.[26] How,
though, might this fit with what seem to be terribly propositional claims:
"We believe in one god," and so on? Still more obviously, can one really
argue that "we believe" does not mean that, in fact, we hold these truths to
be evidentially supported?

One can, but with some care and no small acknowledgment that other
uses of "believe" are exceptional. For most of us, and maybe for all of us
most of the time, "belief" *does* denote a propositional attitude, in which we
implicitly regard propositions as expressing correctly some part of a real
state of affairs. (We may thus regard them explicitly as well, but this is not
required; many of our beliefs are unexamined.) Smith argues, however,
that the primary classical use of "credo" is "to entrust, to commit, to trust
something to someone"—also "to lend" as in money. Credence in this sense
is an intellectual entrusting. He adds, "A secondary meaning in secular

usage was 'to trust in,' 'to rely upon.' . . . There had also developed a derivative usage wherein *credo* meant 'to believe' (usually a person); but that was tertiary. To believe a proposition was quaternary and relatively rare."[27] The creeds' earliest use, he argues, is liturgical, as in the dedication of oneself marked by baptism, which entrusts one to God and community. They mark commitment to a new way of living, rather than to a new set of beliefs. Indeed, says Smith, "Contrary to modern impressions, the classical creeds of the Church include no propositional statements."[28] They do not declare "we believe that there is," but rather "we believe *in.*" Smith's argument here seems a better fit, then, with the fiduciary senses of faith that I shall shortly discuss than with cognitive versions. But there is in that very *in*, that sense of commitment, no small cognitive possibility too.

The English word *believe*, says Smith, similarly begins as a verb of allegiance and dedication[29]—thus, our problem arises not from poor translation, but from semantic shift. One does not believe in one god (or anything else) as an act of accepting a proposition, but rather as an act of devotion. Or, perhaps, the propositional sense is the one that Keller identifies:

> Theological truth . . . cannot be captured in propositions, no matter how correct. But neither does it happen *without* propositions. . . . Theology—not the truth it seeks—comprises a shifting set of propositions, frayed and porous at the edges. . . . To propose is not to impose, but to invite. A proposition may be more like an erotic appeal than a *compelling* argument: we get propositioned![30]

We get propositioned; we are invited into.

Indeed, we could argue that even before the *credo*, faith leads not teleologically *to*, but, as David Miller etymologically notes, into. He points out that *pisteuo*, based on *pistis*, "is never followed by the preposition 'in,' as our translations would lead us to believe. It is always used with the preposition meaning 'into' (*eis*). Hence, where we read 'believe in,' the original text literally means 'faithing into.'" We might hope that a creed and a *credo* will continue that active enticement, but Miller warns, "The problem of mistaking faith for belief arises because Latin, French, English and other Western languages do not have a verb based on the noun meaning faith. Latin has *fides* for 'faith,' but the verb meaning 'to believe' is *credere*."[31] The problem with credence, perhaps, is not its sense per se—its devotional, directional sense—but our tendency to still that sense, to let it lead to belief and stop, rather than to lead into question and continue.

Jean-Luc Nancy writes of a kind of faith he finds suggested in Heidegger, which is: "Neither firm knowledge (science) nor weak knowledge (belief). Neither belief in God, nor belief in man, nor belief in knowledge, nor even in art. Yet a firmness, yes, and a fidelity, even a *devotion* [*dévouement*] in an extraordinarily strong sense of the word (an act of 'vowing or—voting oneself' the way one de-votes oneself to a task or to a devil)."[32] This is a faith in which devotion to the divine is expressed in statements that grow stranger with every reflection. It is possible for this devotion to take all manner of forms. It may simply be affective; it may be practical (which may in turn be a matter of ritual practice, of an entire *ethos*, or of many points in between)—and it may be epistemological, too.

Epistemologically, I have begun to argue, faith is devotion to question, to mystery—a claim, of course, that works best for faith with an element of apophasis and negative theological devotion. But this makes for some deep weirdness: how would one dedicate oneself to what is not, to what does not exist, except perhaps as a gesture of absurdist futility? Does the move from the modern English sense of belief to devotion or dedication really just conceal the former within the latter, necessarily *believing* "God exists" as a prerequisite to devoting oneself to that God? It seems fairly evident that we need to look more at the mode of this devotion—and at the deeply peculiar issue of whether it has an object. To devote oneself to the open question is an odd sort of effort.

Noting, as many have, that belief "is in no way proper to religion," not because there are no religious beliefs—of course there are—but because most beliefs have nothing to do with religious matters, Nancy makes a provocative suggestion about faith, asking: "Should it not form the necessary relation to the *nothing*: in such a way that we understand that there are no buffers, no halting points, no markers, no indeconstructible terms, and that disenclosure never stops opening what it opens (the West, metaphysics, knowledge, the self, form, sense, religion itself)?"[33] In the modern and contemporary sense of the term, we *believe in* what is, in the ontological clarity of entities and the truth value of propositions. In the sense for which Smith and others argue, we *believe in* that to which we devote ourselves. We *have faith in* this "disenclosure" or unceasing opening, where clarity is closer to illumination than it is to comprehension, or rendering definite: where we are drawn into. Our devotion, then, is to an infinite opening: no thing. Intriguingly, we are returned to Merleau-Ponty, who notes that seeing, speaking, and thinking all form "the repeated index, the insistent reminder of a mystery as familiar as it is unexplained, of a light which, illuminating the rest, remains at its source in obscurity."[34] The mystery, the question, the enticing enigma is also what makes sense of much that is itself clear. Clarity needs mystery too.

Not least mysterious is the question of that "repeated index" that seems nonetheless not to point. Even if the affirmation of existence as the sort of attribute we affirm of some object is logically permissible,[35] it properly eludes theology. Even in the straightforward-seeming Aristotelian logic of a Thomas Aquinas, as Denys Turner notes, the proofs that "God exists" must mean something elusively strange—"they are meant to show that we are bound to have lost most of our grip on the meaning of 'exists' as thus predicated of God."[36]

This leads us into some of the cognitive or epistemic strangeness of faith, the peculiarity that attaches to its propositions such that no standard sense of belief can quite attach to them. Staunch believers (in the narrowest sense) and devout atheists (staunch dis-believers) alike err not in the propositions they affirm, but in their certainty that those propositions, "God exists" or "God does not exist," have ready, familiar, easily definable meanings—that whatever is called "God" exists or fails to exist like a rosebush or a unicorn. The point here is not that we don't know enough of the details about God to be confident in what sort of being God is, or what sort of attributes God has, which we might with proper information affirm or disavow. It is rather, and more deeply, that we don't know what *existence* is in this instance—but we also don't seem to have a much better term available. The One, says Plotinus, is beyond being and not-being. Perhaps that is better, but it is certainly no less elusive. Pseudo-Dionysius says much the same of the Christian God, who at the pinnacle of existence nonetheless cannot be said, in the manner of beings, to exist.[37] If we were affirming propositions, this would be a problem. If we were devoting ourselves clearly to a figure of power or authority, it would remain a problem. But if we are devoting ourselves to an infinite opening, to the strangeness that haunts propositions, the questions that haunt answers, seeking that necessary relation to dis-enclosure, it need not be. Indeed, to take such openness as an object of faith (of devotion, of what propositions or entices us even in affirmative theological claims) is necessarily to dwell in the absence, not of affirmation, but of the illusion that affirmation has given us answers.

To shift this devotion or affirmation is also to shift our sense of the right ways of saying, so that we speak to search and not simply to declare. No small part of the problem of faith is the extent to which our search for verifiable truths has excluded us from myth, or from poetry, where language is at its most evocative, its most deliberately aporetic even as it may be at its most precise. As Mackey puts it, modernity creates "a demand for literal language univocally transparent to being, coupled with a corresponding renunciation, or relegation to the exteriority of poetry, of all the forms of figuration by which, as in Holy Scripture, the truth is obscured and the deceptions of priestcraft are sheltered from critical inquiry. . . . It is difficult for us, moderns that we are, to resist the rhetoric of liberation by which modernity has presumed to define itself."[38]

The difficulty is all the more pronounced because we so often conflate evocation with obscurity, and that obscurity with downright malicious confusion. Thus we come to associate faith precisely with a refusal to seek light, with eyes clenched shut against The Facts. Reason regards itself as liberating precisely in this respect; the light that shines in the darkness is that of reason devoted to the understanding of facts. Immensely valuable in its own right, this view of light and of truth becomes a problem when we assume that it is universal, not just in the sense of being shared across different people (it is), but in the sense of being the only right thinking. This makes us assume that faith too has claimed the possession of such truth, is engaged in such reasoning, but is doing it extraordinarily badly by resting in received wisdom and not bothering with exploration at all. This stance must be critical not only of faith as rigid belief but of the openness to query—the former for its inflexibility, the latter for a lack of rigor. As Mackey continues, "Faith, however, is inherently and essentially, even if not all professors have honored the fact, a self-critical stance."[39] I want to argue that it is self-critical not simply because it is willing to alter its answers, but because it is implicitly, inherently, *about* questions—and about the sense that questions matter. Faith is not simply a lazy contentment in not getting around to answers.

Religious faith seems to me more proper to the kind of truth that poetry is, with its spaces and silences, its openings and interruptions, than to our popular image of the kind of truth that science is (though I find that scientists themselves are far more open and curious and contentious than their popular image suggests). Poetry, as I have elsewhere argued (not terribly originally, so I trust that the point will not be controversial), makes use of the power of language not merely to designate, but to evoke.[40] Asked the meaning of a line from "Ash Wednesday," T. S. Eliot is said to have replied, testily but accurately, by repeating the line.[41] This is not a truth that establishes—it is a truth that opens, or, to use Nancy's term again, dis-encloses. I am not suggesting that we must write poetry in order to do theology; either one is hard enough. But I do want to suggest that in thinking theologically, we might do well to treat words poetically, as openings. And that in this sense, the language of faith is poetic—evocative, provocative, and unsettled.

Such poetic theologies find themselves drawn, too, to that same strange puzzle of in/existence. Exploring the wide range of thought that has come under the heading of "theopoetics," David Miller notes the centrality of responding to the notion of the death of God—whether that response is to view the notion as something we are now past, as if unambiguously negative, or as properly attributed to religion rather than to God proper.[42] We may find a "theopoetry" in "an artful, imaginative, creative, beautiful, and rhetorically compelling manner of speaking and knowledge that is and always has been in our possession and a part of our faith," Miller writes. But we may also think a "theopoetics" as it emerges from "the continuing impact of an understanding of the times as severed from any dependencies on transcendental referents."[43] A seductive theology must take up a bit of both, never settling in a transcendental—nor, for that matter, an immanent—referent; engaged by the artfulness, the unendingness, in all language, even that as clumsy as Augustine once thought Christian scripture to be. Theopoetics has long linked back to apophasis, attracted to the notion that faith and the speaking of it may assent to the very limits of thinking without thereby being reduced to meaningless nonsense.

In sum: faith is done a grave and slightly silly disservice in its modern reduction to propositional belief. Even what the faithful seem, in devotion to truth, to believe—to affirm propositionally—turns out to render the proposition so strange that it becomes not a declaration, but an inquiry. Before we can get to more details regarding that inquiry, however, we ought to look briefly at a few other traditional versions of faith, versions that will help to complicate the sense of thinking with assent.

Trust and Fidelity

I really want to say that a language game is only possible if one trusts something. (I did not say "can" trust something.)

—Ludwig Wittgenstein, *On Certainty*, §508, "What Can I Rely On?"

One reason that faith is so readily linked to stubborn, evidence-proof belief is that (like seduction) it clearly participates in will as well as in intellect. (Thomas Aquinas is concerned, in his exploration of "thinking with assent," with whether will or intellect is proper to faith.[44]) So, we easily think, faith could mean the displacement of intellect by will, clinging to belief by sheer stubbornness. The devotional senses of *credo* and *believe* in Smith's work likewise emphasize the willful aspect, as does the "assent" of thinking-with; the *yes*-sayer in assent is the will, the faculty and the force of desire. The other traditional senses of faith on which I'll touch here emphasize the involvement of the will, as either fidelity (being faithful to) or trust (having faith in), or some combination of both. The sense of faithful rite and practice I shall leave until the next chapter, which takes up the particular signifying practices of sacraments. Neither version of faith quite captures the combination of volition and intellect by which I would wish to characterize a seductive *epistemology* of faith, but, like the sense of proposition when we turn it to enticement and not just declaration, they will not turn out to be irrelevant either.

If I say to someone, "I have faith in you," it is quite unlikely that I mean "I affirm the truth of the proposition 'you exist.'" In fact, it's pretty unlikely that I even mean "You exist." Rather, I am likely to mean something like "I trust you" (to do what, or to be what, will vary), or "I believe that you can accomplish what you intend to." This kind of credence is faith as trust. Often, this plays out as a sense of the rightness and the power of divine will and action.[45] Acquiescence to this power can be immensely difficult, and so the danger is that what faith as trust ends up meaning—though seldom overtly—is something like "we believe that a God exists who will what we want, as we think is right."[46] In a less cynical version, this faithful trust covers the assumption that there is a divine plan according to which all unfolds, such that we may be sure that what happens is good, regardless of immediate appearance or the pain it may pose for us. Or, more simply, that there is a God who will keep us in some ultimate sense safe, that our good or at least the good matters. (In this we may also hear echoes of Socrates, who believes that goodness cannot be damaged, as the only harm that could come to it would be to make it something other than good.[47]) This, as much as rigidity in belief, can account for the sense of certainty that may be attributed to faith. Our resistance is grounded only in our incomprehension. Such faith is often a source of great comfort to those who hold it, and of corresponding frustration or annoyance to those who do not.

The view of faith as trust is most strongly associated with Luther, for whom this trusting faith (along with some propositional beliefs) is also the source of justification—so profoundly associated that the Council of Trent, deeply irritated with all things Lutheran, declared the emphasis on trust (or, to be fair, the emphasis on trust as solely constitutive of faith) to be anathema.[48] This attitude of trust is quite distinct from the anxiety and rejection of unpleasant facts that so easily characterize belief. It is classically opposed not to skepticism so much as to cowardice. Keller glosses Mark 4:40, "Why are you so cowardly? You still don't trust, do you?" by noting, "We glean from Jesus' irritation that the opposite of faith (*pistis*, trust) is not doubt, but *cowardice*. Faith here signifies a trust that is kin to courage. It cannot be identified with belief, with knowledge, with any stash of propositions."[49]

Trust also makes more sense than belief for those who would argue that it is our doing, our choice, whether we have faith or not: one can choose to trust much more readily than one can choose to believe, though our human experience of the former reminds us of its difficulty. And trust can be manifest not only in one's attitude toward a God as an entity, but also, both ethically and epistemologically, in an openness to what comes in the world, a sort of anti-paranoia. "It is the attitude that appears in all the wariness and confidence of life as it moves about among the living. It is fundamentally trust or distrust in being itself," says H. Richard Niebuhr, "an ingredient in all knowing."[50] Of course, at its extreme, trust slides into a more worrisome fatalism or quietism, excusing us from further action once our trust is engaged, but its lesser degrees seem less problematic, especially where they do not entail a predetermined divine plan.

Clearly this is no insignificant sense of faith. But is this "thinking with assent?"—does it have both cognitive and willful aspects? Assent seems clear enough, and the standard elements of will—desire and decision— are clear too. But the intellectual component of trust is harder to ascertain, unless we want to make of it a trust in a certain kind of knowing. John Calvin does something like this: "As soon as the minutest particle of faith is instilled into our minds, we begin to behold the face of God placid, serene, and propitious; far off, indeed, but still so distinctly as to assure us that there is no delusion in it."[51] In this assurance, we may also be sure that "Faith consists in the knowledge of God and Christ."[52] Karl Barth echoes and endorses the sense of *certainty* that "knowledge" implies, and argues for living in a trustful security: "In God alone is there faithfulness, and faith is the trust that we may hold to Him, to His promise and to His guidance. To hold to God is to rely on the fact that God is there for me, and to live in this certainty."[53]

Trust seems to become problematic only when trust becomes certain that it knows what it is trusting, slipping back into the troublesome smugness of narrow belief rather than entrusting itself to unknowingness. This is not unseductive: we sometimes wish things were nice, and easy; that there might be a plan behind the evident chaos is indeed an enticing thought. But the easy provides at most a brief seduction, not a continuing enticement, and so it may be inappropriate to the infinite. A seductive trust, a trust in seduction, must allow us to be drawn, must assent to enticement without security in a certain *telos*. It is the sort of trust that allows us to be propositioned.

At least one more traditional answer is apropos. If we understand trust as faith-in, its flipside is fidelity-to, being trust-worthy.[54] Fidelity is opposed not to doubt, but to what has long been conceived as a sort of theological adultery in idolatry. Nancy links, as one must, this fidelity to a sense of trustingness:

> Christian faith is distinguished precisely and absolutely from all belief. It is a category sui generis, which is not, like belief, a lack of . . . a dearth of . . . , not a state of waiting for . . . , but faithfulness in its own right, confidence, and openness to the possibility of what it is confidence in. What I am saying here would be perfectly suitable to our modern definition of faithfulness in love. . . . This is even, perhaps, what we mean more profoundly by love, if love is primarily related to faithfulness, and if it is not that which overcomes its own failings but rather that which *entrusts itself* to what appears to it as insufficiency.[55]

It appears to be something like fidelity for which Augustine struggles in the prelude to his conversion, as he attempts to channel and unify his scattered desires. Such fidelity is not simply an absence of mis-directed desire but the actual, active force of desire divinely directed, an attentiveness found as much in his response to beauty as in his more overtly religious practices. Religious faith as fidelity would be the direction of desire to God—a definition that still leaves a great deal to be decided, but which must include an active attentiveness and an absence of, at least, intentional rejection.

But the existential puzzle emerges again: in being faithful, is one not assuming, thus implicitly believing, in the existence of the one to which one is faithful? Just possibly, instead, might we be faithful to thinking, and to the kind of thinking that leads us to think of the sacred, the kind that that persistently finds wonder in the world? We could then believe in being pulled by the seducing-opening; trust not in a clear outcome but in the value of the draw, be faithful not to a list of commandments but to the sustained difficulty of honoring the enticement. I want to argue that to trust in thinking, to be faithful to its movement, to seek knowledge, is to assent not to a fundamentalist foreclosure, but to the openness of the question, which preserves, I think, some of the character of the revelatory or epiphanic, which also grant a sense of an opened world. But "question" here may still be a little too vague. Let us ask after it more precisely.

So What Was the Question?

> For thinking is a movement, a process. . . . To think of something, especially thinking of it continually, is to be ever transforming it.
>
> —Stephen Theron, "Faith as Thinking with Assent," *New Blackfriars*

Many thinkers oppose questioning quite directly to belief. Jacques Ellul, in *Living Faith*, seems at first not to; he declares that faith (particularly faith in scripture) is not what provides answers, but rather what questions us. Revelation (for him the proper object of faith) is, he argues, not explanatory but rather meant "to confront us with questions . . . to get us to listen to questions."[56] Thus queried, we are obligated to responsivity, and to the risks that responding entails.[57] Ellul, perhaps like many earlier Christian thinkers, says of faith that it *knows*, by revelation, the existence and power of its God; what it *doubts*, under that same revelation, is the rightness of its own acts and knowledge.[58] His doubt has an Augustinian edge; he too has become a problem to himself.

This gives new sense to the link between faith and doubt. Here doubt is not merely a contrary of faith that can function as a strengthening test of it. Rather, at least some kinds of doubt *are* faith, are what it means to be faithful. To be faithful to divine revelation, in this view, is to place oneself always in question. This seems a promising start. Security in or firmness of knowledge, though, remains a problem—it is promising to find an open question here, but the question of God, the sense of "God" as a question, appears to be foreclosed.

Still, Ellul is right to emphasize the *direction* of the question—it matters a great deal who is asking, who is being answered, and who must do the answering. Questioning can line up on either side of authority, of possession, of power. The very term *inquisition* reminds us that those with power may arrogate to themselves the right to wrest information from other, however reluctant, subjects. In *Torture and Truth*, Page duBois argues for an unexpected link between epistemology and metaphysics, in which our very understanding of what counts as knowledge is linked to our cultural history of violently extracting "truth" in the form of confessions from the bodies of "others," most notably slaves. Truth is conceived as what matter—reductively understood, even in those living bodies—hides within it.[59] It is the job of the torturer, or the metaphysician, to rip truth out of the bodies that hold it or hide it. In this view, truth is never immediately evident, and the task of those who would *know* is not merely discovery, but uncovering. Tracing this line of thought from Plato through Heidegger, duBois quotes the latter on the former: "At first truth meant what was wrested from a hiddenness. Truth then is just such a perpetual wrenching-away in this manner of uncovering."[60]

DuBois traces the history of violence as it is linked to the idea that truth is elsewhere than, or hidden by, what appears, especially when what appears are bodies. In this theory of truth, to know is not only to see, but to denude and so to see what was once invisible, to make the world reveal without reserve. (It is, to return to Baudrillard's terms, to deny seduction in favor of the pornographic.) Just that reserve, however, is essential to the character of the divine, which tells us not merely that there is more than we do see, but that there is more than we can see; it demands we allow the possible, the inquisitive, the strange to draw us into asking and to give answers that question us back. We do not cease to ask, but we can no longer assume that an answer is a possession, or that it is the sort of thing that will hold still in our grasp.

The very idea of divinity as the always-more that seduces our thinking suggests that this violent unveiling or denuding may not be the only option for inquiry. It is at least possible that there is also a rather different implication to the notion of the truth as hidden (or at any rate never utterly revealed): the incomplete revelation of truth (the impossibility, indeed, of anything like "completion" in revelation—or in truth) is what allows us to allow ourselves to be seduced. DuBois' historical outline throws into relief the importance of care in the kind of questions and style of questioning we choose.

The torturous approach presumes two things about questions: that they can be answered, and definitively at that; relatedly, that they are possessible and assignable, to be asked by those with power and answered by those with less. We think of authority as the possession of answers (to be authoritative is to have the final answer), but there is authoritative power, too, in being the one who asks the questions. It is certainly a play for power to claim to have all the answers, but "I'll ask the questions here" claims authority just as strongly.[61] On this version of truth as hidden but knowable by forced revelation, the question is not, and must never be allowed to become, reversible. One does not inquire of the inquisitor. This is a theologically dangerous authority, too—the power of the Inquisition, after all, is claimed by the church.

The inquisitor as torturer, the one who will rip out the truth, avoids the perilous reversibility of the seductive question, in which any query is on the verge of turning around and subjecting the questioner to another question, of opening up a question that might force the questioner not just to admit to incomplete knowing, but even, sometimes, to have been asking the wrong sorts of things to start out with. Suppose that we reject this model of inquiry; suppose instead that we and our world are perpetually and mutually in question and under question: that we do not simply interrogate it, but live open to its curiosities, and ours; to being questioned, but also to being enticed by questions, letting them present themselves and seeking them out avidly. Asking how to know, how to say, we shift from declarative discourse to inquisitive conversation, with its more relational, less propositional logic. We shift, that is, to an Augustinian interrogation of the world, which is answered by the beauty that calls forth the question; and away from interrogation under torture, which demands an answer and will tear the world apart in order to get it. We question by attention, and what our attention finds will draw our questions further.[62]

Inquisitive attention always opens further questions. In this is what Turner calls theology's childishness. The contentious issue between theology and atheism is not one of belief, he argues, but rather

> the legitimacy of a certain very odd kind of intellectual curiosity, about the right to ask a certain kind of question . . . the sort that you can make sense of asking, but not a lot of the answer. They are, if you like, rather infantile questions: adult questions are questions you have some sort of control over, questions you have disciplined procedures for dealing with, since the sense of the questions determines what kind of answers stand as good answers to them. . . . Scientific questions are adult, intelligible questions demanding sensible answers arrived at by explicitly controlled methodologies. Theological questions, on the other hand, are childish.[63]

Like the questions of bright children, they are asked with an eagerness not only for hearing answers, but for asking more. Turner adds, particularly apropos of Thomas Aquinas, that the theologian, like the child,

> asks the question "why?" once too often, where "once too often" means; when there is no intellectual possibility of understanding an answer . . . where language itself has run out. And that, for Thomas, is where theology begins. . . . Philosophers seem happy enough to say, after Aristotle, that philosophy begins in wonder. Alas, all too often their philosophy ends with its elimination. Instead of leaving us, as it were, in a condition of *instructed awe*—what Nicholas of Cusa called a *docta ignorantia*—it leaves us instead with Russell's blank and indifferent stare: that there is anything at all is just a brute fact.[64]

The infinitely iterable "why" of theologian and child is grounded in a dual amazement: at the sheer fact of somethingness, on the one hand, and at the nothingness that dis-encloses, as Nancy describes it. That the world *is* is astonishing, wonder generating. It astonishes when we attend, and what is wondrous about it is what draws our attention. Absence is mysterious, enticing, but so too is what there is; it is in this interplay that the world opens up to a query that never intends to get to the bottom of it, for which more is always possible.

Of course Nicholas of Cusa, with his instructed ignorance,[65] must be among our exemplars here. Nicholas argues that, although we need affirmative theology—statements about God—for the purposes of worship, the denials of negative theology, telling us only that God is not that, come closer to "truth," which is to say, closer to God. (He is not, of course, unique in this claim; Pseudo-Dionysius, to take only one famous example, argues something similar.[66]) Nicholas says that God's ineffability arises from divine infinitude: "Sacred ignorance has taught us that God is ineffable. He is so because he is infinitely greater than all nameable things."[67] Keller links Nicholas's knowing ignorance to "a constructive theology, but one already assisted by the uncertainty, indeed the aporetic undecidability, of deconstruction . . . which does not relieve anyone of the need to decide."[68] There is a seductive double pull here, decidable against undecidable, belief against faith, confidence against uncertainty. We need the pull of the paradox, not some simplifying resolution. And for Nicholas this is the only way to "know" the divine: "For you," he says to God, "have shown me that you cannot be seen elsewhere than where impossibility confronts and obstructs me."[69] Theology is just this confrontation—and the willingness not to avoid it. Just this, but with an important inclusion: the child's *delight* in the question, the thinker's delight in assent when an answer arrives and the space for a brand new question is thereby opened.

To question and be questioned—to be seduced by the question as knowledge in the form of possibility—is central to faith within a seductive theology. To "know" the divine in and indeed as the profane is not to apprehend with confidence, but neither is it to relax in easy ignorance. It is, rather, to assent to thinking, which is not nearly as easy as it sounds. And it is not to assent to some knowing either removed from the world or ripped out of its flesh, but rather to pay attention, to pay attention to the question and to being questioned. The desire for knowledge that takes the infinite as its object is itself an infinite desire. Turner even argues that, for Augustine, "the love of learning *is* the desire for God."[70] Query seduces us not out of the world, but more deeply into it, into its play of signs.

The paradox is built in and fairly obvious: we seek the reserved, the mysterious, the infinite as at once breaking, speaking through presence and as already withdrawn. But if we think that we have found it, that we have stripped away its veils and seen its secrets, then we have not, in fact, found the reserved or mysterious at all; we have, instead, destroyed it. To seek the mystery, then, must be not only to wonder, but to continue to seek to wonder, to seek to continue to wonder. And that must mean to seek both questions *and* answers, because the desire to find answers is no small part of what it is to wonder or ask questions in the first place. The answers have the character of never being quite enough, never quite perfect, and this is both our frustration and our delight. Answers, when we have been seeking them (when we have been thinking), have the character of revelation—they seem sudden; they delight and astonish us; they make new sense of old facts and narratives. Pseudo-Dionysius writes of the Christian incarnation, "Sudden is what comes against all hope and thus passes from shadow to light. As for what concerns Christ's love of men, I believe theology uses this term to indicate that the hyper-essential has gone out from its secret and become manifest to us in assuming a human essence. But it is also secret beyond this manifestation, or rather, to speak in more divine fashion, in this manifestation itself."[71] The secret is in the manifest, not as hidden beneath or behind, but as part of it, as the revelation of its character as worthy of wonder. (Seduction, argues Baudrillard, has nothing to do with the distinctions between latent and manifest content.) We do not break open what is given to find what is hidden about it.

This is an epistemology in which we "know" as much in seeking to wonder as in wondering's objects. "Wonder," too, retains its dual sense. First is the perhaps casual inquiry of "I wonder if" which is potentially (though by no means necessarily) violent, allowing the acquisition of knowledge to the benefit of the subject alone. But there is also the "I wonder at," the sense of astonishment.[72] This dual wonder seeks a kind of knowing not easily reducible to the logical or empirical facts that count as knowledge to the modern mind. Mackey, writing again of the incarnation, says "Augustine of course was not trying to prove the existence of God either *ex parte Dei* or *ex parte creaturae*. He was composing the metaphor of the Incarnation. . . . His philosophical theology was an expansion in rational terms of the mystery of faith, a mystery Truth itself had revealed, speaking as Man to men."[73]

So the truth revealed (incompleteable and always seductive) in theological wonder, the truth divinely enticed, is a revelation not of fact, but of mystery; the truth of such a theology does not declare doctrine but composes metaphor, even poetry, with its own power and its own sense. As Nancy concisely remarks, "All the questions thus aroused continue to yield to scholarly and complex investigations that leave an infinitely fragile but resistant kernel of obscurity intact."[74] This too is a notion at once contemporary and premodern, with a conspicuous gap at modernity. Mackey dates "the beginning of the end of the Middle Ages" to the literalist interventions of Etienne Templar in 1277, which condemned, he argues, not only particular propositions, but "the whole of Christian metaphor." As a result, theology moves from its poetic sensibility into something "literalistic and positivistic, consisting more and more of the simple univocal affirmation of Scripture and creed. Luther's insistence on the *unus simplex solidus et constans sensus Scripturae* is the end of that way in theology."[75]

The open query, attention to wonder and the entanglement of beauty with truth, demands a poetic theology, one that sustains possibility as more straightforward discourse does not. Affirmations and negations of faith become poetic statements—statements that, like Eliot's "three white leopards sat under a juniper tree," mean just what they say, yet the meaning of which is perpetually elusive. As Smith has it, "*Not* to believe ancient doctrines is as old-fashioned and as unintelligent as to believe them. . . . The problem lies not in the doctrines, but in conceiving of them as beliefs. This is the modern West's most massive reductionism."[76] One does not believe a poem; one is, however, seduced by it, precisely by its irreducibility to literal and comprehensible paraphrase. So let us turn to the openness that the question, like poetry, sustains when literal language falters. Certainly one of the most troublesome propositions to emerge is one we have briefly considered already, particularly in relation to the poetic, the one so often held to be the fundamental faith-defining belief: God exists.

Poetic Existence: Divine (Not) Being

It is precisely because there is nothing within the One that all things are from it.

—Plotinus, *Ennead* 5.2, "On the Origin and Order of the Post-Primary Beings"

The poet Edmond Jabès puts strikingly the puzzle of existence and belief.

"Whether God exists or not is not the problem," Reb Yasri admitted, scandalizing his audience.
"If I believe God exists, it does not prove He does.
"Not believing so in no way proves that He does not.
"If we have been able to imagine God it is because we are able to conceive of Him and to drown in our own invention.
"God remains out of reach, entrenched in His mystery and safe in His secret."
And he added: "Mystery and secret are but the vertiginous distance between a recognized word and an unacceptable set of phonemes."[77]

It seems a foundational difference between atheism, on the one hand, and theism (or perhaps even agnosticism), on the other, whether one finds poetic questions as they reach toward the out-of-reach mystery interesting and is seduced by them, or whether one instead finds them irritatingly and quickly dismissable, a pathetic effort to cling to belief by redefining the most basic of terms, such as "is." I will not pretend to resolve nor even to persuade in this distinction, but I do want to explore what it is that catches hold of the intellectual will in those who are indeed seduced by such queries (and who, accordingly, find the "-ism" of theism a bit discomforting). It is easy to dismiss as illogical these claims of mystery and imagination, but that assumes they were meant, in the first place, to be logical propositions—and often specifically existential propositions. In fact they seem rather more to be dialogical: their open spaces, their elusive meanings, invite a speaking back.

Retaining our sense of a knowing more interrogative than declarative, let us consider this sense of existence in a conversational mode; let us consider the play between wonder and ineffability, the question and answer, the call and response. Immediately upon asking the question of God, we are confronted by the most puzzling of responses—by poetry and indirection, and within them also by silence—that is, by all the sorts of things that raise (further) questions. The best thinkers of divine questions, of divine names as naming those queries, are as well our best thinkers of silence. The French Nietzscheans, perhaps bearing in mind Nietzsche's insistence that we approach some matters with clean-handed reverence, have been particularly drawn to the questions of silence in speaking. Bataille notes of "silence" that it is a self-denying word, an apophatic word, we might un-say, unable to keep itself.[78] Blanchot further remarks upon the impossibility of silence *kept*.[79] In *Dis-Enclosure*, Nancy offers the converse of this insight: "In order to keep language, in both senses of the word *keep*, one must except oneself from its *goal-oriented* regimen. That which withdraws from the injunction of sense reopens the possibility of speaking."[80] Neither language nor silence admits of keeping, of grasp; each requires its own withdrawal into—and yet its own opening of space for—the other. Yet in them, through them, we find meaning. Is it any wonder we so readily conceive of God as word?

In *Reluctant Theologians*, Beth Hawkins writes of Paul Celan, "All at once the speaking God of the covenant is superseded by the mystical, silent God, but a trace remains, a longing for a dialogical relationship."[81] This trace is epistemologically essential; it is our own desire at play in the seduction of meaning by the sacred, as the sounds of praise and prayers are drawn into silence. Our dialogue speaks with silence—not a simple absence, but the silence within speaking.[82] We enter this dialogue in questioning and in question, gradually realizing that the only trace of an answer leads us into further query, raising questions in its silences and sounds.

This opening-up series of questions means that we are not deceived by the catechismic simplicity of the inquiry, *What is God?* Nancy, reading Blanchot (no one thinks silence more lucidly or more elusively), tells us why:

> Blanchot . . . neither asks nor authorizes any "question of God," but he additionally posits and says that the question "*is not to be asked.*" This means that it is not a question, that it does not correspond to the schema of the demand for the assignment of a place within being ("What is . . . ?" or 'Is there . . . ?"). God is not within the jurisdiction of a question. That does not mean that he falls within an affirmation that would answer the question in advance. Nor does he fall within a negation. It is not that there is or is not a God. It is, quite differently, that there is the name *God*, or rather that the name *God* is spoken. This name corresponds to the *statement* of the question, whether it is a question of the being (the "What?"), of the origin (the "Through what?"), or of the sense (the "For what?"). If all questions intend a "what," a something, the name *God* corresponds to the order, the register, or the modality of what is not, or has not, any thing.[83]

The very name is the name of a question; faith called into this name is faith in the tug on the mind, on the intellect and the memory, that we find and we feel in the thought of the divine. "God," says Jabès, "is a questioning of God."[84] The name is a question, and the question calls. The faith is in the naming, which is not to be confused with decisive declaration.

Names are language's most seductive sounds. It is not (merely) that they pick out more specifically than other nouns do, but that they *mean* otherwise; they call toward, they draw in, and most profoundly when they name something as seductive as the question. Nancy points out that for Blanchot, the name *God* can either impose itself "as the keystone of an entire system of sense," (the assumption of those who critically identify theology with a stabilizing and ultimate metaphysics), or it can reveal the "nonsignification of names" as it names "a sovereign power of the name that beckons—which is very different from signifying—toward that absenting of sense such that no absence can come to supply a supposedly lost or rejected presence."[85] ("Signifying" here has the sense in which I've used the term "designating.") The divine name beckons us to the limit of language, to the withdrawal of sense, to the place where we lose our ways and meanings.[86]

In this curious connection, in the way that inquiry finds its answers in silence, the negativity of theology becomes important; this is where, as Blanchot notes, we are in relation with what properly excludes all relationality: "what we owe to Jewish monotheism is not the revelation of the one God, but the revelation of speech as the place where men hold themselves in relation with what excludes all relation: the infinitely Distant, the absolutely Foreign. God speaks, and man speaks to him."[87] Of course, Blanchot, as clearly as anyone, will link that speaking to silence. Like Augustine, Jabès too reads the infinite in the unknown—"There is no unknown but is infinite."[88] Nancy's discussion of the thought of the infinite likewise shows its apophatic connections; thought demands that we think that there is something beyond our thinking.[89] All of these famous thinkers of the question are thinkers of the divine precisely as query.

But how can this silent, nonontological divinity, this God in absence and exile and yet in traces, be the God of Augustine's exuberantly overflowing beauty, a divinity of delight and not only of bewilderment? For Christianity, this query only renames the recurrent puzzle of the incarnation. Nancy writes:

> With the figure of Christ comes the renunciation of divine power and presence, such that this renunciation becomes the proper act of God, which makes this act into God's becoming-man. In this sense, the god withdrawn, the god "emptied out," in Paul's words, is not a hidden god at the depths of the withdrawal or the void (a *deus absconditus*): the site to which he has withdrawn has neither depths nor hiding places. He is a god whose absence itself creates divinity, or a god whose void-of-divinity is the truth, properly speaking.[90]

It is thus we find the divine doubly in the world, where it speaks to us and where there is silence—but it speaks to us of silence, and the silences intercut and resonate within all of poetic and theological speaking. Theological language means right up to its incomprehensible edge, where it opens onto other questions, makes space for other words. And this, necessarily, in the flesh, with all its transience, its elusion and decay, its embodiment of loss. This is the carnal truth of the *logos*.

We know this at the edge of unknowing, as Blanchot remarks with no small echo of John of the Cross:

> Understanding seeks what escapes it, and advances vigorously and purposefully towards the moment when it is no longer possible: when the fact, in its absolutely concrete and particular reality, becomes obscure and impenetrable. But that extreme limit is not only the end of comprehension, its moment of closure, but also its opening moment, the point at which it illuminates itself against a background of darkness which it has brought to "light."[91]

When thinking is thus pushed, or drawn, to its limit, we must, says Nancy, attend to what is revealed.[92] In language close to Blanchot's, he declares, "the same requirement of reason emerges insistently: that of casting light on its own obscurity, not by bathing it in light, but by acquiring the art, the discipline, and the strength to let the obscure emit its own clarity."[93] Clarity illuminates the very mystery that it also requires. Thinking that is drawn into questioning must itself always be questioned. The open as such, the sacred possible, is not found solely in the abstract, but in the materiality of the world and its voices, human and otherwise, in relation and in conversation. The difficult openness of listening, which will be crucial in the consideration of seductive ethics, has its place in the consideration of epistemology too. In his discussion of "learned ignorance" (a term he attributes to the Socratic tradition), Chrétien writes that all we have of knowledge is "that there should be a question, that I should allow myself to be dispossessed of what I thought I knew by the words of the other, which are thus the occasion of a reciprocal openness. In other terms, what is at stake is what the Socratic tradition calls learned ignorance—the act of knowing what I do not know. Knowing that you do not know means knowing how to learn, knowing each time how to learn."[94] That to which we must be open is encounter: "knowing each time how to learn means encountering the other and allowing the other to encounter you and speak to you."[95]

What we have to offer is not mastery, but insufficiency, and therefore openness itself; we make, we even are, here in our flesh, the space of revelation—endless revelation, not some final truth to be found by tearing away the mysterious. What we know is never quite ours; it is that to which we listen.[96] We can approach inaccessibility, the reserve and remove of everything other, with impatient and univocal demand, or with mutual and seductive engagement (or, of course, we may do our best to ignore it altogether).

This openness to the question is not about indeterminacy alone; it is an openness to mystery. Paradox, suggests Mark McIntosh, "might recall a way of speaking about and understanding God that seemed to have been lost among the deists and free-thinkers, a way of living in relationship with mystery that patiently exposes the mind to what it cannot grasp."[97] Exposure involves not simply questions that we happen not yet to have answered—not even just those we aren't yet sure how to answer. It is uncomfortable in our usual epistemic culture: "In such a culture of knowledge, there is no real room for the radically new or other or incomprehensible; everything is massively clear, explicable, quantifiably appreciable. . . . This kind of formation does not *really* have a use for the ability to encounter the unknowable."[98] This ability is constitutive of faith.

Of course, this doesn't sound like what most people consider faith, any more than it sounds like what most people consider thinking—let alone the thinking or cognitive aspect of faithfulness. As I've noted, it is easiest to read "thinking with assent" as not really thinking at all, but rather, at most, presenting a proposition to oneself as something prejudged to be true or real. That is, assent to truth value has already been given, and the thinking is thereby narrowly constrained. One might consider various aspects of the proposition, maybe even some of its implications, but not its truth.

Aside from the problems noted above in considering religious truth simply to be a matter of propositional belief, this kind of assent seems to provide a kind of security and to try to hide a measure of fear: the "yes" is less a fullness of assent, still less of curious and delighted assent, than a "no" to the consideration of any other possibility.[99] Here the encounter with mystery is forestalled. But thinking with assent is *not* providing in advance the answers to one's questions (thus keeping them from being questions at all), but assenting to thinking—whatever we may call it. "God" is the name of the question, which makes it a reversible name, a name that calls. It calls to language; it calls to thinking. And sometimes thinking says *yes*, answers to that call with assent; says yes to the name of the question, and not as an answer to abolish it.

Assent

> ... tho' he is under the world's splendour and wonder,
> His mystery must be instressed, stressed;
> For I greet him the days I meet him, and bless where I understand.

> —Gerard Manley Hopkins, "The Wreck of the Deutschland"

The link between questioning and negation, between infinite inquiry and negative theology, is mirrored by the question's link to affirmation. Assent is the converse, not the antithesis, of negation. It is essential to a sense of faith as fidelity, including fidelity to thinking, where commitment is maintained and reasserted.[100] As Smith writes, "Faith . . . is 'assent' to the truth as such, in the dynamic and personal sense of rallying to it with delight and engagement. It is the exclamation mark in saying not merely 'yes' but 'Yes!' to the truth when one sees it. It is the ability to see and to respond."[101]

For contemporary readers, the philosophical name most readily associated with assent, with the *yes* (and the exclamation mark, too), is Nietzsche's. For Nietzsche, affirmation is thought together with repetition, specifically with the infinite repetition of eternal return or recurrence. To say *yes* at its fullest is to say it infinitely: that is, to say *yes* to a "tremendous moment"[102] is to assent to that moment so profoundly that its infinitely repeated return, just as it is, can be affirmed with joy and without hesitation. To say yes, then, is to will to re-will, to say, within a moment of desire, that desire must multiply itself, always will this, again. Thinking with assent cannot be simply a thought held as already finished.

Two consequences of this link between repetition and assent are relevant here. The first is simplest: in such an affirmative moment, we also, I think (going beyond what Nietzsche has to say, and affirming Freud's rather commonsensical point that pleasure brings with it a desire for repetition), will "smaller" or imperfect repetitions, repetitions that are not precisely of this moment, but of things very like this. If, for instance, I am thus transported when hearing music, I am likely to want, and to want rather intensely, not just this moment infinitely, but in a more mundane way to hear more music that will have a similar effect, or even to hear this composition again (and again and again, in some cases, until the neighbors begin to object).

The second is more complex. As I shall note in more detail in the conclusion, Pierre Klossowski, in his enormously influential reading of Nietzsche's eternal recurrence, argues that a real "yes" to any moment must be a yes to every one of that moment's possibilities. That is, any given moment splits off in inexhaustibly many possible directions, only one of which we experience as actual. Yet a full affirmation of the moment in its own fullness must mean that we affirm this shattering, this infinitely other possibility. Far from closing off any other option, recurrence actually *opens*, demands the opening of, such options.

Both of these points bear upon the concept of thinking with assent. To begin with the simpler point, questions, however open, are in search of answers—at least where those questions are not purely rhetorical, not posed with their answers already in mind. The point of the infinite question is not that it is divorced from the answer, but rather that it approaches the answer with an openness to further questioning. It is restless—but this is not to deny the profound delight and excitement of answers, or insights; of thoughts that work. In this childlike query is a delight both in asking and in hearing, coming upon, answers. This *pleasure* is the assent to the revelatory moment, with its accompanying eagerness for repetition. Like other pleasures, these delights of the intellect bring with them a desire for more. But, to remind us of the obvious, we can't have more of them without going back to the question, without descending again into the obscure. When we assent to thinking, when we assent in thinking, we assent as well—indeed, we demand—questioning, and puzzlement, and doubt.

This we do in a richer and more complex sense than is immediately apparent. In affirming what we might not too unreasonably call a moment of truth, a *yes* in thinking, we affirm not only the possibility of not reaching that moment or of the insight that doesn't hold up (these are always discouraging), but of every other answer as well. Real assent cannot foreclose other answers in the way that fearful belief must do. Affirmation says of its insight: *this is* so great that, so long as this is, anything else may be: in the actuality of this answer, we find also the possibility of every other; it is this openness of possibility that we affirm. This in no way implies that the answer affirmed, the revelation, is in itself irrelevant. Openness cannot be taken for indifference; "yeah, whatever" is at best the bare minimum mode of assent. The affirmation says, rather, "this is worth anything" with an intensity that pushes it into the paradox of opening to the pure possible (which cannot, as I shall note later on, be quite clearly distinguished from the impossible). When, for instance, Augustine reads the opening lines of Genesis toward the end of his *Confessions*, he reads with this kind of assent: with an intense and prolonged attention, with answers that themselves elude any chance of comprehension (the "formless," for instance, persists in presenting itself falsely as a blobbish sort of form)—with the knowledge that every answer opens questions, and with a willingness to allow other answers that in no way undermines his own.

Here we may return to belief. There is, of course, an element of belief in affirming what is so fully that we affirm it as the space of the possible. It's not that we cannot assent to what is not, but we assent to it precisely in that mode of not-being; we wish for it, which is an assent with dissent, a refusal of what is in the desire for what could be. When in a moment of insight I say *yes!* to an idea, I *believe* that the idea is in some way right, or true, or good. The problem with simply translating this fairly evident point to a "belief in God" is that where the very notion of what it might mean to exist is problematic, so too is the notion of what it might mean to believe; where we "believe in" mystery, every answer returns to the question. Faith becomes, then, a faith in the worth of questioning, of the reserve of mystery itself. The delight of thinking with assent is complicated by and implicated within the struggle, the darkness, of its own necessary and negative condition.

There is trust here as well, but, again, not in the sense in which we might most readily think it. Trust, we have seen, can be narrowly constrained; when we trust someone or something, in many cases that trust is to a specified end ("I trust you to get this project done on time"), and in others an expectation of a kind of behavior ("I trust you to behave professionally"). These simple senses of trust suggest the confidence that control has, a confidence in an outcome that accords with expectations. Yet trust also assumes a willingness not to manage and control. The most irritating aspect of the epiphany is that it cannot be forced. It comes, as Nancy says of the gods, or it does not come.[103] We can only be hospitable, and in this we are already vulnerable to the dangers of that which arrives. Fidelity to the question is just this hospitality.

It is oddly popular to assume that if one believes in—that is, propositionally affirms as existent—just the right God, one will get prizes, ranging from riches to weight loss to inner peace to eternal salvation.[104] This is a crude reduction of trust, however. Just as fear and foreclosure of hope ground "belief" blinded to alternatives, so too are they foundational in the "trust" that a divine assistance will yield exactly one's specified result. An epistemological trust, however, must emphasize trust's element of openness, its willingness to cede control—the element that precisely does *not* guarantee outcomes and answers. We must be cautious to avoid the contrary reduction, as well—among those matters not guaranteed is some divine plan or reason to which even the most bizarre or disagreeable event may be attributed. We trust simply in the value of what we pursue and of what comes upon us; we are faithful not to a truth already seized upon as authoritative, but to the pursuit itself. And because, again, questions are about something (even when that something is nothing), this is a fidelity to the object of inquiry, too, to its value: to the value of the open question.

Origins and Repetitions

The fact is that every thing has its beginning in a question, but one cannot say that the question itself begins. Might the question, along with the imperative which it expresses, have no other origin than repetition? Great authors of our time (Heidegger, Blanchot) have exploited this most profound relation between the question and repetition.

—Gilles Deleuze, *Difference and Repetition*

Through Nietzsche, we have noted that assent has a curious recurrent timing. This is especially so for theological assent, for thought seduced by faith into an unfinishable return. Turner describes vividly the insatiability of the desire for knowledge and the sense that to know is to know again, to return:

> our desire has but an infinite horizon, a horizon whose infinite discloses to us an infinite capacity for it. This unknowable horizon, this unseeable light, which surrounds and governs our learning, is no predetermined boundary at which knowledge must stop, some point of finality which could extinguish the desire to know. It is an enticement, a seduction, a sort of *ecstasis* of mind, which draws the mind out of itself into the infinity of space which is its own natural object, its "home"—in that sense, the place it *already* knows. In the meantime, therefore, the human mind has no place of rest, but only a place of restlessness, of one single unsatisfiable passion: the desire to know.[105]

Our heart is restless until it rests in you.[106] But this resting space is infinitely withdrawn, only read where it is traced, and the time of *until* becomes infinite; the place we already know recedes indefinitely. Chrétien complicates the time of faithful assent by linking remembrance to hope—and both to the untimeliness of forgetting. For Paul in particular, he writes, "Faith is essentially remembrance, but remembrance of God's promises, and it thus constitutes the place where remembrance is transfigured into hope, passing through the fires of forgetting—a fire which burns and consumes every memory of our own in us."[107] What is "remembered," then, is remembered in the mode of forgetting,[108] a restless mode, in which knowing that we have forgotten keeps both forgetfulness and memory incomplete, keeps pulling at us, seductively, entangled with hope.

And this, in fact, *is* home. We begin here in forgetting and in promise, in the double pull of memory and futurity, the seduction of the infinite. We begin with the space of the possible created by the withdrawal of the guarantor. The pull on memory suggests that, first, we forget, though "the very possibility of an initial forgetting seems contradictory, which is to say absurd," as Chrétien points out. We think of forgetting as a deprivation, and so it seems that it could only come after that of which we are deprived. He continues:

If there is an initial forgetting, what it would make emerge must be an absolute immemorial: not a past that, having been present and thus already open and destined to memory, would afterward become inaccessible in memory or for memory, but a past that is ... originally lost: a past that is, in advance and essentially, in withdrawal from all future memory, a past that, simultaneous to its own passage and slipping away, is always already past, always already disappeared and exists only as having disappeared.[109]

We seek the divine in traces, in signs, and so we are not looking only for what is. We are asking after absence too, and the queries of faith turn as well to the absences of memory. Chrétien writes that, for Augustine, "It is therefore necessary that what is primary is this memory by which God himself comes to our mind. But our fidelity to this gift lies in willing to receive still more, in tending toward what it promises, and in paying the price of the forgetfulness that responds—and can only respond—to the unforgettable."[110]

Here again, but now in more temporal terms, is the particular relation to nothing of which Nancy writes—the relation to what cannot even be remembered, yet always pulls at us as something we almost knew. Such is the truth of myth, and perhaps especially of myths of origin, or better, of ante-origin, of what eludes remembering yet seems too desirable to forget altogether. Ultimate forgetfulness, as Augustine notes, is double; when we remember that we have forgotten, when we are troubled by it, our forgetfulness is incomplete.[111] Origin is given to us not historically but mythically.[112] Myth tells us what we cannot simply, discursively "know;" tells us in the mode of poetry, with its always-opening of evocation, tells us to remember, and that we have always forgotten. It tells us of an infinite recurrence and of a mutual infolding of remembered and forgotten. And Christian myth especially tells us of flesh: the principle, the word, that is (in) the beginning, in time as flesh, where this absence and withdrawal pull upon us, as we find ourselves meaning-full, as we embody our signs. We learn the world by heart, by a willful openness to astonishment, by a sensuous and intellectual unknowing. We have no other way to "know" any "god," unless in retreat and in fear.

We begin in forgetting, a forgetting often linked (at least since Plato's *Phaedrus*) to the flesh: the myth of the fall is a myth of descent in which an unconstrained spirit is subjected to the limits and strictures of matter. It is perhaps most clearly here that Christian interpretations have something interesting to contribute to Platonism, a positively Nietzschean revaluation, an incarnation in which flesh is not made less than *logos*.[113] Even if matter "puts us in forgetting,"[114] it is in flesh, only in flesh, that we remember too. Material traces, Chrétien argues, inscribe themselves as flesh,[115] and all our scars argue the same.[116] Divine incarnation reminds humanity of the trace of the divine in the body, and all memory has its "carnal character."[117] And yet somehow, in this slippery and elusive kind of knowing and unknowing that faith embodies and bodies hold to faithfully in their transience, there is also a sense of a contrary demand against slippage, against elusion, in favor of answers. This is faith's paradox: in all of this questioning, in order to believe that it is worthwhile to ask, in order to trust that inquiry leads us and does not merely scatter us randomly, in order to be true to the object of our asking, faith demands as well what cannot be questioned. It demands an unquestionable and perhaps an ineluctable. One often hears, at least from those who are not given to claiming predestination, that faith is a choice, though this is most often attached to faith understood as belief or trust. I suspect, however, that Louis Mackey is right when he remarks, using "believe" in its more complex sense, "I have spoken as if there were a choice: to believe or not to believe. ... The most abstemious rational inquiry is inevitably guided by commitments of which it may or may not be aware. Faith only makes these commitments explicit."[118] There is a commitment of desire made explicit in faith, or a commitment that directs desire, but not a temporally orderly decision— "there is at the heart of faith a decision of faith that precedes itself and exceeds itself."[119] As Hawkins points out in *Reluctant Theologians*, Franz Kafka writes in his notebooks, "It cannot be said that we are lacking in faith. Even the simple fact of our life is of a faith-value that can never be exhausted. You suggest that there is some faith-value in this? One cannot not-live, after all. It is precisely in this 'Cannot not, after all' that the mad strength of faith lies; it is in this negation that it takes on form."[120]

I wonder sometimes if all theologians are not more or less reluctant. Thinking and theorizing lead many of us here simply because we cannot

not, after all. Theologizing is not, of course, to be identified with faith. Indeed, in some senses of faith (and maybe some senses of theology) the two are antithetical. But where faith is the ineluctable devotion to the mysterious question, and theology is unforecloseable exploration in wonder, they must at least come much closer than we have traditionally suspected. Again, I do not deny other forms of faith commitments, nor the value they may have for those who hold them, but neither do I pretend to describe them here. Faith as an epistemic seduction carries on elements of those other senses, of belief and hope, and the fidelity and trust they inspire. It is the willingness—more strongly, the will—to dwell in question, in mystery, and so, paradoxically, in the pursuit of answers. It is thus learning's constant enticement. It has, of course, parallels in any kind of knowing; a committed scientist or obsessive musician, for instance, can work quite similarly without the slightest religious or theological component. What characterizes theologically relevant faith is the deeper inherence of the question in every one of its answers. Its answers precisely *are* question; the answer is questioning, wonder, absence and excess, knowledge at its most restless, pulled by memory and desire. In the Christian version, this is characterized by a most peculiar time of incarnation.

Too often, faith within Christianity is triumphal, a firm belief in historical "fact" linked to exultation in the victory of the battle over death. But I would argue for a faith incapable of dwelling in victory, of being fully answered, no longer called and calling. Blanchot reminds us that all thought, at least all preserved or written thought, unworks itself; the texts in which triumphal faith so firmly grounds itself are in fact seductive and not merely expository, questions and not merely answers. The assembled congregation at several denominations of Christian service declares that Christ has died, is risen, and will come again—a time of incarnation begun as already passed, given only as a time of waiting and recurrence. Faithful time is the time of the question, of memory and hope, of unknowing, and saying *yes, again*, and of calling once more the name of the question, the name called out to us by the world.

2

Reading Rites: Sacraments and the Community of Signs

The eyes of all of them were opened, and they saw the beautiful things; not a single one existed among them that could not see.

—I Enoch 90:35

If all the world's a sign, and all things to which signs point become caught in signification again, then our world is full even as it is fleeting, traced with absence even in what stays. With the modern turn away from a sense of saturated signification, the world's signs are lost not merely, perhaps not even primarily, in their ability to refer indexically; the world at once desacralized and insignificant loses still more its power to seduce.

Faith may work to re-enchant if it opens the world as a seductive question, asking after traces, after a particular kind of presence and absence. Yet this makes rather strange the concept of sacrament, which is perhaps most readily understood either as a re-presentation (of divine action or real presence) or as an act intended to bring about a divine or gracing presence. Augustine, however, reads sacraments more enticingly—as particularly potent signs. He writes in the *Confessions*: "And then to instruct the unbelieving peoples, you produced from physical matter sacraments and the sounds of the words of your book.... Believers also are blessed by them."[1] In *On Christian Teaching*, he admires those signs that are "simple when performed, inspiring when understood, and holy when practiced, given to us by the teaching of our Lord himself, and the apostles, such as the sacrament of baptism and the celebration of the Lord's body and blood.'"[2] What a sacrament enacts is not a divine presence, at least not in a simplistic sense, but the seductive sign of the divine—not a sign that eliminates others, but a sign of exceptional vividness, one that draws attention to the very character of signs. I want here to take up both the particularities of these signs and the vexed questions of their working. As I did with the question of faith, I take up a view of sacraments and the communities that practice them that is at once grounded in long tradition and yet more hopeful than history might justify.

Communities are not unlikely to be closed to otherness, stubborn in belief, convinced in their ontologies. But if a faith in the value of questioning is possible, so too may be the kind of sacramental sense I optimistically outline here. As Catherine Keller has it: "communities of faith will naturally and necessarily speak their own traditional codes; they will play what Wittgenstein called 'language games,' with their own peculiar grammars and rules of communication nowhere more apparent than in the liturgy. But I have come to trust that members of these communities must not be insulated from their own doubts."[3] Sacraments, as a special class of signs, must both bind a community in the shared rules of the game and yet leave it open to the possible and the strange.

Early thought on sacramentality is optimistic indeed. According to late ancient and medieval thought, when Christ redeems signification (as we noted in the Introduction), one of the ways in which he does so is by establishing these particularly clear signs.[4] And, as we have also noted, Christ figured as inner teacher teaches that signs *are* signs, that they mean—or call. So sacraments become linked, and tightly, to this figure of redemption.

Thus, Augustine's thought runs, though every sensory encounter *should* be turned or at least turn-able to delight in the divine, there are certain signs made exclusively for that purpose, and such signs are particularly likely to be efficacious. The sacrament is an active sign, as Denys Turner indicates in comparing Meister Eckhart's sermons to sacraments in their ways of working: "it does not merely *say* something: it is intended to *do* something by means of *saying*, in fact to do precisely what it says; and on the classical medieval account, that is exactly the nature of a sacrament: it is 'a sacred sign which effects what it signifies.' "[5] There seems to be something of a contradiction here, between the purely semiotic *sign* and the performative deed by word or standardized (either ritualized or legislated) gesture. Sacramental signification is brought into a somewhat curious and sometimes tense conjunction with causality or efficaciousness, echoed in the tension between words that describe, words that perform, and words that evoke. If the objects, movements, and words of a sacrament are a description, they seem worrisomely to describe as real what is not evident—bread made flesh, or freedom from the penalty for original sin, or forgiveness of an invisible debt—or else they have no weight of their own, that being borne by what they describe. If they are illocutionary—if they perform or do—then they seem to be a bit of a magic act, shortcutting the laws of nature as well as the rules of reason. If they are purely theatrical, they seem at most to entertain. We will find that these tensions haunt the history of sacramental theology.

The formalized doctrine of what counts as sacramental, the list of the current seven sacraments[6] in Catholic Christianity, was not officially established until the Council of Lyons in 1274 (following the sacraments' designation in Peter Lombard's *Sentences*).[7] Orthodox churches define a similar list, while those of various Protestant denominations may be narrower or less formal. The use of the term *sacrament*, however, is much earlier; it appears in the work of Tertullian, around the year 210. Tertullian, one of the Church's first Latin writers, uses *sacramentum* where the Greek Fathers had used the term *mysterion*. Clement of Alexandria, for instance, "spoke of mysteries . . . as representations of sacred realities in signs and symbols, metaphors and allegories which only the initiated could understand."[8] John Chrysostom declares that "A mystery is present when we realize that something exists beyond the things that we are looking at,"[9] suggesting a close link between mystery and the sign that tells us of—or draws us into—more than simply itself. The mystery is a secret, that which is not to be, and perhaps cannot be, spoken (except perhaps to a select few); the sacrament as visible word signs, sign-ifies, more or other than it speaks. The Latin and the nearly cognate English terms retain some sense of the "mysterious." That sense is not original to the Latin, where *sacramentum* had previously indicated "a pledge of money or property which was deposited in a temple by parties to a lawsuit or contract, and which was forfeited by the one who lost the suit or broke the contract," and "later came to mean an oath of allegiance made by soldiers to their commander and the gods of Rome."[10] There is in the sacrament both mystery and promise (and a connection, we can see, with the devotional faith of allegiance).

As Tertullian often emphasizes the spiritual effects of corporeal action, it is not especially surprising to see him discussing these bodily actions and spoken words as spiritually significant—though he does not go so far as eastern Orthodoxies in emphasizing the goodness of created materiality as a reason for the use of material elements in sacramental rite. The development of a sacramental theology, however, really takes off with Augustine about two centuries later—a development that makes sense alongside his semiotics, given his understanding that sacraments are particularly clear or vivid signs. Augustine's theory takes into consideration baptism and the Eucharist, which will become two of the standard seven sacraments for Orthodox and Catholic Christianity and will be retained by Luther and Calvin as sacraments even after the Reformation's paring down of what was sometimes seen as ritual excess.[11] In fact, though, because of his sense that anything in the world is potentially a sign, for him "the number of possible sacraments was infinite: everything in creation was a reflection of God, and so in a sense even the universe itself was a sacrament, a sign of God. On the other hand, Augustine also taught that the number of really important sacraments in the church was relatively small."[12]

The move from rite to sign, however, is not especially obvious. Clearly sacramental rituals are still performed, but we can see that from a more rationalist perspective, as reason joins forces with production and utility, rite is nearly as problematic as belief. Sacraments, unless they are understood as purely symbolic, may seem oddly anachronistic, a form of magical thinking—perhaps most vividly in the two most widely acknowledged. If we attempt, more promisingly, to understand them as performative speech acts—after all, they effect what they signify, accomplish what they say—we find ourselves still at a bit of a loss: Who performs such an act, and what does the act really accomplish? And so, as Joseph Martos notes in *Doors to the Sacred*, his influential history of Catholic sacramental theology:

> Although the Catholic church officially still recognizes the doc-
> trines of the Council of Trent as its own, Catholicism in general is
> quietly laying them aside. Its theologians no longer speak about the
> mass as a sacrifice, its preachers and catechists no longer urge special
> devotion to the blessed sacrament, and its congregations no longer
> attend the Latin mass that the Tridentine dogmas defended and
> explained. The term transubstantiation, once found in every Catho-
> lic catechism, is virtually unknown to younger Catholics.

And so on.[13] The sense of sacramental rite as something *efficacious*, something that works, seems to be reduced here to a kind of anachronism, as if
it were simply too offensive to the modern mind to think that sacraments
might *work*. To figure out whether there is any sense in which they do work,
we might begin by asking what work they set out to do: Are they simply
causes? Just signs? Both? And for whom?

Cause

Knowledge is the object of our inquiry, and men do not think they know a
thing till they have grasped the 'why' of it (which is to grasp its primary
cause).

       —Aristotle, *Physics*, bk. 2, pt. 3

Let us begin with the most obvious formulation: to do work is to cause
effects. The effect of a sacrament is widely conceived as grace, itself a notoriously elusive term. Grace traditionally has to do with an unearned gift
of divine benevolence (it is gratuitous), whose consequences can extend
from temporary good behavior to salvation. Sacraments may also be understood as having more specific effects, often effects of jointure, such as the
joining of a person to a community in baptism, to a spouse in marriage, to
an order in holy orders. It is no accident, I think, that the kinds of rites
that make communities (even the micro-communities of couples) are made
by them as well—communities both make and are made by their languages,

and sacraments broaden the sign-sense we have about words. These effects of grace and unity are complex enough, but their causality is more elusive still.

Within sacramental theology, questions of cause become central pretty early on—they are especially so for the Scholastics, with their Aristotelian interests in sorting out causal types. Even Scholastic thinkers do not, however, give dogmatically definitive answers. Questions about the efficacy of sacraments remain theologically and doctrinally open, even in the most doctrinal versions of Christianity; no view on the matter of sacramental cause was officially adopted in the considerations of the sacraments at the Council of Trent, for example, nor has any such view been adopted since,[14] leaving a wide range of possible understandings as to both type of cause and causal agent—and, of course, the possibility that we are not dealing here with any standard sense of causal production after all. (Thus also, to be sure, we assume that we understand what causal connection is, a very dubious presumption, as we've known at least since Hume,[15] but still seldom recognized as such.)

And range these understandings have. For (highly influential) instance, Thomas Aquinas holds that the sacrament has instrumental efficient causality; that is, it is the instrument of the effect of which God is the primary moving agent, rather as a hammer is an instrumental efficient cause of a driven nail, its own movement caused by the carpenter. A few theorists, especially among the medieval nominalists, have held to the somewhat stranger occasionalist view.[16] Occasionalism in general is the theory that an apparent cause is just the *occasion* for a real cause—God—to act; in the case of the sacrament, to act by conferring grace. That is, though God bestows grace at the time of the sacrament, which is, as it were, a particularly appropriate or propitious occasion for this bestowal, the sacrament is in no other way causal. There are, by the way, occasonalists about causality more broadly, such as the rationalist French priest Nicholas Malebranche or Descartes' Flemish follower Arnold Geulincx, but they are, as one might guess, rather few and far between, and they seem to have had their heyday in about the seventeenth century.

A roughly contemporaneous but currently less strange-sounding theory is advanced by the Dominican Melchior Cano, who, writing around the same time that the Council of Trent was meeting, argues that sacraments are without efficient causality at all. Rather, they have a "moral causality," functioning as requests for divine intervention.[17] As it was for Thomas, the actual efficient cause, the agent who makes things move in the world, is God; the sacramental effect is a kind of prompting.

Most theories of sacramental causality, then, turn out to argue for some kind of indirection. The theorists have either denied that sacraments are causal in the senses in which we usually understand the term or argued that they are medial in a causal series—from God to sacrament to effect— without having any capacity to be efficacious in themselves. One might, like Thomas Aquinas, trace all causality to God, but at minimum the causal connection in the case of sacraments is particularly clear and direct.

Thomas's understanding is as close to doctrine as the understanding of sacraments has come. As the *Catholic Encyclopedia* notes, "Since the time of the Council of Trent theologians almost unanimously have taught that the sacraments are the efficient instrumental cause of grace itself." That seems pretty definitive, albeit open to all sorts of interpretation given the ambiguities of "grace." But even this quite dogmatic source goes on to acknowledge lingering puzzlements, going beyond the qualification "almost": "The definition of the Council of Trent, that the sacraments 'contain the grace which they signify' . . . (Sess. VII, can. 6, 8), seemed to justify the assertion [of instrumental efficient causality], which was not contested until quite recently. Yet the end of the controversy had not come. What was the nature of that causality? Did it belong to the physical or to the moral order?"[18] In this case, the dogma itself turns out to be inquiry, and so we need to inquire further into some possible answers.

Sacramentum Signum

The very definition of "sign" implies a process of unlimited semiosis.

—Umberto Eco, *A Theory of Semiotics*

One possible answer to the puzzles and peculiarities of sacramental causality is to turn away from the notion of cause altogether and look at sacraments as signs. Augustine describes a sacrament as *sacrum signum* ("sacred sign") or *verbum visibile* ("visible word");[19] as the "sign of a sacred reality" (*signum rei sacrae*).[20] The sacrament is the sign of the *sacramentum*, the contract or, more optimistically, covenant or promise—and, to return to the more evocative Greek, of the mystery. (This may, alert readers will note, make it the sign of itself. The paradox of self-signing will return full force in Chapter 5.) As the sign of the mystery, it also foregrounds the mysteriousness of signs, even in designation; the promise it evokes is not a fixed one, but the "promising" itself, that which offers, without reifying that offering into a gift from an entity. However meaning works here, it is not in a standard referential manner. It again seems clear that the nature of this connection between the sign and the sacred is nothing so simple as indication. I continue to suggest that it is, rather, vocation—invocation, evocation, provocation—and, as I shall also argue below, abduction. Thus it is, as I shall argue in more detail below, neither simply descriptive nor ordinarily performative.[21] The sign in-vokes; it calls out and it calls both us and the divine. It calls us insofar as we read it, but only insofar as we perceive it as given, in fact, to be read—not as an answer to be grasped, but as what touches us and draws us after it.

The emphasis on signs in understanding sacraments is not restricted to Catholic theology. For Martin Luther, sign, along with significance and faith, is an essential part of a sacrament.[22] John Calvin sees sacraments as "signs of God's favor . . . testimonies of God's good will toward men that could open the Christian to an awareness of the grace which was always present to him, if he would but receive it."[23] Ulrich Zwingli argues strongly for a signifying rather than a causal function, denying any spiritual efficacy to the sacraments, but seeing them as "signs of Christian belief; through them a believer indicates that he belongs to the Church of Jesus and has separated himself from unbelievers."[24] (Thus he also emphasizes the communal nature of these signs.) In these instances, signs function *fairly* simply as reminders and symbols—but of course neither memory nor symbolism actually works out to be simple at all. And there are complicating factors: faith, grace, opening, community. Something mysterious—and implicity unfinished or unfinishable—lingers.

In his description in *The City of God*, Augustine argues that the sacrament parallels ritual sacrifice, in which "the visible sacrifice is the *sacramen-*

tum, the sacred sign, of the invisible sacrifice."[25] What we best offer to God is not the flesh of animals, but "a broken spirit," humility.[26] That is, the sacrifice God most desires is not the one that can register upon the senses; however, the evident or "outward" sacrament signifies sensually this invisible, intangible, silent, and scentless humility. In the twentieth century, Karl Rahner will echo this in his sense of sacrament as the exteriorization of an interior decision—if, at any rate, humility can be decided upon. However, as M. B. Pranger notes, there is a risk in such claims: that of reducing the power of the sacrament to a simple description, the outward indicator of an inward state,[27] uninteresting as cause and unexceptional as sign.

However, as Pranger also makes clear, reductive simplicity seldom works with Augustine. The idea that a sacrament is just an unusual descriptor of an inner state is made unlikely by the fact that Augustine mistrusts our intentions, and even our ability to know what they are; he is well aware that we are infrequently, if ever, transparent to ourselves. I do not think that he is inconsistent here, but rather that we must not overread his sense of intention, or, therefore, of indication or description. Augustine's own insistence on the doctrine of *ex opere operato* (by the action performed, or by the work itself), of which more below, argues against the sacrament as the outward sign of an inward psychological truth. The sacrifice makes the very humility it signs. I would argue not that the causal effect is a moral one, dependent upon intention and mediating between the effect of our intent and the effect of divine action, but rather (more semiotically) that, if we already regard symbols as meaningless, we will have no way to read them; if we are already reading them, they are not wholly exterior to us. The "outward" sign means only if we "inwardly" read it as meaningful, read in the proper spirit. As the scare quotes suggest, neat distinctions between inside and out hold up poorly in the invocations of the divine. And so the sign, perhaps, is of the sacrifice of the boundary itself, the pride of self-security, the mastery of knowing; it is a sign that draws inside to out and beckons the outside (the divine, grace, the other in community, the God to whom the spirit in which God is found is sacrificed) in. It teaches us a risky reading.

Causal Sign

> In magic . . . it is expected that a manipulation of the sign (more exactly a
> manipulation of the signifier) causes a simultaneous transformation of the
> "thing."
>
> —M. L. Cameron, "Anglo-Saxon Medicine and Magic"

The apparently dual history of thinking sacraments as signs and as causes
is in fact not so double as it seems. The irresolution of the causal question
itself tells us something of the ways of sacramental working, which are
mysterious ways (and not just in their etymological history). Indeed, not
only may they work as mysteriously as God is said to work, they may even
be a particular divine working. A look back at the line of thought in which
we might best place Augustine will help to make sense of this. For early
Neoplatonists, ritual is often theurgy, the work of God or the work that
humanity does with God.[28] Christianity comes to associate this work particularly with the incarnation, the ultimate God-working of God-self, and
then consequently with the works of that incarnate God: the sacraments
are ostensibly grounded in particular acts of Christ. For many Christian
theologians from late antiquity onward, the ultimate and foundational
sacrament remains Christ's own self, read as God's own embodiment. Thus
for Christian Neoplatonists (such as Augustine, or a bit later Pseudo-
Dionysius), sacrament is both one and many. There are many sacraments,
but this multiplicity is one in that all sacraments ritually work the one
sacrament, the ultimate sign that is the incarnation.[29] These sacramental
acts are ritualized into what Pseudo-Dionysius will call a hierourgy, the
working of holiness, perhaps precisely in order to avoid too close an association with the theurgy of the "magical" Neoplatonisms.[30]

Ambrose of Milan, whose highly philosophical readings of Christian
texts are so important to Augustine's conversion, emphasizes divine work
in discussing the scriptural prefigurations of the sacraments, such as the
Passover meal, which becomes the model for the Eucharist.[31] He argues
that divine working tells us of divine presence; "the Lord Himself says: 'If
ye believe not Me, believe at least the works.' Believe, then, that the presence of the Godhead is there. Do you believe the working, and not believe

the presence? Whence should the working proceed unless the presence went before?"[32] Remembering Ambrose's philosophical complexity (the very source of his appeal for Augustine), we should not oversimplify this "presence." As Blanchot writes of presence in friendship, here "Presence is only presence at a distance, and this distance is absolute—that is, irreducible; that is, infinite."[33] This unity of presence and action, the unseen in the seen, is complicated by the unseeable, by the infinite distance that makes proximate divine desire. This paradoxical multiplicity reminds us to seek for the sign—by which, as Thomas Aquinas puts it, we are enabled to discover the unknown by means of the known.[34] To discover the unknown will not mean its abolition; it is known as unknown, as mysterious, as promising. What we discover by means of this sign is that there is mystery.

Many thinkers have argued that sacraments do their causal work precisely *as* signs—at least in part. That is, what they do is not simply to describe, but to work—but their work is not something distinct from their signifying. It still seems a bit odd to see a sign as a cause; when we do things with words, when we speak performatively, we seem to be neither designating nor calling, but rather making words into instrumental causes in order to bring about a state of affairs. It seems intuitively reasonable to argue that a sign cannot cause anything except, at most, a sort of understanding (or even reminding). Of course, to see sacraments as signs does take the edge off the slight embarrassment one might feel at the anachronistic arguments around causality. The sacraments, one might now argue, are *only* signs, symbols that remind us of a divinity in orderly and somewhat removed relation to the world. But Augustine, as we have repeatedly seen, takes signs very seriously indeed; without them neither theology nor redemption is possible. For him there is no theological or religious causality without signs.

Peter Lombard develops his understanding of sacraments in this context; for him the power and efficacy of the sacrament in bringing about grace is the power and efficacy of a sign (*signum efficax gratiae*). Thomas Aquinas too is well aware of the intricate questions regarding the sacrament as sign or as cause and takes them up in Question 60 of the Third Part of the *Summa Theologiae*, with the general heading "What is a sacrament?"

The first article asks more precisely: "Is a sacrament a kind of sign?" He writes in Objection I: "It seems that a sacrament is not a kind of sign. For sacrament appears to be derived from "sacring" [*sacrando*]; just as medicament, from "medicando" [healing]. But this seems to be of the nature of a cause rather than of a sign. Therefore a sacrament is a kind of cause rather than a kind of sign."[35] In his answer, however, Thomas lists several senses in which the term *sacrament* may be meant. All kinds of things *could* legitimately be considered sacraments—a thing with a hidden sanctity is a sacramental "shared secret"; an object may have a causal relation to sanctity. But, as I do here, he narrows down the use of the term: "now we are speaking of sacraments in a special sense, as implying the habitude of sign: and in this way a sacrament is a kind of sign"; signification even seems here to be more important than causality.[36] A sacrament is a sign. It does something, and it does something particularly significant.

Of course that "seems more important" won't quite do, lest it reduce sacramental practice to pure symbolism, or to rote theatrics void of all sense.[37] The *Catholic Encyclopedia* insists that "the sacraments of the Christian dispensation are not mere signs; they do not merely signify Divine grace, but in virtue of their Divine institution, they cause that grace in the souls of men."[38] The affirmation of the value of sign, or the definition of sacrament as sign, clearly provokes some worry, manifest in cautions and questions. The order of sacramental causality remains stubbornly unclear. What *is* clear is that there lingers a strong, somewhat anxious desire to see sacraments as causes while not letting go of the idea that they are signs, yet to make them performative seems, as we earlier noted, too nearly magical. Much of the concern, I suspect, has to do with that notion of "mere signs"—a notion we have already come to regard with suspicion. Perhaps the sacrament, too, is the sign of a call, or a sign that calls, and perhaps its causality is so deeply peculiar because it does not precisely produce, but seduces—it does its work, its holy working, by drawing into play. That is, it is a sign that causes not a definitive result, but a seduction; as both the mode and the effect of its cause, it calls. Thus if it performs, it is a sustained performance, not an instrumental accomplishment; its importance is not solely, not even primarily, in its effect insofar as that effect might be distinguishable from the signing.

Ex opere operato

But the Sacraments of the New Law not only have been ordained out of their own first institution to signify, but also to obtain grace, and for that reason they have been ordained through themselves to justify; for that reason, speaking *per se*, those (of ours) do justify, those (of old) do not but *per accidens*.

—Bonaventure of Bagnoregio, "On the Difference Between Old and New Sacraments," in *Commentary on the Four Books of Sentences by Master Peter Lombard*

In some of the earliest theorizing on the subject, Augustine argues that the efficacy of a sacrament comes from the rite itself, a notion later referred to by the shorthand phrase *ex opere operato*.[39] The *Catholic Encyclopedia* assures us that the phrase "was happily invented to express a truth that had always been taught and had been introduced without objection."[40] Phrases like "always" and "without objection" must arouse our suspicion, but it does seem true the idea has been widely held. It means roughly "by virtue of the action, [which] means that the efficacy of the action of the sacraments does not depend on anything human, but solely on the will of God as expressed by Christ's institution and promise." The contrary possibility, *ex opere operantis*, "by reason of the agent," would mean that the action of the sacraments depends on the worthiness of the minister (or, arguably, of the recipient, though the latter is less often seen as an agent.)[41] In the first conception, power is in the ritual; in the second, in the one who performs the rite. Though both versions allow that a sacramental rite might be performative, the latter more nearly risks returning the rite to a description of the agent's true action, while the former grants its power to the performance itself.

Augustine defends the doctrine of *ex opere operato* against the claim that sacraments administered by corrupt or heretical priests must be invalid. Ambrose likewise writes, "Do not consider the merits of individuals, but the office of the priests."[42] Thus worries about whether, for instance, one is actually baptized if one's ministering priest turns out to have been corrupt are ameliorated. This is not intended to excuse the priests for wrongly performing their function. But such wrong performance is a worry of another sort; it is not about the sacrament itself.

But it *is* a worry, and in fact, "always" and "without objection" not-withstanding, there are grounds for some doctrinal nervousness here. Pierre Klossowski presents us with some rather dramatic—albeit altogether fictional—instances of the kind of corruption that might motivate both concern with the doctrine and, for that matter, the doctrine in the first place. But in so doing, he also points to some perhaps unsuspected, more interesting doctrinal consequences. He writes in *The Suspended Vocation* of an utterly cynical, "euthanasian" abbot, of whom the church "demands nothing . . . other than that he administers in God's name: whatever his own interpretations of the sacrament might be."[43] The minimal nature of this demand, which seems to exemplify *ex opere operato* rather precisely, is also one of the provocations to the main character's crisis of faith. In these cynically administered sacraments, as Ian James analyzes it:

> There is no real priest but only someone "acting" as a priest. . . . The priest is only an imitation, a copy, a forgery of a real priest. Yet since the priest is only ever "real" in so far as his gestures evoke and coincide with "Real Presence," it follows that as soon as his acts become infected with role-play the possibility of there ever being a "real" priest is undermined.

This undermining depends upon a difference between being and acting or appearing, the truth of a depth beneath a surface, inner truth described by outer sign: seriousness and sincerity versus role playing. Yet this possibility of reversal may actually be integral to the sacrament. Considering, in particular, the prayerful *Confessions*, Pranger argues for a way of reading in which neither the seriousness of the first-person voice nor the pure third-person sense of repetition emerges, but in which voice is arrogated, taken on as if one's own. Voice is taken on, however, as performance in the mode of theater or song, rather than as plagiarism. This analysis transfers intriguingly to the sacraments, where priest and recipient both, playing their roles, play them truly, no less seriously for their ritual theatricality, with no effect save that of the evocative sign itself. If every sacrament echoes the significance, the signing, of the incarnation, we might add, each performance does no less than to continually re-embody, rematerialize, the divine—by reading it once again aloud.

James continues: "The priest . . . parodies 'Real Presence' in such a way as to undermine all possibility of its being either 'Real' or 'Present' because it is only ever an imitation of presence, an illusion of the 'faux prophète,' of the artist actor. This moment of collapse between the two spheres of the theological and the aesthetic is also a collapse of language in its capacity to articulate Truth or to describe a stable and knowable world."[44] We might, to be sure, simply dismiss here any number of terms or ideas: real presence, for instance, or sacramental efficacy. That is, this parodic, destabilizing possibility (and though the example is fictional, evidence does hint that somewhere in the world a cynical priest merely enacts his role) suggests again that we might want to return to the idea that a sacrament is a symbolic reminder, period. But if we do not, remarkably, a new kind of working appears just as easily as a destruction of working at all: a work of the play of the sacramental sign, restlessly, across speakers, across meanings. This work *requires* play—what Pranger calls "a sincerity that, being the performative of attentive action, is theatrical to the core."[45]

At the extreme, then, applying the doctrine of *ex opere operato* seems to undermine whatever sense "real" (as opposed to apparent or seeming) and "presence" (as opposed to either absence or illusion) might have. It therefore seems to undo Ambrose's insistence that we could not find a work where the divine has not been *present*. The sacrament here becomes a play and a pull of signs: it is precisely what pulls truth-ward without a stopping point. In the imitation of presence, what shows itself to the community of readers is presence indistinct from an absence, the trace of meaning. It is thus that both its causality and its signification become so odd. It pulls without reaching a point of pure presence; it performs without being grounded in the depth of orthodoxy. And this sign play is precisely what Baudrillard labels seduction. Perhaps "by virtue of this action"—in this case, the act of signing—might interestingly, if a little anachronistically, be read as meaning just that, rather than as channeling or expressing any will, whether human or divine. It is the sign that seduces. The divine resonates in the calling of the name that is a question. The sacrament opens: what it opens is a reading, and what it reads is that there is, even infinitely, something to be read.

Here in the concept of *ex opere operato* the sacrament begins to appear closer to magic than many might find comfortable. As R. A. Markus points out, "Augustine's theology of the *ex opere operato* efficacy of sacraments, especially of baptism, even if administered by schismatic or unworthy ministers, has often been held to have encouraged a magical view of sacramental efficacy"[46] because of the evident independence of effect from volition (presumably the two will often accord, but this accord is not of itself causal nor even required). Augustine is hostile to the idea of magic, as is most of Christianity, and not just Christianity. Levinas, for instance, worries that magic is a kind of debased sacred, one that in fact, as Virginia Burrus writes, "impedes both the reception and the perception of the holy"—a holiness defined by its purity, in distinction from which the "sacred" takes on a negative valence as a site in which sorcery, or magic, may flourish.[47] Magic is consistently thought in relation to religion, but from within the bounds of the latter this thought is often an effort to disentangle the two. I want, however, both to hold that the sacraments *do* work in some way as magic does and to suggest that we are very likely to misread the sense of "magic" here.

Like sacrament, magic is communal. Some communities may understand their own practices as magical, or, more often, they may be understood by others as practicing magic. More socially dominant communities tend to regard themselves and to be regarded as religious, looking down upon other religious practices as magic or superstition. But in a world in which everything is a sign, the distinction is not especially clear. That we continue to believe that it is reflects a misperception of magic as nothing more than bad science. That is, we presume that magic is to be understood as an attempt at producing an effect by the production of an unusual cause for it, in a procedure that somehow evades or shortcuts the usual laws of physics. Or we might think of it as a kind of causal confusion, as if causality that *can* be effected by words (such as the sentencing of a criminal) were conflated with causality that cannot, such as that governed by biology or physics.

But magic is not bad science, no more than a sacrament is, though both can easily appear to be attempts to bypass the rigors of work by lazy causal practices or to call upon the causal force of a doubtable metaphysical presence. The sacrament, like magic, is not a break in the law but a change in the rules. As Baudrillard puts it, "We are constantly interpreting what falls under the rule in terms of the law. Thus, magic is seen as an attempt to outwit the laws of production and hard work. Primitives have the same 'utilitarian' ends as us, but in order to realize them, they would rather avoid rational exertion." Magic, that is, is widely understood as both intellectual and practical laziness. Baudrillard argues for quite another interpretation:

> Magic, however, is something very different: it is a ritual for the maintenance of the world as a play of analogical relations, a cyclical progression where everything is linked together by their signs. An immense game, rule governs magic, and the basic problem is to ensure, by means of ritual, that everything continues to play thus, by analogical contiguity and creeping seduction. It has nothing to do with linear relations of cause and effect.[48]

Baudrillard in this text carefully distinguishes rule, which governs play (break the rules, and you're out of the game, no longer under those rules' governance) from law, which functions causally—whether that law is physical, legal, or moral. In this reading, magic is not the production of causes but the manipulation, and specifically the seductive manipulation, of the rules governing signs. Like sacramental ritual, it is thus a transfiguration of sense. The "enchantment" of the world, the transformation of "magic" that so concerns those who would explicate *ex opere operato*, is the world's opening. The world of the ritual community bursts into possibility—in forgiveness (as in reconciliation), in memory (as in the Eucharist), in love (as in marriage), in membership (as in baptism, charismation, confirmation, and holy orders). Connections are multiplied and desires are drawn. The meaning of such openings is neither productive nor even referential; such meaning retains the secret, the mystery. "Neither magic nor seduction concerns belief or make-believe," says Baudrillard, "... their logic is not one of mediation, but of immediacy, whatever the sign."[49] The secret (the mystery) is, as we have seen, not what is hidden-beneath.[50] It is not the depth of truth latent behind a misleading surface. Rather, the secret is what is already present and always elusive, what continues to draw. The sacrament is a sign made for drawing: that is, a sign read and re-read as mystery and promise, the secret and the contract both.

We might be tempted to say that, if sacraments work like magic, if they do not produce clear effects or refer with some finality, then the sacramental is in just about every sense meaningless—possibly pretty or aesthetically satisfying, but scarcely important. It is here that the conventions of signifying, with their communal role, become especially important.

Communal Construction: Reading a Shared World

They said to him, "Tell us who you are so that we may believe in you."
He said to them, "You read the face of the sky and of the earth, but you have not recognized the one who is before you, and you do not know how to read this moment."

—The Gospel of Thomas, verse 91

Baudrillard writes: "make no mistake about it: conventional or ritual signs are binding. One is not free to signify in isolation while still maintaining a coherent relation with reality or truth. . . . Each sign is tied to others."[51] Convention, then, is not the enemy of the sacred, though it might seem so. We readily think of convention as precisely what in human thought and conduct works against the surprise of newness, against the possibility of being drawn to a mysterious elsewhere. But conventions are also conventions of meaning, and they are constructed in and constructive of communities. "Seeing the liturgy as discursive practice that determines what can be said about the divine and who can speak about divinity locates the constraints on correct naming not within the sphere of a strong individual, albeit graced, privacy," says Ludger Viefhues-Bailey. "Rather, the constraints . . . are . . . social."[52]

Sacraments communally "mean" the very sacred that they work; they read the divine name that they call out, thus making it available for reading. Much more conspicuously than most signs, they perform this call by virtue of rule and communal convention. In Christian sacrament, the ritual enactment of divine working, theurgy, is reworked into liturgy. The etymology of liturgy is that of a public rite or service,[53] but one can hardly help hearing echoes of *littera*, the letter, the sign by which the word is made visible—and these are public or communal words. The liturgy works in words read and heard in a community, a self-selected public. But *how* do such words work in communities? Seduction works in the realm of response, where motility and not ontology is at stake, where the world is choreographed (and the order of the movements matters) rather than photographed. Seductive meaning is not reference but sense at its most multiply sensuous, sense in motion. This is the realm not of *belief*, with its insistence on referential propositions, but of faith—in this case, of communal faith: the words and movements of the rite are the community's language game. Again, this echoes a Baudrillardean distinction. "One seduces God with faith," says Baudrillard, "and he cannot but respond, for seduction, like the challenge, is a reversible form. And he responds a hundredfold by His grace to the challenge of faith. . . . Belief is satisfied with asking Him to exist and underwrite the world's existence—it is the disenchanted, contractual form."[54] The sacramental rite, too, is a place for that hundredfold response, a place that re-enchants, not in isolation but in community.

We may speak of making up or following our own rules, but rules in fact belong to communities, to the players of the relevant games, and are both defined within those communities and helpful in defining them. Not least among these are the rules of meaning, of what it is to be able to say and to read, of how signs mean and which signs are meaningful. There is no private language,[55] no sign so secret that one person can either make or change its meaning (though one person may create a code for an extant language). Languages belong to groups, and groups, to no small degree, belong to their languages. "The power of society, Augustine knew, is the power of language," says Mackey.[56] Markus argues that, for Augustine, community is the main difference between sacrament and magic: "He accounts for magic and ritual in what are essentially the same, semiotic, terms. Both are systems of signs, in use in rival speech communities. One set of signs has validity in a perverse community of individuals working for their own selfish ends and deceiving each other; the other in a community united in their service of God and of the common good."[57] While we might now doubt Augustine as to the veracity of this distinction's details, the insights that magic and sacramental ritual are both hierurgic sign play, and that signs play as they do within particular communities, remain sound.

This sense of the communal extends even to reading. Augustine generally seems to privilege, as Christian theory often does, the spoken over the written word.[58] A spoken word is a sign; a written word is the sign of a sign: "when we come upon written words, aren't they understood more accurately as signs of words than as words? After all, a word is that which is uttered by means of an articulated sound accompanied by some significate. A sound, however, can be perceived by no sense other than hearing. Thus it is that when a word is written, a sign is produced for the eyes, and by means of this [inscription] something that strictly pertains to the ears comes to the mind."[59] It seems possible, at least, that some measure of this privileging is historically conditioned by the rarity of silent reading in late antiquity. (Augustine, in fact, is amazed to see Ambrose reading silently, and this is one of our earliest citations of silent reading.[60]) If most reading is reading aloud, then letters will seem much more the signs of sounds, instructions for speaking, than they do to those who are more accustomed to reading in silence. In reading aloud, the text is made communal. While this notion isn't explicitly present in the late ancient world, it does nonetheless give us a sense of reading, and of the read word, as less simply and securely private, as belonging to those around the reader as well as to the reader. Reading is in common.

More, for Augustine all signification occurs in common, in the context of a group of readers. This is especially true for "conventional" signs, a category in which words are included: "Conventional signs are those which living creatures show to one another for the purpose of conveying, in so far as they are able, the motion of their spirits or something which they have sensed or understood."[61] As John Rist points out, "Thus verbal signs are of circumscribed usefulness and will clearly be effective only in a community . . . which recognizes the relevant 'conventions' of communications."[62] Mackey notes that in this sense of community, language is linked both to desire[63] and to faith:

> It is faith that constitutes the sign as sign. Suppose you are confronted with a pattern of inscriptions or a series of differentiated sounds. How do you know that what you see or hear is language, that is, meaningful marks or noises? You do not know. At least there is no way you could have learned it. . . .
>
> The ambiguity of signs . . . , which makes it possible for faith to regard them as such, also permits their deradication from significance.[64]

The community is the space in which the meaningfulness, and sometimes the meaning, of signs is given by faith, by the sense that they have meaning, whether that meaning is call or designation.

If faith is a sustained trust in the value of the query, then a community that reads faithfully will read the sacramental sign as meaningful in its members' willingness to be drawn after it. It seems quite plausible that one might have a private sense of the sacramental, a sense in which otherwise ordinary events and impressions take on, often suddenly, a sense of revealed mystery. I haven't the slightest interest in denying or downplaying this sense; in the next chapter, I will even argue that it has ethical importance. But the sacramental rites, which are my concern here, take their meaning in the context of communal ritual. Communally, we read, we interpret—not by ostention, but by inference; not by a simply referential inference, even, but, as Umberto Eco suggests, by abduction.

The term *abduction* is generally associated with the semiotic theories of Charles Sanders Peirce, for whom it is "the process of forming explanatory hypotheses. It is the only logical operation which introduces any new idea" (in this, it is unlike either induction or deduction).[65] But like many semiotic ideas, this one may have a much longer history than is generally recognized. In fact, Eco attributes this notion, or something like it, to *The Teacher*, in his discussion of Adeodatus's attempts there to define verbs ostensively (to demonstrate what "to walk" means, for instance, by walking with unusual emphasis).[66] "Obviously," Eco glosses, "the accumulation of ostensive signs does not clarify the meaning of a term by simple induction. A frame of reference is necessary, a metalinguistic (or, rather, metasemiotic) rule expressed in some way, prescribing what rule should be used to understand ostension. But at this point we have already arrived at the mechanism of abduction."[67]

Eco distinguishes among varieties of abductive inference. First is overcoded abduction, which is nearly automatic—we know the rule, we just have to figure out whether the result actually is a case of it. For instance, if I hear the sound represented by the letters *p-i-g-l-e-t*, I must determine whether I have heard someone say the word *piglet*.[68] Next is undercoded abduction, in which the rule must be "selected from among a series of equiprobable alternatives"—when one must understand, for instance, if the statement "This is not a man" is a reference to gender, species, or some other attribute.[69] Finally, Eco discusses creative abduction, "in which the rule acting as an explanation has to be invented ex novo." He gives a cosmic example:

> This could be the case of Copernicus when he had the intuition of heliocentrism. . . . Copernicus felt that the Ptolemaic system was inelegant, without harmony. . . . Then he decided that the sun ought to be at the center of the universe because only in this way the created would have displayed an admirable symmetry. He figured out a possible world whose guarantee was its being well structured, "gestaltically" elegant. As in every case of creative abduction, this way of reasoning required a sort of meta-abduction, which consisted in deciding whether the possible universe (or state of things) outlined by the creative abduction was the same as the "real" universe.[70]

Perhaps this sort of creative abductive rule gives us one way in which the sacramental sign is read as sacred, is the word made visible: in it, the elegant seductiveness of the ritual universe is a "real" presence, or is, rather, the presence of a trace that a sign is, and faith is the sense of the world observed there. That world, like the community's shared words of scripture or prayer, is given its sense by Word. The sign is read under the rule of seduction; that is, under the rule of infinite reading, saying always that there is more to mean (a point that will emerge again in the later discussion of scripture). The meaning read is infinite, and it may be infinitely read—it remains unexhausted by repetition. But clearly this is no reality readily recognizable by the mechanistic materialism of contemporary sensibility. "The body of Christ," says the ministrative priest, but the devout communicant, however fully drawn into the Eucharistic moment, touches her tongue to bread and not to meat. For this sign to make this sense, a sense neither productive nor mechanical, there must be more than causality, more than the productive performance of work, more even than a customary reading of the sensory evidence that signs (also) are—there must be a seduction of signs.

The world that gives meaning, the world structured by the creative abductive rule, is created as an act of simultaneous memory, making, and discovery. Reading-as is making, too. Such is, traditionally, the working of revelation. Sacramentally, we are reminded first in the way in which we are reminded of what came and went in the past—as I noted above, the sacraments are ostensibly modeled on acts from the life of the historical Jesus. But still more, we are reminded in the way in which memory gives us again the divinity of the world, perpetually arriving and departed. Sacramental rites have long performed a strong bonding or binding function for the communities that practice them (as Zwingli suggests), providing (and being provided by) occasions of gathering. In this gathering, memory is not only one's own, but shared, and the rites that join—a child to a church, one spouse to another, the body of a communicant to that of her God—draw as well upon the corporate memory that tradition is. Familiarity risks meaninglessness, of course, as when words are recited by rote, but it permits the attentive, those absorbed by the enactment, to remake the signs of that seductive infinitude, to create and read sacramental language. Being rooted in tradition does not mean that such signs can dwell in fixity. The multiple, fluid, multi-voiced communal body speaks and reads, in its own incarnations, a language that is constantly reaching further than what already is.

It is true that, for Augustine, scriptural and sacramental words go beyond convention.[71] Thus, it might seem that they are independent of community and of the threat of instability. But in fact both "mean" in a world structured by faith—not a belief that they mean some particular proposition, but an experiential capacity for being drawn into them. The community, laity and ritual ministers alike, is drawn into the play of ritual signs, and reopens the mystery in remaking the rite. Thus the structure or the pattern is not formed as a static image, but as a pattern of movement, where meaning reaches for more.

The visibility of the sacramental word does not imply (though vision easily can) something static. The word spoken in the giving of a sacrament is accompanied by act: the baptism by washing with water, the Eucharist by sharing bread and wine, and so on. Neither the material nor the act renders the word visible; they too are signs. The word made visible in the performance of the sacrament appears to be the elusive, seductive, and reciprocal motion of the world toward, though never entirely to, divinity. Such a visible word is not a referential sign (whether that reference is to an inner state or to a metaphysical entity) but the reading of a sign as the call of a meaning so overfull as to exceed all reference, to elude all speakers (who nonetheless open the space for it by their performances), and to keep drawing all readers into further significance; a sense of something meaningfull but insusceptible of designation. A word, or a Word, that calls. In this visibility, what it means to signify, and indeed what it means to mean, are transfigured in being seduced away from finality.

Production Versus Seduction

Only a God's word has no beginning or end. Only a God's desire can reach without lack. Only the paradoxical God of desire, exception to all these rules, is neverendingly filled with lack itself.

—Anne Carson, *Eros the Bittersweet*

Clearly the idea of seductiveness in sacrament, though not generally named in quite that way, is not entirely novel either. Alongside persistent questions of signification, causality, and their possible connections is the sense of sacramentality that Martos endorses and develops, in which the sacraments mark thresholds, functioning as "doors to the sacred, that is, as invitations to religious experiences."[72] As doors, they function both to conceal and to invite, to draw one in and through, but without showing the entered room first (though this is not quite how Martos develops the metaphor). In invitation and opening, we hear echoes even of Calvin's opening of awareness. And if that "room" is in fact an infinite space, it remains beyond comprehension, even when entered. The sacred space into which one is sacramentally transported is, Martos remarks, experienced as more *meaningful* than ordinary spaces, something special[73]—especially significant, we might well say—and he argues that the sacramental experience is both intense and, returning us to the Greek, mysterious.[74] It moves in a dual invitation between human and divine; without response there is no sacramental event: there is, at best, an unsuccessful attempt at seduction. To be invited is already to be inviting, to invoke the provocative invitation.

It is an invitation to what never completely occurs or arrives. As Mark McIntosh writes,

> If the soul learns not to foreclose the signifying power of the sacramental sign but rather is drawn into a never-ending journey by means of it, then the cataphatic and the apophatic are most truly themselves, truly in a dialectical relationship that gathers momentum within the believer's life. Balthasar usefully highlights a distinction in Gregory [of Nyssa]'s thought between the cataphatic *content* of a sign and the apophatic *movement* that is aroused by the sign. The "vision" or growth in understanding is, importantly, not identified with an intellectual grasp of the sign per se but with the transforming action and movement in pursuit of its ever-receding divine surplus of meaning.[75]

Sacramental reading is not a matter of holding as factual an assortment of unscientific propositions about causal productivity; it is instead a matter of the ritual seduction of signs even within our disenchanted discourse, a seduction in which the reading is essential to making the meaning it reads, and the speaker (broadly conceived) takes on in ritual performance words that we might say are made his or her own, but that more nearly make over the speaker. Seduction problematizes boundaries. A sacrament draws closer to performance than to expression, but its performing too is of a strange sort, as it is never altogether accomplishment: indeed, it "performs" un-finishedness, openness, unbounding, Nancyean dis-enclosure.

So what makes a sign sacred, capable of serving in such a "speaking"? Not that there is a sacred entity toward which the sign points; few theories of the sacraments give us such a clear ontology. Not some magic inherent in the signifier's difference from any other. Nor does a sacred sign teach us to *comprehend* what is unknown, as if stripping the *mysterion* of its mystery; on the contrary, it teaches us the non-prehension of sacred touch. A sign is sacred because it shares the character of the sacred: opening, making possible. It shares that character by the rule of a community reading in faith, but it makes that rule too. What makes possible the openness is what draws into always more, not finishing signification or meaning in a definite reference. A sacred sign works in the manner of all words and signs, but under the reading rule of a community willing to open onto mystery. Any signifier may refer indefinitely, and perhaps even infinitely, but the very referent (and not just the referring) of the sacrament is infinite. The world creatively opened by it is a seductive and not a productive world, a world in which every sign draws us further, and not always in expected directions; a communal or conventional world of faith, in which the question is itself meaningful. The rule that sacramental signing follows is that of divine or infinite seduction.

We must also recall that, in the strange relation of words to the interior teacher and inner light, the "first" Word is not (simply) a sign,[76] but neither is it simply signified, by word or by flesh. Yet, far from being thereby removed from signification, meaningfulness, or the realm of sign systems, it *forms* the illuminating and sense-making pattern,[77] the shape and possibility of significance, the abductive rule by which we mean in our signing. The communities in which sacraments mean ground meaning in that pattern— but here there is no ground inseparable from the infinite drawing. Such a groundedness does not imply stasis—nor does it allow us clearly to distinguish outer word from inner intent, description from action, saying from quoting.

Sarah Klitenic Wear and John M. Dillon write of invocation— calling or drawing into—as central to sacramentality: "The concept of invocation reveals two important aspects of the sacrament—because the invocation must follow a particular formula and must take place at a particular time, it reveals the importance of precise ritual. Also, when Dionysius or the Greek fathers speak of the invocation, they go to great lengths to explain that Christ (or the Father or the Holy Spirit) is the ultimate source of the invocation and the power of rites."[78] They go on to add, somewhat surprisingly in the present context: "These two aspects of invocation . . . show how theurgy is an essentially hieratic ritual in technique, and yet it is not magic because it does not involve a commanding of the divine."[79] This too opposes the Baudrillardean idea of magic with which I want to work here, but it is important to note that the sacrament neither manipulates physical causality in itself nor causes a god to do so. Moreover, it does not command the divine, but seduces it and is seduced by it. It is a provocative invocation, a sign that performs evocation.

The sacrament makes a special use of (and perhaps, to employ some-what mischievously Augustine's own terms, finds a special enjoyment in) semiotic incompleteness. As I noted in the Introduction, premodern se-mioticians are vexed by the imprecision with which postlapsarian lan-guage is afflicted—that is, by its failure to specify so completely that there can be no confusion, no ambiguity. Nor is this frustration restricted to the premodern world. Prominent among modern and present-day invented languages are those that attempt to introduce a systematic categorical com-pletion, such that reference is entirely without ambiguity and meaning can-not be mis-taken.[80] Unfortunately for this ambition, the vocabulary and grammatical indicators required for such precision rapidly multiply beyond the range of comprehension—and rapidly lead those who are not their cre-ators to suspect that it is not merely historical happenstance that spaces open in and between our more ordinary words. Languages in common use retain their incompletion, and the people who think about them remain frustrated, but they remain engaged as well.

Our everyday or profane reactions to the incompletions and imperfec-tions of signs' meanings are multiple. As scholars, we allow ourselves to be intrigued by them. As pragmatic speakers and listeners, we often fill in without needing to reflect, making use of context, tonality, and other cues to select among multiple meanings (a simpler mode of abduction). We ignore, in the interests of our time and energy, the further openings, the other meanings—both the more precise specifications and the infinite possible tangents and questions—that any sentence offers. The sacrament implicitly urges us not to ignore these things. The sacramental attitude is close to that of the scholar, but without its properly academic distance. Incompletion, that is, becomes not an object of study but an experience of desire.

Baudrillard, like Foucault, notes the end of the Augustinian world in which this seduction would have made an easier sense, would not have required effortfully re-attuning ourselves to signs: "That universe where gods and men sought to please each other—even by the violent seduction of sacrifice—has ended. As has the secret understanding of signs and analogies that provided magic with its powers of enchantment. And with it, the assumption that the entire world is susceptible to seduction and re-versible in signs—not just the gods, but inanimate beings, things."[81] But if we do read seriously the sacramental signs, we are seduced into the multiple openness of elusive, touching/ withdrawing presence and infinitely full / retreating meaning. The sacrament is a reminder of this suppleness of the world's meaning, and of its beauty right at the "sacred horizon of appearances"[82]—the beauty not of some prelapsarian, long-gone once-was, but of what always "is" in what always passes, traced by it.

That is, the sacrament means not only as the word, but as the world does, but more vividly, more acutely, because it unfolds in a community focused on reading and re-reading the signs of the divine. In so doing, it both bonds the community in the sharing of a language and inclines that community to see sacramentally first in and then beyond ritual—it is hard *not* to read in a language one has learned. The liturgical sanctity of the sacrament is not the establishment of an ontological transformation but the revelation of wonder. The "sacred sign" neither reveals nor points to what is hidden beneath or transcendentally beyond. Rather, it transfigures the always-absenting present by shifting our sense of it to a different reading—more exactly, to any reading, to an alertness to signs within a community in which the conventions are not those of belief but those of faith. Such conventions write and read a world so rich with possibility that it opens without end.

The community's faith, its grounding in the openness to the question, is what creates the rule for reading signs as sacramental. Again, as all readers know, once you're familiar with a language, it becomes very difficult not to read signs presented in it. Reading is about the complex interactions of signification, and when the sign is a call, that interaction is one of call and response, reading together. The rites that share a community, rites that a community shares, join its members. But it is important that joining is not circumscribing. Indeed, like faith, community itself keeps us in question, keeps us open to one another,[83] all the more so if what joins is precisely the open, the inviting, the promise. To dwell in community, argues Nancy, is to be constituted in exposure, as ex-posed,[84] not to be secured against otherness. It is painfully obvious that many "faith-based" communities are constituted exactly in opposition to otherness, but I want to suggest, in keeping with Keller's version of faith, that there is a rather fundamental conceptual flaw in exclusionary communities joined by sacrament grounded in faith. Reading may ground us, but we have not read the infinite if we are not risked in it too.

In such a holy-working semiotics, the community reads the visible word and opens the memory of word and Word in the visible, of infinite possibilities of meaning that draw us urgently on. The visible is layered, interleaved not only with the tangible but with the meaningful,[85] not only with the referential but with the sacred. The sacraments are "grace events,"[86] as Karl Rahner writes, but also (as I once misread Rahner to be saying) grave events, events with the gravity and pull of grace—inflection points,[87] concentrations. In them and into them is drawn the transfiguring sense of opening onto the astonishment of the world. And this is the sort of sacramental rite that sanctifies that world, that re-enchants it: not into a new set of meanings, but into a new manner of meaningfulness, in which meaning is drawn into the infinite, never altogether knowable, but divinely restless, at once intangible and moving with ritual bodies, their own performances successive reincarnations of the mystery they read.

3

Because Being Here Is So Much: Ethics as the Artifice of Attention

Attention is a task we share, you and I. To keep attention strong is to keep it from settling.

> —Anne Carson, *Economy of the Unlost: Reading Simonides of Keos with Paul Celan*

Attention must be paid.

> —Arthur Miller, *Death of a Salesman*

The very notion of seductive ethics is likely to give us pause, to seem more error than paradox. Ethics is more often than not conceived as the very resistance to seduction, if not in fact to any sort of pleasure (or bliss, which seems to undermine the ethical subject).[1] It is dutiful, we think, a little bit ascetic (provided we don't overly enjoy our asceticism), rule-bound or abstemiously virtuous. And if seduction is about sustaining the possible, then to prescribe, whether character or behavior, seems contradictory to it. But the prescriptions of ethics are not always a matter of foreclosure; they may direct us, for instance, toward the virtue that allows us to flourish, or toward *attention*—and attention, to begin with, to delight. Moving in such a direction, we might speak of an ethical discipline of pleasure. But of course, like a seductive ethics, a discipline of pleasure sounds peculiar to the contemporary ear. Discipline is what we do when we are grimly submitting to the unpleasurable, and pleasures are supposed to be easy. (Or else healthy, or educational, allowing us a small but smug sense of superiority over those who fail to, say, run, or read fine literature.) But the discipline of seduction and seducibility is precisely an ethical discipline—without ceasing to be what also threatens ethics.

Our sense of delight's decadence runs deeply. Even those who see such pleasurable traits as wit and the capacity for friendship as virtues (as Aristotle did, and later David Hume),[2] or whose ethical rules are grounded in the search for the maximum of human happiness (as in a basic utilitarianism),[3] nonetheless end up saying no to at least some of the most seductive kinds of pleasures—pleasures to which we're drawn *because* they are pleasurable, rather than pleasures that we derive secondarily from doing what's right. This opposition appears at its most intense in someone like Kant, who worries that if we take pleasure in doing good, we cannot be sure that we are ethical rather than simply self-indulgent.[4]

Many religions, and certainly Christianity, are also thoroughly vexed by that drawing power of pleasure. Augustine is famously worried about pleasures, devoting long passages in the *Confessions* not just to the temptations of sociality and sexuality, but one by one to the pleasures of each sense, intellectual curiosity, and worldly honor.[5] It is easy to interpret him badly on the subject. His worry is not, as it might at first seem, that pleasure is evil: we are right to delight in material creation, and nothing divinely created is bad. The problem is rather that we are too easily distracted by the immediacy of relatively minor pleasures, and so we turn all of our attention and desire to them, neglecting the more difficult, but more profound, joys of the infinite. This is not, however, an either-or. What simplistic readings neglect is that we reject the infinite if we reject all the finite things in which we read its signs. Thus, as I've noted, for Augustine we do not reach divine desire by rising *above* creation.[6] We reach divine desire by deepening our desire in and for creation; we reach the divine only through a deeper desire for the world. In a somewhat less simplistic reading, Augustine seems to decide we must be moderate in our worldly indulgences, restricting them to what allows us best to flourish in the love of God. (This is particularly true of the pleasures involved in eating.) But here too some part of the point goes missing. What Augustine ultimately seeks is precisely a pleasure without any moderation at all, an infinite delight in an infinite "object" in his love of God.

As Augustine does, I want to connect this sense of desirous and inquisitive goodness to our response to beauty, thus invoking the classic Platonic triad at the pinnacle of the eternal Forms—goodness, beauty, and truth. But this too seems problematic, perhaps giving us permission to declare aestheticized evils desirable after all. I want to insist that such tensions indicate not that we have an imperative to suppress our aesthetic sense, but rather that we should train it: we must teach ourselves to *attend*, to wait, to hear.

To train ourselves in seducibility and its attendant pleasures is not so much to train ourselves to feel some particular feelings, not even, say, cheerfulness (which is in any event a bit wearying in its unremitting form), nor simply to permit ourselves to feel without constraint (as if in a sort of inverse Stoicism). It is rather to develop our capacity for attentive response. These responses will often be in some measure affective, even as they are cognitive too. To respond is neither simply to do nor solely to feel; to be responsive is to be particularly alert and attuned in both feeling and doing. This, like most any undertaking, even in the neighborhood of ethics, is doomed to imperfection, but we must realize by now that all enticement has a place for, and takes its place in, the imperfect, the incompleteable. Moreover, it takes that incompletion as a value, as another trace of infinition, of divine infinitude.

The training of attention comes intriguingly close to the disciplines of late ancient and medieval monasticism. M. B. Pranger writes that in "the flourishing of monastic literature between 1000 and 1200," there is a particular discipline of affect, at once circumscribed and slowed and yet infinitely expansive, inherent in the monastic texts rather than simply being the subject of their discussions.[7] This is the kind of discipline, and the particular sense of asceticism, at work in my sense of the ethical here. As contemporary monk Sebastian Moore remarks, "what we learn from the cross is, not to deny our desires, . . . but on the contrary to *attend* to them . . . and hence to begin to learn the difference . . . between the desire of the ego to stay where it is and simply repeat past satisfactions, and the desire that can say, 'I want to want more.'"[8] A seductive ethics reaches for just that possibility.

The Platonic Inheritance, with Divergences

The musician we may think of as being exceedingly quick to beauty, drawn in a very rapture to it . . . he answers at once to the outer stimulus.

—Plotinus, *Ennead* I.3, "On Dialectic: The Upward Way"

The possibility of living in responsiveness to beauty arises obviously in Platonic thought, with the pair of Platonic dialogues sometimes collected as the "dialogues on love," the *Phaedrus* and the *Symposium*, as key sites. Within the *Symposium*, the most influential and theoretical discussion of beauty and response appears in Socrates' speech, particularly in the portion of his speech that Socrates attributes to the prophetess Diotima. (This is not to reduce the complex and multi-layered *Symposium* to part of one speech, but merely to focus on that speech as especially influential.)[9] The speech is well known, so I shall highlight only a few of its most relevant points. Having set up the discussion with the claim that love is a *daimon* born of Poverty and Resource, neither a god (as in many of the previous speeches) nor a human person but something in between, Diotima encourages Socrates to realize that love is in between in many other respects as well: it is between good and bad, between poverty and plenitude or resource (to which its parentage is attributed), between ignorance and wisdom. In every case, it reaches for the better—for the beautiful.[10] Love, Diotima argues, desires the beautiful. More exactly, in love we desire to interact with the beautiful and to create a lasting result of that interaction, because as beings who do not last, we most nearly approach immortality in making what will linger after us. Thus, in a notion that Freud will pick up virtually wholesale, love as our relation to beauty is the desire to beget upon or procreate with the beautiful—to connect actively with the beautiful in a way that creates something new and lasting, in a quest for whatever kind of immortality might be possible to mortal beings (perhaps in offspring some sign of oneself may still be read). Eros is not moderate; it wants, impossibly, more; not least, it wants more time, to extend into the eternal and into the future.

According to Diotima, not all conjoinings are begotten equal. At the most base, but also the most basic, level, desire directs itself toward a single beautiful body. From this passion it ascends by a process of increasing abstraction and sophistication, finally desiring the Beautiful itself, both the ultimate in beauty and the singular source by which or from which all other beauties are derived.

Plato's complexity and elusiveness, quite marked in the *Symposium*, invite multiple readings. Among the ways in which Diotima's speech is or can be read, one fundamental distinction is especially important for our purposes. The description of the "ladder" ascending from the love of one beautiful body to the love of the Beautiful itself has been interpreted most often as an argument against the material, an argument for turning firmly and quickly away from the lustful pleasures of the flesh and toward the higher and more lasting pleasures of contemplation. Here the value of the sensible world is solely in its capacity to remind us or to prompt us to turn to "higher" concerns.[11] Thus, when we speak of "platonic love" or "platonic friendship," we intend a non-physical, asexual—and often peculiarly unerotic—mode of connection.

A different interpretive perspective emphasizes both the necessity and the taking up of the first step, such that materiality is not that away from which we must turn but that through which—or even within which—we must progress. In this version, the last step does *not* leave the first behind; love at every stage or level can be crass or complete (save the last level, which must be perfect), and we can love at all levels through any level. The climbing or advancement is then not a matter of rejecting each step in favor of its successor, but of rendering every kind of love richer and more complex by incorporating each successive relation into the desire for a more complicated beauty, a complexity that ultimately emerges into the perfect simplicity of Beauty itself.

In Plotinus's seminal Neoplatonic interpretation, these levels of love are reconceived cosmologically, the beautiful One at the center of creation and matter at its outer limit, with the love of beauty retaining its power to draw every desire back toward the center from which each of them emanates.

Plotinus emphasizes the temporal twist: while from our perspective, the perspective of time, the processes of emanation and return can only be understood sequentially as unfolding at increasing distances from the center (first this level, then that one, and so on), from the perspective of the infinite and eternal (which includes that emanating source), all *is*, without sequence. Moreover, what we sense in time is traced with the infinite, is "simultaneously imprinted and transversed by a vestige" of it;[12] the two truths overwrite each other. And so, with proper attention, what we sense can begin to draw us beyond our own finitude.

Plotinus's most focused discussion of beauty, *Ennead* I.6, begins, as Diotima's ladder of love begins, in our attraction to the material world. Sensory beauty is seductive; it "attracts the eyes of those to whom a beautiful object is presented, and calls them, lures them, towards it, and fills them with joy at the sight" (I.6.1).[13] Ugliness has exactly the opposite effect; from it the soul "shrinks within itself, denies the thing, turns away from it, not accordant, resenting it" (I.6.2). Our response to beauty and its absence, then, is one of being set into motion—much as we are by signs.[14]

Plotinus speaks eloquently of the beauties of the senses, which appear "to adorn, to ravish, where they are seen" (I.6.3). But he goes on to declare that these are lower forms of beauty, and indeed, the tractate ends with a condemnation of any investment in materiality, as that which drags down and dirties the natural beauty of the soul. The sole importance of beauties known by the senses is that they alert us to what beauty feels like—to the fact that beauty calls us and delights us. Looking within ourselves at the beauty of our own souls, we fall in love, and that love takes us further away from embodiment.[15] The best form of beauty is loved not in the material world but within oneself, once the truth of that self beyond its individuated selfhood is recognized.

Plotinus is firm in his reminders that no sensory stimulation is at work here—"No shape, no colour, no grandeur of mass"(I.6.5). It is in these passages that love of the material begins to acquire negative associations: the ugly soul dwells upon what perishes, lives in "abandonment to bodily sensation" (I.6.5).[16] Such hostility toward matter is atypical in the *Enneads* (despite Porphyry's claim that Plotinus hated his flesh).[17] As Margaret Miles points out, as a rule Plotinus is not especially obsessed with body at all.[18] And he seems to work against such obsession in his readers; he sometimes suggests, for example, that we should take reasonable care of our bodies so that they do not distract us from more abstract contemplations.

But the Platonic ambiguity regarding love of the material reappears as an ambivalence in Plotinus. In the tractate on beauty, Plotinus suggests not only that we must move on from material beauties, but more dramatically that we have to flee them, lest they fool us into mistaking them for a better and higher reality, and so trap us in the low realm of the senses.[19] We find true beauty *only* by withdrawing from the senses, which (in an image perhaps drawn from the *Republic*'s allegory of the cave, 514a–520c) show us only shadows of the truth. This matters a great deal. Failing to find beauty is the worst, maybe in an ultimate sense the only, kind of failure.[20]

It is, importantly, an ethical failure. Miles remarks that, for Plotinus, "seeing beauty is a profoundly moral act" or (citing Martha Nussbaum) "an ethical ability."[21] Noting the deceptive simplicity of this claim, Miles goes on to add, "it is more accurate to say that Plotinus derives a complex metaphysics, morality, and what we might call a spirituality from his conception of the universe as beautiful to the core."[22] Plotinus, that is, starts with value, in this case beauty or aesthetic value, and from that he derives his sense of the very structure of the world, of its moral demands, and of the most desirable experience of the highest love. Miles goes on to elaborate on Plotinus's arguments in favor of cultivating a sensitivity to beauty, which is at the heart of the possibility of a response to the world.

To observe beauty may not seem like much of a foundation for a way of living (whatever we may think of it as a ground for metaphysics). We tend not quite to believe that, as Miles summarizes Plotinus, "Inability to see beauty is a moral failure," even if "cultivating the ability to see beauty is 'within our power.'"[23] All sorts of things that are within our power are nonetheless things that we ought not to do. In fact, Miles goes on to worry about Plotinus's arguments precisely in regard to the ethical concerns of community. She writes, "In omitting relationship and community from his philosophy, he differs significantly from his mentor, Plato, who advocated both committed relationships in which the partners encouraged and stimulated each other to virtue, and communities in which philosophical issues were heatedly discussed."[24]

To be sure, Plotinus's own *practices*, so far as we know, seem to have been of the sort that strike most of us as ethically admirable and socially generous.

"He was able to live at once within himself and for others," [25] Porphyry declares; "He was gentle, and always at the call of those having the slightest acquaintance with him."[26] It seems that he cared for the area's orphans and at least some widows; he had close friends among both women and men; he was an inspiring teacher; he was probably even vegetarian (Porphyry says that he refused animal-based medicines, at any rate).[27] In a reversal of the more common pattern, he seems, by most senses of personal goodness, to have been an even better person than his philosophy would argue for one's being. Miles suggests that Plotinus's emphasis on interconnection (his sense that all ultimately derives from and returns to the One) might hold ethical possibility, but she argues too that he fails to develop it.[28] In these criticisms we are, of course, somewhat imposing upon Plotinus our own sense of right living, and we shouldn't be too surprised if our sense fails to map onto his. We must then wonder, however, whether there is really any value in reconsidering the life lived for beauty. When Plotinus talks about virtue, as Miles points out, his ideal is a withdrawal from the world of sensible materiality, a withdrawal that in some of his tractates appears so extreme that he can alarmingly advocate an indifference to suffering, as it is, after all, ultimately insignificant.[29] This would seem less disturbing if the suffering at issue were only one's own (to which all manner of complicated relationships are possible), but it is not, and indifference to others' suffering seems not only a failure of response, but an ethical failure in most any system.[30] We see such indifference not much later in the Neoplatonically influenced, strongly dualist Manicheans, whose obsessive attention to the purity of their own bodies was matched by a refusal to attend to the bodily needs of others, such as beggars.[31] In more contemporary terms, it seems clear that to dwell *only* on beauty would entail a willful blindness to the misery of many. Can we then live well at all if such attention is at the basis of our relational attitudes?

Plotinus's responsivity to beauty is in fact a better fit with his own behavior toward many kinds of others (adults, children, animals), and a better source of inspiration, than is this advocacy of indifference. The response to beauty, and the sensitivity to beauty that enables that response, really is a fundamentally ethical act, but not because it encourages us to seek increasingly pure forms of beauty and so to reject the world of matter. It is not in the discussions of virtue, but rather in the curious morality of responsivity, in the need to train oneself to be drawn in—and even amazed—by the world, that I believe we find the most hopeful starting point in Neoplatonic ethics. To make that claim at all persuasive, I'll argue that delight in the beautiful is not, at least not necessarily, the self-centered indulgence that it sometimes seems. Nor does it necessarily entail the worrisome withdrawal from the material that Tractate I.6 unfortunately does seem to advocate.

Yet there is the potential for another problematic in-difference here. For both Plato and Plotinus, we fall in love with a B/beauty that we also *recognize*. For Plato, the source of this recognition has to do with the sort of succession of incarnations described in the *Phaedrus*, wherein the soul between embodiments circles the heavens and gazes upon the Beautiful, of which lesser beauties, participating in it, remind that soul when it is "trapped" in a body. For Plotinus, we recognized the Beautiful because we are it. That is, we, like everything else that exists, both emanate from the One and, as its outflowings, are not other than it. The turn within to what is beautiful in us is the turn to what is most truly us, eternally and not just temporarily. Of course, knowing that is also leaving the self in its distinct individuation behind, and we must then wonder if we also leave difference.

Augustine too writes of seeking the divine within oneself, but there is a difference between the inward turns that Augustine and Plotinus both advocate, a difference that echoes the divergence in their cosmologies (for Plotinus, all is ultimately One; for Augustine, the creator is not creation). For Plotinus, I recognize my own truest self in beauty; for Augustine, I recognize the infinite difference between myself and the very beauty that I also find by turning within. What both writers alike require of us is that we work not to diminish desire, but to discipline and direct it such that it may become more responsive, more intense, and not so readily dispersible. Carol Harrison even argues that an "incarnate aesthetics" is central to Augustinian thought, and I am inclined to agree.[32] Neoplatonic ethics comes to take on a potent antisomatic asceticism. Augustine takes us away from this, rightly, I think, with his attention to the voices of worldly beauty.

To strengthen the positive valuation of difference, I'll also use more contemporary theorists, especially Nancy and Levinas, to argue for a sense that beauty and the space of its absence do not simply resonate with what is the same in us, but cut across us, and in the cutting make us as we are. We are not even self-same, but always open to, opened to, difference. But we are also more or less free to try to ignore that openness and to wall it off, to maintain our indifference as much to joy as to suffering. It is in deliberately intensifying responsiveness that cultivating our response to beauty can draw us into the ethical, into a seductive ethics of attention and astonishment, in a world that is at once familiar to us and infinitely strange. In this responsiveness, an attentive listening enables an ethical speaking, speaking with attention to that which exceeds it—the infinity of the world's possibility. And that speaking, in its excesses, names the divine.

As a starting point, I would remark on something that both Plato and Plotinus suggest, though neither emphasizes it, perhaps taking the point as too obvious. If one is not seduced by the beauty of bodies and of materiality, the ascent to Goodness and Beauty will never get started, no matter how one conceives of its levels. If we don't see beauty in the easy and obvious places, if we are not drawn to it, there is no hope for us in abstraction. To say of beauty that it seduces is not only to say that it draws us, but that it draws us in a way that awakens desire and delight and not only satisfaction and satiation, a way that questions at the same time that it answers. Here the "final" level of Diotima's ladder, the "innermost" realm of Plotinian return, is not a place of finality at all, not a resting place, but an openness, a promise of possibility, in which finality makes no sense. The beauties of the world seduce us wrongly only when they seduce us into limited pleasures and quick satisfactions; their beauty holds more than that, signifies more than that. The world's many destitutions call to us to create, or recreate, beauty's sense of possibility. That is: I would argue for an ethics that draws us into, and not out of, the world—and is drawn, in that world, into the infinite "in" and "across" the finite, not least by its easy attraction to what is beautiful.

Christianity, with its outset in an incarnation, should be less ambivalent than classical Platonism or Neoplatonism in its love of bodily beauty. Of course, its history has not precisely borne out this "should," but Augustine takes an important step in the direction that the Plotinian tractates do not go, in the passage of *Confessions* book 10 that I cited in the Introduction, where the relation of the divine to the sensuous is clearly strong as beauty tells Augustine the name of God. For Augustine, as Harrison notes, "the soul can only love and desire something . . . because it already has a general idea of corporeal beauty."[33] Even more clearly than for his Platonic predecessors, then, for Augustine if we cannot love the world then we cannot love at all, and we thereby disregard the God who is for him the source and sense of all love. For Plato and for Plotinus, that someone would *not* be attracted to material beauty is apparently a thought too foreign for thinking. The only issue is what we do with that attraction. For Augustine, the Manichean hostility to matter, a hostility he embraced in his own young adulthood, is a reminder that, in fact, love of beautiful things is not a necessary given. Augustine's rejection of the Manichean tendency wavers sometimes, as he worries about the constant temptations posed to him by the senses, or the pull of old desires against his newfound love of continence. But often, and at his best, he holds onto his view of the material world as good, believing that, as Harrison remarks, "a delight might rightly be felt by the soul for sensible as well as spiritual beauty."[34] Not just felt, but rightly.

There still seems to be a problem somewhere in our love of material beauty. Love remains a relation (not altogether unlike the Socratic *daimon*, which moves between), so perhaps that problem is not in the world, not even exactly in us, but rather in the betweenness of us and world. Harrison writes, "It is . . . man's apprehension of Creation which is fallen, not Creation itself."[35] If it is a relation that is fallen, then it is a relation that needs to be fixed. We must change the way we see—quicken ourselves to beauty, perhaps, develop a willingness, a will to be astonished by beauty, to regard the world and all that is in it as if it were not already familiar to us and a little bit boring in consequence.[36]

The vocative beauty of the world is for Augustine itself a sign of divine creativity—a trace and a reminder and a call to an inexhaustible meaning. As it did for Plotinus, for Augustine desire leads us to cosmology. The beautiful things of the world "tell" him that they are not God, but that "he made us." Beauty itself is an answer, provided we are asking the right question, or more precisely, provided we have the right notion of what questioning means. Augustine does not reject worldly beauties as filthy or even as low in turning his attention to their maker; rather, he listens to them crying out with the answer to his question "Where is God?"—their answer is in their form, in their beauty. Beauty seduces us, not only by calling to us, but by awakening the call in us, calling us (in)to question—and "answering" us with a return that recurs, a return that returns the answer once more to the questioning. Again, a distinction is relevant: for Plotinus, we find the divine somewhat weakly evident in the world and then more intensely within ourselves as a way to recognize the divine oneness of all that is; for Augustine, we read beauty and we hear it, both in the lovely things of the world (despite their potential for distraction) and within ourselves, as calling out the name of the divine with which we are in intense and mutual desire. That desire cannot exclude the flesh, because we cannot refuse to listen to beautiful things without cutting off beauty entirely. The world does not name God by either logical argument or empirical inference, but in a delight that calls out first to the senses.

Call and Response

I am the one who cries out,
And I listen.

—The Thunder, Perfect Mind

After this the Holy of Holies was opened to you, you entered the sanctuary of regeneration; recall what you were asked, and remember what you answered.

—Ambrose, *De Mysteriis* (*On the Sacraments*), 3.5

A seducible faith expresses itself ethically in an attitude toward the world, an attitude that works to apprehend the world as a particular sort of gift—not the sort that comes with demands and provokes resentments, but the sort that comes of the pure delight in giving and provokes a delighted return.[37] As James Wetzel points out, this circle must include a delight that Augustine himself sometimes misses, in the interconnections of flesh and willful desire[38]—a delight, then, in the body's capacity to sense in desire and not merely to register information.

To see the world as a gift is to take ethics beyond a relation between persons, to a more complex relation with the world as it is traced by the sacred—though interpersonal relations remain important. The gift is made in the between. And in between, in all manner of spaces, all manner of possibility is given as well. Merleau-Ponty suggests something not unlike this when he writes, in *The Visible and the Invisible*, "Between the alleged colors and visibles, we would find anew the tissue that lines them, sustains them, nourishes them, and which for its part is not a thing, but a possibility, a latency, and a flesh of things."[39] A few pages later, he adds, "What is proper to the visible is . . . to be the surface of an inexhaustible depth."[40] This depth is not simply an interiority corresponding to an outside; it is possibility, which gives us astonishment, and newness, and sometimes even hope.

A gift is the possibility of delight; we give gifts hoping that those who receive them will receive them as gifts, will find in them possibilities for pleasure. It is not the case that there is a gift, and then we notice and politely say "thank you." Rather, our thanks makes the gift, and we are grateful because of it.[41] The world ceases to be a gift when I cease to be grateful for it. Just as this cannot be only a lazy reception on my part, so too it cannot be made into the sense that I have obligations only—even infinite, unmeetable obligations of the sort Levinas describes, important though those will turn out to be (of this, more below).

Giving is not so unidirectional as it might seem. "True," muses Paul Celan, "some know that you can give a flower to a person. But how many know that you can also give a person to a pink?"[42] Remembering that persons, ourselves included, can also be given helps us to avoid the risk of regarding any gift as having been given over entirely, to do with as one sees fit. If a gift is that for which I am, and ought to be, grateful, then to see the world as gift is precisely *not* to see it simply as at my disposal. To respond to the world as that for which one is grateful is to open oneself to it, to respond to it in ways that allow it, as well as oneself, to flourish. It, as well as oneself: the response to the gift is a response to the call that gratitude itself makes. To see beauty responsively is to see it as a gift. But response itself demands more exploration, not least in its relation to that which calls for it. The entanglements of response and call are crucial.

The tradition of beauty as a call is long-standing, and runs deep in Platonism and Neoplatonism.[43] There, as Jean-Louis Chrétien points out, it extends even to etymology: "Plato in *Cratylus* uses *kalein* to mean naming, bestowing names," he writes, noting that Neoplatonists reading the *Cratylus* "will awaken in *kalein* its second meaning, namely that of sending out a call."[44] These two senses come close to one another: we are given our names (and so we might say that the name is language as a gift), and names become words by which we call and are called. Chrétien goes even further than the etymological link, attributing to the Platonic tradition a necessary association between the beautiful and that which calls:

> the Platonic tradition, from antiquity to the Renaissance, has thought beauty to be, in its very manifestation, a call, a vocation and provocation. . . . things and forms do not beckon us because they are beautiful . . . Rather, we call them beautiful precisely because they call us and recall us. Moreover, as soon as we are able to call them beautiful we must do so, in order to answer them.[45]

We answer to beauty by calling its name. We answer for beauty by calling out for it. To name is not to still, but to seek; Socrates says in the Cratylus that the very word *onoma*, "name," signifies "being for which there is a search," adding that the sense of mobility "is still more obvious in *onomaston* [notable], which states in so many words that real existence is that for which there is a seeking [*on ou masma*]; *aletheia* is also an agglomeration of *theia ale* [divine wandering], implying the divine motion of existence; *pseudos* [falsehood] is the opposite of motion."[46] Granted that it is hard to know in this dialogue just where (or if) Socrates is serious, we may at least note the presence of the connections between naming and seeking, motion and truth.

In this connection, gratitude emerges as closer to query than we might have thought; in calling for one, the world calls out the other. Most simply, the giftedness of the world is made by the question that attention is, or rather by the play between attention and what calls for it and that to which it calls. When we pay attention, we find that our attention is called for. Even visual attention hears that Augustinian voice of beautiful things— the eye, says Chrétien, "sees truly only by listening."[47] Hearing implies more strongly than seeing, though perhaps less strongly than touch, a sense of movement.[48] Attention to the beautiful is practice in attention at the easiest level, but it is no less important for that. Attention is both a question that calls for an answer and an answer that that responds to a call.

The very role of response here, of the *daimon* of desire moving between, suggests to us that we are out of the realm of modernist metaphysics. Seeing already incorporates interpretation; to see is also to read, and to listen. Seducibility is lived not in the imposition of a secondary layer of interpretation onto a received sensorium, but in the very mode of openness to signs as means of seduction—in the very fact of listening, of reading. The doubleness is not consecutive; interpretation is built into seeing and hearing the world.

Attention requires that we must sometimes read slowly, and in fact one of the most difficult aspects of attentiveness is that it demands a kind of slowing, a patience that neither hurries nor directs the world, a willingness not to be too multiple in our tasking, to focus upon something as if it were worthy of all of us, even if only for a moment. That moment is the place of pure attention; as Pranger argues, "for Augustine the dynamics of temporality are to be found in the 'sed tamen perdurat attentio / and yet attention lasts' rather than, as Ricoeur and others suggest, in the distention animi proper."[49] Seduction places particular constraints and requirements, perhaps most obviously patience. Impatience seeks immediate satisfaction. Desire, especially eros, can certainly be impatient, and is maybe the better and more intense for it. But seduction uses that impatience against itself, as a source of further intensity, a deeper need to know. This doubleness—the intensity imparted by impatient urgency and the sustaining by an infinite draw—seems to demand no less than the infinite object, the infinite as its object.[50] Astonishment is sudden, but it requires a practice of attentive slowness.

Unexpectedly, but just maybe rightly, Franz Kafka declares that all human sin comes down to impatience.[51] Patience must not be taken for passivity; it is attention, working with rather than solely imposing upon. In this, it is an asceticism, and we are, again, connected to the ascetic aesthetics of monasticism. Pranger writes in *The Artificiality of Christianity*, "my focus will be on slowing down, on retardation verging on immobility, and, indeed, on eternity."[52] The eternal *now* is found not by extending the moment, but by slowing the temporal flow in an intensity of focus until the moment can appear. Paying attention cannot be rushed; we cannot always flip ahead to the parts we already know we want to see and hear, or close the tab to view a more interesting window. Attention moves at the pace of the flesh of the world, of its movements and its voices. It may be that this attentiveness is becoming increasingly difficult for us—but if it is, it may well be correspondingly more important.

It is important in part because there is a kind of speaking that can only be response, a speaking grounded in listening and the call of the name—and listening takes time. We must be careful that we do not deprive others (speaking human others, or the analogical voice of the world, or in both the name that calls the divine) of meaningful speaking just because we cannot be bothered to listen. This is not selflessness; it is not only others we deprive of voice by our failure to hear. "We speak for having heard," writes Chrétien; "Every voice, hearing without cease, bears many voices within itself because there is no first voice."[53] The relation of call to response is not linear; here too we face the infinite retreat of an origin. What we put forth as our own voices are the entangled echoes and traces of infinite voices listened to before us and listened for after us, and the effects of all of our listening to them. That toward which we are seduced is, we might say, an origin, that first calling out, in its absence. Chrétien adds, "the call, as recall, repeats no first call: it is first at the moment when it repeats; its second time is really its first."[54] No doubt we can speak without listening, and most of the time I'm afraid that we do, but we cannot speak very well.

Beauty calls to us, and we call it beautiful. The world queries us, and when we find it beautiful we answer it in praise; we question the world, and it answers us with beauty, though not, as we must already suspect, with beauty alone. Understanding the world as gift, as divine sign, comes about not through logical analysis but "in the flash of a trembling glance,"[55] as a transformative revelation that the beauty of the world is not a dead end— but not because it takes us to some definitive where.

Just as we can understand theological "knowing" as both necessary and elusive, so too we must understand even this clearest call, that of beauty, as beyond our capacity to master it—that is, to respond in full, to answer in turn the call that responds to our attention. Like any good seduction, the draw of the beautiful entails neither the triumph nor the repression of the will. In this it is like Levinas's response to the call of infinite need, a responsibility that always exceeds my responsive capacity (a call, therefore, that importantly qualifies the celebratory sense of the world as gift, and so of the kinds of attention we have to pay).

The capacity to be engaged in call and response, the openness to the call that is and forms responsivity, is itself, says Levinas, a grace.[56] Grace entails openness—or, as I shall argue below, vulnerability. And this too is a Levinasian point, as Jeffrey Bloechl notes: "Levinas points to the source of goodness in an openness anterior even to this; 'grace' would then stand not for something in me, even if put there from the outside, but rather for the primordial fact that my interiority is wholly *for the Other*. . . . the word [grace] will have to refer simply . . . to a radical responsibility given eternally in advance."[57] This is not only the imposition of an obligation: the relation of call to response is a grace, meriting gratitude. And grace, the other-giving of the interior, is to be desired. While I shall differ from Levinas in some important respects, I would join him in this sense: that to be able to give is itself, as all graces must be, a gift. It is, sometimes, the gift of speaking.

The implication of call and response complicates more than it simply loops. It does not begin; it cannot be foreclosed; and it does not come to rest in an ontological security at either "end." Chrétien says that both the query of the original call and the answer of the final term are "abyssal," sending us "into a destiny of eternity."[58] That this is an abyssal cry, a cry of infinite depth and not only height, is vital.

The call is also an awakening of desire. No doubt we can, and often do, attend simply because we are fairly sure that we should, because we are dutiful. But even at our most dutiful we do as we should because we desire to—we want to be virtuous, or to act ethically. There is a pleasure in so doing, and a displeasure in our failure.[59] To think an ethos of call and response, then, we must think of desire even more, to understand both why and how we pay attention, why and how we might rightly be astonished.

I want to suggest that what rightly astonishes us is the peculiar object of faith, the mystery—what is of the world and yet not exhausted by it, the *more* of what is. The love of mystery is the love of questions, *not* a willful ignorance that refuses to ask. In such a willed ignorance (not to be confused with a learned ignorance) we would encounter at the start the impossibility of any response at all. We respond not in denial, but in desire.

Desire, Yes, Always

Anyone who has seen this knows what I mean when I say that it is beautiful. Even the desire of it is to be desired as a good.

—Plotinus, *Ennead* I.6, "On Beauty"

Classical Platonists and Neoplatonists would be unsurprised to find desire at the heart of the good life—that, after all, is where Plotinus clearly puts it, as does Plato in at least some of his guises (though he elsewhere seems to subordinate it to reason). But desirable desirousness seems a much odder fit for Christianity, which has had from very early on a potent ascetic element and, as I've noted, a complicated relation to desire, particularly that of the senses and the flesh—even though it gets much of this asceticism from its integration with Platonism. At least as early as Paul, we get the impression that desire may itself be undesirable, because in humanity after the Fall desire is so disordered as to be beyond redemption. It is a common enough notion that we are redeemed in the overcoming of desires (by our actions, by our faith, or by divine intervention, depending upon just whose version of the common notion we're dealing with). *Concupiscence,* understood by Augustine as the tendency toward sin that is consequent upon original sin, now has as its primary dictionary definition "sexual desire, lust," followed by "ardent, usually sensuous, longing."[60] Small wonder we conflate the senses of the term, and conflating them, small wonder we see *eros,* desirous love, as an ungracious obstacle and not as a grace in itself.

However, as James Alison points out, the fairly Augustinian Catholic dogma on the matter of desire is not so exactly a condemnation. It holds that desire is itself a good. It has become disordered in us, but it is not "radically corrupt." Not being bad in itself, desire is transformable (back) into a good.[61] So the idea that postlapsarian desire is corrupt remains, but even dogmatically the prescription for dis-corruption is not abolition: it is discipline and direction. Augustine declares that we must "fully and perfectly love" the good we seek, a love certainly of desire and not mere admiration. However, Augustine's Pauline sense of original sin means (at best) a perpetual reconversion. That is, he does not think that we can simply mend desire and then happily find ourselves only ever desiring well; rather, we must be on the mend perpetually. What mends us is a greater desire, and I want to argue not merely that desire is redeemable, but that, caught up in infinite enticement, it is redemptive.

This infinite desire, though, may mask another problem. Even if we allow that desire for the world's beauties might direct us toward divinity, we must hesitate a little bit before the notion of contemplating desire *between humans* as a response itself to be either ethically or divinely desired. We are more accustomed to thinking the call of other persons in terms of need or at least of want, of their lacks and demands and rights of inquisition—the infinite demand that Levinas makes so clear. Our desire for others has a kind of greediness to it, even if the greed is only of the senses. Can our responsiveness to the beauty of finite otherness really be ethical too?

I think that it can. Even Levinas acknowledges some parallel. Both desire and ethical response, for all that he wants to hold them apart, are deepened rather than fulfilled by their objects—although seductiveness is for him associated strictly and rather disapprovingly with desire, as an infringement upon the pure freedom to respond to the absolute demand.[62] In fact, we can already see some of the traits traditionally ascribed to eros in the foregoing discussions of response and attention. Erotic interest sustains attention better than nearly any other force or factor—indeed, it can introduce downright obsessiveness. It is likewise responsive, alert to what it loves, mobile in interaction. We love what we find beautiful, and what we love becomes more beautiful to us, not only in eros, but most vividly there.

This cannot, of course, be a narrowly sexualized view of desire. An expansion in the sense of what it means "to see beauty" is helpful. Augustine writes:

If there is no beauty in righteousness, why is a righteous old man loved? What is there in his body that may please the eyes? Crooked limbs, brow wrinkled, head blanched with grey hairs, dotage everywhere full of plaints ... what good do we see with the eyes of the flesh? None. There is therefore a kind of beauty in righteousness, which we see with the eye of the heart, and we love, and we kindle with affection: how much men found to love in the hideous martyrs, though the beasts tore their limbs![63]

This sounds at first rather more like a turn to the immaterial than a proper sensualist might prefer, with an inner vision of virtue privileged over the pleasures of sight. But a richer and more sensuous reading is also possible. Harrison says that Augustine's aesthetics allow for "an outward perception of inner beauty."[64] I would emphasize the genuinely *outward* character of this perception. We don't perceive that only inner beauty really counts; rather, our perception of what seems to be a non-sensory beauty interprets the evidence of our senses in the very process of perception. (Interpretation, we recall, is not just secondary.) We love with our eyes here, and not just with our minds—with our eyes, and with our ears and all of our abilities to sense. That association of love and beauty is no more unidirectional than the relation of call to response.

That is, our perception of what we consider "good" really does change the appearance that persons, but also objects, present to us. Moreover, our perception is changed simply by our attention. (We need only consider how fascinating a well-framed photograph of a very ordinary object can become.) There is a perceptual alteration caused by an intellectual and affective appreciation. We love—we desire—what is beautiful. (We can only love what is beautiful, Augustine insists).[65] But we also beautify what we love. Beauty calls because we are listening; we have to ask with our attention if we're to receive a response. Our attraction even to abstract beauties—righteousness, intelligence, humor—does not take us out of the world, nor replace the beauty of it, but deepens both its beauty and our attraction to it.

As Paul Moyaert writes of the Levinasian understanding of desire, "A love-relation is distinguished by a hypersensitive attention for the concrete."[66] The world into which beauty draws us is this one, in its emphatically concrete materiality. It draws us because it is beautiful, and it is beautiful because it draws us.

Destruction and Destitution

One cannot be deeply responsive to the world without being saddened very often.

—Erich Fromm, interview with Mike Wallace, ABC TV, 1958

So far I have focused on the kind of delighted desire that responds to beauty, but complex though this response is, it still gives us much too simplistic a sense of relationality. The openness to the mysterious, to the problematized boundaries of inside and out, arouses desire, but it creates trepidation too. Beauty draws us, I have said; it draws us not merely to but beyond its immediate presentation (thus sharing in the character of the sign). In this draw there is both a calling and a questioning, and there is an urgency and importance in our response to that beauty. Beauty, in being that toward which we are drawn, gives us a sense of space, of the drawn-into. Ugliness, correspondingly (if, of course, oversimply) closes off spaces, pushes us away. Beauty thus shares with the gift a relation to the possible, a sense of opening. It gives us a sense of delight in possibility.

But an ethical response requires the complication of destitution. The world's beauty is *not* always evident, perhaps most particularly where humanity is involved. (At the very least, we would have to admit that the world is not *simply* beautiful.) The notion that beauty everywhere sings the name of the divine is hard to hold to in a world in which the absence of goodness and beauty, whether or not we think that this indicates some active presence of evil and ugliness, has often been so much more obvious. Indeed, we focus narrowly upon some kinds of beauty—some simple prettiness, perhaps—at our peril, at the cost of our fullest flourishing and of our richest reading.

Levinas is clear about this, and it is one ground for the otherwise somewhat puzzling distinction he draws, and draws sharply, between the ethical and the desirous, though each is a mode of attentive response. He declares that to respond to the other aesthetically is to fail in ethical response:

> I think ... that access to the face is straightaway ethical. You turn yourself toward the Other as toward an object when you see a nose, eyes, a forehead, a chin, and you can describe them. The best way of encountering the Other is not even to notice the color of his eyes! When one observes the color of the eyes one is not in social relationship with the Other.[67]

There is here a deliberate *in*attention to all of the sensuality I've been emphasizing. Indeed, Rudolf Bernet adds in his gloss on Levinas's remarks, "Apprehending the form of the Other's body instead of responding to the infinite demand his 'face' expresses would be both a theoretical and ethical fallacy."[68]

To observe the color of the eyes, the shape of the chin—that appreciation of and attentiveness to concrete detail seems the quintessential desirous response to beauty, a response of obsessive attention. Levinas does not declare eros evil, but he does set it firmly apart from ethics. That to which he would have us ethically respond instead, the dual imperative and impoverishment expressed by the face, is behind or beyond the visual and not, it seems, emergent *as* the visual (not even in its marvelous transfiguration by love). For him, we ought to avoid being seduced by whatever beauty the face might possess, by the voice of delight called forth by the world, in favor of hearing the cry of the destitute voice even in its silence.

This face—this fully human, needy otherness—carries an interesting mix of attributes and meanings. It is vulnerable, impoverished, exposed. Its vulnerability might seem to invite violence, simply by making it so easy: we realize in the faces of others how very fragile they are. Yet the face is precisely thus the source of the imperative against violence, especially against homicide. The face-to-face encounter creates the ethical imperative by also offering the temptation to behave unethically—without that temptation, we have and need no imperative. The imperative against violence is the fundamental demand made by the presence of the other, says Levinas: "[The face] is the most destitute . . .: there is an essential poverty in the face; the proof of this is that one tries to mask this poverty by putting on poses, by taking on a countenance. The face is exposed, menaced, as if inviting us to an act of violence. At the same time, the face is what forbids us to kill."[69] For Levinas, the face *calls.* It is important, however, that it calls not as a seduction but as an imperative: it does not lure; it summons. In this its call is quite unlike the provocation of beauty. Like beauty, however, the face calls not for a specific response (though certain specific responses, notably homicide, are foreclosed by it), but rather for responsivity itself, and especially for speaking. Precisely because we must respond to the call, the content of this response cannot be set forth in advance. Here again, we will find the phrasing familiar: "Face and discourse are tied. The face speaks. . . . I have just refused the notion of vision to describe the authentic relationship with the Other; it is a discourse and, more exactly, response or responsibility which is the authentic relationship."[70] In the fullness of response, in speaking with the resonance of infinitely (many) other voices, we must consider destitution as well as bursting fullness, obligation as much as eros. The other, destitute and vulnerable, speaks to us synaesthetically, draws us into listening, demands of us that we speak—and though Levinas is paradigmatically interested in human relations, it seems at least possible that this is true of our relation to the rest of the given world as well, though not in exactly Levinasian terms. We too might sometimes have to speak for the trees, not least should they face imminent devastation. Is there anything of a seduction here in this rather grim obligation?

To answer in the affirmative requires that we complicate our terms still further. An ethics of enticement must modify an ethics of beauty in at least a few ways, to be able to respond not only to the gorgeous astonishment of beauty's presence, but also to the negative astonishment of destitution, of beauty's absence or apparent absence—and perhaps most vitally, the absence of the sense of the possible, of the world as inviting and opening, carried and created in beauty. Indeed, the two deepen and complicate one another. The first indication that there is more common ground here than there might seem occurs when we realize that destitution is not emptiness, not without power or force. For Levinas, the destitute other is not powerless, but, in her capacity to impose, oddly dominant: "The first word of the face is the 'Thou shalt not kill.' It is an order. There is a commandment in the appearance of the face, as if a master spoke to me. However, at the same time, the face of the Other is destitute; it is the poor for whom I can do all and to whom I owe all."[71] This combination of impoverishment and power, resourcefulness and indebtedness, is already familiar to us; Diotima claims resource and poverty as the parents of Eros. Like beauty, need calls us to answer to it; it does not usually call to more erotic forms of desire, but as in such desire, our mutual need to meet the needs of others is drawn to the creative potential of the future, our need not to have possibilities foreclosed. The opening of the possible is the call of both beauty and destitution, the call to enter spaces and the call to make them. We do not occupy the world alone (it would be no world if we did), and futurity—as, indeed, the fullness of the present—demands that possibilities be open in common—it is impossible that the possible be only for me. To attend to the present, then, is to see and to desire its openness, to the rest of time and to the eternal, to all of the possibility in it.

Levinas links this future to the otherwise than being, to ethics beyond ontology.[72] And he links it to the secret, which for him is the possible: that unknown which is not yet, but might yet be.[73] What is exposed, the bare face of the other, also imposes. But what it imposes is not a determinate actuality. It is rather the sustaining of possibility that life is. It imposes the demand of the possible. Not quite a seduction, this is yet not in every way distinct. Seduction cannot be imposed, yet it too exposes. It too must work to sustain possibility, and so, unless its impatience outweighs its desire, it forbids much impatient destruction. It too will forbid us to kill, but not by anything quite so direct as imposition. Rather, because the possible is the very matter of seduction, because seduction demands the open space of time in which it might yet play, it turns desire against death and against foreclosure—the seductions of desire deeply complicate our sense of mortal passing.

Destitution, with its impoverishment and insufficiency, belongs to the answer as well as to the call. Chrètien writes:

> In order to answer what Claudel . . . terms the "relentless gentleness" of the call, the soul, he says, must "kneel in a state of silence . . . weep in a state of creation . . . be crowned in a state of desolation." "I lack absolutely all means, says the soul, with which to answer," yet it "calls upon the inexhaustible resources of its own nothingness in order to provide what is required of it."[74]

More is always demanded, but this means too that we are always drawn further; in both our desire and our response to need we are impoverished, but resourceful too. Responsiveness to the seduction of the world is not the same as the ease of finding the world ever-friendly and abundant; it is rather allowing oneself to be called to uncertainty, even to impossibility, precisely *because* we respond so strongly to the call of the possible. We respond to need and to sorrow, but this we do *because* we respond so powerfully to beauty and joy that we hear the silence that falls on them, or the outcry of their absence, the voices that are missing from the possibility of harmony (or of a particularly lovely dissonance). When we resist responding to beauty, we resist not only our own discipline, but the sorrow and the demand that we know we will often find implicated in the beautiful. Responsiveness is our alertness to, and our astonishment at, the possible—in the cosmological models, to the very making possible and (as I shall suggest in the final chapter) the possibility before making. The possible and the strangely other, the mysterious draws of perpetual desire, are the demands of destitution too. Here too is mystery, and the infinite. Beauty entices more directly than does need, more easily, but need draws us with the possibility of its transfiguration into the enticing, the possibility of its reopened future—and our response includes our sense of responsibility for the pain of possibility's foreclosure.

This too is a trace of the sacred. Our vulnerabilities to the fullness and the deprivation of beauty are inextricable. "Theophanic beauty," says Chrétien, "is a theopathic beauty: the manifestation of God can be expressed only through a suffering of God, and enduring of God."[75] Divine sorrow answers to Beauty too.

The summoning space of the possible is at once open—not fulfilled or foreclosed, insofar as it remains possible—yet not empty in the sense of an empty space in which nothing can be done because there is no material with which to do it.[76] There is a necessary emptiness in this more positive sense, the sense of opening, traced through the plentitude of things. Beauty, the call to creation ("He made us"), calls not only where it is, where we see or hear or otherwise sense it, but also where it is not, where we feel its absence as the trace of the possibility that it could be—the possibility of making possible. We respond best by making most possible, whether we do so by a generosity of gentleness in which we allow ourselves to be drawn without imposing, or by a constructive generosity in which we re-create the space that was too empty for creativity to be possible. We respond in destitution too, responding to the imperative to speak even as we know the inadequacy of speaking: we must speak, knowing we cannot capture, knowing we cannot know. We must speak in order to listen.

Thus we might, and perhaps we must, reconceive "destitution" not as pure lack, but as both space and insufficiency, in the call and in the response alike. (It is not irrelevant that insufficiency characterizes all language, and indeed all signing.) The response is always tempered by the other aspect of emptiness, the creative possibility of space: emptiness and fullness are both dual. This is not to deny, but to complicate, the fear, the anxiety and frustration, of confronting a space one cannot fill, a need one cannot meet—or a beauty that overwhelms to the point of terror.[77] But we face here not so much an empty despair as dispossession and inadequacy—a never enough. My very words, by which I make myself, by which I enter into the world, are other than my own, and not only because I share a language: "The response of others is the future of our speech. . . . Such a future is intimately our own, yet without belonging to us."[78]

The Levinasian demand is infinite, interminable—in this lies the weight that has made his ethics seem at times an unbearable burden. But seduction too may be infinite. We do not respond only to the demand placed on us as a burden; we respond to the invitation opened to us, perhaps as a delight, perhaps as a sorrow, but at least as a possibility. Delight in beauty, as a wide-ranging desire, and the obligation to the other, as the demand of response, both belong to the discipline of attention, and both are drawn by the divine as it is traced in the world, beauty in its presence and in its imperfectly distinguishable absence. Both are the world's enticing trace of divinity, keeping us always in question.

Destitution reminds us that there is always an edge of sadness in our love of beauty, not least because beauty is fragile, and we are too, scarcely around long enough to enjoy it. We despair in the love of the beautiful, in the love of joy, because the very dispossession that delights us also reminds us that we cannot stay, and beauty will not last. There is terror in the love of beauty, because we can be annihilated, but also because we can so easily annihilate it.[79] We may love what is in the love of what is not, of what was or could be—of the memory or the restoration, the preservation or the creation, of the world as the astonishing gift of possibility. The presence of beauty opens our sense of the possible, of the world as promising; the absence of beauty opens the demand for possibility. The complexity of joy does not diminish it in the least; it may well, however, make it far more difficult for us to be willing to open ourselves to this strangeness. We must pay attention; this does not mean that we must always accept. Indeed, when we attend we shall find a great deal that is unacceptable.

To love the beautiful is not only to be attracted to it, but to desire both to be susceptible to attraction—to be a participant in one's own seduction, to want to want more—and to go on being attracted, to desire to hear the other's voice and meet her needs, but also to go on listening and trying to answer. In delighted desire we answer to beauty—but we must answer *for* beauty's absence and our destruction of it, too. We are drawn by the trace of beauty, by the trace of the divine left by its presence and its absence alike, the answer in the beauty of things inseparable from the questions they ask us, and keep us asking. When we stop asking, when we lose the question, we lose too the world as sacred. Such a responsiveness cannot be indifferent to suffering, not despite, but because of, its discipline of attraction to joy. Destitute otherness, like delightful mystery, exceeds infinitely both my ability to comprehend and my capacity to respond. Thus I too am in need, am not enough; the destitution of the other is also mine in my (in)ability to respond. I am called to respond by a dual vulnerability, my own where the call can enter, and that of the world into which I can step forth, and speak.

Vulnerability: Desire and Dispossession

Jesus said, "Let him who seeks continue seeking until he finds. When he finds, he will become troubled. When he becomes troubled, he will be astonished."

—The Gospel of Thomas, verse 2

As soon as I speak, my words are not simply my own—nor could I speak words if they were. For Plato (as he speaks through Diotima), beauty first draws us by our desire to possess it; recognizing the mortal impossibility of fulfilling that desire, we develop the more complex desire to unify ourselves with it such that some new beauty is created, in which we and the beautiful are joined forever. This version of eros—uniting and immortalizing—returns in psychoanalysis, with an added emphasis on desire's pull against itself (desire seeks satisfaction, which is the abolition of desire) and complication by our destructive urges. We may further remind ourselves that, for Plotinus, all response is grounded in likeness. The eye responds to light, he says, because it is structured like the sun. The soul resonates to beauty because it is itself beautiful, drawn to and by the Beauty that made it and that it eternally remains. So in these traditional interpretations, either I want to make the beautiful mine, or I want to make it me (by making myself it).

But we must recognize a counternarrative to this story of purely unitive desire, one at which the reversibility of such "possession" already hints. Chrétien asks "whether beauty says adieu," that is, "whether there is within it a power which breaks presence, which separates and invites separation, a power of denudation and dispossession, a demand for itinerancy."[80] Such a power would not be a simple lack or absence, but a far more complex relation of absence to the presence it breaks, a power a-dieu.

Such a dispossession is suggested by Levinas, precisely in his discussion of eros: "It is only by showing in what ways *eros* differs from possession and power that we can acknowledge a communication in *eros*. It is neither a struggle, nor a fusion, nor a knowledge. One must recognize its exceptional place among relations. It is the relationship with alterity, with mystery, that is, with the future, with what in the world where there is everything, is never there."[81] Eros, like ethics, is fundamentally addressed to alterity.[82] It is a relation to the mystery of the possible. In other words, for Levinas as for Augustine, we do not respond so strongly to beauty because we recognize it as being the same as us, but because we recognize the mystery of its otherness—the mystery, and not the simple numerical or qualitative fact of difference. And yet, I would add, we *recognize* here too. The mystery is not only outside of us.

As a relation to mystery, no desire attains (or ever entirely seeks) possession, but neither is its dispossession complete. Both possession and dispossession entail contact and elusion at once, moving without completion. And we cannot always tell these things apart, any more than we can perfectly distinguish touching from being touched, withdrawal from being withdrawn. As this suggests, responsiveness, whether to beauty or to need, must move us beyond easy divisions between subject and object, active and passive, and even same and other. Beth Hawkins writes: "In the transformation of the look, desire, too, is reconceived. Desire no longer suggests a passion for ownership or possession, but, rather, for reciprocation—'desire to see, desire to be seen.' In reestablishing the look as a potential source of relation, communion, the look is stripped of the violent tendencies it displayed before."[83] To be seen keeps me from being the invisible all-powerful. It may hold me desirable, but it holds me accountable too. The desire to be seen is a constraint upon my power-over. "But what happens," Chrétien asks, "...if the visible itself, through beauty, calls us and speaks to us? Beauty's call reaches us irresistibly and caringly and without our being able to master it.... From the start, to see is to respond to what in the visible calls out to us."[84] I look into visibility; I listen into speaking and speak into listening; I listen in seeing and speak in being seen.

This seductive reciprocity, with its echoes of Merleau-Ponty's in/visible, entwined world-flesh, is ethically crucial. It suggests a kind of synaesthesia, in which the look, becoming less static, becomes also more like voice.[85] We can practice speaking not to impose (not to force others to hear us), but because we listen, knowing that listening will help us to speak and vice versa. We enter into conversations; we speak with; we question and answer; we praise and we mourn, without a goal, drawn by the mutual pull of words and things. Beauty, again, provides us with the most obvious case; delight calls to language in a way that misery or obligation does not. But once we have learned to attend slowly to what calls us in fairly pure pleasure, we may begin to attend to other desires and other needs. Once we interpret the world as gift, open in grace, we can begin to see both the delights that open possibility and our own ungenerosity and the foreclosures of grace endemic to human relationality. The mystery that draws us out of ourselves is both radically other and our own otherness too. Response and attention open us to our own disappropriation.

Otherness is unknowability, infinite rather than susceptible to comprehension or possession. But the multilocation of mystery suggests that otherness is not the same as utter foreignness, which so eludes my thought that I cannot even be drawn to it. The strangeness that draws me out is neither quite me nor quite alien. Self and otherness, inside and out, are troubled here, as Nancy points out: "But the *self* of the other is already within the 'same' that is not itself. It trembles through the 'same,' shudders *through* it so that all at once the 'same' gives way and finds itself determined. The other *transits*, or *entrances*, the 'same' and makes it come to pass."[86] Nancy is not claiming indifference, as if everything were somehow the same, as if same and other simply got muddled in transition. On the contrary, difference dwells within all apparent identity, such that "within" becomes not quite the right word. We are as we are because of what is other than us, what passes through us and entices us beyond ourselves. Nancy's point echoes Levinas's: "Through sight, touch, sympathy and common work we are *with* others. All these relations are transitive. I touch an object, I see the other; but I *am* not the other."[87] Our relationships are "transitive" not merely grammatically, but because we are transited and entranced. We are in transition: our boundaries are not fixed. This means, too, that we cannot simply possess what we desire. Both the strange beauty of the other and my own strangeness draw me out, the world resonating with my own within-ness, with the seductive possibility of reversal. Calling into the spaces of the world, we call to divinity too; we ask with our attention.[88] To call the name, Derrida says, is not to hold possessively onto it, but to traverse toward the named other.[89] To be *with*, dispossessively, and to speak to by name, are both in motion toward, but not a motion that can reach or grasp.

Thus the "same" that here calls to and "recognizes" sameness is mysterious strangeness itself. What traces within the sensory and finite entices us as an infinite name, abstract and yet sensuous too. Following this trace, we are drawn to that infinite—we, who are also traced through with this absent divinity, transited by it. "In" us, it also exceeds us, to draw us to itself (never the self-same) in the other. It is the other's mystery, too, that cuts through me: makes, within me, new spaces. The "finite other," says Levinas, "is a trace of the infinite." [90] What draws us as a relation to this mysterious trace of infinite mystery draws "out" the mystery "in" us too.[91]

What desires sustaining must sustain mystery too. We find reemergent the important difference between a seductive questioning and a teleological interrogation. We attend to matter, to flesh, not as if it were in the way of the answers we need, but as that which will draw us into infinite query. The carnality of divine enticement, its attention to the fact of flesh, marks a difference from the Levinasian approach as well as from the (Neo)Platonic. Robert Gibbs points out that, though Levinas's emphasis on the absolute demand of the other can lead to an emphasis on suffering sometimes regarded as too Christian,[92] it is important to Levinas that the divine is not made incarnate, even or especially in the face of the other. Rather, the other manifests God's transcendence, is "where the difference opens up."[93] Elliot Wolfson, however, points out some complications in this resistance. In the Levinasian face-to-face relation, he argues, there is "a residuum of incarnational thinking," though not of the Christian variety. Rather, embodiment is part of one's moral stance: "One's own materiality can be considered the locus of infinite transcendence in the sense that it is dependent on the immediacy or proximity of the other, on the sensibility of being there for the other."[94] Levinas, Wolfson argues, misses or misreads the kind of incarnationalism at work in the Jewish mysticism that nonetheless influences his thought. From the Kabbalistic standpoint, " 'Body' does not denote physical mass . . . but the phenomenological sense of the corporeal as lived presence," a sense given an interesting turn in the Kabbalistic entanglements of textual body and bodily text.[95] The face may not be quite disconnected from the body after all, so long as we read in bodies the constant emergence, the possibility, that keeps them from static materialism.

We are seduced not simply by the presence of beauty but by the tantalizing slippage of present and absent, of delight and desire—of the eternal cutting through the present even as presence withdraws from us, of meaning as it slides before our senses. Desire keeps us from being wholly our own, traces us too with the track of infinite transition. We neither fully perceive nor entirely miss the infinite in the finite, neither within us nor altogether without. But unless we properly attend to finite things, in their fullness and in their emptiness, we cannot see that they are also more.

The othering within myself, as I am passed through and remade by who and what is not me—this dispossession by the shock of the beautiful and the sorrowful—reminds me vividly that I am not invulnerable, and this too is a point of no small ethical significance, requiring considerable delicacy in attention. Beauty reverberates not simply with sameness (myself found in the outside) but also with otherness (what is also other in me, but as wound, a constitutive self-rupture.)[96] Need arouses empathy, but also incomprehension. Both awaken us by reminding us that we are not just us. This is why vulnerability is so important: without it, we close ourselves off and are, so far as possible, only us, untransited, perhaps intransigent. Mary-Jane Rubenstein suggests that Levinas considers "the possibility that responsibility relies upon vulnerability rather than mastery or uncertainty."[97] We naively think of the balance in vulnerability as one between protecting ourselves, our fragile interiors, and investing ourselves, our energies and emotions, in something other, such that it is permitted to affect that interior. But in fact vulnerability is as essential to self-making as it is to unselfishness. A perfect unselfishness is impossible; as Jeffrey Bloechl points out, a certain self-absorption is even essential for the revelation of absolute otherness, for the exterior/interior contrast—and, we can add, the troubling of that contrast—to make any sense.[98]

The troubling of interior and exterior, self and other, has a perhaps unexpected consequence here: among the beauties and needs to which we must attend are those we experience as our own. To delight in our own beauty is not the narcissistic silliness it must at first sound, particularly once we get past the notion that our boundaries are determinate; it is to delight not only in what gives us the capacity to enter into the world, but also in the transitions in which the world enters us. It seems almost equally odd to insist that we must attend to our own needs, especially if we have just insisted on the ethical importance of vulnerability—our very capacity to be wounded. But if we trouble inside and out, which is precisely what vulnerability must do, then we must attend *to* our own vulnerability, to the limits at which we are not able to delight or to listen or speak—not able to listen because we cannot speak.

We are not simply ourselves, not our own self-possessions, and the desire, delight, and compassion we exhibit are caught up in the subject-troubling of call and response. When what calls to me calls from what I experience as "within," I need no less to listen. Thus, though the obligation of seduction is as infinite as that of Levinas's demand, it is not as depleting, precisely because it must circle back upon the obligated, precisely because I cannot listen if I cannot speak, and not just vice-versa. The troubling and transiting of subjects (which is not their annihilation) thus also tells us that we must attend to what comes to us as or through ourselves, to our own delights and emptinesses, to mystery wherever it is. Because we can no longer be so certain of inside and out, we should not fail to answer the call that seems to come in no other voice than our own (it is never only our own). Nor is this to fall back into unquestioning comfort; we are great enigmas to ourselves.

To be vulnerable is to be open, not only to the chance of wounding, but to the mystery, to the possible; it is to let go of the protection of rigorously imposing predictability. To be seduced, I allow myself to be seducible, to risk. To be seduced by beauty is not to find myself outside myself, same to same; neither is it is to be faced with absolute otherness in its infinite and nonreciprocal demand. It is, instead, to respond precisely to the play of same and other, to delight in what is also other in me, to ache for what is missing or destroyed, to read the trace of the question asked by my own attention. I am drawn by what is other, and not the same, and by what is other within my sameness.[99] As Bernet nicely puts it, I respond to "a strangeness in me"—to which I have a "pre-originary" susceptibility.[100] This strangeness is not a transcendent infinite; it is the astonishment of what in the "immanent" nonetheless cannot be captured, of the so-much of just being here. As strange, as unknowable rather than as simply unknown, it is inappropriable. We respond as awakened, enlivened—yet as opened, even wounded, too.

Levinas argues that it is only through the infinitude of otherness that we know the divine.[101] I would add that it is not only in others that we encounter this otherness. The ethical response to the mysterious difference in and out of the same is neither to appropriate nor to make the same. It is to enter into, to be entered into: to be cut across. It is an unsettling of our secure individuation, but not via entry into an absolute whole, nor by the incorporation of a previously distinct other. This response is the experience of the inappropriability not only of other persons but of the world, the aching insufficiency of it, the seductive extraordinary overburstingness of it and the spaces that make making possible.

Chrétien returns vulnerability to call and response: "The call of the beautiful is a call that recalls itself to us by recalling us to ourselves. To wound us in the heart brings its utterance to life. It draws us out of our poise and makes us lose our immobility. It calls only to disquiet us."[102] Not least disquieting is the finitude of beauty, the mortality it shares with us. We are vulnerable especially to the sharpest reminder of finitude—to death, which is the end of all wounding—and so, it seems, of possibility. Yet generosity is possible out of the relations of mortality. ("Each knowing that the other was going to die," writes Blanchot, "everything was enlarged by a generosity of space.")[103] We are drawn by this duality, the trace of the infinite in the fact of our finitude—in it, and not transcending it. Mortal passing is mutually implicated with eternity, and we see divinity in passage too. As Wetzel notes, "Augustine never claims to be able to see divine perfection other than in the visible things of creation, whose corruptibility is his usual notice. When he loves God in these things, he sees something immortally beautiful in a mortal offering."[104] What sustains the seductiveness of mortal beauty is paradox: the infinite is not traced *despite* the finite; they are in need of one another. Though Augustine thinks that his more impatient desires for mortal things pull him away from God, it is through those things that he is drawn beyond the ending implicit in time. In his *Confessions*, Augustine remarks that he has erred in loving mortal things as if they could be immortal.[105] Ending is always a problem for him, and always happens too soon. But *in* the movement before and toward that end is the eternal outside of all ending, not because it lasts, but because it is not only temporal.

In his comprehensive survey of the early Christian practice of permanent sexual renunciation, Peter Brown says of Augustine that he always considered death and not the fugitive quality of bodily pleasure to be "the most bitter sign of human frailty." He writes:

> For death frustrated the soul's deepest wish, which was to live at peace with its beloved, the body.... And apart from some such recognition about him, it is easy to misconstrue his sense of the weightiness of sexual habit.... The weight that pulls him away from immortality is, in his mind, his own perverse and inexplicable love of the corruption of things, as if he were harboring a death-wish for what he loves. [106]

Rather than being a denial of mortality, responsive living is mortality directed to living in the full intensity of attentive vulnerability, living not in denial but toward something other than its end. Seduction in its imperative to sustain is always in play with death, as what keeps us from being only toward death, that which entices us off the straight path toward dying, and what is given its sharpest edge by finitude. The relation between us and the other, us and the flesh of the world, is not only death, with the obligations mortality imposes, but the draw of desire: not only the future, but also the eternal in the moment. Both are spaces of the possible.

Astonishment: Mortal Speaking

I have found my music in a common word
Trying each pleasurable throat that sings

—Gerard Manley Hopkins, untitled early poem

I have said that to find the eternal and the possible, we attend; we slow down. The discipline of this seducibility is one of newly perceiving what already is—like a monk, or like an artist, who sees with a care that makes the ordinary strange. Here I would differ more sharply from Levinas, who argues against art: "To make or appreciate a novel and a picture is to no longer have to conceive, is to renounce the effort of science, philosophy, and action. Do not speak, do not reflect, admire in silence and in peace—such are the counsels of wisdom satisfied before the beautiful." [107] To prolong the process of perception, to make even seeing difficult, is not to renounce effort but to pronounce attention.

This again is the discipline of paying attention, and then prolonging attentiveness, by attending first to the strangeness of the ordinary. "Know what is in front of your face, and what is hidden will be disclosed to you,"[108] says Christ in the "Gospel of Thomas"; the mystery is not only in some elsewhere. Moreover, this prolonged perception, like attentive listening-speaking, reveals not just the otherness and unknownness of things and of persons, but their *strangeness*, which astonishes us—their mystery. Attention, which familiarizes us with things, must also be able to defamiliarize, opening the possibility of amazement, and so of gift.

Here too is a perception grounded in a particular faith, not unlike the epistemology that accepts the value of the open question: the faith that we may be astonished. "We encounter the extraordinary with astonishment, though we should be astonished at . . . ordinary things too," says Plotinus.[109] We are amazed by mystery not only as we realize how much is elusive or hidden, but precisely before the revealed. Chrétien writes, "Revelation does not abolish mystery, but reveals mystery as such."[110]

And mystery is everywhere revealed. Nancy writes: "At the heart of thought, there is *some thing* that defies all appropriation by thought (for example, its appropriation as 'concept,' or as 'idea,' as 'philosophy,' as 'meditation,' or even as 'thought'). This thing is nothing other than the immanent immobility of the fact *that there are things.*"[111] This most ordinary and inescapable aspect of the world is also beyond grasping. We cannot quite think this. But we can desire it, and echo to things as to others the praises they voice in the world. Nancy reminds us that "To give and to withhold, to give oneself and to withhold oneself, these are not contradictories here."[112] We withhold our impatient urge to speak over all other voices, including those we only see or touch. In so doing, we give ourselves as attentive, and we are given back the gift of the very speaking we resisted rushing forth. The world as gift is given not in totality but in relation. Our relation to it, our seduction into call and response, begins as Augustine's begins: we have to pay attention. And it continues as Augustine's glorious voices continue in the city of God: it says. That *there are things* exceeds them all.

This too echoes a Levinasian point. Rubenstein writes: "The ethical relationship that Levinas designates as the occurrence of the Good entails a reciprocal openness: the abject vulnerability of the other is mirrored by my own vulnerability to that vulnerability. This exposure that responds *as* exposure *to* exposure . . . goes by the names of *discourse, speaking,* or, in Levinas's later work, *saying.*"[113] Speaking is only possible where language has already entered; language can enter only where there is speaking. Rubenstein adds, "Taken from itself, the self is restored to itself as a reference to otherness—a *sign.*"[114] This possible restoration can present a problem—if I simply get myself back, my vulnerability seems irrelevant, perhaps ungenuine. But if self-restoration always restores a changed self, a self always changing, then this sign too, speaking in exposure and shared vulnerability, may say the name of the divine. In my speaking is the responsive echo of infinitely other voices.

What we perceive demands our attention, exceeds our thought and our words. What we say exceeds material, entices our flesh. Words and things seduce one another. We are called to say the beautiful and the good (in their absence too); without reduction to simple facticity, we are called to say the truth, a truth necessarily incomplete. We are called to answer as we are called to and into question. And we can be called only because we listen.

As Chrétien writes: "The call that recalls us is also a promise that keeps us beholden; it gives us speech only by gripping us by the throat. No hymn will be able to keep it. Yet every hymn, torn and heartrending, must remit itself to this promise for safekeeping, entrust itself to it, give itself to it and lose itself, always already, always more, never enough."[115] The secret cannot be kept; one cannot hold onto mystery or *capture* it in words—but one is no less called to say it. To say it, but responsively, which is to know that mysteries slip into silences too: to be called to speech and to be called to hear are as inextricable as any call and response. Ethical speaking is truth telling, but we can only know the truth where we have listened.

The beautiful, like the question, compels us to repeat it,[116] and beauty, like everything strange, nonetheless exceeds our capacity to say it—exceeding that capacity, it calls us further to speech. That is: when we attend, the world is revealed in the mystery of its strangeness; the strange calls to us, and we can respond only by reaching toward it, incompletely, addressing it in query and praise alike. Thus Celan: "The poem holds its ground on its own margin. In order to endure, it constantly calls and pulls itself back from an 'already-no-more' into a 'still-here.' The 'still here' can only mean speaking. Not language as such, but responding."[117]

Language rushes toward silence, toward not-being, like the other it addresses, like the world it describes. But it responds in still-speaking, naming, even so. Call and response are infinitely looped: we respond to what calls our attention, we call to it by calling it beautiful, and thus we too call to Beauty. We try to say the world as it is, we try to address others as they are, as part of this complex call, this infinite name that *is* the name of the question, of the reach and address. But the world as it is, others as they are, are also the very possibilities of what they have not yet been.

Perhaps the saying of things reflects, through the desire implicit in all language, our sense of the deep desirability of the world. Wallace Stevens even imagines immaterial spirits returned to hear the saying of things, as close to matter as they can get. "There were ghosts that returned to earth to hear his phrases," he writes in "Large Red Man Reading":

There were those that returned to hear him read from the poem of
    life,
Of the pans above the stove, the pots on the table, the tulips among
    them.
They were those that would have wept to step barefoot into reality,

That would have wept and been happy, have shivered in the frost
And cried out to feel it again, have run fingers over leaves
And against the most coiled thorn, have seized on what was ugly

And laughed, as he sat there reading.[118]

In language, the ghosts can feel again the world directly accessible only to those still enfleshed (and in their delight in flesh, even ugliness is transfigured, not unlike the flesh of that righteous old man). Rainer-Maria Rilke likewise imagines language as reaching from material to immaterial, bringing delight in its reach.

Perhaps we are here just to say: house,
    bridge, fountain, gate, jug, fruit-tree, window—
    at most: column, tower. . . . But to say them, understand,

oh, to say them more intensely than the Things themselves
ever dreamed of being.

For Rilke, saying seems to exceed beings, but only as it is superadded to
what is, as a recognition of beauty:

And these Things, that live
on impermanence, understand that you are praising them;
  transient,
they look to us for deliverance: us, most transient of all.[119]

Our saying exceeds the swiftly lost time of both sayer and said; even as it
passes, it attends to the moment. Thus it addresses eternity, and when we
"praise this world to the angels, not the unsayable one, they will stand astonished."[120] Matter in its passage, word slipping into silence, and eternity
all call to one another, and in the moment of that calling is what exceeds all
of them, the response of an infinite name.

The call calls across times to otherness. If beauty, pleasure, fearful seductiveness "mean," if they signify, they do not do so in the manner in which we
are accustomed to think of signification, with meaning neatly set apart from
the signifying form of sound or letter. Rather, the sensuous sign entices
infinitely. Even Levinas, with his hesitancy about desire, declares: "For my
part, I think that the relation to the Infinite is not a knowledge, but a desire.
I have tried to describe the difference between desire and need by the fact
that Desire cannot be satisfied . . . It is a paradoxical structure."[121] Desire, not
knowledge, relates us to the infinite because desire is without finality—
but knowledge caught up in the desire to know is transfigured too. And the
world faces us: we attend, and it answers us and it questions us. It calls to us,
if we make ourselves vulnerable. It shows us the astonishment of possibility,
to which we answer with our own openness, terrified, delighted, or both.
The answer is finite unless it is a question too. We must answer to beauty,
answer for beauty—and for our careless inattentions, too, to all the divine
names that it calls, to the world as the very sign of divine enticement.

The world is seductive, but seduction is never single-sided. We are
in and of the very world that seduces us, complicit—and seductive
ourselves—in our own vulnerability and desire. We are, we can be, seduced
by the world, by people and by things. But this requires, far from the lazy

self-indulgence it implies, a careful discipline of attention. The call of beauty may be ubiquitous, but it is easily drowned out by our impatience, our inattentiveness, and even our caution, which urges us to know in advance what the next moment will bring. The call of destitution is difficult and demanding, and we would rather not hear it, not hurt for the echo of the possible so nearly silenced within it. We are deeply reluctant to stand astonished in the world; we don't want to take the time to praise it. We want to contain ourselves without the threatening bother of transition by the other—and especially not by the infinite. And thus we're able to treat the world and others in it not as spaces for the openings of possibility, but as raw material for the worst kind of domination, that which is unable to pick up on the thousand subtle cues that could transfigure it (seduce it) into interaction, that would speak without speaking-over.

We must in fact estrange ourselves, make the world and the other strange, to encounter them with astonishment, as always new, as reborn. Our dispossession is not least a matter of the words we are called to speak. Words call us and reach out, but in them we are strangers too. William Franke writes, "In language . . . we are essentially estranged from ourselves and from every possible source or ground for our world."[122] Yet far from undoing any chance of an enchanted reading of the world, this re-enchants and re-entices us: we are opened. Language does not make present; it does not freeze in time. It designates, to be sure, but it also calls, and the calling reaches out to a mystery—to incarnational ghosts, to concrete things. Certainly there may be something extraordinary, exotic seeming, about the mystery of all otherness. But even within its extraordinary character, the mystery is everyday too: we are attentive to it in something as simple as a conversation in which we await responses rather than presuming them, creating an actual space for speaking by the rare act of listening. Mystery is everywhere in the space of the possible. We are called to hold that space open. We must find or create in ourselves the capacity to be seduced, to be drawn into the world; not beyond it, but into the infinite possibilities that shimmer across it and within it, calling the name that infinitely withdraws its meaning and opens the space for new questions.[123] It is in silence that meaning is gathered, but we find no meaning if we only stay silent. Words reach in and out of their own impossibility, toward others, toward things, toward a name beyond saying. Trembled-through by silence, words and the subjects they make, words and the subjects who make them, stand astonished. "But I think," says Celan, ". . . that the poem has always hoped, for this very reason, to speak also on behalf of the *strange*—no, I can no longer use this word here—*on behalf of the other*, who knows, perhaps of an *altogether other*."[124] On behalf of the infinitely strange beauty of the world, we praise; on behalf of the other, we call by name: the poem moves toward an approachable *you*, across an abyss of difference. The elusive, transient touch of otherness, gone through us before we can quite grasp it, is as close as we come to Beauty itself: "And once," says Celan, "by dint of attention to things and beings, we came close to a free, open space and finally, close to utopia."[125] Such attention is the seductive: it can only remain in question.

4

Prayer: Addressing the Name

Yet every sentence is not a proposition; only such are propositions as have in them either truth or falsity. Thus a prayer is a sentence, but is neither true nor false. Let us therefore dismiss all other types of sentence but the proposition, for this last concerns our present inquiry, whereas the investigation of the others belongs rather to the study of rhetoric or of poetry.

—Aristotle, *On Interpretation*, §4

Ethical speaking is a strange, intercut mode of address and listening. As some of the peculiarities of the sign are made vivid in thinking of sacraments as divine signs, so too the strangeness of speaking is especially evident when it calls upon an infinite addressee. In considering the peculiarity of prayer as an address from finite to infinite, I have followed Nancy, for whom "The singular address to a singular God—my god!—is prayer in general."[1] The singular address links prayer to love, with an echo of Augustine's "what then do I love when I love my God?"[2] But the idea that this is "prayer in general" is not universally shared. Levinas, notably, insists that true prayer is communal, because it opens and shares, functions he believes private prayer fails. Community is for him necessary for an interrogative opening, and as such it is the only proper place for this most open of addresses.[3] I would certainly join Levinas in valuing opening and interrogation, but find my own thought closer to Nancy's sense of the "self" as already made in being transited, always opened or exposed to an outside. The particular opening that community makes possible may turn out to be closer to the earlier considerations I have made of the fundamentally communal sacrament; the point is not that one or the other opens more, but that they do so a little bit differently. The distinctions are not as sharp as we might at first think; the consideration of sacraments as formalized rituals in community also inflects the sense of the world as sacramental, with its ethical implications. And that sense in turn, with its emphasis on call and response and the resonant sounding of voices, becomes central to the consideration of prayer. Prayer is a curious interrogation no matter who may pray, or how many. Individuation is necessarily troubled in any relation, but the trouble is especially vivid in the call that would relate one to a singularly infinite divinity.

As Nancy realizes, the address or outcry "my God!"—characteristic of joy and devastation alike, of ecstasy and abandonment—is grammatically a little bit odd. We use the phrase, he says, "as we say 'my friend' or as we used to say 'my Lord.' . . . In each case, behind the apparent possessive there in fact lies what we ought to call an interpellative: you, here, now, are entering into a singular relationship with me."[4] In fact, "my God" (as Nancy fully recognizes) is still more puzzling than "my friend," despite the deep complexity of my relation to any other person. When I call my friend, I call by her individuating name; when I call "my God," as Nancy says, "I am entering into a singular relationship with the lack of a singular name."[5] The name of my friend calls in part because it also designates, though its call is not limited to its designating. How do we call a name without designation?

Nancy echoes Friedrich Hölderlin's argument that "holy names are lacking."[6] For Nancy, this has a profound impact on our ability to use such names, to call (on) *my God*. Divine names "no longer refer to gods," leaving us unable to use those names for the beings they once designated. "They are, as *divine* names (and not as the nomenclature of worship), strictly unpronounceable: they no longer call upon 'My God.' "[7] In this lack of names, says Nancy, prayer is suspended. We can celebrate the divine, but we cannot pray without names; at most, we cite those names and those prayers.[8]

I have argued here (not least under Nancy's influence) that holy names do lack a certain kind of referentiality. Prayer cannot provide a name as definite referent, but it can call upon and respond to the sign of infinite enticement. It can address, both as we always address, reaching toward without quite reaching, and as we address nothing else, reaching toward what is itself question. It is suspended in the sense of remaining always between, yet we do call upon the name in suspense, the name that is lacking designation but abundant in seductive evocations. There is a poetic quality to this kind of addressing. Blanchot quotes Kafka as answering the question "Do you mean that poetry tends toward religion?" with, "I will not say that, but toward prayer, certainly."[9] More extensively, Celan writes of poetry, "A poem, being an instance of language, hence essentially dialogue, may be a letter in a bottle thrown out to sea with the—surely not always strong—hope that it may somehow wash up somewhere, perhaps on a shoreline of the heart. In this way, too, poems are *en route*: they are headed toward. Toward what? Toward something open, inhabitable, an approachable you, perhaps."[10] Poetic language is not an arrival but a reach, always approaching. So too is prayer. What the genres share is also what sets them aside from most prose—not just their frequent musicality and sensory beauty, but the very fact of address, evident in their frequent use of the second person.

This grammar of address is fundamental to prayer. Merold Westphal writes: "To address God as 'you' would seem to be a necessary condition for prayer. To present oneself as 'yours,' in which that you is *aufgehoben*, would seem to be the necessary and sufficient condition of prayer."[11] That "you" is the pronoun for a most elusive name. The prayer, as Celan says of the poem: "is lonely . . . . Its author stays with it. Does this very fact not place the poem already here, at its inception, in the encounter, *in the mystery of encounter*?"[12] The encounter with mystery, which is not quite grasp, not quite rest, is itself mysterious. It is not quite a meeting, with not quite a presence. The address to mystery must also render its language strange. "Each time Augustine addresses God," Pranger notes, ". . . he evokes the newly found source of his life. Yet, by nature of his timelessness, this same addressee of his prayers is also the black hole in his remembering mind, in his prayer, his thought and his narrative."[13] This beauty so old and so new is before what he can remember, later than his newest love.[14]

The one who reaches out, who calls, will be transited and complicated by the very question, the question proper to the caller (the *you* is *my* God, even as the *I* is *yours*), yet without the bounds by which propriety is set (*my* God is infinite, unbounded, always question and in question). Every question makes an opening and so is just a little bit improper. (So your mother might have told you, suggesting that you not be quite so inquisitive with strangers.) The most profound question, says Blanchot, "places us in relation with what evades every question and exceeds all power of questioning."[15] Prayer addresses itself to what not only exceeds it, but even evades it. No matter how manifest, Blanchot says, the profound question "still flees." Yet, he adds, "perhaps this flight brings us into relation with something essential."[16] Blanchot sees some measure of such evasive strangeness in all address. The other approaches indirectly by evasion and retreat—not out of a perverse hostility, but so that the separation or space necessary to speaking is maintained.[17] The distance in all speaking is "infinite" in a sort of Zeno's paradox fashion—it is uncrossable, uncloseable. This infinite distance imposes an impossible demand—the demand of response, that we "engage with speech."[18] The mere act of address carries its own demand; failing to meet it, as Barthes reminds us, we risk boring the addressee. He writes to the author of the boring text, "You address yourself to me so that I may read you, but I am nothing to you except this address . . . for you I am neither a body nor even an object . . . but merely a field, a vessel for expansion."[19] Instead, "the text you write must prove to me *that it desires me*."[20] Address is a desirous relation, or it is a failure. Prayer's address reaches beyond a single body or object, but it must address, still, must seek more or other than its own expansion.

Prayer brings us into relation with what exceeds both us and the language that is our means of relating; the nature of that relation—its modes of address, its implicit responsivity, its revelations, its embodiment—forms the questions for the rest of this chapter.

Calling the Name, Responding to the Impossible

You? Can that be you?
Imagine! And here, of all places!

—David Markson, *Wittgenstein's Mistress*

In *Dis-Enclosure*, Nancy refines his sense of non-referentiality to declare that divine names have meaning *only* in calling: " 'God!' " he writes, "only takes on 'sense' in calling, in being called, and even, if I may say so, in calling himself."[21] The call in its seductive reversibility (a reversibility that may even allow the name to call itself) is enfolded in the sense of the singular yet lacking name, a name lacking reference to a thing: we hear the call that we echo; the call that we hear echoes our own desire. The divine name is a name that calls and calls forth, even when it calls out to itself.

Attending to desire, the prayer doesn't only call, but necessarily listens, to the divine. In exploring Samuel's *here I am* (I Samuel 3:4–10), Westphal points out that one prayerfully reveals oneself as an *answer* to a divine call, an answer that is in its turn an invocation. Samuel "is called, called forth, even called into being by a voice not his own,"[22] and he in response to the call presents himself "as a listener."[23] Augustine in the *Confessions* likewise (though more complicatedly) presents himself both as a listener eager, or maybe desperate, for the word, straining to catch God's meaning, and as a speaker who tells of himself, as he says, "for love of your love" (2.1). For both (and they are exemplars among many others), to speak *is* (once more) to listen—when Augustine prays, when Samuel answers, they strain to catch the traces of God's voice in their own.

In this grammatical interpellative, the act of prayer unsettles the very relation and distinction on which it seems to be founded: the self over here and finite, and God infinitely out there. Samuel's "here I am," says Westphal, is an entirely free statement; nonetheless, "He does not originate the conversation but is called."[24] The response to address "decenters" us. Samuel presents himself, reveals himself, but he is not alone in revelation. So too when Augustine confesses himself to God (and not so much to his readers, causing centuries of frustrated fascination): so that God might "come into" him, he reveals himself too. It is to God Augustine wants most to reveal himself, God he wants to read him in the seductively graceful text. This desire displays the reversibility of seduction: Augustine hopes that God will read him in the beautiful text as he reads God in the beauty of scriptural text and created world. Failure to reveal himself to God has a curious effect, the reverse of what we might anticipate: "I would be hiding you from myself," he writes, "not myself from you" (10.2.2). Augustine reveals himself to seduce divine revelation, tells his story to call God toward him and to learn how to read sacred signs—how to hear God called out by the world. What he reads in the world calls out to the divine, which in turn calls Augustine into himself. As Pranger points out, "In a sense the first and third person are sublimated into the second, as in—confessional—prayer which is the ultimate literary rendering of the 'object' bestowing itself."[25] The address has a graceful gravitation.

The one who prays does not call and *then* find that God is revealed; rather, the revelation is in the calling, in the answer that is another call, that has a question built into it. "Surely when I call on him," Augustine writes, that is, when he uses the second person in relation to God, "I am calling on him to come into me" (1.1.1). This doubly reaching invocation is typical of prayer. The divine is the perfect *you*, *my God* the ultimate address. But address multiplies. "Do not be vain, my soul," writes Augustine; "Even you have to listen. The Word himself cries to you to return" (4.11.16). We too call upon ourselves, if only to remind ourselves to pay attention to the call.

Even a third party may be drawn in, as in the case of the Augustinian text, which seductively leads its readers into temptations, and not only those Augustine describes as his own: he entices us with his desire to praise (a desire, we come to realize, that he desires to share); he draws us with his desire to describe the infinite "object" of that praise; and he makes us want to join in, to enter into this relation.

All language is relational, belonging wholly neither to speaker nor to listener, but the language of prayer is unusually unlikely to speak from a clearly defined subject position. For Blanchot, Kevin Hart argues, "we might say that we do not experience God," with we the subjects knowing a divine object, "but rather encounter Him by way of an infinite relation."[26] We encounter in a proximity without meeting, without grasp. "Nah ist / und schwer zu faßen der Gott," writes Hölderlin. The grammatical structure makes the English hard to render; Michael Hamburger wisely goes for a fairly literal translation: "Near is / and difficult to grasp, the God."[27] Prayer is reach and just possibly passing touch, but never grasping; nearness, but never co-location. Nancy links the very space that differentiates proximity from full contact with God—or what is left after God, after the death or loss of the solidity of the God who is some-thing: "The interval, the space between us—which makes 'us' possible—is all that remains when there is no more God. God filled the intervals; he was himself without interval."[28]

Nothing fills the intervals, but we cannot simply identify the divine with nothing (particularly not if we retain any trace of the Augustinian; for Augustine, nothingness is evil). There remains the interval itself, not a nothing between somethings but the space that makes us and speaking and communication in all of its imperfection, the sound interval of silence in which an infinite moving toward is signed, the space-interval moving between written words and between bodies; moreover, there is the interval as itself a trace, a space *left*, perhaps by a withdrawal itself seductive. Blanchot's approaching other is relevant here: "The other who draws near you does so, Blanchot says, by turning away, backing off out of your reach, out of your ken."[29] Backing off with, perhaps, a Nancyean "wink," the divinely enticing gesture that is what we have left in the lack of divinely referential names.[30]

Speaking is drawn by an other whose approach is not distinct from its withdrawal, across an infinite distance: prayer then would be a conspicuously pure or intense speech, or a speaking with an exceptionally profound question. As we have seen with desire in other contexts here, the relation of this query and call to desire is complex; an infinite draw is enticing, but not altogether satisfying, certainly not satiating. It is perhaps more "the communication of a disappointment, of a nonpossibility, of a withdrawal of communication itself,"[31] as Nancy says that speaking is for both Bataille and Blanchot. The disappointment occurs because "no subject of the utterance comes in touch with another subject."[32] So if communication means completely crossing the abyssal interval between subjects, full comprehension, then every communicant is disappointed. All the more so anyone who prays, especially if that praying is trying to reach and to grasp the divine. If it is not just disappointment, prayer must seek something other than comprehension and conclusion.

Prayer addresses itself to a mystery, to an unknowable that is not just incidentally unknown, to a distance that is proximate too, to the impossible fullness of possibility—to the element within speaking that gives to all of it a trace of prayer, here without illusions of finality. Prayer, says James Mensch, makes the space in which the sacred can appear.[33] Or, we might also say, can speak. Making that space and enticing across it are paradoxically coincident. Speaking of Blanchot, Ann Smock remarks in a conversation with Nancy that our obligation of response to the other is "answering the demand, which his nearness is, that you should hear him—hear him and thus let him speak; make it so he can; let him come up close and be there, speaking."[34] The space opened by hearing also entices speaking nearer; the space opened by speaking (and prayer, like the question, speaks to open, not to speak over or foreclose) also entices the listener.

The tradition of such paradoxical, apophatic address turns out to be a long one. Oliver Davies notes that even one of the most stubbornly elusive Christian thinkers, Meister Eckhart, "cannot be seen to be operating with apophatic reference to the exclusion of address. . . . The individual is . . . in the most profound sense addressed by God through the *gotesgeburt* or birth of the Word in the ground of the soul. Christian apophatic language is not pure reference therefore, but rather reference which has been transformed by divine revelation as address."[35] Virginia Burrus writes that, for a still earlier figure, the fourth-century Evagrius Ponticus, "the Trinitarian naming—the matter of divine address—involves a relation, rather than a metaphoric, linguistic practice."[36] It is not only the referential element here that is deliberately apophatic, but the address itself, and the relation to which it calls: the call does not end, does not arrive, but it does draw toward, into a space in which we may speak, and be heard, and encounter the mystery of the voice.

That notion of non-arrival, or arrival infinitely deferred, belongs most famously to Blanchot and, in intellectual conversation with him, to Derrida. Davies notes of the latter:

> Derrida points out too that negative theology is a mode of address, an encomium or hymn, which bears the distinctive trace of the other to whom it is uttered. It is preceded by a prayer. . . . This prayer Derrida describes as a living conversation, and he speaks of it in most

un-Derridean terms as language that can never be written: "Does one have the right to think that, as pure address, on the edge of silence, alien to every code and to every rite, hence to every repetition, prayer should never be turned away from its present by annotation or by the movement of an apostrophe, by a multiplication of addresses?"[37]

Like Nancy, Derrida emphasizes the singularity of the addressee, even where that addressee is a *theos* whose logic is negative. Yet Derrida too acknowledges the echoes of Augustinian confession in prayer, and that echo problematizes the notion of the unwritten. Augustine's confession is a prayer recorded in writing not as some sort of definitive result, but as if (we must always be wary of underestimating Augustine as a polished rhetorician) caught up in the midst of its outpouring, a writing intriguingly close to speech, or a writing deliberately evocative of speaking. If prayer can be written, then it must be read; if in its reading it is to function as prayer and not simply as an account of prayer, then it must be read in an unusual kind of re-creative performance, in which the reader takes on the voice and the curious decentered positioning of the one who prays.[38] Like the sacrament, it opens and unsettles even when it seems to be spoken as rite or by rote.

Conversion

You spin me right round, baby
Right round

— Dead or Alive, "You Spin Me Round (Like a Record)"

Every address turns itself toward. This is as true carnally as in any ostensibly disembodied sense; calling out to somebody, to another body, I turn toward if I can—at least calling over my shoulder, if not in fact shifting my torso. When we speak without such a shift, it is often because we are angry, or resistant and resentful of the need to address the other at all. Prayer is conspicuous in its embodiment, though complex in its direction. Every call, and every response, is a small conversion. Derrida suggests that the Augustinian sort of confessional prayer "is a matter of a singular movement of the soul or, if you prefer, of a conversion of existence that accords itself to, in order to reveal in its very night, the most secret secret."[39] The revelation of a secret, though, is not its unsecreting, but the revelation that there are secrets, that there is mystery; the Augustinian conversion is vivid, yet the God to whom it directs its passion is no precisely defined or located thing. Chrétien calls prayer "a speech that . . . turns towards God,"[40] and Blanchot, still meditating upon the incompletion of speaking, notes that to turn and to find may be closer than we think: "To find is to turn, to take a turn about, to go around. . . . No idea here of a goal, still less of a stopping. To find is almost exactly the same word as 'to seek,' which means 'to take a turn around.' "[41] We turn about the unfindable, around the center that is everywhere.[42] When Augustine asks, "Where then did I find you in order to learn of you?" he finds the answer in memory, but he remains puzzled. "You were not already in my memory before I learnt of you," he declares, deciding that it is God's exceeding of place that answers, still mysteriously, the peculiar question of "where."[43]

In studying Augustine's *Confessions*, Pranger links conversion to the performance of a promise, which, like a seduction, must be sustained[44]—and which, like a secret, cannot be kept, or at cannot at any rate be kept by Augustine, who is constantly having to turn himself round again.[45] We keep promises by remaking them; we keep them as we keep making them.[46] Not definition but possibility, the promising, opens in prayer—not least the very possibility of turn and return, the possibility that "To be converted is something that is always ahead of us as well as behind us."[47]

Conversion, then, is not once and for all, but is a matter of re-turn. Prayer does not describe conversion, but enacts it. Thus, as I shall note again just below, it is not especially surprising to find that it so often takes up, and makes up, the language of scriptures. Augustine's act of reading scripture "itself turns into conversion,"[48] says Pranger, a conversion in which multiple voices sound at once—in which Augustine voices Paul's text, after hearing the voice of a child who seems to speak for a God.[49] Prayer's duality of revelation is also a duality or even a multiplicity of voice; one reveals oneself as a listener by speaking, and one may even speak in the voice of the addressee, or of other listeners who have sought the divine in address. This too is part of the search to know: to speak as a listener to multiple voices. Hart, in a scriptural citation, echoes our sense of the mutuality of revelation, here in the mutuality of speaking: "In the words of Isaiah, 'before they call, I will answer; and while they are yet speaking, I will hear' (Isaiah 66:24)."[50] As Pranger has eloquently argued, in prayer or prayerlike speech the speaker takes on other language and voices—especially, as in his analysis of Augustine, the language of scripture—as the speaker's own.[51] The times of prayerful speaking and hearing are not linear and distinct.

Speaking Through

What matter who's speaking, someone said what matter who's speaking.

—Samuel Beckett, *Stories and Texts for Nothing*

To say that there is a connection between knowing and speaking is hardly unusual—we ask in order to know, we say what we know, we even learn what we know (and what we want to ask) by working it out in the saying. The nature of that connection is somewhat strange in prayer, where we do not simply speak what we know, nor simply learn by extracting information from what is spoken. We cannot altogether distinguish who is speaking here, who knows and who is learning, any more than, say, Augustine is able to distinguish the source of the childish voice that has urged him to "take and read" the transformative text from Paul. As Pranger points out, "the two aspects of turning inward on the one hand and the sheer exteriority of language on the other have to be taken together and analysed as one corpus presented to us in the shape of uninterrupted prayer."[52] This blending and slipping among voices, the appropriation of the scriptural voice that is itself in some way said to have God speaking through it, is not some confusion or mistake on Augustine's part, but a remarkable and graceful performance of the inwardness of desire in the outwardness of words. That is, it is a performance of prayer, and it shows us something of prayer more generally. Desire draws forth speaking; words, in turn, draw desire. Prayer, however brief, is taken up in, to steal Blanchot's lovely phrase, an infinite conversation. "Such, then, would be my task," he writes, "to respond to this speech that surpasses my hearing, to respond to it without having really understood it, and to respond to it in repeating it, in making it speak."[53] *In repeating it,* we make it speak: the prayerful appropriation of ritual words and scriptural phrases is something more than rote.

Prayer is mutually implicated with the divinity of its address, and as some measure of that implication, it repeats responsively; it arrogates other voices that are also addressing, and reading themselves as addressed by, divinity. In its reach across an infinite distance, "Prayer reflects exactly this process—or rather this ever repeated moment of arrogating voice," writes Pranger. He notes that, in Augustine's prayer, "It is language (seemingly) external to himself which is proven to have been carrying and creating his self all along: before you were born I have chosen you."[54] Even those divine names, lacking or exuberantly overplentiful, may thus be re-performed. Westphal notes, for instance, that Pseudo-Dionysius's divine names "are those given to us in Scripture. The very call to which we may respond 'Here I am' . . . typically comes through the words of Scripture, directly or indirectly. . . . Before prayer is a . . . speech act on our part, it is listening to the word of God as found in Scripture."[55] Prayer is at once both our listening and our speaking, but the very nature of the speaking makes it something other than simply our own.

As thus multiple, prayer can no more be attributed to the divine than to the one who prays. (The number should begin to sound suspicious as our opening distinction begins to blur: those multiple voices suggest something communal in the most solitary prayer; the singular address to a singular name nonetheless begins to sound polyphonically.) As Mark Cauchi points out, "The prayer, like the question, cannot simply come *from* the other."[56] If it did, my speaking would serve no point. We are not simply returning some possession in our words; even if I return to you your words, they must be changed by the resonance of my voice and the direction of my address. Prayer is not parroting, not quoting, but performing and sometimes, rather sacramentally, reperforming. And no repetition, we know by now, is ever exactly the same.

The address of prayer is thus complicated not only by the duality of its revelation, but also by the words it takes up and re-voices as its own. It is complicated by its search for a language in which to address and to say an infinite that stubbornly exceeds and evades words. We might reasonably wonder if it doesn't make more sense, if we are trying to hear divine voices, just to shut up. Augustine himself sometimes warns of praying that talks too much and listens too little: "Lord, why should I so much as pray at all? You would not that I should use long prayers, yea rather Thou dost even bid me to use near none at all."[57] Moreover, if we share any of the Augustinian worries about the ease with which language misleads us, silence would seem to be the safer option.

If we want to make sense of prayer, then, we must seek a language that not only speaks in many voices (some of them the scriptural voices ostensibly of its own addressee), but also carries its silences in it, one that serves to listen even as it speaks. It is not only speaking that enters us, but silence too. Chrétien writes: "Far from enclosing ourselves, in some dark crypt, [silence] is that which opens us, in the only way that anything can be opened: irreparably. Nor is it, even in the highest of its possibilities, a purely spiritual silence. Only what has a body can throw itself bodily into the fray. All attention takes place body and soul."[58] Both calling out and drawing breath pull the infinite in; both speaking forth and listening to the meaning are acts of gathering.

Prayer becomes the overflow of divine voices in our speaking; it requires its silences, its intervals, even more dramatically than does other speech. (It is becoming clear that much of what I have said of prayer is true of all speaking, especially of attentive speaking, just as much of what I said of sacraments is true of all signs. In both cases, the introduction of an explicit infinite intensifies the ordinary into something strange.) Prayer is desire welling up in the world of words. As I've suggested, the mutuality of revelation is already seductive and indeed, I would further suggest, erotic; the gaze of eros, unlike that of scientific inquiry or even aesthetic judgment, is unusual, perhaps unique, in the urgency with which it seeks to be seen as well, to draw and not merely to be drawn by desire. But the better metaphors here may not be visual; prayer is an aural medium, meant to be heard even when we read it in print. The one who prays asks to be heard rather than seen, and asks the divine not to show its shape but to speak in turn, to offer answers that open the questioning further—answers, like beauty, that are vocation and provocation, that call us and recall us, always into question.

That to which we listen, says Nancy, is "first of all presence in the sense of a *present* that is not a being (at least not in the intransitive, stable, consistent sense of the word), but rather a *coming* and a *passing*, an *extending* and a *penetrating*."[59] When we are called and when we call (especially when we in our finitude call on the infinite to "come into me"), we complicate ourselves and are complicated, with a vulnerability that echoes the ethics of an openness onto the world.

We are transited, as Nancy says, or wounded, as Chrétien has it—in fact, he calls prayer "a wounded word." Chrétien's sense of prayer reminds us of the vulnerability of speaking and listening—of the important element of prayer that is lament, and not just joy, and of the entanglements of the two. Prayer "is the very event of a wound by which our existence is altered and opened, and becomes itself the site of the manifestation of what it responds to. . . . the wound can bless and . . . benediction can wound."[60] Intriguingly, Jabès uses the same terminology to describe the project he shares with Celan, with whom he says that he is joined "by everything, . . . but in particular by 'one and the same interrogation and one and the same wounded word.' "[61] Prayer reaches toward what eludes saying, such that a word becomes only "the trace that it leaves;"[62] crossed through by the question and the silence that enters its words. Our speaking is traced through by silence, our silence by those sounds whose meanings it gathers.

Words and silences are traced through each other, and so too are those whose words and silences they are, those who are as unsettled in their possession of words as in their positions as subjects. Nancy writes that when we listen for sense, we are also attentive—attuned, even—to resonance ("in resonance, there is source and its reception"). Like the divine, such a sense withdraws even as it barely touches: "Sense . . . reaches me only by leaving in the same movement. Or: there is only a 'subject' (which always means, 'subject of a sense') that resounds, responding to a momentum, a summons, a convocation of sense."[63] This sense of *resonance*, shared sound, shared sense, is the sense in which we communicate the ungraspable: "the incommunicable is nothing other, in a perfectly logical way, than communication itself, that thing by which a subject makes an echo—of self, of the other, it's all one—it's all one in the plural. Communication is not transmission, but a sharing that becomes subject: sharing as subject of all 'subjects.' An unfolding, a dance, a resonance."[64] Resonance keeps speaking from being speaking over, drowning out. Ann Smock summarizes Blanchot: "The other who approaches speaks and asks you to make it so that he can speak. Blanchot says you hear him asking you to find the words with which he'll make you hear him."[65] Making space for the sacred, for sound, for the other, comes in the strange listening character of invocation, the silence of speaking traced throughout prayer.

Prayerful Genres

Many have tried, but in vain, with joy to express the most joyful
Here at last, in grave sadness, wholly I find it expressed.

—Friedrich Hölderlin, "Sophocles," Epigrams from 1799

I have spoken primarily of the prayer of praise or adoration, a prayer that may describe, but does not inform (at least, its purpose is not to impart information about what it finds admirable). Rather, it invokes and reveals, though, to follow Nancy's distinction, it does not manifest; its praise resonates.[66] Praise is interestingly entangled with confession; listening to the praises we make in prayer, we perceive the praiseworthiness of their subject; telling the truths of ourselves, we perceive our entanglements with the *you* to whom we tell them. We continue to seek in the delight of finding, to desire even more of what we desire, and so to ask and to praise find their way into the same prayer, the same invocation. We can only hear prayerfully by listening to what resonates in what we say.

In this section, I want to argue that in fact this strange intersectionality applies beyond praise, that is it is true too of prayers of both petition and lamentation. All three forms are movements of desire, and as that desire they are mutually revelatory movements of address, conversionary and subject transiting.

All these forms of prayer are driven by desire, and it is through desire that they make their revelations. Praise is the most obvious instance. As I have suggested, it may well describe, but there is no presumption that it offers that description as new knowledge to the one it praises or to an uninformed audience; primarily, it expresses desirous, astonished delight. In the prayer of praise, meaning and language are themselves full of desire, reaching toward an impossible completion—in which all speaking would already have ceased, becoming pure resonance, words echoing the joyful, delightful character of that which they praise, of the one they address. The language of prayer, of praise and desire in excess of denotation,[67] is for Augustine (and not only for him) nonetheless the very deepest and most important meaning of language—as close, perhaps, as fallen speech can get to the mythically unfallen word, the least distorted echo of the word of God. Language will never grasp divinity, but it can still praise.

In fact, for Augustine, praise is primary in the glorified and redeemed speech of resurrected bodies. Prayer, as we see both in the attentive response to worldly beauties (in the *Confessions*) and in the eternal commentary of the resurrected on the beauty of risen bodies (in *The City of God*), *is* the joy of speaking, and of writing; it is the joyful call in response to the call of joy; it is mutual revelation. The beauty of glorified bodies causes those who live as those bodies to call out praise to the creator. Praise says of the world that it is good—a goodness caught up with vulnerability, not least with that in us which we cannot protect from beauty. The imperative to speak is not an imperative to report, or even to impart information. It is wholly unspecific as to what is or may be spoken; it may indeed speak about as well as to, or it may, better still, speak about to. Praise, most conspicuously of all speech, is drawn out of us, imparts no information. It may express astonishment, but it does not say that it is astonished (not, at any rate, as its primary point). Thus it is an expression, rather than an informational discussion, of desire. Augustine is again paradigmatic, declaring, "For he who desires, even if his tongue is silent, sings from his heart; and he who has no desire, whatever the cry with which he strikes men's ears, is mute for God."[68]

One might wonder whether prayer as praise is purely ornamental. Ornament, I hope I have indicated, is not without importance. But it is important to remind ourselves that praise serves a revelatory function as well, by calling upon an infinite name, and what it reveals, dually, are caller and respondent—in their mutual implication, which is no small measure of the content of the revelation. Delight is caught up in desire, the Augustinian essence of prayer. "If you would pray without ceasing," he writes, "do not cease to long. Your ceaseless longing is your ceaseless voice. You will be silent, if you stop loving."[69] Praise is speech seduced by delight in the desire of delight's returning.

Petitionary prayer too speaks desire, desire too intense for a simple, informational "I want X" statement to suffice. A petition at once exemplary and a little unusual is taken up in Derrida's *"Sauf le nom,"* as Derrida considers Angelus Silesius's lines "Giebstu mir dich nicht selbst / so hastu nichts gegeben," "If you don't give yourself to me, then you have given nothing."[70]

Derrida points out that: "this particular prayer asks nothing, all the while asking more than everything. It asks God to give himself rather than gifts. . . . Which interprets again the divinity of God as gift or desire of giving. And prayer is this interpretation, the very body of this interpretation."[71]

This is stranger even than it seems; Angelus asks the gift for its giving, and the asking is a giving too, a giving over of self in the very demand—because for Angelus, as for Eckhart, one does not receive God and retain separation.[72] That is, this petition, and any petition that interprets the divine as gift, also troubles the petitioner's subjectivity, because if she is given that gift, she is no longer simply the self that requested it but, in some strange measure, is crossed through and remade by the very gift requested.

Praise reveals to us the problems of trying to retain that separation, but also of the impossibility of overcoming it—it reveals the reach of desire. As Denys Turner argues in his discussion of Augustinian prayer, prayerful petition is also the discovery, if we pay attention, of the call of the desires that are deepest in us: in this sense too, it gives us ourselves. Noting that we have come to use "will" rather badly, as if it were opposed to desire, Turner insists that prayer is an act of will in an older and richer sense:

> For the great spiritual writers of classical and premodern times meant by "will" something more like our deepest desires. . . . And many of those desires lie very deep within us indeed, so that we do not know them, they do not fall within our experience. . . . Prayer is the process of discovering in ourselves that with which we can truly love God: that is our will, that is where our hearts are. . . . [For Augustine and Thomas] prayer is a kind of revelation to us of what our wills truly are, it is a kind of hermeneutic of the opaque text of desire.[73]

The petition, if it is not made glibly, tells us what we want, shows us to ourselves.

Petition is a special case in that it is so easily misconceived, in a manner not altogether unlike the misconception of faith as ill-grounded belief. Both errors oversimplify and demystify. As Nancy writes: "Prayer does not ask in order that its request be granted, nor does it produce that result. To have one's prayers answered—that is the expectation, as self-interested as it is illusory, of religion, which consequently is doomed to content itself with imaginary satisfactions."[74] He insists that prayer is essentially adoration, "not primarily a request made in order to receive a response, retribution, or reparation."[75] If petitionary prayer were simply a matter of presenting a request for fulfillment, it would scarcely be discursively unusual; we make requests of one another all the time. Indeed, it is generally more effective to call upon my spouse, for instance, to help me find my keys than upon St. Anthony of Padua, for all the latter's patronage of those who seek lost things. For that matter, we may even make requests of inanimate objects, as when we urge our cars to start on nasty cold days. What characterizes a petition as prayerful is also what characterizes the prayerfulness of praise: its revelatory character and its curious subject position. Like praise, the petition that arises out of meditation upon the depths of desire is a revelation of the praying self even as it addresses that self's outside; desire is itself drawn out in its expression in address, revealed in its saying. The prayer of petition, then, is caught up with the prayer of praise precisely by the commonality of desire. It too functions as a revelation, a revelation of will and desire to the speaker through the act of address, through address to what draws desire infinitely.

There remains an important third category: the prayer of lamentation. Desire prays, says Augustine, but so too does sorrow: "For, as soon as we feel sadness, we already pray."[76] At first lamentation evokes anything but revelation; as Michael Purcell notes, it is "associated with the scriptural notion of a God who has hidden his face . . . and will not respond."[77] Purcell links this hidden God to the demands of the Law, the keeping of which is the way both to love and to experience the hidden God—an ethical way that does not keep us from experiencing the terror of absence.[78] Purcell argues that suffering, expressed in the lament, can be redeemed from meaninglessness only when it works toward justice, when suffering is for the sake of others.[79] Yet the same emptiness that creates the lament's sorrow and longing is, he says, the condition of hope, which ends if it is fulfilled in specificity.[80] Lament reaches back to memory, forward to the hope for justice. Purcell argues that it is solitary, occurring in the absence of interlocutors. I would suggest that, in the very specificity of lament's address, we hear that its solitude is not the simple condition of being alone, but rather the more complex one of experiencing and addressing a particular withdrawn or hidden other: an absent interlocutor, to be sure, yet one who is importantly different from the absence of address at all.

Responding to Purcell, Kevin Hughes argues that lament is the first and paradigmatic Christian prayer, noting Christ's reiteration of the Twenty-second Psalm—"My God, my God, why have you forsaken me?"—just prior to his death in two of the gospel accounts.[81] Hughes wonders if the Lurianic sense of divine withdrawal or contraction fundamental to Purcell's understanding of the absent and hidden God is in fact useful to Christianity.[82] He argues instead that

> What we see on the Cross is precisely the Lament, and the Lament without answer. But, precisely as such, the Cross points to a God who is found in the Lament, and thus is no stranger to those who lament in turn. The paradox of the cross is that the one who laments and is not answered is himself the revelation of God, the coincidence of full humanity and full divinity in suffering is the coincidence of lament and God's presence.[83]

The "scandal" is not, he argues, the withdrawal of God, but the revelation of divine weakness, God's taking up in the incarnation of everything human, even the non-heroic, unimpressive aspect of mortality.[84] The divine embrace of this suffering and so of those who suffer "anticipates the end of suffering," he adds.[85]

Both accounts begin with lament, but diverge from it in an effort to make it meaningful, thus redeeming it by anticipating, hoping for, its end. Divine vulnerability appears differently in the two accounts—as a shattering in need of regathering, as the capacity to suffer—but it is important that it does appear. But both cases also look to some redemptive move, and for both, to redeem lamentation requires stepping outside of the lament. Lamentation in its own time of unbearable, inescapable attention does not anticipate suffering's end, nor wholeness reassembled; it may well ask "how long?" of its abandonment, but this is a sense of the hollow stretch of time, not of a measured discipline of endurance. It cries out. Both Purcell and Hughes, very reasonably, seek a way out of the sense of meaningless suffering that lamentation expresses; I am more engaged, here, in the moment of the lament itself, which like praise and petition is a revelation: of vulnerability shared, of the passionate desire for what is profoundly missing—a reminder that a name, a trace, a sign is not a full-fledged presence.

Here I recur to poetry as prayer's sister speech, to look at Rilke's poem "The Olive Garden." The poem retells the story of Christ's night in the garden at Gethsemane:

> . . . and why is it Your will that I must say
> You are, when I myself no longer find you.
>
> I find you no longer. Not in me.
> Not in the others. Not in this stone.
> I find you no longer. I am alone.
>
> I am alone with all of human grief,
> Which through You I undertook to lighten,
> You who are not. O ineffable shame . . .[86]

The theory of lamentation at work here seems closer to Purcell's; certainly it emphasizes solitude, though not its mending by justice. It calls to a *you*, but precisely in that addressee's absence, or withdrawal. Its grief is all the stronger in the absence of the one who was to lighten all grieving. The address could not be more direct, and if *my God* defines prayer, this is praying at its clearest. It is almost petition, but not quite: it is petition within abandon, petition that not only does not expect satisfaction, but that arises in the destitution of desire. And it is as destitution that it too is revelation. This is not suffering that hearkens toward its own end:

> For angels don't come to the prayers of such men,
> And nights don't grow large around them.
> The self-losing are let go by everything,
>
> And they are abandoned by their fathers
> And locked out of their mothers' wombs.[87]

The loss here is complete; the sense that resounds in the speaking and the reading and the hearing is the sense of forsakenness. To lose *my God* is to lose myself too.

Praise reminds us of the trace of the divine in all that is, the delight of reading it, the memory invoked by every sign in a mutual revelation of "within" and "outside." Petition reveals to us in the outpour of words our own inmost desires, and perhaps the entanglement of those desires with the no less desirous divine. And lamentation reveals to us the double, and sometimes devastating, vulnerability, at the extreme of loss, of human and divine. Just as there is some sense of praise, Nancy's "adoration," in all prayer, so too is there a touch of lamentation: lamentation also shows to us the paradox of signification, because the sign is not what it signifies, whatever its mood or its mode. If we *read* divinity in ourselves, in others, in the stones, we do not *find* it there. The sign is not the thing: We are not God, say the beauties of the world to Augustine, and finally, even the query "Where then did I find you?" has as its only answer a memory without an origin. The lament, to be sure, cries out when the trace cannot be read, but it also reminds us that we are *never* wholly fulfilled, never lastingly in a presence, even when we read most clearly and take pleasure most fully. Seduction is often delight, but it is never satiation, and that must mean that it is sometimes sorrow. As we are ethically impelled, by our very vulnerability to beauty, also to be open to destitution and loss, so too we find expressed in prayer a sorrow that is not simply hurried toward its absence nor set as a prelude to praise. We do not have everything.

It is too easy for us—certainly for me, I find, writing—to focus optimistically. The open space of the possible, as Purcell points out, is the only space of hope, and that space of the possible is the space of seductive enticement. But true possibility opens onto darkness too, and the dark nights of the soul are not just trials endured for the prizes that come after. Lament calls upon the retreating, withdrawn divine when the trace is too faint to read. It may well call bitterly—*you*, who are not, not even to be read anywhere, and yet retain this address, this remnant of a name by which *you* are called. It remains prayer because it calls, and infinitely. It calls despairingly, but not in the despair of not calling at all; it retains vulnerability and indeed woundedness. Here too the sacred speaks.

Here, too, if we pay attention. In his famous "Meridian" speech, Celan writes of the sites he has sought in his poetry,

None of these places can be found. They do not exist. But I know where they ought to exist, especially now, and . . . I find something else.

Ladies and gentlemen, I find something which consoles me a bit for having walked this impossible road in your presence, this road of the impossible.

I find the connective which, like the poem, leads to encounters.

I find something as immaterial as language, yet earthly, terrestrial, in the shape of a circle which, via both poles, rejoins itself and on the way serenely crosses even the tropics.[88]

The connective, immaterial as the breath of the word and earthly as the stretch of the desiring body, reaches out and crosses around. It addresses, it attends, and it prays. It speaks because it is paying attention, "the natural prayer of the soul."[89] It attends to fullness and to absence too; we are connected not just to what is, but to passing and to passion.

Body

And henceforth movement, touch, vision, applying themselves to the other and to themselves, return toward their source and, in the patient and silent labor of desire, begin the paradox of expression.

—Maurice Merleau-Ponty, *The Visible and the Invisible*

The connective, again, is not wholly immaterial. Prayer is strongly physical language; written on the page, it comes to life only when vocalized; breathed into voice, it is often accompanied by postures (spontaneous or prescribed) or gestures, movements and repetitions.[90] It demands attention to its sounds and not only its sense. Or rather, "here there are two senses," as Nancy writes, "and listening aims at—or is aroused by—the one where sound and sense mix together and resonate in each other, or again through each other. (Which signifies that . . . if, on the one hand, sense is sought in sound, on the other hand, sound, resonance, is also looked for in sense.)"[91] Sense in sound: we neither desire nor find sense without embodiment. "Each time," says Nancy, "it can only be a matter of a close combination of analysis and touch, each one sharpening or strengthening the other."[92] The body that listens, like the body that prays (itself, we see by now, a form of listening speaking), is resonant, mutual in its speech and revelation: "Timbre can be represented as the resonance of a stretched skin . . . , and as the expansion of this resonance in the hollowed column of a drum. Isn't the space of the listening body, in turn, just such a hollow column over which a skin is stretched, but also from which the opening of a mouth can resume and revive resonance?"[93]

Chrétien notes of this mutual, resounding revelation: "If [prayer] corresponds to a theophany, it is first of all an anthropophany. . . . This act of presence puts man thoroughly at stake. . . . It exposes him in every sense of the word *expose* and with nothing held back. It concerns our body, our bearing, our posture, our gestures." That the addressee of prayer is not a material entity, or any entity in any conventional understanding, does not alter the corporeality of prayer: "Even he who turns toward the incorporeal does so corporeally, with all his body."[94] Prayer is no disembodied speech, even if it is silent, even if it forgoes traditional postures and gestures. Drawing us into the world with all of our senses, the divine name we call out resounds at once beyond the time of speaking and in the depths of our hearing. "The *body* [is] unique bearer of speech, . . . the very site of any response to the appeal," Chrétien declares. "This is what founds the central character of *voice*, *breath* [*soufflé*], and *nudity*: this will not be the speech of angels!"[95] We praise and desire and mourn this world, reaching into it for what transits it, for what it cannot hold.

When prayer is put into words, it is attentive to sound, to the music and the poetry of language, to its flesh. This is important not only because it reminds us to praise what our senses give us and to give sensory beauty to praise, to desire with all of ourselves, to allow the bodily vulnerability and physical ache of mourning—but because it reminds us to link prayer to the body, to the dual capability and vulnerability of the flesh. Prayer, says Chrétien, is "wounded by this hearing and this call that have always already preceded it, and that unveil it to itself, in a truth always in suffering."[96] The speech that is prayer is ordeal throughout, he argues, always called and always struggling toward an impossible perfection in which God speaks to God in an embodied human voice.[97]

Prayer gives to the divine to listen, as music gives itself to us, and prayer speaks and listens to music and not only to meaning. "Perhaps," as Nancy suggests, "it is necessary that sense not be content to make sense . . . , but that it want also to resound."[98] *Resonance* emphasizes the sensuality as well as the mutuality of sound. Nancy writes:

> It returns to itself, it reminds itself of itself, and it feels itself as resonance itself: a relationship to self deprived, stripped of all egoism and all ipseity. Not "itself," or the other, or identity, or difference, but alteration and variation, the modulation of the present that changes it in expectation of its own eternity, always imminent and always deferred, since it is not in any time. . . . In resonance the inexhaustible return of eternity is played—and listened to.[99]

Chrétien argues for a resonance of the will as well: "My obedience in this case could hardly be mute: to respect beauty is not to regard it silently but to sing it. This obedience, however, does not relate us to the will as such. . . . Here, too, obedience resonates in the sound of our own voice, through prayer, but also through the words that we exchange, since this is how the voice of the Word reaches us."[100]

Language resonates, and so does desire. In prayer there is no object presented to a subject, but the reach of the voice in address. To listen, Nancy argues, is to strain toward a meaning not immediately accessible[101]—to be seduced, I would suggest, by sound and meaning both, not stopping with either—coming and passing rather than finding and halting. It is not simply coincidental that Augustine searches in poetry and hymns for the ways in which language, distended across time, is nonetheless collected in meaning; some measure of the meaning even of words is, like the answer to his attention, in beauty. And for him as for us here the sense of the divine is *always* seductive, even into sorrow, always drawing us on, always a coming and a passing. We do not simply dwell in some "standing now," but neither are we simply distended over time; eternity too comes to us and passes as we live temporally.

Seduction in language, as language's poetic element—that is, as what evokes and speaks in sounds and spaces—does not, and cannot, confer meaning in the narrow sense. It is precisely what in language eludes discourse and representation, even narration and description.[102] Lacking the completion of meaning, the one who calls out in prayer has the seduction of faith, a lived experience of the infinitely incompletable, the eternal coming and passing—joyful, hopeful, and sorrowful too. Prayer is, we might say, the resonance of the divine trace in the human voice.

In the in-finition[103] of the call, we are reminded of the impossibility of fully *knowing* the name we call out. The completion of what "infinite perfection" could possibly mean is as impossible as the saying of it; thus to say *is* all the knowing and showing we have, and we can never say enough. In language as it seeks understanding, divine enticement is dual, showing again the reversibility characteristic of all seductions. God draws Augustine's language, leading him to declare that "I tell my story for love of your love" (2.I.I), but Augustine's language is likewise a seduction, to God and to reader both. "Here I am," says Samuel, drawing God's attention to his attentive response, in response to God's searching attention. Give me what you will, says Angelus, but what I will is you (that very desire is my gift to you). Desire desires address, desires to direct itself. *My God* is that which pulls on desire to the extent of address—as the beauty read in the trace and mourned in its absence, called by the dispossessive name: *my God, you*.

A name that confronts us again with the depth of its strangeness. "This is an outcome we will once again be tempted to find disappointing if, at the moment when the sacred present declares itself for us in its now, we have with it no relation other than that of desire and are still only able to reach, in the very name by which we establish it, our fervent wish to name it. Desire is very little, says Blanchot, ". . . but perhaps it is much more."[104] We will be disappointed if we think we might grasp, or even if we desire to end our desiring. The open name calls out desire, question, a revelation of a relation rather than of a presence. Or, as Nancy has it, a being-unto: "*Here*—on a face, but equally, perhaps, in a name—the divinity lets itself be seen, manifestly invisible and invisibly manifest. God reveals himself—and God is always a stranger in all manifestation and all revelation. Revelation—if such a thing must be conceived of—is not a presentation, or a representation: it must be the evidence of a possibility (never a necessity) of a *being-unto-god*."[105] It is a revelation of mystery.

To Call by Name

Father,
Great is our need and we beg,
...
That your name be not
Darkened within us.
Tell us your name again
lest we forget.

—Hildegard of Bingen, "Antiphon for God the Father"

Name calling too is reversible. In the scriptural example Westphal explores, Samuel is called by name, and in that call is made (a listener) and makes himself, presents himself, as he is made. To call and be called by name is itself a revelation. Prayer calls the divine not into being, but into coming, into proximity. Since Hegel, or at least since Kojève lectured on Hegel in the 1930s, those who take seriously the entanglements of subjectivity and human interrelation have reasonably assumed that being a subject is tied to the use of the subjective pronoun, the use of the "I." Kojève writes: "Man become conscious of himself at the moment when—for the 'first' time—he says 'I.' To understand man by understanding his 'origin' is, therefore, to understand the origin of the I revealed by speech."[106] But perhaps we come to another kind of consciousness, a more complex selfhood, when for the first time, rather than designating ourselves in the first person pronoun, we are called by name. Novelist Muriel Barbery gives us a vivid instance of such a possibility in *The Elegance of the Hedgehog*. Remembering a revelatory moment of her childhood, the character Renée Michel thinks:

> We are mistaken to believe that our consciousness is awakened at the moment of our first birth—perhaps because we do not know how to imagine any other living state.... The fact that for five years a little girl called Renée, a perfectly operational machine of perception blessed with sight, hearing, smell, taste and touch, could have lived in a state of utter unawareness both of herself and of the universe, is proof if any were needed that such a hasty theory is

wrong. For in order for consciousness to be aroused, it must have a name.

However, a combination of unfortunate circumstances would seem to confirm that no one had ever thought of giving me my name.[107]

When Renée is finally called by name, at the age of five, the result is extraordinary. Not only does she come to consciousness, she is also given the world, "brought . . . into the world"; "I looked around me and saw a world that was suddenly filled with colors."[108] Though she has been designated, probably at birth, by her name, she has never been *given* it, as if it were a gift. She has never been *called* by it—and so never brought into the world that calls out beauty. Names are words we are given, not words given about us. As given language, they call us into the world as given, as something worth enjoying, and not just using up. As the dual call of names, finite to infinite, prayer gives the world as divinely significant.

But it does not, not even as a revelation, give us a full divine *presence*. As Elliot Wolfson points out, "In traditional kabbalistic lore, the mystery of prayer involves the invocation of the name that cannot be invoked, but such an invocation is based ultimately on the paradox of an absence that is present in its absence."[109] In the sense of prayer as I have tried to develop it here, too, the invocation of the name is an incompleteable call, a call into mystery. As mystery, this "necessitates an authentic lack, an absence that cannot be represented even as absence."[110] It is thus that the mystery and query avoid degenerating into the ontotheology of which Derrida suspects even apophasis. The seductive mystery draws language to what "in" language nonetheless exceeds it, at once *before* as if at an origin, *after* as if at a telos, yet *within* as if eternally. It does not posit an ontology, but neither is it certain that it calls only to other signs; in this, it remains mystery, otherwise than being or than words. The language of prayer functions rather like that of the Valentinian *Tripartite Tractate* in Patricia Cox Miller's description: "The accent here is on the search, for to speak is to search, and that is how the ineffable 'origin' can be conceived. What language as search yields, however, is neither the presence nor the absence of the unfathomable one, but rather 'traces' of him. All words are traces which mark out the paths of the search."[111] Without invoking the particularly Valentinian cosmology implied, we can nonetheless echo the sense of speech as search, a search provoked by traces and leaving further traces of its own.

Without the designation of a being, the name that calls mysteriously is not a representative sign. It is not a common or a normal noun. Burrus notes: "The name of God uttered in prayer is . . . a 'proper' name. And, as Nancy points out, a proper name is not 'part of language . . . in the way a common noun is.'"[112] A proper name calls even when it cannot call properly. But it cuts in, it transits, as well, as Barbery shows us: "Renée. That meant me. For the first time, someone was talking to me, saying my name. . . . here was a woman with clear eyes and a smiling mouth standing before me, and she was finding her way to my heart, saying my name, entering with me into a closeness I had not previously known existed."[113] In calling out the name that traces through the world, the language of prayer echoes the world's elusive speaking, calling out (to) the trace, the interpellative name, of the God who is nonetheless not a presence.

Nancy reminds us of one last peculiarity of the divine trace. For Augustine, as Nancy puts it, the created world is a "world traced, simultaneously imprinted and transversed by a vestige . . . , that is to say, traced by that which remains withdrawn and by the withdrawal of an origin."[114] And so we are returned by the sign—the name traced and the name called out—to the impossibility of an ultimate return that would finalize the process of conversion, and give us completely back to ourselves. We are returned to the elusion of the origin, not knowing where to start to speak. We answer with a call, and what is revealed to us in answer is a calling, a sensuous and full-bodied desire out of our own deepest will. We begin again.

"It is with prayer that the redemption of humanity and language must begin," writes Mackey. "But prayer itself is a problem. . . . The *Confessiones* begins . . . with the impossibility of beginning."[115] So too do less extended prayers. The impossible origin, the beginning that is never in the first place, calls out from within an infinite cycle of call and response and response again, calls to the *you*—to a singular and yet infinite name.

5

Take and Read: Scripture and the Enticement of Meaning

There is a great struggle in the language of God.

—Origen, *de Engastrimutho* 4, quoted in Patricia Cox Miller, *The Poetry of Thought in Late Antiquity*

In his analysis of scripturally based faith as an opening of questions rather than a settling of answers, Jacques Ellul declares, with not unmerited irritation, "We must vigorously reject that nasty habit of turning to the Bible for an answer to the banal problems of everyday . . . or, still worse, the custom of opening the Bible at random to find some providential verse."[1] It is hard for those of us who love books not to approve immediately of this, to find it disrespectful of a text with such historical and literary weight to treat it as if it were a sort of typeset magic eight-ball. And then we remember Augustine.

Few can ever have had a more intense or productive respect for Hebrew and Christian scripture,[2] yet in the famously dramatic passage of his *Confessions* detailing his conversion, Augustine seems to do exactly what Ellul so sternly forbids: he takes and reads, letting the book fall open where it may and taking the first verse he finds as an urging directed at himself.

More vexingly still, he places himself in a long tradition of others similarly converted. To argue that Augustine is doing something far more interesting than the condemned sort of fortune telling, we must look more extensively at his conversionary reading, at what leads to it and what succeeds it. This we may use as our starting point for a look at the seductiveness of scripture more generally, or at seduction as a way of reading these sorts of texts, texts that seem uniquely well suited to turning and drawing seducible minds and bodies toward themselves. Augustine's example, and his theorizing, suggest that there is a way of reading scripture that makes sense of its particular semiotic richness.

Augustine's highly textual seduction is described in the conclusion to the drawn-out conversion scene of *Confessions*, book 8. He is seduced by a text enfolded in multiple retellings, a text that draws him seductively back through those retellings toward both a word and a Word that remain perpetually elusive. The conversion has a long narrative setup. As the story opens, Augustine is a catachumen in Milan. Though his formidable mother has been hoping for, urging, and perhaps expecting his conversion to Christianity for quite some time, he conceives his desire to convert not out of filial devotion but as an imitation of other conversions. More specifically, the conversionary moment is set up with the descriptions of several other turns to Christianity. The first is that of Marius Victorinus, who begins the process in "reading and inquiry" and makes his gradual way to public profession at the urging of Simplicianus, teller of this tale and also the teacher of Milan's bishop, Ambrose, by whom Augustine is in turn instructed (8.2.3–5). We don't hear a great deal more of Marius here, but it is not irrelevant that in order to begin, he reads, nor that, like Augustine, he finds his readings most persuasive under the instruction of a subtle mentor. That is, he is engaged most by reading when it is not straightforward, but seductively layered in meaning. Augustine presents himself as being straightaway enticed by Marius's story: "As soon as your servant Simplicianus told me this story about Victorinus, I was ardent to follow his example" (8.5.10).

Ardent he may be, but the following takes some time. More immediately influential is a complicated story that Augustine hears from Ponticianus, a court official and fellow African who has come to Milan on business. The presence of a text inspires Ponticianus to recount the story: "we sat down to talk together," Augustine says:

> and it chanced that he noticed a book on a game table before us. He took it up, opened it, and, contrary to his expectation, found it to be the apostle Paul, for he imagined that it was one of my wearisome rhetoric textbooks. At this, he looked up at me with a smile and expressed his delight and wonder that he had so unexpectedly found this book and only this one, lying before my eyes; for he was indeed a Christian and a faithful one at that. (8.6.14)

Augustine, though not yet considering himself quite converted, admits his own interest in this text. Ponticianus responds with the story of another conversion—which turns out to be the story of five conversions, one of which inspires the next two, which in turn inspire the two after that. In Ponticianus's story, two highly placed government officials are out walking one afternoon when they come across a copy of the *Life of Antony*, which includes one of Christianity's most famous conversion scenes.

The story of Antony itself is only hinted at in Augustine's text, but it is clearly one he knows, and in fact one that comes to mind at the moment of his own conversion ("For I had heard how Antony happened to be present at the gospel reading, and took it as an admonition addressed to himself..." 8.12.29). As Athanasius tells it in his *Life of Antony*, Antony at the time of his conversion is "about eighteen or twenty" and newly orphaned. He is on his way to the church, contemplating the asceticism of Christ's disciples: "Pondering over these things he entered the church, and it happened the Gospel was being read, and he heard the Lord saying to the rich man, 'If thou wouldst be perfect, go and sell that thou hast and give to the poor; and come follow Me and thou shalt have treasure in heaven' [Matt. 19.21]."[3] Though of course what Antony hears is someone reading the Gospel, and we know that the reading entails a quotation, nonetheless what we are told is that he hears the Lord. There is an important notion at work here: that in scripture, too, we hear a divine voice speaking.

The story of Antony continues with another scriptural passage and a further leap of faith:

Antony, as though … the passage had been read on his account, went out immediately from the church, and gave the possessions of his forefathers to the villagers. … And all the rest that was movable he sold, and having got together much money he gave it to the poor, reserving a little however for his sister's sake. And again as he went into the church, hearing the Lord say in the Gospel, "be not anxious for the morrow," he could stay no longer, but went out and gave those things also to the poor.[4]

After being thus addressed through the medium of a text read aloud, Antony embarks on his life of eremitic asceticism. He is clearly not converting from one set of propositional beliefs to another, nor even from one communal identity to another; he is already headed into a Christian church, considering the lives of Christ's disciples, when he hears the inspiring passages. This is, rather, a turning in his mode of existence and desire, an irresistible will to be, and to behave, and to read the world, otherwise.

Whether or not Ponticianus retells Antony's story, he does describe the conversion of the two officials who have come across the text (like the texts of Paul, the story of Antony appears to present itself where it is needed). One of the officials "began to read it, to marvel and to be inflamed by it" (8.6.14). The agent's conversion, like Antony's, is abrupt; he is "suddenly … overwhelmed with a holy love and a sober shame" (8.6.15), and he decides that being a "friend of the emperor" (a member of the imperial inner circle) is nothing compared to the eternal blessing that comes with being a friend of God. His fervor persuades his human friend to join him in conversion, in which they are further joined by their fiancées, whom they successfully persuade, on the basis of the text, to join them in the delights of a chaste and celibate life. The quartet is persuaded not by scripture as such, but by a text about scriptural power.

Augustine is strongly drawn by these entangled stories of texts and tellings, by the repeated resonance of written and spoken word. What the previous beliefs of the imperial agents might have been is not quite clear, but their inward change seems, like that of Antony, more attitudinal and behavioral than propositional, a change less in ideas than in allegiance (a seduction in an early sense, then, as a turning-about of loyalties). Conversion here is not about beliefs, though beliefs may lie beneath it or come before it. It is rather about what draws us, about what we turn to follow. Augustine's way of reading the world is inseparable from his way of reading scripture; his turn around in desire, changing the way he's drawn into the world, is entangled with the sudden transformation of that way of reading.

That is, as he desires conversion and struggles toward it, Augustine does not seek to make himself believe particular claims. Belief he has long since established.[5] Persuaded by Ambrose's complex and intellectual Neo-platonic readings of the Judeo-Christian scriptures that had previously impressed him as mere children's stories, Augustine has come to believe that the dogmas of Christianity are true, and he does not seek to have that belief strengthened (nor does he conflate it with faith), though one senses that he mightn't mind greater clarity about its particulars.[6]

Before we come to the famous conversion scene, then, two conversionary steps have already occurred: intellectual persuasion and a desire grounded in example—the example of those who are enticed by words into turning themselves about. It is not immediately clear what it is that Augustine is so frantically seeking as his next step. Certainly he seeks freedom from the bonds of previous (mostly sexual) habit, but as he isn't indulging in those habits at every moment, it's hard to see how he'll know when he's unchained, or what will count as evidence of that disenchainment—how many minutes, or days, must he go without a particular kind of desire in order to say that such desire is absent? He prays, it seems, in a desperate desire for the turning of desire, for a conversion that, though it won't stop him from turning round again (his is a lifelong process of re-turn), will give him a greater sureness of his capacity to make that turn—which he must, if his present desire is any indication, already have begun. Past and future are tightly pulled into the intense, attentive moment of prayer: "Let it be now."

As Augustine in the courtyard garden of his dwelling in Milan weeps and tears at his hair, dramatically bewailing his incapacity to release himself from the (bad sort of) seductions of the world, he hears a child's voice directing him to a text. "Tolle lege," the androgynous child says; "take up and read" (8.12.29). As the child is unseen, unidentified, and speaking for no apparent reason (Augustine cannot recall any children's games featuring the phrase), we might be pardoned for suggesting that the text itself, the collection of childish stories, beckons him in its childish voice. A book lies conveniently in the garden, and Augustine obligingly takes it up and reads: "Not in riots and drunken parties, not in eroticism and indecencies, not in strife and rivalry, but put on the Lord Jesus Christ and make no provision for the flesh in its lusts [Rom 13.13]." Augustine is drawn in by this passage, and correspondingly drawn away from his old attachments: "I wanted to read no further, nor did I need to. For instantly, as the sentence ended, there was infused in my heart something like the light of full certainty and all the gloom of doubt vanished away" (8.12.30). This is his conversion, his dramatic turn. What it takes to change that vital something in him—the direction of his allegiance and his desire—is text. His heart is enlightened "as the sentence ended"—in the silence after the sentence, in which its meaning is gathered. The book that was so hopelessly unengaging when read for a single and straightforward meaning acquires a seductive conversionary capacity when it becomes layered, multiple, and even elusive, no longer giving up its secrets quite so easily. This, as R. D. Williams notes, helps to insure that "learning from Scripture is a *process*—not the triumphant movement of penetration and mastery, but an extended play of invitation and exploration." As Williams points out, "the resonances of these metaphors are deliberate, and not wholly absent from Augustine's vocabulary."[7] The text is also seductive when it directs desires—when it is a text *about* the direction of desire, even, as it is for both Augustine and Antony. The text of pleasure need not be the text that describes pleasure, nor the text of desire one that directs desiring—but it just might. Such a text may even rewrite its reader.

Augustine thus illuminated no longer doubts the direction of his loyalties or his desires, though he knows better than to think that their steadiness will remain absolute. To turn himself around, he has followed a circle: Ponticianus is reminded by the presence of a text of Paul, whose own conversion is among Christianity's most famously dramatic (Acts 9:3–9). He is reminded of a story about the conversion of four Romans, itself grounded in a story in which another scriptural text prompts Antony's conversion. The stories arouse Augustine's desire for conversion, but the full development or intensity of that desire must wait until he is mysteriously directed back to scripture, until he, like Ponticianus, takes up and reads. (In fact, both may be taking up the same copy of the same book.) The text is not one of his rhetoric textbooks, but it does turn out to be a book about a kind of rhetoric, a book that is also about signs and meanings. Augustine is led back around.[8] Though the text turns him toward God, the God ostensibly at the inspirational origin of the text itself, that same God eludes the very writing in which Augustine finds him. In this play of presence and elusion, language meets with desire and the divine, a divine not presented but signed, throughout both the text and the world.[9] As Catherine Brown has it, "the word made flesh is twice incarnate: once in the Virgin Mary and once in scripture."[10] It is this curiously incarnational value of scripture, the fleshiness of its words, that also makes it so seductive as to turn around Marius, Antony, the officials, their fiancées, Augustine, his friend Alypius, who has joined him in the garden and who "takes and reads" after him, and many more of its readers and listeners.

Conversionary textual seductions occur, then, in texts that somehow incarnate the infinite desire for the infinite by telling of that desire (though perhaps indirectly: the text that Augustine reads tells him to put on the flesh of infinite Word, to dwell in the pull of desires that do not stop short) and by telling of the infinite in its relations to the world, such as creation and incarnation, which manifest that desire in the reverse direction. As I shall suggest in more detail below, scriptural texts do this in part by their particular play with the materiality of language. But first, yet a few more words about desire.

Desire, Rich and Insufficient

What happens is the insatiable desire for what does not happen.

—Georges Bataille, "Beyond Seriousness"

I offer more words not just because "never enough" is characteristic of desire, but more immediately because to see what language is doing here, we must also see what desire is up to. Though Augustine's conversion clearly has a great deal to do with the direction of his desire, it is not one of volition simply, any more than of cognition.[11] As Nicholas Woltersdorff points out in *Divine Discourse: Philosophical Reflections on the Claim that God Speaks*:

[At the moment of conversion,] the language of *decision* has disappeared from the account. Earlier in the text, when Augustine was describing his state of mind before the final turning, will was central. . . . Now, when Augustine is describing the actual moment of turning, there is not a word about will, not a word about decision, not a word about resolution. . . . The language is not the language of *being overcome*: Rejecting his former way of life and embracing the new way was not something he *decided to do* but something he *found himself doing*.[12]

Such conversion is a consequence neither of deliberative reason nor of divine (or maternal) bullying and overcoming. Instead, we see the duality characteristic of seduction: neither deliberative decision nor overwhelming compulsion is at work. Augustine has been utterly seduced by the childish voice and the Pauline passage, by the sound of words and the written text. His seducibility was prepared (all good seductions take groundwork) by the example of Marius and the seductive layering of stories in his encounter with Ponticianus; he was already drawn toward being drawn further. He finds, in a rare moment of peace and confidence, that his will is so perfectly unified that it seems no will at all, because it encounters no resistance. This perfection does not remain, but the memory of it does. And that memory will have the power to turn him again, to return him, to draw him back—indefinitely back, around again.

This drawing back is arguably the power of scripture, "calling us from beyond memory, . . . always elsewhere,"[13] to quote Derrida on the intensely scriptural poetry of Edmond Jabès. What we are turned-toward, what draws us, will not hold us safe, not even in memory; it will keep on drawing us in, remaining elusive. In the possibility of any scripture is an essential separation, even a break;[14] there is a space of absence in its very presentation, and so the possible space of a seduction too.

We recall that language is seductive both in its overfullness and in its inadequacy. In scripture, more clearly than in most texts, the meanings toward which a reader is drawn, meanings not quite given in the given text, are fabulously multiple, as Augustinian readings of such texts as Genesis make clear; yet those meanings are never perfectly conclusive. Augustine is not, of course, alone in this reading of scripture as multiple in its meanings, strange though that may sound to those of us wearily accustomed to dogmatic or fundamentalist versions of literalism. In this there are intriguing commonalities, though by no means perfect accord, between his ways of reading and those of the Valentinians. Both the *Tripartite Tractate* and the *Gospel of Truth* are fascinated with the polyvalence of language, the multiplicity of meaning animated by desire, the simultaneous richness and incompleteness of words.[15]

Augustine does not, to be sure, give wholly free reign to the would-be exegete, but he does give quite a lot more leeway than one might expect. In *On Christian Doctrine*, having discussed the use of rhetorical tropes and figurative language, he declares, "When . . . two or more interpretations are put upon the same words of scripture, even though the meaning the writer intended remain undiscovered, there is no danger if it can be shown from other passages of Scripture that any of the interpretations put on the words is in harmony with the truth."[16]

Augustine does assume that the writers of scripture had some intent, and that we should seek the authors' meaning. But he makes this assumption without thinking that this intent is exhaustive. Moreover, we should seek it knowing that we won't know if we've found it. We should avoid readings that clash with other biblical passages or with "right faith," but there will always be many right readings. This, in fact, is a sign of the richness of scriptural truth—that the text can tell us so many right things at once, can so reward continued interpretation.[17] Augustine confronts this multiplicity with delightful exuberance and a surprising measure of tolerance—even for himself, toward whom he is more usually unforgiving.

Markus argues that Augustine's belief that there is some real but not self-evident, intended meaning serves for him a usefully restrictive function: "like Origen, Augustine saw the necessity for restricting the multiplicity of interpretations. . . . it may be that several alternative readings break [the text's] richness into manageable fragments; but in the end, this 'semiotic anxiety' is allayed by the assurance that the text does have a definite, if unattainable, meaning."[18] But this guarantees only meaning, not conclusion: we may be certain that there is at least one meaning, but we must suspect that there are always more (I confess myself unsure about the finitude of that "definite"). Indeed, Augustine may share with Origen as well the flipside of this claim; for Origen, as Burrus notes, "the cosmic generativity of the Logos correlates directly with its linguistic fecundity . . . an insight that Origen shares with many 'Valentinian' Christians in particular, despite his strong resistance to certain aspects of Valentinian cosmology and soteriology."[19] We will not by now be surprised to see reference to the fourth gospel; "Origen observes that the Word, God's only-begotten Son, 'is called by many different names' (I.2.I). He discovers in the *Gospel of John* striking evidence of the inexhaustible plenitude of divine epithets by which the Logos reveals itself to a differentiated creation . . . (*Commentary on John*, I.52)."[20] We recall, as Miller points out, that for the Valentinians the danger of reading lies in trying to finish the story of the ineffable, to complete the narrative.[21] This is quite a different danger from that of coming up with a "false" interpretation. The worry about misreading is a worry about stopping too soon—or perhaps at all, dwelling in an unfounded certainty. This multiplicity opens up the possibility of a wandering among meanings, an endless search. "When the language of a text gapes," writes Miller as she too considers Origen, "its surface or obvious meaning disappears and plural possibilities of meaning appear."[22] The tease of the text is this unending allure of multiple meanings.

Yet that a text can say innumerably many things does not mean that it can set any thing forth completely. This is especially true of the things that can be said about the divine—in a truth that cannot be apart from the language that cannot hold it. For Augustine, Louis Mackey notes:

> the inscription of truth distances and defers the presence of truth that would confirm it. The moment of presence is lost as soon as it is written. But was it ever not written? Augustine's life is motivated by language, and his conversion is mediated by the language of Scripture. . . .
>
> The experience of God cannot be contained within the text that proposes to (re)capture it. It subsists only as an unwritten and unwritable excess of the text.[23]

Augustine, of course, goes on to dwell in and contribute to this particular kind of excess, devoting considerable text of his own to the question of reading scripture—seeking, perhaps, to write the central mystery of his own conversion, the sudden sense of rightness and even joy that comes after his having willed it (strenuously, dramatically, and at length), yet comes abruptly, without his willing it at all. In a life motivated and converted by language, he writes, and writes around, a sacred absence that can nonetheless seduce both his words and the desires of his flesh: a text that tells him to re-embody that flesh in Christ, whose enfleshing scripture will also provide a text. The origin is not presented as an entity, but as what entices the very texts it exceeds. Thus, rather than grounding the text in a singular source, the idea of a scripture inspired by divinity here enhances the text's polysemousness, multiplies its enticements. Conybeare notes that: "The translation of human language to the divine—and, at the same time, the way in which the divine simply cannot be summed up in human language—is something with which Augustine has been concerned throughout this work."[24] Scripture in any language is written in translation, teasingly evoking an original speech that we neither read nor hear.

Enticement is not wholly distinct from frustration. In struggling with his intensely logocentric God, Augustine also struggles against the absence inherent to God as truth and the site of meaning, the absence essential to divine presence, the elusion already in the contact. "Let it be now," he prays, until finally it is *now*, in the will-less perfection of a conversionary instant—but only a few books later, Augustine will famously realize that in time, in the slip from a not-yet future to a no-longer past, *now* has no when-ness at all.[25] It is never, though always, now. Words always slip, meaning unfolding behind them and new possibilities opening ahead. Word and flesh are both at once passing (already past by the time we can measure their passage) and more than temporal.[26] They are not just vessels of eternal meaning but rather are transfigured by their role as that in and through which meaning *is*, as the signs no less necessary than what they signify. Yet the secret of their connection is persistently elusive. It is for this secret that incarnation will become a particularly potent image. In the canonical fourth gospel, Word is made flesh in a retelling of the divine speaking of Genesis I; in the Gospel of Truth, that Word is written in the body that also publishes the divine Book.[27]

That elusive connection is generally an imperfect one too. Augustine is frustrated by language's inadequacy in expression—"understanding flashes like lightning through the mind, but speech is slow and sluggish, and hopelessly inadequate."[28] Indeed, we must recognize not only our frequent sense that we have not managed to say what we meant, at all, but that we are wholly unable to guarantee that our words will be heard or read in accord with our speaking intent. The inadequacy of written and spoken words to immaterial truths is an ancient concept.[29] For Platonically influenced religious thinkers, language is most notably insufficient when it purports to be the word of God, though scripture is a word that, for many of them, cannot properly be said to be in *error* as such. Such a peculiar claim means that we must ask what it is that these texts do successfully, in what strange sense they might be "true." Clearly they make for bad science and often dubious history, and their predictive use is notoriously unreliable. (Augustine notes certain discrepancies in the scriptures' historical descriptions; that he is untroubled by them suggests more a sophisticated reading than a willful indifference.) But they make for excellent enticements of desire, and for fascinating sources that, accumulated tradition suggests, may instruct us, in the very act of reading, as to how we ought to read them—or perhaps just how we ought to read. Most seductively, in their most enticing and conversionary passages, they promise a secret, show us a mystery.

We read restlessly, enjoying on the way to richer pleasures. Augustine's heart is restless, and not merely until it rests in God, who is no place nor time of restfulness, no time or place at all. Language, in its impossible fragility, nonetheless bears the full force of desire (we recall that for Augustine desire is the moving force of all language).[30] Miller notes in parallel that in the Gospel of Truth, "The life of that journey [of the living ones] is the desire in language, the lure of meaning set in motion by words."[31] The God of desire is a God of words. "Language in its fluidity and displacements is inseparably interwoven with the restlessness or openness of desire," declares R. D. Williams.[32] The God who is love is the Word, but is words, too, restless in seeking to establish meaning, too restless to leave meaning as established—and meaningful in a way that can only slip between and among those words.

Such is exactly the seduction of scripture, a lure toward meaning. In a conversionary reading, these are the texts that promise us knowledge of knowledge's source, the truth about truth, the impossible/necessary link between signifier and signified. They tell us how to read themselves while they tell us how to read at all, how to find the traces that they (also) are—and that we must read them for more than they can designate.

The simple transmission of information, lacking the performative or demonstrative element, could not be seductive enough to turn around desire—or not very often, at any rate. What draws Augustine into Christianity through a complex of seductive texts is not merely knowledge, but love; not a peaceable and contented love, but desire more intense than any other he has known—a desire so strong as to cut the bonds by which other urges had held him. This God in the fullness of its truth eludes the very articulation that desire demands;[33] Augustine both interprets and praises the God who cannot be said. We are seduced by sight and sound and by meaning too—precisely by the intensity of the desire to know, by the intermixing of knowledge and desire, by the divine dissatisfaction and incompletion of both.

If we can turn one way, we can turn another. Mackey links linguistic desire to both destruction and redemption:

> Language . . . redeems when the Word itself speaks in the silence of our words. Augustine's conversion is precipitated by the voice of a child saying, 'Take and read,' and by the first words of the Apostle his eyes fall on when he opens the codex and reads (8.12.29). But it is language that effects the fall, by soliciting humanity's legitimate desire to conform to the divine likeness.[34]

We must note the place of this redemption—this speaking in silence, into language's own stillness. Language is redemptive in creating the spaces of its own absence; destructive when it speaks over the stillness it might create. But it must speak to create these still spaces. The illuminative Word in its silence creates the space of possibility, the stillness into which words speak, the infinite breaking the moment, the opening of astonishingly multipliable meanings that draw after them our greed for understanding. "As what allows the production of meaning, the unnameable one says nothing; rather, he permits saying," writes Miller.[35] The act of creation, as it calls into being, makes the space for speaking too.

Desire, historically and controversially linked to lack, is more rightly at once lacking and overfull, and both are relevant to language.

Incompletion and excess are one another's flipsides. Incompletion entails the multiplication of meanings, that further interpretations are always possible. The desires satisfied by language give way to desires aroused and left unsatisfied by it. Mackey notes Augustine's own efforts to capture Word and word, to capture scripture in his own multiplication of its meanings: "In the Scriptures as in Augustine's book, the Word is never fully incarnate. It eludes the text as a presence always already and ever yet absent from its alienated traces. Mythically recalled, prophetically foreseen, always desired, it is never possessed."[36] When by faith we know a sound to be a sign and not just noise, we are set into motion toward both signified and signifier; we want to know the word better, know its meaning. In some simple cases this desire is satisfied by a definition. Sometimes, especially when the words at stake are held to name the divine, it is not. Meanings multiply.

The value of scripture for Antony, for Marius Victorinus, for the readers of Athanasius, for Augustine, for Valentinus or Origen is not the value of propositional truth, though each may believe that such truth is there. This too is the excess of the text—the seductive draw of divinity evoked, thus signified, but not captured. Because of the presumptive infinity of this divine truth, it has to an unusual degree the value of desire, a desire so strong that will can present no obstacle. Throughout the present work, and hardly originally, I have argued that all language speaks desire, is drawn and driven not so much *by* desire but rather *as* desire, desiring desire—that is, desiring to draw, but also drawn by desire. And language read as divine sign speaks, not more loudly,[37] but most seductively of all—its draw is infinite, because it is precisely the sign for infinity, but more, because it promises the secret of signs, *meaning* itself, *reading* itself. It is time to begin to see how.

The Text That Says Flesh That Says Text: Take This, All of You, and Read of It

There is no more reading where signs no longer are removed from and deprived of what they indicate. There is no more interpretation if no secret sustains and summons it. There are no more words if no absence founds the waiting that they articulate.

—Michel de Certeau, "White Ecstasy"

D. Moody Smith notes of the fourth gospel: "The prologue concludes with the affirmation that Jesus (God the only Son) has made [God] known.... It is interesting, and perhaps significant, that the Greek verb translated 'to make known' (*exegeomai*) means to explain or interpret. The nominal form is literally *exegesis*.."[38] A line from Elliot Wolfson similarly reminds us that we begin in commentary; "In the beginning," he says, "there is interpretation."[39] Despite the often-differing roles played by Jewish and Christian commentaries, this curious primacy of the interpretive ("secondary") source seems to be shared. "In the beginning was the Word," says John's rewrite of Genesis, but both this word enfleshed and the text that tells of it are already interpretations—the Word exegetically sets forth the God with which it is in some mysterious fashion one. Exegesis is the function and the nature of both words and Word.

Where it begins again with Christian texts, scriptural exegesis already also begins to pull words toward enfleshed Word. The incarnation here functions exegetically, but what makes this so odd is that it has this function *in* and *through* the very text that presents it. The textual exegesis tells of the incarnational exegesis that exegetes itself, if we may be permitted the awkward verb. Divine meaning cannot be contained in the text that is its sign. Commentary and incarnation alike not only sign again, but tell us an essential something of what signs are. And that strange, central sign, the sign that is what it tells, is the most seductive draw upon the intellectual desire of those turned toward it. This is scripture's seduction for those who read it in the faith of open questions: that of which it tells is that which it tells us cannot be told, and this telling occurs when the text performs own exegesis doubly with its exegesis of God. In the Gospel of Truth, "The mystery of the incarnation is framed . . . as the declamation of the name of the nameless, the 'great name,' that the Son 'to whom the name belongs' bestows upon the 'sons of the name in whom rested the name of the Father, (who) in turn themselves rested in his name'" (38.25–30).[40] The mystery is in the strange doubleness of the sign of what cannot be signified, the name of what cannot be designated. And the mystery is written in the flesh. What exceeds the text, going beyond its propositional truths or falsehoods, may nonetheless be given by it, as the surplus of its propositions: the elusive, allusive silence of poetic space, the exuberant resonance of praise, the sensuousness of its syllables; the satisfaction, even, of precision.

Even more than other words as signs, this purportedly inspired text, this divine word, is conceptually entangled with divine Word, with the notion of the incarnation in which the Christian God becomes Word and flesh both. As Wolfson points out, there are both parallels and differences here between Jewish and Christian thinkings of textual bodies: "For Christians, the body is the embodiment of the book; for Jews, the book is the textualization of the body."[41] What, then, do these Christian converts hear or read in a book about a body that embodies the book?

In the world of time and of saying, the materiality of language sets it into complex relation to a God who is likewise a materialized, enfleshed abstraction, yet no less flesh for all its abstractness. All words, it seems, come back to God (in whom, according to some traditions, both Jewish and Christian, they also pre-exist), but without fully arriving, without staying, because the god of those words is not itself a being in a place; it is not finally and fully arrived at and found. Like the moment in which conversion happens, it is not *there* to be found—only turned-toward, in and by conversionary texts.

The materiality of language is linked not only to desire, to our pleasure in the sight and sounds of words, but also to the multiplicity and insufficiency that we have already noted as characteristic of language. The sensuous words of the scriptural text and the Word made sensible flesh both multiply the meanings of divinity, even as they exemplify divine elusiveness. In order to be perceptible, knowable, at all, truth must enter into the sensuous, where givenness is never complete.

Nowhere is sensuality a greater puzzle than in the question of divine language, where neither the look of the text nor the sound of the voice, still less the feel of its vibrations, lends itself to being concretized in an image. Augustine deals extensively with questions of God's speaking, determining that the divine word cannot pass in time and so cannot be sensual, any more than it can be fallible, in the manner of ordinary speaking. John Rist notes, as we have, the fragility, and frequent failure, of language. He points out that in use (and not mere mention) words mean by convention,[42] by an agreement itself unspoken and unwritten, probably unspeakable and unwritable. But he also notes an important exception: "for Augustine at least one set of signs is not merely conventional . . . ; that is the signs of God given in the Scripture (or in the liturgy and 'sacraments,' i.e. in religious acts). Part of the explanation of why these are not conventional is because they are not mere *attempts*, but accomplishments of what God wishes to achieve. For Augustine believed it is impossible for God to try and fail."[43] We might consider that the gap in signification is not, then, a failure. As Catherine Brown writes of the provocative, evocative opening invocation of the fourth gospel, "Here is something to desire, perhaps, for a use of language, something one might ache to know. For one who loves words precisely for their imperfections and double-talk, here also is food for ambivalent thought, a stab of difference between human words that are lovable, as Gertrude Stein said, because 'they can be so mistaken,' and a word simultaneously so like and so unlike them."[44] The gap entices, seduces, eludes even when what is signified, what is being told, is the story of a perfect sign. To make sense of this, we can look more closely at the crucial role that the incarnation plays in reading, a role that turns out to be entangled with divine as much as human writing. As Origen suggests in his commentary on the Song of Songs, "wisdom offers the flesh of the word."[45] Here too, as Miller points out, "a reader dwells profoundly in the textual reality of Scriptural language." And here too, "that profound dwelling is erotic."[46] The divinely seductive is scripturally embodied in words as the traces that draw meaning past measure, pulling toward body itself, toward incarnation.

We recall that Augustine associates the second person of the trinity both with our ability to understand language (when it functions as Teacher) and, more mysteriously, with our ability to generate language, to create using words. This inwardly creative Word is pre-sensory; indeed, it lacks sensory existence altogether, which is why it cannot itself be a sign. The Word within is neither sign nor signified; rather, it is the condition of the possibility of signification, an elusive sort of meta-meaning.[47] Like the Inner Teacher by which we know, this meaningfulness is at once ground and final destination, but still more, within that circle is the luminous space of meaning's possibility, a light that darkness can neither overcome nor comprehend. The light can only shine in the world when it enters that world, when it too becomes flesh. The truth, if it is to have any *meaning* at all, needs signs as much as sense, and that means that it needs its sense to be sensuous too.

Indeed, for Augustine, the incarnation—not just the second person of the Trinity abstractly or interiorly—is essential to meaningful speech.

Marcia Colish writes, "In Christ, says Augustine, God speaks to man as man, 'proclaiming aloud by words,' through the sensible, temporal media of his life, deeds, death, descent, and ascension [*Conf* 4.11.10. See also *De civitate dei* 11.2–3]. The Incarnation conveys the knowledge of God to the world by communicating God himself. It also enables man to respond to God in human terms, by restoring man's words to God in Christ."[48] The puzzle of the relation of word to corporeality is the puzzle of sensible materiality; most particularly, of the sensuous character of signs. Language, like the incarnation, renders sensuous the elusive presence of truth. But a sensory "presence" can never *capture* any truth; words pass across our eardrums or vocal chords or eyes; the "presence" of meaning is saturated with absences, leaving us to read meanings in the spaces as much as in the letters,[49] in the openings of the body's wounds as well as in its reassuring solidity.

As we began to see already in the introduction, in premodern Christian semiotics, the incarnation is at once paradigmatic and unique, granting human access to word and reason and meaning itself. Uniquely, as Mackey notes, "It confronts us directly with the reality it signifies, a reality with which it is consubstantially one in the unity of the divine Person. Yet Augustine knew—for that matter the evangelists and the apostles had already known—that the divine presence is not immediately discernible in the fleshly sign. Else the Christ could not have been rejected."[50] So in this sign most full of meaning, closest to its own meaning, a body of divine truth, there is nonetheless the space for misreading. We can miss the point no matter how nearly direct our access to it may be. There must, then, even here, be some measure of indirection, and some gap in the match of sign to signified. So too with words as they reach for their truth: imperfection is necessary to them, and, as I noted above, I am not so certain we want to see this as a flaw. It is in the imperfect match that possibility and enticement exist: the perfect sign is not perfectly matched.

This becomes stranger (but richer) still when we consider the tradition that scriptural texts are themselves somehow divinely worded and that, in these divine words, they tell the story of an incarnational meaning already past. Even this long after the "death of the author,"[51] when we learned "that a text does not consist of a line of words, releasing a single 'theological' meaning (the 'message' of the Author-God), but is a space of many dimensions, in which are wedded and contested various kinds of writing, no one of which is original,"[52] we still want to ask who is telling. Somehow, we think, it matters who is speaking. And we want to ask that even more when what we are told is that there is somehow a god-author behind the text; we want to ask what that could possibly, *if* that could possibly, mean.

But Who Gives the Text? Speaking, Writing, and Divine Publication

As an institution, the author is dead: his civil status, his biographical person have disappeared . . . but in the text, in a way, I desire the author: I need his figure (which is neither his representation nor his projection), as he needs mine.

—Roland Barthes, *The Pleasure of the Text*

That only God can designate God adequately is a commonplace thought for premodern theory.[53] The Gospel of Truth goes further, arguing that, beyond designation, God alone, who makes all things by calling their names, can *call* his own name: neither representation nor evocation is possible from some source external to the name(d). "God" names the elusive "cause" of meaning, which is at the same time a call in all its confusing reciprocity. In keeping with this curious evocation, the texts purporting to tell about God are purported to be, in some imperfectly direct fashion, God's telling as well.

Our fragile words, meaningful by an underlying semiotic faith, must be susceptible to failure,[54] and as we've noted, there are many ways to read scripture as failed. Language, Augustine suggests after his conversion, eludes the proud by its apparent simplicity. With Christianity, even the beginning begins again, a duplication of creation warning us against reading as if we were children, or as if the stories were simple and not complex, repeated, and contradictory. Scriptural texts, Augustine warns, rely heavily on indirection, and some instances are easier to follow than others.[55] Not least complex is the layering of authorship.

Augustine is especially drawn to parts of scripture in which divine word is presented explicitly, such as the opening of Genesis, in which God's speaking is the act and source of creation, and its restatement in the prologue to John, in which Word is identified with God as the (nontemporal) "beginning." The combination of cosmological and semiotic, in fact, makes these very popular texts among late ancient and medieval exegetes more generally. Augustine worries considerably about those of God's words given scripturally as quotations, such as "Let there be light" from Genesis 1:3, arguing, as I've noted, against their unfolding in time in the manner of human language. He worries too about the fourth gospel's originary Word, and just what a beginning could be before time is. The text, of course, *does* unfold in time as it is read, even as its written form leaves it ready for another reading, another unfolding. So we find a curious and perhaps paradoxical narrative. On the one hand, the quotation of God's speaking, or the story of the beginning in which the Word is (with) God, must be the temporal telling of a non-time, an eternal present or a realm ontologically prior to the temporal. But on the other, the words unfold one after another, into silence or the end of the page, finding their meaning in an after. If these are not texts that make their points and then end, but rather texts about the absence of ending, then perhaps we can find something of their strangeness in the beginning, in claims about their source.

That source is held to be, usually in some odd and indirect fashion, God's own word or words or at least words that God has caused in and from humans:

> To speak of the matter as it is, who is able? I venture to say, my brethren, perhaps not John himself spoke of the matter as it is, but even he only as he was able; for it was man that spoke of God, inspired indeed by God, but still man. Because he was inspired he said something; if he had not been inspired, he would have said nothing; but because a man inspired, he spoke not the whole, but what a man could he spoke.[56]

The notion of divine inspiration of scripture, the claim that it *is* of divine inspiration and does not just indirectly quote divine speaking as something that the author or a friend of the author's friend once heard somewhere, tends to have a circular justification. Those who hold to the claim often point to second Timothy 3:16, which reads, "All Scripture is inspired by God and profitable for teaching, for reproof, for correction, for training in righteousness." The evidence for divine inspiration of scripture is that scripture says so. As a logical argument, this is less than spectacularly persuasive, but perhaps we can find a more seductive circularity, a more graceful ground for the sense of Antony or Augustine that the texts they take and read and hear speak divine words to them.

Again, for Augustine all words are given meaning and intelligibility by their relation to some inner, unspoken (and unspeakable) word. But what makes that teaching possible is the event of *publication*, the Word made sensible so that we can read the sense of words. So for a Christian exegete thinking along Augustinian lines, what distinguishes scripture from other texts is the claim that in it the relation of words to Word is unusually direct; that it *is* in some sense the word of God by virtue of the stories that it tells, words that tell both of God's speaking and of the Word made words, both in material text. What we find in such a text is not a fullness of presence, but that always-interaction of presence and absence, touch and withdrawal, that characterizes the theologically seductive. The divine speaks without when.

The problem of divine speaking, placing in time a word seemingly without sensuality, recurs and intensifies in the more limited and rather peculiar scriptural passages evoking divine writing. I would like to dwell upon these in succession, and upon some important noncanonical examples as well, as it may be in these strange small moments that we best see the particular draw of reading this language. As Wolfson has noted, the Christian tradition has associated God with the spoken *logos*, while the God who writes appears more prominently, though certainly not only, in Jewish texts and traditions,[57] and we see more extensive instances of divine writing in the Hebrew Bible. Without insisting that writing works just the same in every one of these cases, I do want to see if there mightn't be some peculiar elements in common.

The best-known and most extensive of the God-writing stories appear with slight variations in Exodus and Deuteronomy as they recount Moses' receipt of the commandments, written by God on tablets of stone (Exod. 24:12, 31:18, 34:1; Deut. 4:13, 9:10, 10:4).[58] Moses is given not only God's words, but God's writing, the materiality of the text divinely created, as the text in Exodus, on which I shall focus here, emphasizes: "The tablets were God's work, and the writing was God's writing engraved on the tablets" (32:16). But while Moses is up on the mountain, receiving these texts, the people are worshipping a calf made of gold rather than the writing God with whom Moses has just intervened on their behalf. Displaying a rather godlike temper of his own, Moses "threw the tablets from his hands and shattered them at the foot of the mountain" (Exod. 32:19). Thus the only one who reads God's writing (and even this is an assumption: the only one who *could* have read God's writing) is Moses, who is also alone in his ability to speak directly with God.[59] To endure the divine language is beyond the rest of us; we can approach the meaning we desire only indirectly or mediately.

Recovering his temper, Moses once again pleads with God on behalf of his obstinate people. As part of a covenant with those people, God agrees to reissue the commandments that had been inscribed on the shattered tablets: "Now the Lord said to Moses, 'Cut out for yourself two stone tablets like the former ones, and I will write on the tablets the words that were on the former tablets which you shattered'" (34:1). Moses obligingly returns, two stone tablets in hand (34:4). But God does not inscribe them after all: "Then the Lord said to Moses, 'Write down these words . . .' . . . And he wrote on the tablets the words of the covenant" (34:27–28). With these tablets he descends back to the people, the divine word, well mediated, now in hand.

Among these passages is another important kind of divine writing—and erasure. After smashing the first set of tablets, "Moses returned to the Lord, and said, 'Alas, this people has committed a great sin, and they have made a god of gold for themselves. But now, if You will, forgive their sin—and if not, please blot me out from Your book which You have written!' The Lord said to Moses, 'Whoever has sinned against Me, I will blot him out of My book'" (Exod. 32:31–33). The letter gives life: to live is to be written.[60]

What God writes, in the book and on the stones, no ordinary person reads. Here the materiality of the divine text is elusive, and we can read only what is written secondhand. Whatever the original may have been, it is beyond reading; it is written in stone, but it reveals to us not stone's durability but the fragility of all matter, even that touched by a divine hand. We are vividly reminded of textual materiality, and of the tight alliance of the name that may be called with the self in the presence of divinity: God also keeps a book, a book of names, by which only those who have not displeased him, those he still desires, may be called.

Another passage cited as an instance of divine writing, once again mediately read, appears in the fifth chapter of the book of Daniel. King Belshazzar has arrogantly taken two goblets from the Temple, and has the extraordinary bad taste to use them to serve wine at a feast. "Suddenly," the text tells us, "the fingers of a man's hand emerged and began writing . . . on the wall of the king's palace, and the king saw the back of the hand that did the writing. Then the king's face grew pale and his thoughts alarmed him, and his hip joints went slack and his knees began knocking together" (5:5–6).

This writing is distinguished by its lack of intelligibility. The letters can be made out, but neither the king nor any of the many advisors he calls in has the slightest idea what the words might mean. Finally, the queen suggests that Daniel, known for "insight and wisdom like the wisdom of the gods," be brought in to interpret or translate the text on the wall (5:11). Summoned to the palace, Daniel prefaces his reading by sternly pointing out that the king, who ought to know better, has allowed himself to become proud and careless, making no effort to glorify God. "Now this is the inscription that was written out: 'Mene, mene, tekel, upharsin.' This is the interpretation of the message: 'Mene'—God has numbered your kingdom and put an end to it. 'Tekel'—you have been weighed on the scales and found deficient. 'Peres'—your kingdom has been divided and given over to the Medes and Persians" (5:25–28).

The prophecy proves accurate, but the reading is deeply strange. Daniel reads in a way to which no one else has access, seemingly akin to the kind of divination involved in conversations with oracles, or the reading of omens from natural phenomena. If we assume the impossibility of a private language, this is at least a language with exceedingly few speakers or readers—perhaps only two, if one counts God. Moses is unique in his ability to withstand God's words and so to mediate them to his people. Daniel is unique in his ability to read words that others can perceive directly with their senses but not at all with their intellects. Through both figures, divine writing preserves its general indirection; it can be read or even heard only by one person, a prophet outside the standard run of humanity, with special access to the divine writer. There is in the Daniel story another level of remove, as well; the hand is "sent down from Him," not so clearly "His," adding a sensory mediation to the intellectual one, as when the hand of Moses inscribes the word of God.

God the father does not appear to write in the Christian gospels, but Christ does, in a peculiar little episode in the fourth of them, where the scriptural Jesus most nearly approaches his later status as a person of the Trinity, declaring "The Father and I are one" (10:30). As Jesus is teaching in the Temple, those who are hoping to trick him or trip him up bring to the Temple a woman "caught in adultery" (John 8:4), and they raise questions of the law: "Now in the Law Moses commanded us to stone such women; what then do You say?" (8:5–6) Famously, Jesus will urge that the woman be stoned only by the sinless, upon which suggestion all of his would-be accusers slink off, and he instructs the woman to leave, adding, "from now on sin no more" (8:11). But in between these well-known sentences something unexplained, perhaps even inexplicable, happens: "But Jesus stooped down and with His finger wrote on the ground. But when they persisted in asking Him, He straightened up, and said to them, 'He who is without sin among you, let him *be the* first to throw a stone at her.' Again He stooped down and wrote on the ground" (8:6–8). As with the divine writing in Exodus, there is no indication at all that anyone reads what he writes. More frustratingly, the text does not clue its readers in either.

This, of course, leaves people to wonder, and wonder they have. One interpretation suggests that Christ alarms his accusers by recording their names—a sort of inverse blotting out, or an inversion of the eternal book of the living in which the names of those rendered wholly mortal are inscribed in the vanishing dust. Augustine has a more ingenious suggestion, in which he juxtaposes this story with the one we've just read from Exodus: the hard law was originally written in stone, he says, but with the coming of Christ, it is written more gently in the softer soil, also the place of taking root and sprouting.[61] Thus it may live on.

Though the episode is probably not a part of the earliest versions of the text,[62] it nonetheless serves to echo intriguingly other Johannine reflections on writing. George Aichele considers the episode at some length in "Reading Jesus Writing," and suggests that the story fascinates because "in this text the scripture—that is, the writing that is John—tells of another text (another writing) that can never be subdued or controlled, that resists every attempt to read it."[63] Thus the maximally resistant, unread and perhaps unreadable writing in the dust parallels the always-overflowing text of the gospel in which we find it, a text that declares its own inexhaustibility at its "end":

> In its final sentence, the Gospel announces, "there are also many other things which Jesus did; were every one of them to be written, I suppose that the world itself could not contain the books that would be written" (21:25). This phrase is frequently regarded as a rhetorical flourish. . . . However, if this statement is taken more seriously, then the Gospel of John denotes the failure of denotation itself . . . not merely the limitation of this particular book, but rather the impossibility of ever completely presenting or re-presenting any object.[64]

Any object—but especially the non-object of the divine itself, calling in excess of all language. Again, I do not mean by this assortment of examples to propose a grand overarching theory of divine writing, but only to note some among its undoubtedly many peculiarities. It is, perhaps most dramatically, unreadable except by a few persons in exceptional relation to divinity, persons who can act as intermediaries, themselves perhaps providing the necessary spacing and distance. The divine texts come to our language secondhand, as copies or bodies or reports or translations. In the Christian texts, even this limited legibility is mediated by the dual possibility of generating and understanding language: that is, through God as Word, or the Word that is somehow atemporally co-original with God, before the beginning of any writing at all. Elusion writes—and erases—itself.

All texts are written in dust or on what will become dust—even stone crumbles, or is angrily smashed into pieces. God's own writing, then, would have to inscribe the intersection—or the deeper relational infolding—of timelessness with time, of the eternal with the material. Even more than divine speaking, divine writing emphasizes the very materiality of language that presents it with problems. Small wonder that the incarnation becomes a favored metaphor. But it is more than that too: for some of its subtlest exegetes, it is the site of meaning itself, a site that appears, disappears, re-emerges, and promises in its materiality and its sense. In it, the book of the Living lives again.[65]

As I have previously suggested, the Gospel of Truth is surprisingly close to some of Augustine's claims about the exegetical role of the incarnation—at least in its theory of reading and naming. (Wolfson argues that these claims may also reflect the influence of Jewish wisdom traditions, from which the Valentinians would not have sharply distinguished themselves.)[66] In this text God, as both knowledge and love, is contrasted with forgetfulness, which is the consequence of not knowing the Father. We know and we remember in textual flesh. To know and to be known are coincident; of those who are taught by the Word, the gospel declares, "They knew, they were known, they were glorified, they gave glory. In their hearts the living book of the living was revealed, the book that was written in the Father's thought and mind and was . . . in his incomprehensible nature."[67] Augustine similarly remarks, "There is a word about God in your heart."[68] There are some parallels, clearly, to the book in which the names of the pleasing are inscribed, but this book seems both broader in scope and more complex in its interior/exteriority. As Wolfson points out, there is a "circularity of salvation" here: "those within whom the name dwells gain knowledge of the name, that is, the name is bestowed upon those who bestow the name. . . . the content of the revelatory act can be construed as self-knowledge (epignosis) that is at the same time contemplation of the divine."[69] In the hearts of those located in this reversible double knowledge is the book that is in the ineffable divinity, the book that calls to life. But how do they learn how to read it?

This is where the self-signifying sign steps in. This book, with life as its subject and its nature, appears together with, and in some senses as, Christ. He does not merely read, but "puts on" the book—as another book will encourage Augustine to "put on Christ," to draw his desire into evocative signification. There is another Augustinian parallel: the inner Word by which we know parallels the inner book inscribed within those who know the Truth that is the Father. But something more complex happens in the Valentinian version:

No one had been able to take up this book, since it was ordained that the one who would take it up would be slain.[70] And nothing could appear among those who believed in salvation unless that book had come out. For this reason, the compassionate, faithful Jesus was patient and accepted his sufferings to the point of taking up that book, since he knew that his death would be life for many.[71]

Life can only be taken up by one who will die, memory by one who is willing to subject its eternal divine perfection to human distractibility in the extension of time. Taking up the book into mortal flesh *means* life: the text that comes to an end means the endlessness of the divine traced through it. "Jesus appeared, put on that book, was nailed to a tree, and published the Father's edict on the cross."[72] In this marvelous passage is a seamless shift from the taking to the being of the book, from "take and read" to "take and be": the book of the Living is the book by which living is possible, and this transfiguration can only occur by crossing the boundary of living flesh, flesh and text alike affixed to the place of death, made readable in a way that pure Life, the Book unpublished in or of the mind of the Father, cannot be. The W/word is published, and so its knowledge is given. When we read, we know the words "within" ourselves. As Wolfson notes, there is an unusual convergence of graphic and phonic here; "To be inscribed in the book is to have one's name enunciated by the Father."[73] The Son is spoken Word, published Book, living Breath.

The unreadable primordial Book is perfectly polysemous; it is written by the Father for revelation to the Aeons, and "each letter is like a perfect book."[74] In this book, that is, each letter opens up another book, in which, perhaps, each letter opens another. The revelation of meaning is infinite; in every letter an infinite Borgesian library unfolds.[75] Christ appears as the one who will in turn reveal the book to humanity, the one who makes reading possible; before him, those who claimed textual knowledge were themselves ignorant. The reading he teaches cannot be finite, finished, closed.

The incarnation is, for Augustine as for Valentinus, both thing and sign, because the incarnation is where the two cross; it is the making of meaning, the connection of signified to sign by which we both read and speak, both write and hear. The incarnation, says Williams, is God's entry into the world of signs,[76] the knowledge that ours is a signifying world.[77] This is what the Teacher has to teach theological semioticians: not the rules for using particular words, not the interpretation of a particular text, but *that* signs mean, that the sensuous has a sense too. And this is thus the peculiarity of scripture, which writes that story. "If we had known how to 'read' the created order," Williams notes, "we should not have needed the incarnation."[78] Christ teaches reading by linking truth to sign, by being meaning: not designation, but evocation. Scriptures become seductive because what they mean is meaning; that is, because they are read as telling the story of the very way in which meaning (and storytelling too) is made possible: in word that becomes world, in Word published as flesh. One would have to be quite incurious not to be seduced by such a promise—but this promise too is kept only as one keeps a secret. When the sign tells itself, we have not finished with meaning, but can only read in amazement at the limit of comprehension, watching every word and every letter open onto more.

In both the book of the living and the Gospel of Truth, words—especially names—take on a creative force echoing the verbal creativity of Genesis: "If he wishes, what he wishes appears when he gives it form and a name—and he does give it a name. He brings into being those who before coming into being were ignorant of the one who made them."[79] And to be created is, at the same time, to be called (by name) to return. "Those whose names he knew at the beginning were called at the end, as it is with every person who has knowledge. Such names the Father has uttered. One whose name has not been spoken is ignorant, for how could a person hear if that person's name had not been pronounced?"[80] So we must not only be written in the book of life, published in the flesh of Christ, but read aloud and brought at once to life and to knowledge, in a double reading by which knowledge is brought into us. Unless we have been taught how signs mean, we will never know if we have been signified, called forth and inscribed. Here names have power, have a direct connection to what they name, and the connection is that of evocation, of calling. "The name of the Father is the Son,"[81] we read, and so we know that in this flesh in which all of our names are published, God is called in all persons.

In the unpublished book in the ineffable primal Father, *language is identical with its own meaning.*

> He revealed it as knowledge that is in harmony with the expressions of his will—that is knowledge of the living book, which he revealed to the eternal realms at the end as his letters. He showed that they are not merely vowels or consonants, so that one may read them

and think them devoid of meaning. Rather, they are letters of truth; they speak and know themselves. Every letter is a perfect truth like a perfect book.[82]

But again, we can only read this Living Book when it takes a distance from its meaning, affixed at the site of death, held still for a moment so that we can take in the text. The body of Christ puts on, becomes, the book of the living by being mortal flesh, naming life even at the site of death. The allusions and reversals here are dizzying. The "tree" of the cross echoes the tree of knowledge in the second and third books of Genesis, the one from which Eve and Adam eat, attain forbidden knowledge, and so unsettle God that he makes them mortal. The fruit of that first tree is death; what hangs on the second tree and delights those who eat it is the legible version of the book of life. The figure who urges in the canonical gospels "take and eat" in offering bread that "is my body" here silently urges, like the Augustinian mystery child, "take and read"—take this, all of you, and read of it. The published word appears to be dead, to be fixed in place, nailed to the page, but the mystery of it is that it lives. Its stillness is that not merely of death, but of attention, and its mystery is what calls. "He was nailed to a tree (and) he became a fruit of the knowledge of the Father. It did not, however, cause destruction because it was eaten, but to those who ate it it gave (cause) to become glad in the discovery, and he discovered them in himself, and they discovered him in themselves."[83] Platonic though the Valentinians are, they do not seem to share the Socratic critique of writing as fixed and dead, incapable of living communication.[84]

We do not quite find in this published book either a primal speaking or an originary writing. Rather, we find a non-transparent, because more intimately sensuous, focus on the elusive meaningfulness of words as we have them. In sensuous language, transparent telling remains a dream.[85] The very Word that illuminates words' meaning remains elusive of language. The divine language eludes human words; it is readable only in the intersection of passing and eternal in the flesh, an intersection in which forgetful death and eternal life in full remembrance meet. The word that passes away into silence passes also into the gathering of meaning—and so, too, of desire. And yet I would say, again, that this inherent loss is not a flaw in it. The modernist God of metaphysical stability, the guarantor and granter of the truth of propositions, gives way here to the stranger, and even in these deep abstractions far more carnal, subtleties of premodern theological thinking about the reading of signs.

Among canonical texts, perhaps the closest we come to a similar emphasis on a book that is God's is in a work that Augustine attributed to John, as he did the fourth gospel—the book of Revelation, or Apocalypse. Here the divine identifies itself alphabetically, as "the Alpha and the Omega" (1:8, 21:6, 22:13). While we ought not to overliteralize the letter here, the emphasis in the text on what is written adds further significance to this metaphor of first and last (those terms are also found at 1:17 and 2:8). The narrator of this text is instructed to write, first in general, and then more specifically to the individual churches (1:11, 2:8, 2:18, 3:1, 3:7, 3:14). He encounters in a vision one "like a son of man," who instructs him, "write the things which you have seen, and the things which are, and the things which will take place after these things" (1:19). This is perhaps a more direct account of divine inspiration of scriptural production than the verse from Timothy usually cited, and a more self-reflexive one: included in this text is the command to create it.

In the fifth chapter of Revelation, we encounter another divine book. Like the book of Life in the Gospel of Truth, it is initially unreadable, in this case because there are no suitable readers (5:3). But "the Lion that is from the tribe of Judah, the Root of David, has overcome so as to open the book and its seven seals" (5:5), and, in the form of a Lamb, takes the book (5:7–8) and is declared worthy of so doing (5:9). Christ, it seems, can read this awe-inspiring text; as in the Gospel of Truth, though in quite a different way, he acts as intermediary between divine word and human understanding. If the words are to be understood, Word must illuminate them, open them up, and make the written text readable. The opening of the book is the opening of a deeper seduction; at the breaking of each of the first four seals, a voice beckons "Come" (6:1–7), drawing in.[86] The sign is not an answer but a summons.

There are other curious books in this altogether curious text, such as that of chapter 10, which is to be ingested. At the outset an angel appears, holding a "little book" (10:2). "So I went to the angel, telling him to give me the little book. And he said to me, 'Take it and eat it; it will make your stomach bitter, but in your mouth it will be sweet as honey.' I took the little book out of the angel's hand and ate it. . . . And they said to me, 'You must prophesy again concerning many peoples and nations and tongues and kings'" (10:9–11). The *take and read* and the *take and eat* have become completely entangled. The words are taken in not by sight or by hearing, nor even by Braille-like touch, but as food; as words do, especially when they teach, they then give to the one who has taken them in an ability to make more words—words that will tell of "the things which will take place after these things." Once the narrator has the book within him, he has the possibility of making books himself.

And again we find the book of Life, in which names are written. The person saved becomes the very site of writing: "He who overcomes, I will make him a pillar in the temple of My God, and he will not go out from it anymore; and I will write on him the name of My God, and the name of the city of My God, . . . and My new name" (3:12). Though it is not interiorized here, "on" rather than "in," once more the one who bears the name can dwell in the space of the divine. There is likewise an anti-salvational text: "Then I saw a beast coming up out of the sea, having ten horns and seven heads, and on his horns *were* ten diadems, and on his heads *were* blasphemous names" (12:18). It matters where names are written, apparently, for the direction in which they will be called, blasphemously or redemptively.

Called in blasphemy toward, perhaps, a blotting out, a washing away in the sea, or a recording in transient dust. The call does not give us an original word legible in time; it gives us, instead, an elusive and seductive drawing toward a knowing that never quite becomes known—thus, toward an always-distancing origin of meaning, an immemorial natality of the always-past and ever-new eternal. In scripture the faithful read the impossible divine word, a word unspeakable and unwriteable in time. God as writer withdraws from the text, and the text writes that absence even as it says the fullness of life, writes (of) forgetfulness even as it tells the forgetful what they most need to remember—tells it in the passing truth of the flesh, of which the Word itself is made. In that absence, the world and the word are created; by it, they are made possible. The seduction of scripture is the seduction of all writing, but writ impossibly large: what if, we ask ourselves reading, an author could be *infinitely* absent, and infinitely, world-makingly overfull in textual presence too? This too, after all, is signification, telling us of both sides of excess even as it tells us that meaning is. The text itself is on both sides of excess. Mark Vessey asks,

> But what if the Bible, in the sense taken for granted by theory, were in fact absent and *yet* to come? We know that Augustine "never saw a Bible." Nor did he have any word for such a thing. Suppose that scripture, instead of being there "in the beginning," like the tablets of the law or the books of Moses, began like the literature theorized by Derrida, "with a certain relation to its own institutionality, i.e., its fragility, its absence of specificity, *its absence of object*."[87]

The book itself, whatever its status as the Book, has a strange, open unfinishedness, and that of which it tells is stranger still. Again we hear resonance with Augustine, for whom, Conybeare notes, "the important thing might be the res behind the uerba—but it might not, in fact, be a 'thing' at all." She adds, "human language is in itself grounded in ontology, in notions of being. This ontology can approximate the non-material, but it cannot conceive of anything that simply is not, that does not exist."[88] It cannot conceive or hold, but it can evoke and remind, and the body of every letter offers us more.

Absence and Open Spaces

A space must be maintained or desire ends.

—Anne Carson, *Eros the Bittersweet*

Christian gospels, canonical and not, tell the story of the embodied, materialized, sensuous sign itself. But they have to use signs to tell it, and so they begin again the infinite enticement: they begin, excessively. Beyond proposition, language is the evocation of its own excess, an excess to which it can deliberately call attention—an excess particularly of desire, manifest alike in praise and in silence. Excess is entangled with absence. Signs re-call to mind; the visual signs of words hold the quickly passing vibrations in the air in a more stable form on the page,[89] but words cannot be held indefinitely before the gaze—and the longer we look, the more they lose their meaning. Playing on the Meno-like paradox of *The Teacher*, Mackey remarks, "The problem is iterated in the solution. Knowledge of the immediate is not immediate knowledge. The self-consciousness essential to cognition—knowing that one knows—disrupts the immediacy that is also essential to cognition. The recognition of presence defers presence, so that knowledge is never more than the inscription of a truth that is always elsewhere."[90] Knowledge is inscribed: thus it is written, we say; that is how we know. But the truth of its inscription, the meaning of its sign, is always elsewhere, even and perhaps especially when it is the sign that tries to tell not just truths, but the untellable truth as such. That this idea of knowledge evokes some origin ought not to be taken as demonstration of the canonically Platonic notion that human knowing only copies a perfect reality: rather, it might suggest that the origin is only ever evoked, and not produced, not present even as a precise or locatable *then*.

The divine as eternal absent-present is signed in the text as the text's own reflexive grounding, the inspiration behind meaning making and the inspiring possibility of hearing or reading significantly. Text, and especially text read or heard as scripture (canonical or not), only concentrates the significance of the world, reads it a little less distractedly, focuses desire. "Let it be now," prays Augustine, his desires painfully scattered, and "now," in all its slippage, comes only when he reads. The passage from Paul is not his own special fortune or prescription, but rather his own concentration: *now*, as he reads; *here*, in this text in this garden, his scattered desire and wandering attention gather perfectly for just an instant into the God of the book. The moment of text unfolds and demands interpretation and commentary—"like poetic necessity," says Derrida, "... the very form of exiled speech."[91] Mackey points out:

> The absence of God—his excess of our inscriptions of him in memory and in time and in texts produced by memory in time—is an essential mark of his divinity. His absence is as critical as his presence. A theologian would say that the divine transcendence and the divine immanence must be asserted together at no matter what cost of intelligibility. God is the necessarily remote term of a necessary allusion, the irreducible *allos* of a mandatory allegory.... a God

who allowed himself to be contained within our knowledge would be an idol.[92]

Divine writing is elusive, especially in the book of the body published on a life-giving tree of death, in a flesh that gives itself as a book to be eaten.

Regardless of their canonical position, scriptures are unsettled texts—and sometimes the texts of an unsettledness, of an exile in the desert, of light in a world where dark is preferred and more readily understood. Their writers are absent in many senses: not merely deceased, or deceased and anonymous, but anonymously giving way to a tradition of an ultimately present-absent authorial inspiration. Divine writing seems perpetually hidden, either unintelligible from the beginning or already smashed and erased and nailed to the place of death before we can read it. But the traditions of reading scripture raise the possibility that language may be a divine enticement, calling attention to our words' impoverishment and richness, their inability to denote precisely when faced with paradox and their extraordinary capacity to evoke well beyond denotation. "Those divine letters spell out absence," says Derrida of Jabès,[93] suggesting that even in the primordial text presence cannot be simply full; to write, even to make the possibility of writing, is to spell out the absence in presence, the spaces and silences too. What the word says is its own slip, its own impending absence drawing us into the absence of meaning in it, from it, its fullness eluding us. "God" is not the name of a final answer in which meaning rests secure, but the opening of the infinite question, in the text as excess and insufficiency. God's writing even in those texts is only present as absent; is only ever presented as absent. The original is never there to be read, always shattered into fragments, coded by a strange hand, or scuffed out in the dust. "Far from letting itself be oppressed or enveloped within the volume, . . . repetition is the first writing," Derrida insists—not so distant from my thought here, though more insistent, perhaps, on divine absence rather than on the mystery of absent-present. "The writing of the origin, the writing that retraces the origin, tracking down the signs of its disappearance, the lost writing of the origin. *To write is to have the passion of the origin.*"[94]

At the origin is the Word, but words give us the beginning (as a) yet again. The word is a sign, but signs are remembered, repeated. In the beginning is the Word and the Book before words, that which illuminates, motivates, grounds and eludes signification. In the beginning is the open-ing of a possibility that seduces exegesis into multiplicity. In the beginning is the elusion of the origin that draws, seductively, into the overfullness of praise. And in these texts, as they tell of the voice that makes and the finger that writes and the book of the Living that is published (even and only) in death, we hear the voice of living creatures saying "Come."

Indeed, in such seductive potential, scripture is itself released from the fate of being either rather muddled and frequently inaccurate history or pedantic and often puzzling prescription. When Augustine obeys the injunction to take and read, he isn't seeking answers—he will have plenty of questions, but at that moment they aren't troubling him: desire is. He seeks to be seduced by God, by *meaning*, and so he is by this text in which meaning is its own subject, in which desire is sustained by the meaning that makes possible, makes possibility. Scripture seduces in its promise of the secret of signs: it promises truth itself, and it tells of the material-ization of that truth. It tells in words we know through our senses the story of word and flesh, speaking and world. And because bodies and words alike arouse and sustain our desires, so too, so much more, does the body of a text about the body that somehow is the book, the text that tells us how meaningful the sensuousness of our world is, but also that that mean-ing is as elusive as it is saturated.

Explicitly, the text that converts Augustine urges him to focus his de-sire; implicitly, that desire is thereby seduced. The "key to the text," says Williams, "is conversion to Christ."[95] And yet it is *by* the text that Augustine, like so many others, is converted in the first place. This is not simply a falla-cious logical circle. It is, rather, a passing back over the same point, a crossing over Celan's meridian. The embodiment of truth is the elusive key to reading the most elusive writing: it tells us that signs are. There is a crossing where sign meets signified, in a mystery we are nonetheless shown, but *as* a mystery, as a secret. The secret is esoteric and exoteric at once; it "secrets itself in the concealment of disclosure wrought by the disclosure of its concealment."[96] Scripture seduces by promising the secret of meaning. It keeps the secret—only thus can it keep the promise.

Thus the thoughtful faithful may read scriptural texts, for the infinite layers of meaning, for new ways of opening questions, for the pull of body and breath upon written text and vice versa. Scripture tells the deep truths of myth, of the absent origin that pulls infinitely at our memories, intensely at our desires, that calls us by name, saying *come*. And for those converted by words, the most seductive such summons is the echo of the name that is what it says, the secret of meaning at the chiasm of sign and signified, the word of the Word in the flesh.

In Place of a Conclusion: Thoughts on a Prior Possible

Jesus said, "Have you discovered, then, the beginning, that you look for the end? For where the beginning is, there will the end be."

—The Gospel of Thomas, verse 18

Seduction resists conclusion—"the melancholy of everything *finished*,"[1] as Nietzsche aptly has it. It depends upon recurrence and sustaining, on the continued emergence of a new or re-newed and not quite comprehended possibility, on something we know we want even if we aren't quite sure what it is (even the desire of it is to be desired as a good). To conclude a work on seduction thus seems a bit misguided, so in place of a conclusion I would like to offer this very brief meditation on the coincidence of two inconclusive possibilities, of new emergence and infinite recurrence in the call of the strangely numbered name(s) of God. That is, I conclude with a return, but I argue that that to which we return is the possibility of an always-new beginning: and so, even at the end, we may be seduced again. The thought of the impossible, of the limit and its outside, is enticed by and enticed into all possibility. And what returns us is the same as what draws us: the calling of our names in one divine naming.

I have argued that in a seductive theology the divine name is called and not simply told, and that this calling that is not a telling is caught up in the tradition of a God who is not a being—who thus cannot be designated. Divine seduction resists ontologizing, resists the identification of an entity which, separate from the seductive draw, does the seducing. It finds its sacred in signs, in the incarnate gift of infinity traced in flesh.[2] We must also remind ourselves that this God who is not a being is also not a thing that isn't; even the most thoroughgoing of apophatic theologies do not predicate in-existence of God as of leprechauns—that is simple, and rather boring, atheism, which shares, as Catherine Keller puts it, "the same smug concept of God" as the theism it dismisses.[3] This much we saw in arguing for a seducible faith.

"God" is a name that is called, an improper name; perhaps, as we saw in the Valentinian variation on the uncaused first cause of Aristotelian or Thomist cosmology, the only name that can call itself. Might this name resonate in every evocation? In his sermon on Acts 9:8, Meister Eckhart departs from the text at hand to analyze a line from the Song of Songs, a line in which the speaker seeks and calls out to "he whom my soul loves." Eckhart's take is provocative (his listeners surely expected no less), though he shares with other medieval exegetes the assumption that the beloved must be God. There are four reasons, we are told, for the speaker to say "whom my soul loves" rather than to give the name of the beloved. First, God is above all names. Second, the soul, dissolved "entirely by love into God," knows nothing but love, not even how to name the beloved. Third, it cannot turn away from loving long enough to name him. In all of these, intriguingly, "all names" and "not nameable" coincide—the maximum and the minimum of naming meet in desire. The final meaning of the phrase is that the soul "saying 'love' . . . pronounces at the same time all names."[4] I want to focus especially upon this last possibility here, which I think will help to illuminate the first three. It is clear that, for Eckhart, to name by all names is not to designate by all words. Indeed, he declares in another sermon, "God is nameless, because no one can say anything or understand anything about him."[5] It is in this sense that God is above all names, or cannot be named by the soul wholly attracted and distracted by love, wholly caught in the moment of perfect attention. "God" is named when a name is called in love, and the name of God is a desirous calling out—a calling by all names, by every name of the beloved.[6] "A name of God, in a tongue, a phrase, a prayer, becomes an example of the name and of names of God, then of names in general,"[7] says Derrida—an example and an exemplar, I add with Eckhart, of the name that calls.

This is not an indifferent name: though it calls by all names, not all names always so call. Here is a perhaps unexpected parallel with Pierre Klossowski.[8] The names that repeat in his work are names cognate with particularly intense desires: Sade with his eponymous passion in the analyses of *Sade My Neighbor*, the masochistic Roberte in the fictional series on the *Laws of Hospitality*; even Nietzsche, who for Klossowski is centrally the thinker of recurrence as it is linked to affirmation. Names differ even as they return; repetition is never so simple as identity.[9] "If what returns at any given moment never returns in exactly the same way," Klossowski worries, "how can we justify the use of the same signs?" The "unique signs" of names at the limit of desire name moments of the greatest attentive intensity, breaking the structuralist order of "quotidian signs."[10] Such a unique sign repeats as the same name, yet the name that can call all things without denying their difference.[11] The name of the one, for instance, whom my soul loves.

Calling out the name, an act of desire, is also an act of creation. God and the world, suggests Eckhart, call one another; as God says "Let there be," so too does the responsive world in its praise. "Let there be" is not permission but the double desire of summons and response.[12] *Credo*, says the heart, and we perceive the world as a sacrament, and we seem for a moment to glimpse the newness of creation itself, once more naming, word giving, in the beginning, declaring in the beauty of its form, "He made us." For Eckhart, this calling is more than an origin; it is an always again, a constant birth. It calls again to every name; it calls in the name of every love. The origin and the *again*, the emergence of the new and the already once more, are called together. (Or, to be more traditionally Neoplatonic, divine love overflows into what, precisely as love, it always pulls back toward itself.)

This conjunction of recurrence and newness seems odd to us in part because possibility and novelty appear necessarily linked to futurity and opposed to the already-given. Aristotle, as we have seen, explicitly distinguishes this future potentiality from givenness, which is past or present actuality.[13] For him, potentiality is the capacity of a thing to move or change from one actuality to another. Sometimes this term implies the power to change, sometimes it suggests a more passive susceptibility to alteration, but in any case, it is either already actual (actually real, and so not potential in respect of the same qualities), no longer actual (once real, but not anymore), or not yet realized. A possible future may or may not become actual. The future as the time of the possible seems to elude the logical demands that establish the either/or truth or falsity of the past and present. This is a source of puzzlement to Aristotle, for whom any statement, even one about the future, ought to be either true or false (this is the law of the excluded middle), and not both (this is the law of non-contradiction).[14] Yet he acknowledges that there really are possibles beyond actuality. The logical status of a purely possible statement such as "There will be a sea battle tomorrow," from *De Interpretatione*,[15] is thus rather difficult to discern (at least until the development of modal logic, which is meant to take just such issues into account).[16] For a good Aristotelian (and so, later, for a good Thomist), actuality is primary. Potentiality belongs to what is actual; future possibilities arise out of the actualities of present and past. Like many Aristotelian ideas, this seems to formalize common sense: first what is, and from it, what might be.

In his theological study *The God Who May Be*, Richard Kearney is likewise, though in a quite different manner and to a different end, engaged by the puzzling openness of the future. He argues against ontotheology (the belief that God is an actual and existing being, a "disembodied cause, devoid of dynamism and desire") and for an eschatological God who may be, a possible God who "calls us beyond the present toward a promised future."[17] The divine promise is not a determination: its fulfillment requires our assent. If we do not say yes, argues Kearney, the promise is not kept; it will not be fulfilled against our acceptance.[18] The God who may be is the promise of the future, a promise kept if and only if we accept it. The grammatically elusive "I am who am" is transfigured into "I am who may be,"[19] a phrase that names the possible God, generous in relation to human desires.

Catherine Keller also considers the generosity of a God for whom emergence is interconnected with human activity. She does so through the thought of, among others, the fifteenth century Nicholas of Cusa, influenced by both Eckhart and Dionysius. Keller argues that, for Cusanus, God works not by imposing an omnipotent will onto the world of possibilities, but by *enabling* things to be otherwise than they already are.[20] Thus, as she notes, our understanding of divine power may shift from the overbearing "omnipotent" to the intriguing "omnipotential."

In a three-way dialogue, Nicholas labels God with a neologism as the "possest," the possible-being, the "being" of the possible itself.[21] "I am who am" he boldly reconceives as "I am the actuality of every possibility";[22] "I am who am" and "I am who may be" become rephrasings of the same strange sentence. The possibilities we may or may not actualize are all here, placelessly, *without* losing their character as possible. If all things and all time are, as Nicholas argues, enfolded in God, and all unfolds from him, then the was and the is and the may be are implicated alike.

Here Nicholas argues that in God alone actuality and possibility are at once wholly fulfilled and indistinct from one another: "God is the simple Beginning of the world; He exists before actuality that is distinct from possibility and before possibility that is distinct from actuality. But all things that exist after Him exist with their possibility and their actuality distinct."[23] In this text Cusanus thus does not deny possibility in God, but insists that it is fully realized; he does not deny actuality, but insists that it is fully possible. "Absolute possibility coincides with actuality," he says;[24] that which is necessarily possible, says the modal logician, is necessary.[25] Rather than scholastically privileging actuality in this perfect indistinction, Nicholas insists on the indistinction itself, the complex perfection of what is enfolded here. And indeed, he will move from here to privilege the possible itself, seeing the possible as prior.[26]

In his final text, *On the Summit of Contemplation*,[27] Nicholas moves further even than this provocative new possible-actual. God is newly named as *posse ipsum*, possibility itself—and, as Keller also notes, in this move Nicholas decisively distances himself from the Aristotelian and Thomist divinity that must, however potent, be purely actualized.[28] Keller makes use in her analysis of the dual senses of power and potential (a duality we find both in Nicholas's Latin *potentia* and in Aristotle's Greek *dynamis*):

> the divine power is not operating as an efficient cause upon the world, from its outside; it does not *do for* or *to us*. It is the potentiality which we actualize—or not—within the constraints of our creaturely freedom. It is our own ability, congruent with our understanding (which is always a knowing of the limits of our knowing), our *pouvoir/savoir*, by which the *posse ipsum* is actualized. For what could satisfy the longing of the mind other than *Posse* itself, the *posse* of every *posse*, without which nothing whatever can?[29]

Thus the distinction that Aristotle unfolds is re-implicated. We may well be tempted to re-conceive this by reducing the possible—the actual/possible or the possible itself—right back to the actual. That is, we make of Nicholas's implication a kind of statistical determinism, a set of probabilities, just the opposite of the openness that Keller's more precise reading gives us. We need to avoid this temptation.

Though Nicholas certainly knows Aristotelian logic,[30] he does not follow Aristotle's claim that possibility is a relation among or capacity of actual things, taking its meaning only from those things. Rather: "Possibility exists . . . possibility itself exists." We must, of course, thus open and alter our sense of what existence might mean. "God" turns out to name in a fashion intriguingly and familiarly odd; it is "equally the name of each and every name and of no name."[31] Certainly there is an echo here of Eckhart's God, at once called to in love by every name and described by no name at all—and named by the strangest and most seductive sort of naming, the sign without de-signation, the word at play that calls and is called. Keller argues that *possest* "allows a new name to be revealed as something more than a qualification of the substance called 'God.'"[32] So much more the substance-defying name and non-name of the possible itself.

Every name is called out from here, and called back too, an aural doubling echoing the visual doubling of knowledge ("the eye with which I see God," says Eckhart, "is the eye with which God sees me.")[33] "For everything that in any way either exists or can exist is enfolded in this beginning," says Nicholas, "And whatever either has been created or will be created is unfolded from Him, in whom it is enfolded."[34] It is this complex relational *all* that allows *any* possibility to be fulfilled in the unfolding of creation. It is difficult to be certain, but it seems that enfolded in God are not merely the actualities that do unfold, but those that *could*—or perhaps, in the long extension and sharp intensity of time, the two are the same, and all things are possible.

If they are—if it is possible that they are—we find a resonance not only with Eckhart, a fellow Dominican, but more surprisingly with Nietzsche, who understands his own Platonism as inverted.[35] (The Platonic "inversion" occurs primarily in the value Nietzsche gives to the transient material world, though this value is not so distant from at least some possibilities of Platonism as he might have believed.) The unfolding of the possible resonates more particularly still with Nietzsche as read by Klossowski, read as the name that affirms recurrence. The return is complicated by the call of singular every-names. In this eternal recurrence, every possibility plays out, unfolding over infinite time, and infinitely plays out again.

Nietzsche does provide a physical or metaphysical explanation for this claim—that matter is finite and time infinite, so that every possible configuration and even every order of configurations can only reappear[36]—but this explanation does not seem to be what persuades Nietzsche himself. Nor is this version of eternal recurrence new with him; we find precursors not only in Schopenhauer,[37] but at least as far back as the Stoics.[38] What *is* new is what brings him to his concept of eternal return: not a logical deduction, but an experience of the shock of the world's beauty, an experience with oddly Augustinian echoes. Klossowski argues for the character of this thought as a revelation or unveiling, rather more than a reasoned conclusion.[39] Nietzsche's first published reference to the eternal recurrence, §341 of *The Gay Science*, presents the return as a thought experiment, and a question: how would the thought of an infinite "again" affect you?

If we say "yes" to the thought of recurrence, that affirmation is a revelation, not of the impossibility of newness, but of its infinity.[40] A no to the thought, a sense of the crushing weight of repetition, unveils the contrary revelation, the exhausting boredom of the nothing-new. The revelation, then, comes in the affirmation; it is not simply what is affirmed. Chrétien, though he does not consider Nietzsche, reconnects the affirmation to the Augustinian outpouring of praise by beauty: "A song that offers the world to the light of its origin, which illuminates it by virtue of offering it, and illuminates itself as the place where it comes to offer itself—such is the horizon of all human speech, and already the horizon of the air that we breathe in and out. Every yes that was not uttered by reluctant lips, taking itself back, refusing itself, was always filled by the desire and the hope for this oceanic acclamation."[41]

Every moment is transfigured by the "yes" of this return. What transfigures is not a logical confirmation of the reality of recurrence within the laws of physics, but rather the act of affirmation itself. The affirmative and revelatory thought is the moment as an act of praise. Nietzsche, like Augustine, is brought by the beautiful to a temporally strange revelation. The newness of creation and the infinitely old time of recurrence coincide, says Klossowski, in "the fundamental *eros* that makes man, as Nietzsche says, *the animal who reveres* (Gay Science §346). What becomes apparent, then, is that the event of the 'death of God' stirs the *eros* of the soul at its root; it awakens the instinct of adoration, this *instinct that generates gods*, which in Nietzsche is both a *creative will* and a *will to eternalization*."[42] Nietzsche's God who is dead is the God of guarantees, a stable and certain entity. The release of this certainty arouses the instinct to generate gods, which may ground itself quickly in new certainties, and too often does. But it may also will the endlessness of creation, of divine newness, of astonishment, always again. In this return, even the name of the subject is shattered across all possibilities. "I am one of those machines which can explode,"[43] Nietzsche declares to his friend Peter Gast, around the same time that he has the transformative thought/experience at Sils-Maria.

It is here that Klossowski's interpretation becomes particularly important, as it will take us back to the puzzle of names. Klossowski points out that the thought of eternal recurrence cannot come as something remembered; it is not a particularly intense *déjà vu*. The moment *remembered* would not, in fact, be the same; it would be changed by the very fact of memory. Rather, it must come each time as an astonishment, a revelation, of the implication of the again and the new in each other. If we remembered, as Klossowski and common sense alike point out, we would not be returning.

The return would seem, if anything, deterministically to fix all change in advance and to disallow possibility: nothing could ever be new again; indeed, nothing could ever have been new. Possibility would be entirely subsumed into actuality. But fixity is undone when what matters is the affirmation. And the affirmation re-enfolds every possibility into the actual moment. The moment is not stretched, but gathered: "it is precisely the non-extendedness of the present as activated in *attentio*," writes Pranger, "that does not cease to be what it is: concentration containing the whole."[44]

Klossowski's crucial insight is that the full affirmation of any given moment must be an act of such concentrated attention, including not only that moment's actuality but its possibility, meaning every possible development of that moment, every alternate reality that might also emerge from it. The promise of the future is kept if we accept it, but the promise is the future itself, not a particular outcome: the possible, the open, the *more*. In recurrence, possibility opens even onto the past. This eternal moment is so full that it shatters; even its subject, whose affirmation is the force of eternity, is lost in it—and multiplied, as the revelation "brings about, as necessity, the successive realizations of all possible identities."[45] In the return, says Klossowski, "I deactualize my present self in order to will myself in *all the other selves whose entire series must be passed through*."[46] Klossowski's fiction shares the preoccupations of his Nietzschean analyses; as Mark Jordan notes of Klossowski's odd novel *The Baphomet*, "In a world of repetition, subjects are never singular."[47]

Interestingly, it is not only in the name of Nietzsche that Klossowski makes his striking de-subjectivizing, mobilizing move. In 1938, while his work is still more deeply or obviously Catholic than it will later be, he writes, "The notion of the 'enemy' responds, then, to the more or less concerted ignorance I show regarding one of my own potentialities, and the more I think I experience this potentiality as a difference from someone other than myself, the less I am able to recognizes it within myself as a difference from myself."[48] Ian James notes that: "Klossowski elaborates here a plural view of the Self. The infinite variety of others expresses, in reality, the infinite possibility and multiplicity of my own identity. Or put another way, because Catholic doctrine [of original sin] excludes no human from sin, it must include all humans within its community."[49] "Self" is rendered plural by sin and glory alike, and this is so not only for the subject living that sudden thought of recurrence, but also for the object of joyous desire, the one whose name calls all the names that desire takes. In saying *love*, in saying *yes*, the lover names with all names a singular delight and desire.

The desired one recurs across a series of characters, the same and not the same, called by a name that seems to multiply, so that we are never certain just whom it is naming. The same in being called by desire and calling to it; not the same in places or in times. Sometimes in Klossowski's fictions the same story unfolds once and then unfolds again with changes, like another possibility opening off from that infinite set of recurrences. Each of the uniquely signed names, in "a body of writing which seeks to void the proper name of its identity to overturn the notion of a stable self which would allow names to name, to designate properly, a body or bodies,"[50] is a name called in desire and the name of a desire—Sade's iterative apathetic urgency, Nietzsche's powerful will to recurrence, Roberte's elusive combination of matter, memory, and masochism. The desirable, the beautiful, is called by all names, and its name calls too to every "object" of desire. The names do not *designate* types of desire any more than they do objects, but rather call out in them and to them.

The various theories I have arranged here call one to another. Augustine reads in the world the name that Eckhart will call every name, Cusanus's every and no name (every *possible* name), the name that is and may be and lets be. For Augustine, once we learn how to read it, the whole world is signs, signs calling one name. The significant world is Nietzschean as well as Augustinian, for all the seriousness of their differences. Arguing against the interpretation of the Christian gospels as guarantors of punishment and reward, Nietzsche writes, "Blessedness is not promised, it is not tied to any conditions: it is the only reality—the rest is *signs for speaking* of it."[51] Nietzsche's "only reality" is no more a being than Dionysius' or Eckhart's or Nicholas's. He reads in the world the sign of the return, the name of blessedness traced in flesh. This name too is called, and not told, called in the sudden lived thought wherein we see, Klossowski argues, "the identification of lived time with eternity."[52] This is the moment in which the subject shatters, and names multiply even as they narrow to one: the love, the desire, that names with all names.

Every potential is *willed* in the affirmation of the moment, says Klossowski: "To re-will all experiences, to *re-will* all possible acts, all possible joys and sufferings—this means that if such an act were accomplished now, if such an experience were now lived, it would have been necessary for one series to have preceded and for others to follow—not within the same individual, but in everything that belongs to the individual's own potential—so that one day it could find itself *one more time*."[53] Every possibility is enfolded in every moment, calling out all the names that will always call us back.

This potential must exceed the individual to whom it nonetheless "belongs." The will as *mine* is undercut by the very return *I* affirm. One must lose the security of selfhood to find oneself one more time, to have one's name re-called. Jordan writes, "If the will releases memory, the self scatters across other bodies and their times, is swept into a dance of spirits through every life, every body"—and this too, he notes, is the lived experience of the return as Klossowski describes it.[54] Or, to rephrase the point in the language of one of Klossowski's favorite saints, Teresa of Avila, "The soul is suspended in such a way that it seems to be completely outside itself. The will loves; the memory, it seems to me, is almost lost; the intellect does not work discursively, in my opinion, but is not lost. For, as I say, the intellect does not work, but it is as though amazed."[55]

Releasing its grip on sustaining the individual self, remembering nothing but its own intensities, willful desire re-collects everything, disperses everything: enfolds every possible moment and unfolds itself into every subject. Memory is *almost* lost, scattered so widely across all the possibilities of the shattered subject; almost perfect, taking in everywhen—but always newly, and so never quite remembering, neither fully present nor lost altogether.

Creation, and not just of the self, emerges with repetition in the dual will to generation and eternalization. Beginning over, we return to our beginning in cosmology. Potentiality may always materialize;[56] matter is always potent. Here again, Augustine is less anticorporeal than we usually think. Catherine Conybeare writes: "Augustine expounds nothing like [Philo's] non-material blueprint for matter. In fact, he does exactly the opposite; for in Augustine, there is matter as potential (the *informis materia*), but not form. . . . Material (in *De Genesi contra Manichaeos*) is not in fact matter, but what may potentially become matter. It is in fact better described as a state or condition of potentiality."[57] The association of matter with potential, which must be formed in order to be anything, is hardly uniquely Augustinian; it is very old and very common,[58] and it sounds as if it might fit easily back into a neat division—matter/potential versus immaterial divine act. But Conybeare offers a subtler and better reading: "In his quest to counter dualism, Augustine succeeds in finding the bridging notion of potentiality. It is not exactly liminal, for it is not a threshold between one state or concept and another; it is far more comprehensive, containing always the possibility of presence."[59]

The dual, nondualist possibility of newness and return that emerges in affirmation is the possibility out of which all time unfolds, into which all time enfolds; this is the possibility that touches time, for which time stretches itself into contact; this is the possibility that cuts through the dull trudge of progression and says now, always. Not only "out of the possible, everything," but more: "within everything, possibility." This entices us, frightens us, seduces us. This is not the creation of a God who as a firmly established divine being stabilizes and settles, the God Nietzsche had declared dead—with whom, Klossowski adds, the self dies too.[60] Deleuze, reading Klossowski, points out that the instability of identity of self and God must be connected: "As long as we maintain the formal identity of the self, doesn't the self remain subject to a divine order, and to a unique God who is its foundation?"[61] The God who is beyond the comprehensible categories of being, "God" as the unique name called by all names, seduces us as the possible within the mundane actuality of the world—by which the actual is revealed as not so mundane, after all. This is the possibility of a name that calls all names, is called by all desire, repeated across all subjects not to designate them, but to call them forth and to call them back. It is, as Pseudo-Dionysius says, "rightly nameless and yet [it] has the names of everything that is."[62]

We are called by the question, called into question rather than into security. Nietzsche associates eternity with *Lust*, the German ambiguous between delight and desire, naming the blessedness of the world.[63] The will is all love, says Teresa. Where desire shuts down, so too does the openness of the possible. The new emerges whether we make it or find it or find ourselves made by it; it emerges as a seduction does, neither wholly from nor quite against our wills, as our *yes*. In the eternal return, "The feeling of eternity and the eternalization of desire merge in a single moment," which is not the extension of the self across infinitely iterable time, "but rather the *same life* lived and experienced through its individual differences."[64] Even the same is not.

But surely this is nightmare time, combining both the unbearable boredom of infinite sameness and the unbearable loss of all of one's memories?[65] Nietzsche argues quite otherwise:

To take all this upon his soul, the oldest, the newest, the losses, hopes, conquests, and victories of mankind: to have all this at last in one soul, and to comprise it in one feeling—this would necessarily furnish a happiness which man has not hitherto known—a God's happiness, full of power and love, full of tears and laughter, a happiness which, like the sun in the evening, continually gives of its inexhaustible riches and empties into the sea—and like the sun, too, feels itself richest when even the poorest fisherman rows with golden oars! This divine feeling might then be called—humanity![66]

In the full experience of affirming, of taking on, humanity emanates like sunlight and in this, like God, overflows. Human and divine are mutually reborn, made possible once again. This appears absurd if we consider joy and sorrow as oppositional and quantitative, if we assume that we would weigh them and find the preponderance in human experience, which must surely be of sorrow. But the happiness is *in* the *yes*, the name that says the soul's love. The yes names a trust, not that recurrence is true in the manner of facts, but that it will transform us—and that it has, infinitely many times and every time new. Affirmation, as I noted in the discussion of faith, does not give us answers. This is a luminous thought, shining like the evening sun, from which the darkness is irremovable.[67] "In the end," writes Elliot Wolfson, "as in the beginning, indeed in the origin before the beginning, darkness itself will become an aspect of the light, for the two cannot be distinguished in the essence of the Infinite."[68]

Against the reassuring but not particularly seductive stability of the purely actual being that is *designated* by the name "God," then, we call the name from the love that opens possibilities, from desire, from the sense of the opening possible, from the creative and eternalizing *eros* emergent from the death of perfect actuality. The name is called out, and in it every possibility is called out too, affirmed by its naming. And the name calls to all that is possible. It is there in what we say and in what we leave space for saying, sounding paradoxically in the silence within our words and not just in the sounds of our saying.

In Pseudo-Dionysius's God other than being, Eckhart's divine indistinction, or Nicholas of Cusa's divinely possible, all names are named in one non-thing; in Augustine's beauty, all things call one name, every possible name. By such names, things are not designated, still less gathered as if in a collection of objects. Rather, things are called forth; like Samuel, they answer. In the affirmation of recurrence, the will is all love, the memory scattered over an infinity of subjects all called by that beloved name, and a scattering of names all calling to the infinite desire. In the intensity of that call, the creative, disruptive moment of pure affirmation, purely seeing that it is good, we call not just one possibility at a time, limiting ourselves to the actual, but all at once and again. In saying "love," we call all names. This is no simple identity, as if every name could be replaced by "love" or "God" or "Roberte" or "recurrence" without loss of meaning. It is rather a complex and infinitely transfigurative repetition. The divine name is repeated in every name called out in desire; this is paradigmatically the name of the call itself. The Name of all naming. The call and response extend across an infinite renaming, and we call the name of the infinite too: in profound question, in sacramental community, in attentive reading of text and of world, in prayer. Every *again* and *already* emerges with the enticing astonishment of the new.

Notes

Introduction: From the Presence to the Sign

1. Roland Barthes, *The Pleasure of the Text*, trans. Richard Miller (New York: Hill and Wang, 1975), 38.

2. David Miller offers a different understanding of the idea of "make-believe" that brings it closer to the seriousness of children's play. He writes: "Faith is being gripped by a story, by a vision, by a ritual (game). It is being seized, being gripped by a pattern of meaning, a pattern of meaning that affects one's life-pattern, that becomes a paradigm for the way one sees the world. It is not belief. . . . Belief is beside the point. Faith is not belief. It is not intellectual assent. It is not some ritual played *so that* something will happen. Faith is being turned on by an incredible vision. It is make-believe. Questions of truth and falsity remain irrelevant. . . . Faith is make-believe. It is playing as if it were true. It is not that the religious story is not true. It is simply that questions of truth are irrelevant while in the midst of make-believe, while in the midst of faith." David L. Miller, *Gods and Games: Toward a Theology of Play* (New York: Harper and Row, 1970), 168–69.

3. Jacques Derrida, "Khora," in *On the Name*, ed. Thomas Dutoit, trans. David Wood, John P. Leavey, Jr., and Ian McLeod (Stanford: Stanford University Press, 1995), 102. Derrida cites Hegel's defense of Georg Creuzer's *Symbolism and Mythology of Ancient Peoples, Especially of the Greeks* (1810–12). In the English translation, the citation is from Georg Wilhelm Friedrich Hegel, *Lectures on the History of Philosophy*, vol. I, trans. E. S. Haldane (London: Kegan Paul, Trench, Tübner and

Co., Ltd., 1892), 88: "It is not worthwhile to treat seriously of those whose philosophy takes a mythical form" (citing Aristotle, *Metaphysics* 3.4).

4. " 'Pleasure' here (and without our being able to anticipate) sometimes extends to bliss, sometimes is opposed to it." Barthes, *The Pleasure of the Text*, 19.

5. Ibid., 21.

6. Ibid. Cf. Giorgio Agamben, *Potentialities: Collected Essays in Philosophy*, ed. and trans. Daniel Heller-Roazen (Stanford: Stanford University Press, 1999), 35: "The thing itself is not a thing; it is the very sayability, the very openness at issue in language, which, in language, we always presuppose and forget, perhaps because it is at bottom its own oblivion and abandonment."

7. Jacques Derrida, "Parergon," in *Truth in Painting*, trans. Geoffrey Bennington and Ian McLeod (Chicago: University of Chicago Press, 1987), 46.

8. Derrida, "Sauf le nom," in *On the Name*, 37; italics original. Vladimir Lossky argues that Augustine is only modestly apophatic: "the Pseudo-Areopagite insisted on the 'superessential' character of the Thearchy, whereas St. Augustine saw the excellence of 'Being-itself.' A God beyond being is, above all, the God of apophasis.... More modest apophasis is however sufficiently conspicuous in St. Augustine for us to be able to speak at least of the elements of negative theology in his religious thought." Such elements include frequent cautions, professions of ignorance, and praise of acknowledging not-knowing. Vladimir Lossky, "Elements of 'Negative Theology' in the Thought of St. Augustine," *St. Vladimir's Theological Quarterly*, 21, no.2 (1977): 68.

9. Augustine, Second Homily on the Gospel of John, sec. 10. In *Homilies on the Gospel of John 1–40*, trans. Edmund Hill, O.P. (Hyde Park, N.Y.: New City Press, 2009), 63.

10. Catherine Conybeare cites *de ordine* 2.18.47: "This is the system for the study of wisdom, through which each person becomes capable of understanding the order of things, that is, of distinguishing between the two worlds and the actual father of the universe, of whom there is no knowledge in the soul except to know how one might not know Him." Catherine Conybeare, *The Irrational Augustine* (Oxford: Oxford University Press, 2006), 132. She later reminds us that when Augustine urges us to return into ourselves, he urges too, "remember that you are transcending your reasoning soul." *De vera religione*, 39, cited and translated in Conybeare, 150.

11. Only close: the world is transient, not wholly in being, and where there is not being there may be absence, even nothing—not a presence of evil, but a decrease of good.

12. Catherine Keller, while not working on Augustine specifically, offers several of these subtle variants in *Face of the Deep*. What they tend to have in common

is a refusal of the simplistic "intersection of two entities" (21) and a more complex and fluid relationality. These sources are not always unorthodox; she cites, among others, Irenaeus (55) and Athanasius (63). Catherine Keller, *Face of the Deep: A Theology of Becoming* (London: Routledge, 2003).

13. That all seduction is the seduction of signs is central to the argument of Jean Baudrillard's *Seduction*, trans. Brian Singer (New York: St. Martin's Press, 1991). Catherine Conybeare argues that in Augustine's early dialogues, in particular, when his commitment is fresh and his sense of institutional constraint least powerful, the point of his work and thought lies in the seeking (ix). That this work elicits an affective and not merely a rational response is no accident: "When he elicits an emotional response from his readers, it is not merely a bid for verisimilitude; it is a crucial argumentative stance" (56); "The emotional responses, especially, prepare the ground for a type of argumentation that leaves more to the human actors, and more space for what cannot be controlled" (57). Persuasively arguing against earlier received opinions, Conybeare points out that the dialogues

> have repeatedly been read . . . as a rather dry charting of Augustine's progression into a Neoplatonic version of Christianity which denies all things physical and prefers to avoid thinking about the implications of the Incarnation. It has been claimed that Augustine is too reliant on the power of the intellect, and over-confident about its ability to discern divine truth.
>
> But can we consider the implication of these works as precisely the opposite? What is remarkable is the way in which Augustine allows quite other considerations and interpretations to intrude. This he effects principally though his full-blooded use of the dialogue form. (Conybeare, *Irrational Augustine*, 143)

14. Roland Barthes, *A Lover's Discourse: Fragments*, trans. Richard Howard (New York: Hill and Wang, 1979), 215.

15. Patricia Cox Miller, "'Words with an Alien Voice': Gnostics, Scripture, and Canon," *Journal of the American Academy of Religion* 57, no. 3 (1989): 459. The quotation is from Edmond Jabès, *The Book of Questions*, vol. 2, *The Book of Yukel*, trans. Rosmarie Waldrop (Middletown, Conn.: Wesleyan University Press, 1972), 37.

16. Augustine, *Confessions*, trans. Henry Chadwick (Oxford: Oxford University Press, 1991), 10.6.9.

17. In the event that there are any readers of this work who have also read my "Carthage Didn't Burn Hot Enough: Saint Augustine's Divine Seduction," in *Toward a Theology of Eros*, ed. Virginia Burrus and Catherine Keller (New York:

Fordham University Pres, 2006), 205–17, I apologize for the repetition. I have tried to keep it to the minimum required to bring other readers up to speed.

18. Barthes, *The Pleasure of the Text*, 27.

19. Ibid., 6.

20. R. A. Markus, *Signs and Meanings: World and Text in Ancient Christianity* (Liverpool: Liverpool University Press, 1996), 111–12.

21. See Elena Lombardi, *The Syntax of Desire: Language and Love in Augustine, the Modistae, Dante* (Toronto: University of Toronto Press, 2007), 10f.

22. M. B. Pranger, *Eternity's Ennui: Temporality, Perseverance and Voice in Augustine and Western Literature* (Leiden: Brill, 2010), 6.

23. Irenaeus of Lyons, *Adversus Haereses*, 4:21. Thus cited and translated in Leonardo Boff, O.F.M., "The Sacrament of Marriage," in *The Sacraments: Readings in Contemporary Sacramental Theology*, ed. Michael J. Taylor, S.J. (Staten Island, N.Y.: Alba House, 1981), 195. The Irenaeus text is available in English as *Against the Heresies*, in *Irenaeus of Lyons*, trans. Robert M. Grant (London: Routledge, 1997), 55–187.

24. Michel Foucault, *The Order of Things: An Archaeology of the Human Sciences* (New York: Vintage Books, 1994), e.g., 30, 57. I am grateful to Merold Westphal for reminding me in conversation of this point.

25. Max Weber famously speaks of secularization as the disenchantment of the world. *Max Weber: Essays in Sociology*, trans. and ed. H. H. Gerth and C. Wright Mills (New York: Oxford University Press, 1946), 155.

26. Roland Barthes, *A Lover's Discourse*, e.g., 63, 67, 68.

27. See Derrida, "Sauf le nom," 55–56.

28. Denys Turner, "How to Be an Atheist," in *Faith Seeking* (London: SCM Press, 2002), 8. Keller quotes an intriguingly similar point from John Wesley: "we should use and look upon nothing as separate from God, which indeed is a kind of practical Atheism." John Wesley's third sermon, "Upon Our Lord's Sermon on the Mount," quoted in John B. Cobb, Jr., *Grace and Responsibility: A Wesleyan Theology for Today* (Nashville: Abingdon, 1995), 50. In Catherine Keller, *On the Mystery: Discerning Divinity in Process* (Minneapolis: Fortress Press, 2008), 52.

29. Jean-Luc Nancy, "Of Divine Places," trans. Michael Holland, in *The Inoperative Community*, ed. Peter Connor (Minneapolis: University of Minnesota Press, 1991), 145.

30. Ibid. More completely: "But I cannot answer the question 'what is a god?' by saying I am he. 'A god' signifies: something other than a subject. It is another sort of thought, which can no longer think itself identical or consubstantial with the divine that it questions, or that questions it."

31. Derrida, "Sauf le nom," 58.

32. Winfried Noth notes that, for Plato, verbal signs represent incompletely, and immediate knowledge of things is regarded as superior. *Handbook of Semiotics* (Bloomington: Indiana University Press, 1990), 15.

33. Lombardi, *The Syntax of Desire*, 6.

34. Eugene Vance, *Mervelous Signals: Poetics and Sign Theory in the Middle Ages* (Lincoln: University of Nebraska Press, 1986), x.

35. R. Howard Bloch, *Etymologies and Genealogies: A Literary Anthropology of the French Middle Ages* (Chicago: University of Chicago Press, 1983), 17.

36. Stoics see the signified as propositional, somewhat in the manner of contemporary logic, while Epicureans see it as a part of nature, somewhat in the manner of naïve common sense. See Markus, *Signs and Meanings*, 72–73.

37. Noth, *Handbook of Semiotics*, 16.

38. At this point, semiotics is less concerned than it will later be with the result-oriented sense of meaning's *production*. Andrew Cowell notes that in the twelfth and thirteenth centuries we begin to see "a new model of the essential nature and social function of literature, a model that posits not theosis but semiotic play and overproductivity—profit—as the central feature of literature." *At Play in the Tavern: Signs, Coins, Bodies in the Middle Ages* (Ann Arbor: University of Michigan Press, 1999), 4.

39. John M. Rist, *Augustine: Ancient Thought Baptized* (Cambridge: Cambridge University Press, 1996), 24–25.

40. Markus, *Signs and Meanings*, 78: "Before Augustine, I have found only one hint of an attempt to bring the notion of 'signification' to a central place in a theory of language. It occurs in a brief suggestion made by Plotinus which might well have been known to Augustine. In his discussion of the categories of being, Plotinus asks to what category do words belong." Markus cites Plotinus, *Ennead* 6.1.5. Contrary to Aristotle, who categorized words under quantity, Plotinus says that they belong to the category of meaningful action—*poiēsis sēmantikē* (ibid.).

41. See Augustine, *On Christian Doctrine*, trans. D. W. Robertson, Jr. (New York: Prentice Hall, 1958), 2.1.2f; *The Teacher*, in *Against the Academicians and The Teacher*, trans. Peter King (Indianapolis: Hackett Publishing, 1995), 120.

42. Augustine, *On Christian Doctrine*, 2.1.1.: "A sign is a thing which causes us to think of something beyond the impression the thing itself makes upon the senses."

43. Augustine, *The Teacher*, 98, 102.

44. Ibid., 110.

45. Ibid., 136.

46. Ibid., 137.

47. Ibid., 138.

48. The echoes of Plato, of course, are powerful. See especially *Meno*, in *Meno and Phaedo*, ed. David Sedley, trans. Alex Long (Cambridge: Cambridge University Press, 2011), and *Phaedrus*, trans. Alexander Nehamas and Paul Woodruff (Indianapolis: Hackett Publishing, 1995).

49. Lewis Mackey, *Peregrinations of the Word: Essays in Medieval Philosophy* (Ann Arbor: University of Michigan Press, 1997), 57.

50. Augustine, *The Teacher*, 145–46.

51. Lombardi, *The Syntax of Desire*, 3.

52. Aristotle's arguments against an actual infinite (as opposed to a potential infinite, such as in the system of numbers or the divisibility of spaces) are found primarily in the *Physics*, trans. with commentary by Daniel Graham (Oxford: Oxford University Press, 1999), ll. 205 and following.

53. Markus, *Signs and Meanings*, 97: "Augustine's theory of the 'word' approaches language from the side of the speaker, unlike the sign-theories of the *De magistro* and the *De doctrina Christiana.* The latter are theories of meaning for the spectator and the interpreter, and *prima facie* plausible only so long as we keep to that model."

54. *On the Trinity*, 15,11.20, cited and translated in Markus, *Signs and Meanings*, 94–95.

55. Markus, *Signs and Meanings*, 100–101.

56. Lombardi, *The Syntax of Desire*, 23. Lombardi goes on to argue that in syntax, by which words joined in time acquire their sentential meaning, we find both temporality—one word after another—and eternity, the meaning gathered at the end of a sentence (24–25). A more elaborate form of this play between maximum and minimum will emerge in the thought of Nicholas of Cusa.

57. Bloch, *Etymologies and Genealogies*, 35.

58. Though linked to original sin, the fallenness of language is connected as well to the story of Babel, in which human arrogance is tempered by the destruction of perfect linguistic unity, perfect comprehension. Early semioticians seem to have focused primarily on the Fall rather than on the tower as their preferred explanatory myth.

59. See, e.g., Cowell, who notes of Vance that "Eugene Vance predicates much of *Mervelous Signals* on the medieval concepts of a prelapsarian and postlapsarian semiotics: medieval semioticians, he notes, were preoccupied, and haunted, by the Fall." *At Play in the Tavern*, 101.

60. Barthes, *A Lover's Discourse*, 99, citing Jakob Boehme as cited by Norman O. Brown, no further references given. I have not been able to track down this source outside of Barthes' reference.

61. See Bloch, *Etymologies and Genealogies*, 39. This perfection is understood to be lost at Babel.

62. Ibid., 40, no reference given.

63. Ibid., 54.

64. Karmen MacKendrick, *Fragmentation and Memory: Meditations on Christian Doctrine* (New York: Fordham University Press, 2008), 32–54.

65. Friedrich Nietzsche, *Beyond Good and Evil*, trans. Walter Kaufmann (New York: Vintage Books, 1966), §188.

66. This is true of most, I think, who write after Nietzsche—or, in a slightly divergent tradition, after Horkheimer and Adorno. See, e.g., Max Horkheimer and Theodor W. Adorno, *The Dialectic of Enlightenment: Philosophical Fragments*, trans. Edmund Jephcott (Stanford, Calif.: Stanford University Press, 2002).

67. Martha Malamud remarks of Prudentius's poem *Hamartigenia* (The Origin of Sin): "I will suggest in this essay that the puzzling substitution of Cain for Eve (whose role is drastically reduced) is best comprehended in the light of the poet's preoccupation with the schism between language and truth that originates from original sin. It is this same schism, which forces man to rely on imperfect attempts at interpretation, that lies at the root of heresy. The schism dividing language from truth opens a gap, an abyss. Long before poststructuralism, the writers of late antiquity gazed into this abyss." Martha Malamud, "Writing Original Sin," *Journal of Early Christian Studies* 10, no. 3 (2002): 330. She argues that the characters of Discordia in the *Psychomachia* and Satan in the *Hamartigenia* "both represent the divisive, imitative properties of language, both are emblematically represented by serpents, both are associated with snares and traps, and both are incarnations of Heresy. Thus it is no surprise to find that the splitting of Discordia's tongue in the Psychomachia has its counterpart in Hamartigenia 201–2." Ibid., 337.

68. Bloch, *Etymologies and Genealogies*, 60, citing Denys from Pépin, "L'herméneutique ancienne," 298, and Eusebius from *Ecclesiastical History*, ed. E. Capps and T. E. Page (London: Heinemann, 1926), 2:22.

69. Bloch, *Etymologies and Genealogies*, 43, citing Dante, *De Vulgare Eloquentia*, ed. P. Rajna (Florence: Le Monnier, 1896), 16. This is intriguingly comparable to the Kabbalistic conception of language's ground. Agamben writes:

According to this theory, the foundation of every human language is the name of God. This name, however, has no proper meaning, nor can it itself be uttered; it is simply constituted by the twenty-two letters of the alphabet from whose combination all human languages derive.

"For the Kabbalists," Scholem writes, "this name has no 'meaning' in the traditional sense of the term. It has no concrete signification. The meaninglessness of the name of God indicates its situation in the very central point of the revelation, at the basis of which it lies." (Agamben, *Potentialities*, 57)

The reference to Scholem is to Gershom Scholem, "The Name of God and the Linguistic Theory of the Kabbalah (Part 2)", *Diogenes* 79 (1973): 194.

70. Cowell, 19, citing *On Christian Doctrine*, prologue 9.

71. See Cowell, who opposes this kind of reading to one that develops in the twelfth and thirteenth centuries, with a rhetoric of profit and play, asking what it is that we get out of using words. As Cowell notes, this position is not uniquely Augustinian; among its other notable proponents is the ninth-century scholar John Scotus Eriugena. *At Play in the Tavern*, 7.

72. R. A. Markus describes this captivity as "our inability or unwillingness to go beyond and see behind what is immediately given; to seek meaning." Markus, *Signs and Meanings*, 29.

73. Patricia Cox Miller, *The Poetry of Thought in Late Antiquity* (Aldershot: Ashgate Publishing, 2001), 215: "As Harl has pointed out, for Origen, the 'semantic habits' of the Christ as Word, as language itself, are obscure, enigmatic, ambiguous, riddling, dark. Words may indeed reveal what Origen calls 'the depths of the wisdom of God,' but do they not also conceal those depths as well? Is there, in other words, a 'bottom,' an end to the poetic display of verbal polysemy?" Citing Marguerite Harl, "Origène et la sémantique du langue biblique," *Vigilae Christianae* 26 (1972): 161–88.

74. Miller, "Words With an Alien Voice," 463.

75. Ibid., 465. Miller notes: "See, for example, de Certeau (89), who discusses 'the labor of writing which is given birth through the animation of language by the desire of the other'; see also J. Hillis Miller." The reference to de Certeau is to Michel de Certeau, *Heterologies: Discourse on the Other*, trans. Brian Massumi (Minneapolis: University of Minnesota Pres, 1986). The reference to J. Hillis Miller is to "Ariadne's Thread: Repetition and the Narrative Line," *Critical Inquiry* 3 (1976): 57–77.

76. "Like the focus on language," Lombardi points out, "the centrality of desire in medieval culture is theologically based." Lombardi, *The Syntax of Desire*, 10. Cf. Barthes, *A Lover's Discourse*, 15: "Endlessly I sustain the discourse of the beloved's absence; actually a preposterous situation; the other is absent as referent, present as allocutory."

77. Elliot R. Wolfson draws this distinction between mere absence and mystery in several places; e.g., in considering the relations between Derridean and Kabbalistic thought in "Assaulting the Border: Kabbalistic Traces in the Margins of Derrida," *Journal of the American Academy of Religion* 70, no. 3 (Sept. 2002): 506–7.

78. Such as that of which Derrida, rightly I think, accuses Heidegger: "he seems to understand/hear the beyond as the beyond of the totality of beings and not as the beyond of being itself, in the sense of negative theology." "Sauf le nom," 65.

79. Compare a line from Walter Benjamin, cited by Giorgio Agamben in *Potentialities*, 52: "There is no such thing as the content of a language; as communication, language communicates a spiritual entity, that is, a communicability pure and simple." Walter Benjamin, *Reflections: Essays, Aphorisms, Autobiographical Writings*, ed. Peter Demetz, trans. Edmund Jephcott (New York: Schocken, 1978), 320; trans. modified.

80. From Meister Eckhart, "Commentary on John," in *Meister Eckhart: The Essential Sermons, Commentaries, Treatises and Defense*, trans. Edmund Colledge and Bernard McGinn (Mahwah, N.J.: Paulist Press, 1981), 122–76, §12.

81. Sean Kirkland persuasively argues for an ancient heritage of invoking the terms of excess and distance rather than of immanence and transcendence. See *The Ontology of Socratic Questioning in Plato's Early Dialogues* (Albany: State University of New York Press, 2012), esp. chap. 4.

82. Augustine, *Confessions*, 10.27.38.

83. Cf. Barthes, who reminds us that all signs are sensory: "What is significance? It is meaning, *insofar as it is sensually produced.*" *The Pleasure of the Text*, 61; italics in original.

84. Lombardi, *The Syntax of Desire*, 28.

85. Mackey, *Peregrinations of the Word*, 114.

86. Augustine, *Confessions* 10.25.

87. Mackey, *Peregrinations of the Word*, 12; my emphasis.

88. Keller, *The Face of the Deep*, 56. The embedded quotation is from Luce Irigaray, *The Forgetting of Air in Martin Heidegger*, trans. Mary Beth Mader (Austin: University of Texas Press, 1999), 178.

89. Mackey, *Peregrinations of the Word*, 11.

90. Plato, *Republic*, trans. G. M. A. Grube (Indianapolis: Hackett Publishing, 1992), bk. 10.

91. Marcia Colish, *The Mirror of Language: A Study in the Medieval Theory of Knowledge* (Lincoln: University of Nebraska Press, 1983), 10.

92. Augustine, *On Christian Doctrine*, 4.12.27. Cicero's claim occurs in his *On the Best Style of Orators*, trans. C. D. Yonge (Lawrence, Kans.: Digireads.com, 2009), sec. I, on 81.

93. Miller, "Words with an Alien Voice," 460.

94. Like music in Nancy's account, sensuous language "is not exactly a phenomenon; that is to say, it does not stem from a logic of manifestation. It stems

from a different logic, which would have to be called evocation, but in this precise sense: while manifestation brings presence to light, evocation summons (convokes, invokes) presence to itself." Jean-Luc Nancy, *Listening*, trans. Charlotte Mandell (New York: Fordham University Press, 2007), 20.

95. Michel Foucault suggests that this may be so for Klossowski, of whose novel *The Baphomet* he writes: "This is a narrow, numinous region where all figures are the sign of something. Here one passes through the paradoxical space of real presence—a presence which is only real in so much as God has absented himself from the world, leaving behind only a trace and a void, so that the reality of his presence is the absence in which it resides, and in which it unrealizes itself through transubstantiation." Michel Foucault, "The Prose of Actaeon," introductory essay to Pierre Klossowski, *The Baphomet*, trans. Sophie Hawkes and Stephen Sartarelli (New York: Marsilio Publishers, 1998), xxv–xxvi.

96. Ibid., xxxvi.

97. Augustine, *Confessions*, 11.27.34–29.39. cf. Agamben, *Potentialities*, 49–50.

98. Nelson Pike, *God and Timelessness* (New York: Schocken, 1970), 29.

99. For this turn of phrase, see J. L. Austin, *How to Do Things with Words*, ed. J. O. Urmson and Marina Sbisà (Cambridge: Harvard University Press, 1975).

100. We know, of course, that proper names—of people, of cities, and so on—are in fact sometimes shared. But we find that sharing irksome, and we usually try to add propriety in order to narrow the specification—adding a surname, or a state or country, for instance.

101. Nancy, "Of Divine Places," 119.

102. Friedrich Hölderlin, "Heimkunft" ("Homecoming"), in *Friedrich Hölderlin: Selected Poems and Fragments*, trans. Michael Hamburger (New York: Penguin Books, 1994): "Schweigen müßen wir oft / Es fehlen heilige Nahmen" ("Silence often behooves us / deficient in names that are holy"; 164, 165).

103. Nancy, "Of Divine Places," 117.

104. Ibid., 116–17.

105. For this point, I am indebted to conversation with William A. Robert.

106. Elliot R. Wolfson, "Inscribed in the Book of the Living: *Gospel of Truth* and Jewish Christology," *Journal for the Study of Judaism* 38 (2007): 251. Wolfson cites G. G. Stroumsa, "A Nameless God: Judaeo-Christian and Gnostic 'Theologies of the Name,'" in *The Image of the Judaeo-Christians in Ancient Jewish and Christian Literature*, ed. P. J. Tomson and D. Lambers-Petry (Tübingen: Mohr-Siebeck, 2003), 230–43.

107. Augustine, *On Christian Doctrine*, 1.13.12.

108. Markus, *Signs and Meanings*, 97.

109. Barthes, *The Pleasure of the Text*, 61. Note also the highly corporeal character of meaning in *A Lover's Discourse*, 67: "A squeeze of the hand—enormous documentation—a tiny gesture within the palm, a knee which doesn't move away, an arm extended, as if quite naturally, along the back of a sofa and against which the other's head gradually comes to rest—this is the paradisiac realm of subtle and clandestine signs: a kind of festival not of the senses but of meaning."

110. Markus, *Signs and Meanings*, 95. The "mental word" is not a sign because it is not a sensuous reality. See ibid., 100.

111. Eliot R. Wolfson, "Judaism and Incarnation: The Imaginal Body of God," in *Christianity in Jewish Terms*, ed. Tikva Frymer-Kensky, David Novak, Peter Ochs, David Fox Sandmel and Michael A. Signer (Boulder, Colo.: Westview Press, 2000), 254.

112. Ibid., 243.

113. Ibid., 244–46.

114. Ibid., 250.

115. Ibid., 253.

116. Ibid., 247. Cf. 249: "The equation of Torah and YHVH suggests a form of incarnation predicated on the assumption that the nature of corporeality in its most fundamental sense is linked to letters."

117. Ibid., esp. 241: "It may be valid to conclude (and even this is by no means beyond critical assessment) that the particular expression of incarnation in Christianity, the union of the divine and the human in the body of Jesus, is an idea that has neither precedent in the ancient Israelite religion nor parallel in any of the varieties of Judaism in late antiquity that were contemporaneous with the emerging religion. This does not mean that the doctrine of incarnation in general is antithetical to Judaism. On the contrary, the idea of incarnation unique to Christianity should be viewed as a 'special framing' of the conception of incarnation that was idiomatic to a variety of Judaic authors who represented God as a person."

118. Ibid.

119. To echo Merleau-Ponty, "We must not think the flesh starting from substances, from body and spirit—for then it would be the union of contradictories." Maurice Merleau-Ponty, *The Visible and the Invisible*, trans. Alphonso Lingis (Evanston, Ill.: Northwestern University Press, 1969), 147.

120. See Pamela Haag, *Consent: Sexual Rights and the Transformation of American Liberalism* (Ithaca, N.Y.: Cornell University Press, 1999), 181.

121. "Seduction" derives "from L. *seducere* 'lead away, lead astray,' from *se-* 'aside, away' + *ducere* 'to lead.'" *Online Etymology Dictionary*, at http://www.etymon line.com/.

122. We hear echoes of Augustine in Lacan and in Derrida. See, e.g., Jane Gallop, *The Daughter's Seduction: Feminism and Psychoanalysis* (Ithaca, N.Y.: Cornell University Press, 1984), 30: "Since words elicit a desire for meaning, there is a drive to complete the sentence, fully reveal the signification. Yet any 'sentence' can always be added to; no sentence is ever completely saturated. The play of metonymy, the forward push to finish signification, to close meaning, creates the impression of veiled signification." And see Susan David Bernstein, "Confessing Lacan," in *Seduction and Theory: Readings of Gender, Representation, and Rhetoric*, ed. Dianne Hunter (Champaign: University of Illinois Press, 1989), 117: "By deferring meaning, Lacan's abstractions and puns facilitate the possibility of seduction in the form of a reading investment spurred by a desire to know." Cf. Graham Ward: "With Derrida's work the emphasis is on the *economy* of the signifier—the fact that the signification of any word is caught up in the forward pull of the signifiers that follow it. This establishes an endemic deferral of meaning within language." Ward, "In the Daylight Forever? Language and Silence," in *Silence and the Word: Negative Theology and Incarnation*, ed. Oliver Davies and Denys Turner, (Cambridge: Cambridge University Press, 2002), 172.

123. Foucault, "The Prose of Actaeon," xxvii.

124. Ferdinand de Saussure, trans. Wade Baskin, *Course in General Linguistics* (New York: Columbia University Press, 2011).

125. Foucault, "The Prose of Actaeon," xxvii–xxviii.

126. Cf. Elliot R. Wolfson: "The secret is a secret only to the extent that it is concealed in its disclosure, but it may be concealed in its disclosure only if it is disclosed in its concealment." "Occultation of the Feminine and the Body of Secrecy in Medieval Kabbalah," in *Rending the Veil: Concealment and Revelation of Secrets in the History of Religions*, ed. E. R. Wolfson (New York: Seven Bridges Press, 1999), 119. Cited in Mahdi Tourage, "The Hermeneutics of Eroticism in the Poetry of Rumi," *Comparative Studies of South Asia, Africa and the Middle East* 25, no. 3 (2005): 613.

127. Tourage, "The Hermeneutics of Eroticism," 613.

128. Miller, "Words With an Alien Voice," 460. Miller notes that she has: "used the translation of the Tripartite Tractate by Attridge and Pagels (in *Nag Hammadi Codex 1 (The Jung Codex)*, ed. Harold W. Attridge (Leiden: E. J. Brill, 1985), 193–337). Attridge and Pagels remark about 'silence' that 'apparently to protect the absolute transcendence of the Father, he [the author of the Tripartite Tractate] interprets the silence as a quality of the Father's solitary existence' (ibid: 234). My understanding of silence differs from theirs, in that my focus is on the relation of the unnameable one with language (which the text underscores often).

In this context, silence functions not as an indicator of metaphysical status (transcendence) but as a dynamic of language."

129. Barthes, *The Pleasure of the Text*, 10.

130. Miller, "Words With an Alien Voice," 461.

131. Ibid., 461.

1. Seductive Epistemology: Thinking with Assent

1. Aristotle, *Metaphysics*, trans. Hugh Lawson-Tancred (New York: Penguin Books, 1998), Book Alpha, 1, 980a: "By nature, all men long to know."

2. Augustine, "The Predestination of the Saints," in *Four Anti-Pelagian Writings*, trans. John Arthur Mourant and William J. Collinge (Washington, D.C.: Catholic University of America Press, 1992), 222. Thomas Aquinas, *The Summa Theologica of St. Thomas Aquinas*, trans. Fathers of the English Dominican Province (Allen, Tex.: Christian Classics, 1981), 2.2, Question 2, Article 1. Online Edition by Kevin Knight, 2008. Accessed at http://newadvent.org/summa/.

3. Harvey Cox argues that the latter is so on the rise that we may speak of a new "age of the spirit," arguing that "The recent rapid growth of charismatic congregations and the appeal of Asian spiritual practices demonstrate that, as in the past once again today, large numbers of people are drawn more to the experiential than to the doctrinal elements of religion." Harvey Cox, *The Future of Faith* (New York: HarperCollins, 2009), 8, 13.

4. Thomas Aquinas, *Summa Theologica*, 2.2, Q 2, Art. 1, Objection 1.

5. Ibid., "I think that."

6. Kirkland, *The Ontology of Socratic Questioning*, 11; italics in the original.

7. See ibid., chap. 4.

8. Patricia Cox Miller, "Words with an Alien Voice," 466.

9. Maurice Blanchot, *The Infinite Conversation*, trans. Susan Hanson (Minneapolis: University of Minnesota Press, 1993), 18.

10. Ibid., 14.

11. It is not unusual to identify faith with such certainty or security. Cox makes this identification in the act of distinguishing faith from belief: "Faith is about deep-seated confidence. In everyday speech we usually apply it to people we trust or the values we treasure. . . . Belief, on the other hand, is more like opinion. We often use the term in everyday speech to express a degree of uncertainty. . . . We *believe* something to be true without it making much difference to us, but we place our *faith* only in something that is vital for the way we live." Cox, *The Future of Faith*, 3.

12. Cf. Catherine Keller: "when people of faith step out of the mystery and make totalizing claims for our truth and our beliefs, we perpetuate an antagonistic polarity that actually paralyzes faith rather than fostering its living process. Relativity [relationality] dissolves into the indifferent relativism." *On the Mystery,* 4.

13. Derrida, *Sauf le nom,* in *On the Name,* 35.

14. Ibid., 67; ellipsis original.

15. James Carse notes how strongly dependent on a defined enemy or opposition most belief systems are. "Religion is Poetry," interview in *Salon,* July 21, 2008. Accessed at http://www.salon.com/books/atoms_eden/2008/07/21/james_carse /index1.html.

16. James Martin, "A Saint's Dark Night," *New York Times Magazine,* August 29, 2007. Accessed at http://www.nytimes.com/2007/08/29/opinion/29martin .html?_r=2&em&ex=1188532800&en=9e59f11fbd412882&ei=5087%0A.

17. See David L. Miller for a somewhat different take on the value of doubt: "Belief that is not matured by doubt is not true faith. Naive play is no better for the mature man than is ironic gamesmanship. We cannot go back. But we hope to go on. Faith that does not go beyond naive belief *and* rebellious disbelief is not true faith." *Gods and Games,* 169.

18. Carse, 4: "In one respect, it is not a mistake to associate religion with belief. Mystery is difficult to live with, and for some even terrifying. It can often be of great comfort to hide our unknowing behind the veil of a well-articulated belief system." Compare Denys Turner on our sometimes frantic efforts to rid ourselves of temptation, a description readily applied to desperate belief: "Much of what we call 'spirituality' seems to issue from this anxious, threatened condition of soul. . . . Let us at least acknowledge in ourselves the anxiety to become as temptationless as possible, invulnerable to weakness and failure; and let us look, from time to time, at how much work, how much fretting, how much anxiety we invest in the futile pursuit of this invulnerability." Turner, "How to be Tempted: A Homily," in *Faith Seeking,* 102.

19. Alvin Plantinga, "Intellectual Sophistication and Basic Belief in God," *Faith and Philosophy* 3 (1986): 306–12.

20. William Alston, "Perceiving God," *The Journal of Philosophy* 83 (1986): 655–66.

21. Paul K. Moser, *The Elusive God: Reorienting Religious Epistemology* (Cambridge: Cambridge University Press, 2008).

22. John Bishop, *Believing by Faith: An Essay in the Epistemology and Ethics of Religious Belief* (Oxford: Oxford University Press, 2007).

23. Keller, *On the Mystery,* 7.

24. Keller goes on to cite Athanasius: God incarnate as the Word "was not, as might be imagined, circumscribed in the body, nor, while present in the body, was he absent elsewhere; nor, while he moved the body, was the universe left void of his working and providence." Athanasius, "On the Incarnation of the Word," trans. Archibald Roberston, in *Christology of the Late Fathers*, Library of Christian Classics, vol. 3, ed. E. R. Hardy (Philadelphia: Westminster Press, 1954), 70–71. In Keller, *Face of the Deep*, 63.

25. Keller, *On the Mystery*, 7–8.

26. Wilfred Cantwell Smith writes of "the Platonic, rather than the propositional, sense of truth, comparable to our speaking of a true note in music, a true university, a man's being true to his word, not logically true, as a statement." *Faith and Belief* (Princeton, N.J.: Princeton University Press, 1979), 109.

27. Ibid., 76.

28. Ibid., 76–77. The text cites as examples of supporting scholarship: J. N. D. Kelly, *Early Christian Creeds* (London: Longmans Green, 1950; 3rd ed., 1951); J. N. D. Kelly, *Early Christian Doctrines* (London: Adam and Charles Black, 1958); Joseph Crehan, *Early Christian Baptism and the Creed: A Study in Ante-Nicene Theology* (London: Burnes Oates & Washbourne, 1950). Smith notes that "The principle verbs in the classical creeds are performatives: 'I hereby commit myself to.'"

29. Smith, *Faith and Belief*, 105–27.

30. Keller, *On the Mystery*, 20.

31. D. Miller, *Gods and Games*, 166–67.

32. Jean-Luc Nancy, *Dis-Enclosure: The Deconstruction of Christianity*, trans. Bettina Bergo, Gabriel Malenfant, and Michael B. Smith (Fordham: Fordham University Press, 2008), 28.

33. Ibid., 12.

34. Merleau-Ponty, *The Visible and the Invisible*, 130.

35. Immanuel Kant famously argues that "existence is not a predicate." See *Critique of Pure Reason*, trans. Werner S. Pluhar (Indianapolis: Hackett Publishing, 1996), Book 2, chap. 3, sec. 4, par. 55.

36. Denys Turner, "How to be an Atheist," in *Faith Seeking*, 9. Turner adds that "the real challenge for the theologian is not our ignorance of what God is, but rather that presented by those who think that they know what God is, for this is just idolatry. And that problem is presented to us equally by those theists who know all too well what they are affirming when they say 'God exists' and by those atheists—the mirror-image of the first—who know all too well what they are denying when they say 'God does not exist.'" Ibid., 9–10.

37. See *Pseudo-Dionysius: The Complete Works*, trans. Colm Luibheid (Mahwah, N.J.: Paulist Press), 1987, esp. *Divine Names* and *Mystical Theology*.

38. Mackey, *Peregrinations of the Word*, 2.

39. Ibid., 3.

40. Karmen MacKendrick, *Immemorial Silence* (Albany: State University of New York Press, 2001).

41. According to poet Stephen Spender in "Remembering Eliot," an Oxford undergraduate asked the meaning of a line in Eliot's "Ash Wednesday," "Lady, three white leopards sat under a juniper tree." Eliot replied, "I mean, 'Lady, three white leopards sat under a juniper tree.'" "Remembering Eliot," in *T. S. Eliot: The Man and His Work*, ed. Allen Tate (New York: Delacorte Press, 1966), 42. I have heard a similar story told of John Cage's response to an inquiry about the meaning of a passage of his music.

42. David L. Miller, "Theopoetry or Theopoetics?" *CrossCurrents* 60, no. 1 (March 2010): 7–8. Miller identifies these positions with, respectively, John D. Caputo, Thomas Altizer and Mark C. Taylor, and Gianni Vattimo—among many others he mentions or discusses.

43. Ibid., 8.

44. "Further, to believe is an act of the intellect, since its object is truth. But assent seems to be an act not of the intellect, but of the will, even as consent is, as stated above (I–II, 15, I, ad 3). Therefore to believe is not to think with assent." Thomas Aquinas, *Summa Theologica*, 2.2 Q. 2, Art. I, Obj. 3.

45. See, e.g., H. Richard Niebuhr: "When we say that the interpretation of the radical action is made in faith, we use the word, faith, not as meaning some set of beliefs that must take the place of knowledge until knowledge is possible. The aspect of faith we have here in mind is simply that trust or distrust . . . to which theologians, notably Luther, have pointed as the fundamental element in religion. Faith is the attitude of the self in its existence toward all the existences that surround it, as beings to be relied upon or to be suspected. . . . Such faith is an ingredient in all knowing." *The Responsible Self: An Essay in Christian Moral Philosophy* (New York: Harper and Row, 1963), 118.

46. Meister Eckhart suggests something like this in his sermon on the beatitudes, German Sermon 52. In *Meister Eckhart: The Essential Sermons*, 199–203. He goes further, however, to argue that it is well intentioned, but imperfect, to will to fulfill God's will, because so long as we will even this we have not let go of our own willing.

47. Plato, *Apology*, in *Plato: Euthyphro, Apology, Crito*, trans. F. J. Church (New York: Prentice Hall, 1987), 41d.

48. See Richard Swinburne, *Faith and Reason* (Oxford: Oxford University Press, 2005), 142. Swinburne cites Luther's "The Freedom of a Christian," sec. II, in *Reformation Writings of Martin Luther*, trans. B. L. Woolf, vol. I (Cambridge: Lutter-

worth Press, 1952). David Miller writes, "The reformation church . . . and especially Martin Luther, preferred the word *fiducia* to the word *fides*, because *fiducia* can never be confused with belief in something taken to be true. It, rather, means 'trust' and 'confidence.' . . . Faith is not mental assent or emotional assent, either, whose object is a belief in some supernatural or historical datum which dogmatically and zealously insists on its truth." *Gods and Games*, 166–67.

49. Keller, *Face of the Deep*, 214. New American Study Bible: "Why are you afraid? How is it that you have no faith?"

50. Niebuhr, *The Responsible Self*, 118.

51. John Calvin, *Institutes of the Christian Religion*, trans. Henry Beveridge (Edinburgh: Calvin Translation Society, 1845), vol. 2, 3.2.19.

52. Ibid., 3.2.3.

53. Karl Barth, *Dogmatics in Outline*, (New York: Harper and Row, 1959), 19.

54. "This 'truth' has little to do with right or wrong belief or dogma; nor is it some eternal verity engraved in our souls; it is a truth of right relation, to be embodied and enacted. This faithfulness cannot be boiled down to propositions, but it will transform our language, and indeed our propositions. Faithfulness in the genre of truth means *trusty language*." Keller, *On the Mystery*, 37.

55. Nancy, *Dis-Enclosure*, 153. Ellipses in first paragraph are original.

56. Jacques Ellul, *Living Faith: Belief and Doubt in a Perilous World*, 1980, trans. Peter Heinegg (San Francisco: Harper and Row, 1983), 100.

57. Faith "asks a question—a series of questions—that is; it makes people responsible (obliged to respond) and throws them back upon their freedom. Unlike beliefs, faith consists in heeding God's questions and risking ourselves in the answers that *we* have to give." Ibid., 101. See also ibid., 99: "belief provides answers to people's questions while faith never does. And I would say that we have here a decisive criterion to tell the two apart."

58. "Belief is reassuring. People who live in the world of belief feel safe; God is their protector. On the contrary, faith is forever placing us on the razor's edge. Though it knows that God is the Father, it never minimizes his power." Ibid., 112. And ibid., 113: "this doubt concerns myself, *not* God's revelation or his love or the presence of Jesus Christ. It is thus the clean contrary of belief."

59. "I want to show how the logic of our philosophical tradition, of some of our inherited beliefs about truth, leads almost inevitably to conceiving of the body of the other as the site from which truth can be produced, and to using violence if necessary to extract that truth." Page duBois, *Torture and Truth* (New York: Routledge, 1991), 6.

60. Martin Heidegger, "Plato's Doctrine of Truth," in *Philosophy in the Twentieth Century*, ed. William Barrett and Henry D. Aiken (New York: Random House,

1962), 260, cited in duBois, *Torture and Truth*, 130. Cf. Martin Heidegger, *Being and Time*, trans. John Macquarrie and Edward Robinson (New York: Harper and Row, 1962), 265, cited in duBois, *Torture and Truth*, 132: "Truth (uncoveredness) is something that must always first be wrested from entities. Entities get snatched out of their hiddenness. The factical uncoveredness of anything is always, as it were, a kind of *robbery*."

61. Just conceivably, I am too much influenced by detective novels here, but the claim still seems to me accurate.

62. For the Jewish as well as Christian roots of such thought, note, e.g., Beth Hawkins's remarks on Franz Kafka: "Kafka provides the capacity for a faith circumscribed by the question, a faith that is a condition, a way of being-in-the-world, rather than a prescribed set of behaviors." *Reluctant Theologians*, 65. She comments of Edmond Jabès, "the question is exploded; it becomes the symbol of faith par excellence in a world where answers no longer apply." Ibid., 167. Other obvious thinkers of the question in more or less Jewish terms include Derrida and, in the realm of ethics, Levinas.

63. Turner, "How to be an Atheist," in *Faith Seeking*, 19.

64. Ibid., 20.

65. Vladimir Lossky points out that the expression *docta ignorantia* is borrowed from Augustine's *Letter to Proba* (412). For Augustine, such *docta* "obliges us not only to recognize divine transcendence, in a philosophical thought which traverses the order of the created universe, but of transcending all that the human spirit could formulate, while addressing itself to God in prayer." Vladimir Lossky, "Elements of 'Negative Theology' in the Thought of St. Augustine," *St. Vladimir's Theological Quarterly*, 21, no. 2 (1977): 71–72.

66. See esp. the *Divine Names*, in *Pseudo-Dionysius: The Complete Works*, 47–131.

67. Nicholas of Cusa, *On Learned Ignorance*, chap. 26, in *Nicholas of Cusa: Selected Spiritual Writings*, trans. H. Lawrence Bond (Mahwah, N.J.: Paulist Press, 1997), 126.

68. Catherine Keller, "The Cloud of the Impossible: Feminist Theology, Cosmology and Cusa," presented at Harvard University, March 22, 2007, 2. Accessed at http://users.drew.edu/ckeller/essays-download.html.

69. Nicholas of Cusa, *De Visione Dei* (1453). In *Selected Spiritual Writings*, 252; cited in Keller, "The Cloud of the Impossible."

70. Turner, "Dominus Illuminatio Mea," in *Faith Seeking*, 135. More completely: "Augustine knew . . . well . . . that to love learning is to be in love with love. For learning is a kind of loving, a desire whose object is an *infinite* truth and an *infinite* beauty. . . . the love of learning *is* the desire for God. For sure, a teaching and a learning which lacks that 'infinity' to it, are nothing but forms of pedantry."

71. Pseudo-Dionysius, *Exaiphnēs esti to par'elpida*, in *Patrologia grecque* (Paris: J. P. Migne, 1857–1866), 3:1069B; cited in Jean-Luis Chrétien, *The Unforgettable and the Unhoped For*, trans. Jeffrey Bloechl (New York: Fordham University Press, 2002), 116. Chrétien adds in his gloss: "Revelation does not abolish mystery, but reveals mystery as such."

72. In *Strange Wonder: The Closure of Metaphysics and the Opening of Awe* (New York: Columbia University Press, 2008), Mary-Jane Rubenstein carefully distinguishes wonder, with its openness and its potential for terror, from mere curiosity. This parallels the distinction between wonder about things with answers and wonder at mystery as such, but of course both Rubenstein and I are aware that these terms are not always distinct or separable.

73. Mackey, *Peregrinations of the Word*, 228.

74. Nancy, *Listening*, 64.

75. Mackey, *Peregrinations of the Word*, 230–31.

76. Smith, *Faith and Belief*, 147.

77. Edmond Jabès, *The Book of Resemblances*, vol. 3, *The Ineffaceable, the Unperceived*, trans. Rosmarie Waldrop (Middletown, Conn.: Wesleyan University Press, 1992), 22.

78. Silence "is already . . . the abolition of the sound which the word is; among all words it is the most perverse, or the most poetic: it is the token of its own death." Georges Bataille, *Inner Experience*, trans. Leslie Anne Boldt (Albany: State University of New York Press, 1988), 16.

79. Maurice Blanchot, *The Writing of the Disaster*, trans. Ann Smock (Lincoln: University of Nebraska Press, 1995), 29: "Keep silence. Silence cannot be kept."

80. Nancy, *Dis-Enclosure*, 126.

81. Hawkins, *Reluctant Theologians*, 106.

82. Such a seduction appears even within strongly protested atheism. Blanchot disagrees with Pierre Klossowski's claims about Sade: "But does such a scalding hate affirm, as Klossowski seems to believe, a faith that had forgotten its name and resorted to blasphemy in order to force God to end his silence?" Blanchot argues instead that Sade has infinite hate and fury and so seeks an infinite object. But both may be true: fury, like joy, and hate, like love, demand a response to their call. Maurice Blanchot, *Lautréamont and Sade*, trans. Stuart Kendall and Michelle Kendall (Stanford, Calif.: Stanford University Press, 2004), 31.

83. Nancy, *Dis-Enclosure*, 87.

84. Edmond Jabès, *The Book of Questions*, vol. 2, *The Book of Yukel*, trans. Rosmarie Waldrop (Middletown, Conn.: Wesleyan University Press, 1991), 138.

85. Nancy, *Dis-Enclosure*, 88.

86. Cf. Jabès, *The Book of Resemblances*, 3:66: "The imperatives of the question lay down the order of our wandering, and vocables spell our steps or, rather, pass us and plunge ahead into the unknown."

87. Blanchot, *Infinite Conversation*, 249.

88. Jabès, *The Book of Resemblances*, 3:83.

89. "The argument rests entirely on the movement of thought, insofar as it cannot not think the maximum of the being it is able to think, but thinks also an excess to that maximum, since thought is capable of thinking even that there is something that exceeds its power to think. In other words, thinking (i.e., not the intellect alone, but the heart and the demand itself) can think—indeed, cannot not think—that it thinks something in excess over itself. It penetrates the impossible, or rather is penetrated by it." Nancy, *Dis-Enclosure*, 11.

90. Ibid., 36.

91. Maurice Blanchot, "Madness *par excellence*," trans. Ann Smock, in *The Blanchot Reader*, ed. Michael Holland (Oxford: Blackwell, 1995), 112.

92. "It is . . . a question of opening mere reason up to the limitlessness that constitutes its truth." Nancy, *Dis-Enclosure*, 1.

93. "The same requirement of reason emerges insistently: that of casting light on its own obscurity, not by bathing it in light, but by acquiring the art, the discipline, and the strength to let the obscure emit its own clarity." Ibid, 6.

94. Jean-Louis Chrétien, *The Ark of Speech*, trans. Andrew Brown (London: Routledge, 2003), 12.

95. Ibid., 12.

96. Keller also develops the strangeness of Christian listening in analyzing John 18:37b, "Everyone who belongs to the truth listens to my voice." *On the Mystery*, 31–32.

97. Mark A. McIntosh, "The Formation of Mind: Trinity and Understanding in Newman," in *Silence and the Word: Negative Theology and Incarnation*, ed. Oliver Davies and Denys Turner (Cambridge: Cambridge University Press, 2002), 138.

98. Ibid., 145.

99. For a fabulous example of this approach, see the character of Ida Turpin in Flannery O'Connor's short story "Revelation," in *The Complete Stories* (New York: Farrar, Straus and Giroux, 1971), 488–509.

100. "For mortals, there is an essential identity between maintaining and renewing. Fidelity requires one to reassert the act at each new instant." Chrétien, *The Unforgettable and the Unhoped For*, 22.

101. Smith, *Faith and Belief*, 168.

102. Friedrich Nietzsche, *The Gay Science*, trans. Walter Kaufmann (New York: Vintage Books, 1974), §341.

103. "The gods come or do not come. They impose their presence or they withdraw." Nancy, "Of Divine Places," 131.

104. It was my intent to provide representative urls, but the websites are simply too numerous. I urge readers to do a Google search ("God" with "weight loss," "money," and so on) for hours of fascinating entertainment.

105. Turner, "Dominus Illuminatio Mea," in *Faith Seeking*, 136.

106. Augustine, *Confessions*, I.I.

107. Chrétien, *The Unforgettable and the Unhoped For*, 92.

108. Cf. ibid., 93: "In order to hope in remembering, and remember in hoping, which makes up faith, one must lose something of one's own memory. When we remember an event from sacred history, such as the Nativity, this memory hopes, because it also calls and awaits the Christ born in our hearts. But he can be born only in a heart as poor as a manger, a heart that is empty and dispossessed, and this memory thus also asks for forgetting, forgetting of self as offering."

109. Ibid., 1–2.

110. Ibid., 78–98.

111. See Augustine, *Confessions*, 10.16.24. Cf. Chrétien: "Fear of forgetting is not fear of losing what we possess, but fear of losing what is already lost. For loss of the loss does not form a double negation that would amount to an affirmation." *The Unforgettable and the Unhoped For*, 71.

112. Cf. Chrétien: "For its part, philosophy supposes that first access as its other past, the absolute past that myth alone can express. The original opening to the truth cannot be thought according to the presence of the present. This once again marks an irreducible difference with transcendental idealism and its 'original acquisition' [Chrétien adds a footnote to Immanuel Kant, "Über eine Entdeckung nach der alle neue Kritik der reinen Vernunft durch eine ältere entberlich gemacht werden soll," *Werke* (Berlin: Walter de Gruyter, 1979), 3:339; Ak 8:221–23.] where spirit gives itself to itself what innatism thinks as given. There is indeed an 'original acquisition' for Plato, but this origin is always already forgotten and lost." Ibid., 23.

113. Cf. Augustine: "Again, I read there that the Word, God, is 'born not of the flesh, nor of blood, nor of the will of man nor of the will of the flesh, but of God.' But that 'the word was made flesh and dwelt among us' (John 1:13–14), I did not read there." *Confessions*, 7.9

114. Chrétien, *The Unforgettable and the Unhoped For*, 52. On the same page, Chrétien offers a relevant quotation from F. Ravaisson, *La philosophie en France au XIXième*

siècle, ed. P. Millot (Paris: Fayard, 1984), 22:220: "It is materiality that puts us in forgetting; pure spirit, on the contrary, which is all action, being therefore all unity, all duration, all memory, always present to all and to itself, keeping, without ever lacking, under its regard everything that is, everything that was, perhaps even ... everything that will be, pure spirit sees all things ... under the form of eternity."

115. Chrétien remarks this particularly for memory in its limited sense, as the recollection of the past: "Without the flesh, we could not learn what this is by heart, *par cœur*, according to the beautiful French expression. Incarnate being is by itself power of recalling and remembering, not because the past is inscribed of itself in it in the form of material traces, which are always only present and of the present, but because it alone opens us and relates us to what we can remember. If there is memory only of the past, incarnation is the condition and the place of all memory." Chrétien remarks in a footnote, "This does not rule out that the term *memory* could be given a much larger sense, as occurs in Augustinian thought." Ibid., 69.

116. I go on about this at much greater length in the "Cut" chapter of *Word Made Skin: Figuring Language at the Surface of Flesh* (New York: Fordham University Press, 2004), 137–60.

117. "Knowing that there is in the color and grain of paper, in the curl of script, the fading of ink, more than there is in any image, and that without seeing them I could remember only having forgotten them? Should we not hear in this a confession of the carnal character of memory?" Chrétien, *The Unforgettable and the Unhoped For*, 72.

118. Mackey, *Peregrinations of the Word*, 3. Mackey, it is clear in context, does not use "believe" in the reductive sense I have criticized here.

119. Nancy, *Dis-Enclosure*, 52.

120. Franz Kafka, *The Blue Octavo Notebooks / Reflections on Sin, Suffering, Hope, and the True Way*, ed. Max Brod, trans. Ernst Kaiser and Eithne Wilkins (Cambridge, Mass.: Exact Change, 1991), 54; cited in Hawkins, *Reluctant Theologians*, 1 and 63.

2. Reading Rites: Sacraments and the Community of Signs

1. Augustine, *Confessions*, 13.34.49.

2. Augustine, *On Christian Doctrine*, 3,10,33. Thus cited and translated in Pranger, *Eternity's Ennui*, 214.

3. Keller, *On the Mystery*, 16–17.

4. See, e.g., Lombardi: "In history, Christ is figured as the redeemer of signs. He set their confusion in order, providing a set of few ..., easy ..., elevated ...,

and chaste . . . signs—among which Augustine mentions baptism and the Eucharist." *The Syntax of Desire*, 30–31.

5. Denys Turner, "Apophaticism, Idolatry and the Claims of Reason," in *Silence and the Word: Negative Theology and Incarnation*, ed. Oliver Davies and Denys Turner (Cambridge,: Cambridge University Press, 2002), 31. See Thomas Aquinas, *Summa Theologica*, 2.2, Q 60, Art. 3; see also supplement, Q 30, Art. I.

6. Baptism, penance or reconciliation, the Eucharist, confirmation, holy orders, marriage, and anointing of the sick. Orthodox Christianity has a similar list: baptism, the Eucharist, chrismation (which accompanies baptism), confession, marriage, holy orders, and the anointing of the sick.

7. Joseph Martos, *Doors to the Sacred: A Historical Introduction to Sacraments in the Catholic Church* (New York: Image Books, 1982), 68. Martos notes further that the Council of Florence in 1439 "taught that [the sacraments] were instruments of salvation which contained and conferred grace," while contemporary teaching is traceable largely to the Council of Trent, with minor, more modern modifications. Ibid.

8. Ibid., 41.

9. John Chrysostom, *Commentary on I Corinthians* 1:7; cited in Martos, *Doors to the Sacred*, 41. I have not been able to trace the original.

10. Martos, *Doors to the Sacred*, 11.

11. See ibid., 104, 113.

12. Ibid., 59.

13. Ibid., 292–93.

14. Kenan B. Osborne, O.F.M., *Sacramental Theology: A General Introduction* (Mahwah, N.J.: Paulist Press, 1988), 67.

15. David Hume, *An Enquiry Concerning Human Understanding* (Indianapolis: Hackett Publishing, 1993), esp. "Of the Idea of Necessary Connexion," §§48–61.

16. "This opinion . . . was defended by St. Bonaventure, Duns Scotus, Durandus, Occam, and all the Nominalists, and enjoyed a real success until the time of the Council of Trent, when it was transformed into the modern system of moral causality." Daniel Kennedy, "Sacraments," in *The Catholic Encyclopedia*, vol. 13 (New York: Robert Appleton Company, 1912), Online edition by Kevin Knight, 2009. Accessed at http://www.newadvent.org/cathen/13295a.htm. Later, oddly enough, Samuel Taylor Coleridge would hold this view. On Bonaventure, see also Louis Marie Chauvet, *Symbol and Sacrament: A Sacramental Reinterpretation of Christian Existence* (Collegeville, Minn.: Liturgical Press, 1995), 16. On Coleridge, see J. Robert Barth, S.J., *Coleridge and Christian Doctrine* (New York: Fordham University Press, 1987), 172.

17. Osborne, *Sacramental Theology*, 67.

18. Kennedy, "Sacraments."

19. Osborne, *Sacramental Theology*, 23.

20. Augustine, *The City of God*, trans. Henry Bettenson (New York: Penguin Classics, 2003), 10.5. Thus cited in Joseph M. Powers, "Eucharist, Mystery of Faith and Love," in *The Sacraments: Readings in Contemporary Sacramental Theology*, ed. Michael J. Taylor, S.J. (Staten Island: Alba House, 1981), 118.

21. See M. B. Pranger, "The Unfathomability of Sincerity: On the Serious-ness of Augustine's *Confessions*," in *Actas do Congresso International As Confissoes de santo Agostinho 1600 Anos Depois: Presenca e Actualidade* (Lisbon: Universidade Catolica Edi-tora, 2002), 193–242.

22. Martos, *Doors to the Sacred*, 110, citing Martin Luther, *Treatise on the Blessed Sacra-ment and the Brotherhood*, no page given. See "A Treatise Concerning the Blessed Sac-rament of the Holy and True Body of Christ and Concerning the Brotherhoods," in *Works of Martin Luther* (Philadelphia: A. J. Holman Co., 1915), 2:9: "Like the sacrament of holy baptism, the holy sacrament of the altar, or of the holy and true body of Christ, has three parts which it is necessary for us to know. The first is the sacrament, or sign, the second is the significance of this sacrament, and third is the faith required by both of these."

23. Martos, *Doors to the Sacred*, 110, citing Calvin, *Institutes of the Christian Religion*, 4, 14, 22.

24. Martos, *Doors to the Sacred*, 111, citing Ulrich Zwingli, *On True and False Religion*, no page given. For the standard edition, see *Commentary on True and False Religion* (Jamestown, N.Y.: Labyrinth Books, 1981).

25. Augustine, *City of God*, 10.5, 377.

26. Augustine, "On the Catechising of the Uninstructed," trans. S. D. F. Salmond, in *Nicene and Post-Nicene Fathers*, series I, vol. 3, ed. Philip Schaff (Buffalo, N.Y.: Christian Literature Publishing Co., 1887). Online edition by Kevin Knight, 2009. Accessed at http://www.newadvent.org/fathers/1303.htm, §22.

27. "The discovery of a link between the 'sacramental' and descriptivity hits upon a serious problem in the history of the sacrament proper. . . . since the emer-gence of scholasticism, religious language, both scholarly and devotional, has tended to become descriptive in spite of claims to the contrary. And, paradoxically, to the degree that it has tried to present itself as performative (increasingly record-ing the outcome of an inner experience rather than being 'just' rite), it has become ever more descriptive." Pranger, "The Unfathomability of Sincerity," 197.

28. On the various Neoplatonic authors presenting these options, see Sarah Klitenic Wear and John M. Dillon, *Dionysius the Areopagite and the Neoplatonist Tradi-tion: Despoiling the Hellenes* (Aldershot: Ashgate, 2007).

29. Ibid., 106, citing Dionysius's *Ecclesiastical Hierarchy*, 440aff. See Pseudo-Dionysius, *The Complete Works*, 193–260.

30. See Wear and Dillon, *Dionysius*, esp. 100.

31. Ambrose of Milan, *De Mysteriis*, 2.9–12. Accessed at http://www.cross roadsinitiative.com/library_article/657/On_the_Mysteries_St_Ambrose_on _the_Sacraments.html.

32. Ibid., 3.8.

33. Maurice Blanchot, *Friendship*, trans. Elizabeth Rottenberg (Stanford, Calif.: Stanford University Press, 1997), 218.

34. Thomas Aquinas, *Summa Theologica*, 3, Q60.2, Art 2, in "I answer that": "Signs are given to men, to whom it is proper to discover the unknown by means of the known. Consequently a sacrament properly so called is that which is the sign of some sacred thing pertaining to man; so that properly speaking a sacrament, as considered by us now, is defined as being the 'sign of a holy thing so far as it makes men holy.'" Cf. Peter Lombard, *Sentences* IV, I, 2: "A sacrament properly so called is that which is a sign of God's grace and the invisible form of grace in such a way that it evokes the likeness of that grace and constitutes its cause." Cited in *St. Thomas Aquinas: Summa Theologiae, 3a.60–65*, ed. David Bourke (Cambridge: Cambridge University Press, 2006), xviii. For Lombard, see Peter Lombard, *The Sentences*, bk. 4, *On the Doctrine of Signs*, trans. Giulio Silano (Toronto: Pontifical Institute of Medieval Studies, 2010).

35. Thomas Aquinas, *Summa Theologica*, 3, Q 60, Art I.

36. Ibid.

37. For a nuanced reading of this distinction between seriousness and theatricality, as well as the ways in which it may be troubled, see Pranger, "The Unfathomability of Sincerity."

38. Kennedy, "Sacraments," cites Peter Lombard: "'A sacrament is in such a manner an outward sign of inward grace that it bears its image (i.e. signifies or represents it) and is its cause';—'Sacramentum proprie dicitur quod ita signum est gratiae Dei, ei invisibilis gratiae forma, ut ipsius imaginem gerat et causa existat' (IV Sent., d.I, n.2)" and Thomas Aquinas: "'The sign of a sacred thing in so far as it sanctifies men'—'Signum rei sacrae in quantum est sanctificans homines' (ST III:60:2)." For English citations, see n. 34 above.

39. "The phrase 'ex opere operato,' for which there is no equivalent in English, probably was used for the first time by Peter of Poitiers (D. 1205), and afterwards by Innocent III (d. 1216; de myst. missae, III, v), and by St. Thomas (d. 1274; IV Sent., dist. I, Q.i, a.5)." Kennedy, "Sacraments."

40. Kennedy, "Sacraments."

41. Ibid. The text notes, "see Pourrat, 'Theology of the Sacraments,' tr. St. Louis, 1910, 162 sqq." I have found this reference as P. Pourrat, *Theology of the Sacraments: A Study in Positive Theology* (St. Louis: B. Herder, 1910). Thomas Aquinas worries about something like this in *Questiones Disputatae de Veritate*, Q 26, Art. 1, in the objections: "But one who deliberately resists, especially an adult, is not helped through the instruments of divine mercy, the sacraments" (Obj. 13). *Sed contra*, however, in the same article, "certain corporeal beings act upon the soul for its justification in so far as they are instruments of divine mercy, as is evident in the case of the sacraments of the Church." Thomas Aquinas, "Truth," Online edition by Joseph Kennedy, O.P. Questions 21–29 trans. by Robert W. Schmidt, S.J. (Chicago: Regnery Company, 1954). Accessed at http://dhspriory.org/thomas /QDdeVer26.htm.

42. See Martos, 57. Cf. Ambrose of Milan, *De Mysteriis*, 5.27, where the chapter heading summarizes the argument: "Christ is Himself present in Baptism, so that we need not consider the person of His ministers."

43. Ian James, *Pierre Klossowski: The Persistence of a Name* (Oxford: Legenda, 2000), 104. The quotation is from Pierre Klossowski, *La vocation suspendue* (Paris: Gallimard, 1950), 103, James's translation.

44. James, *Pierre Klossowski*, 105–6.

45. Pranger, "The Unfathomability of Sincerity," 240.

46. Markus, *Signs and Meanings*, 142. Cf. Martos, *Doors to the Sacred*, 96.

47. Virginia Burrus, "A Saint of One's Own: Emmanuel Levinas, Eliezer ben Hyrcanus, and Eulalia of Mérida," *L'Esprit Créateur* 50, no. 1 (Spring 2010): 9–10. Burrus's argument is developed through an analysis of Emmanuel Levinas, "Desacralization and Disenchantment," in *Nine Talmudic Readings*, trans. Annette Aronowicz (Bloomington: Indiana University Press, 1990), 136–60.

48. Baudrillard, *Seduction*, 138–39.

49. Ibid., 75.

50. Baudrillard is careful to distinguish the seductive secret from latent content; see ibid., 54.

51. Ibid., 137.

52. Ludger Viefhues-Bailey, "Displacing Bodies: The Eucharist, Ritualization and Resistance," presented at Calvin College, 2008. Viefhues-Bailey cites Ludwig Wittgenstein, R. G. Bosanquet, and Cora Diamond, *Wittgenstein's Lectures on the Foundations of Mathematics, Cambridge, 1939: From the Notes of R. G. Bosanquet, Norman Malcolm, Rush Rhees, and Yorick Smythies*, (Ithaca, N.Y.: Cornell University Press, 1976), 183–84.

53. "From M.Fr. *liturgie*, from L.L. *liturgia* 'public service, public worship,' from Gk. *leitourgia*, from *leitourgos* 'one who performs a public ceremony or service,

public servant,' from *leito-* 'public' (from *laos* 'people'; cf. *leiton* 'public hall,' *leite* 'priestess') + *-ergos* 'that works,' from *ergon* 'work' (see urge [v.]). Meaning 'collective formulas for the conduct of divine service in Christian churches' is from 1590s." *Online Etymology Dictionary*, accessed at http://www.etymonline.com/.

54. Baudrillard, *Seduction*, 142.

55. The locus classicus for arguments against the possibility of a private language is Ludwig Wittgenstein's *Philosophical Investigations*, trans. G. E. M. Anscombe, P. M. S. Hacker and Joachim Schulte (Oxford: Blackwell, 2009), §§243f.

56. Mackey, *Peregrinations of the Word*, 8. Mackey cites the passages in *Confessions* 10 in which Augustine admits his fondness for the praise of his contemporaries (10.36.59–10.38.63), and *Confessions* 1.13.21, in which Augustine recounts the tears he shed over the plight of Dido in Vergil's *Aeneid*.

57. Markus, *Signs and Meanings*, 142.

58. Elliot Wolfson notes this difference from most Jewish theory, while also citing the limitations of a simplistic distinction; see, e.g., Elliot R. Wolfson, *Circle in the Square: Studies in the Use of Gender in Kabbalistic Symbolism* (Albany: State University of New York Press, 1995), esp. 57–58; or "Inscribed in the Book of the Living," 266.

59. Augustine, *The Teacher*, 104–5. Pranger reminds us of the importance of language's *sound*: "For Ambrose, what counts, as indeed for Augustine, is the primacy of sonority, the *sound* of the word. Realisation of that sound reveals the deep structure of language. As such it requires sufficient acoustic means and space in order to resound. This then is the main principle behind the *Confessions*: reflection and rumination upon the Word in circles of an ever-increasing depth without that Word ceasing to be basically sound-bound. Thus it will always be—in a manner of speaking—the Ambrosian hymn as a sonorous reflection of the Word that will release frozen tears." *Eternity's Ennui*, 240.

60. Augustine, *Confessions*, 6.3.3.

61. Augustine, *On Christian Doctrine*, 2.2.3.

62. Rist, *Augustine*, 34.

63. See Mackey, *Peregrinations of the Word*, 11.

64. Ibid., 74.

65. Charles Sanders Peirce, *Collected Papers*, ed. Charles Hartshorne, Paul Weiss, and Arthur W. Burks (Cambridge: Harvard University Press, 1933), 5:171.

66. Adeodatus, Augustine's son, is also the pupil or interlocutor in *The Teacher*.

67. Umberto Eco, *Semiotics and the Philosophy of Language* (Bloomington: Indiana University Press, 1984), 39–40.

68. "Augustine knew that /ex/ meant the separation of something from something else; he still had to decide how to identify the two terms of this relationship within the co-text he was interpreting. His decision was quasi-automatic;

however, he had to figure out a hypothesis—even though a hardly challengeable one." Ibid., 41.

69. Ibid., 41–42.

70. Ibid., 42.

71. Rist, *Augustine*, 36. I shall make more of Rist's point in Chapter 5, on scripture.

72. Martos, *Doors to the Sacred*, 16. Martos attributes this idea to Mircea Eliade, but without specific citation.

73. Ibid., 17.

74. Ibid., 150. Similarly, Joseph T. Nolan writes: "The possibility of expanding life to the infinite comes from the infinite, or God. But we have often acted with sacraments as if they were an achievement, not an invitation." Joseph T. Nolan, "Do We Still Need the Sacraments?", in *The Sacraments*, ed. Taylor, 3.

Jared Wicks emphasizes both the drawing power of the divine and the necessary receptivity of the to-be-drawn: "In receiving a sacrament, a person is both receptive of God's loving nearness and responsive in worship. Receptivity to grace, or 'faith,' is basic to a life near God. . . . In sacramental events, we are not, however, exclusively passive or receptive." Jared Wicks, S.J., "The Sacraments: A Catechism for Today," in *The Sacraments*, ed. Taylor, 28.

This echoes Karl Rahner's focus on receptivity; he urges us to see "instead of . . . a spiritual movement outward from the sacramental action to an effect in the world, . . . a spiritual movement of the world toward the sacrament." Rahner, "How to Receive a Sacrament," 71; see also 73. However, he adds that "it is grace itself that makes the reception fruitful" (77).

75. McIntosh, "The Formation of Mind," 148. McIntosh cites Hans Urs von Balthasar, *Presence and Thought: Essay on the Religious Philosophy of Gregory of Nyssa*, trans. Mark Sebane (San Francisco: Ignatius Press, 1995), e.g., 98–99.

76. Rist, *Augustine*, 38: "In *The Trinity* (15.10.19ff.) we read of a word which precedes any particular language, but such a word (or divine Word) is not itself a sign."

77. See Markus, *Signs and Meanings*, 100, citing Augustine, *On the Trinity*, 9.7.12: "In this eternal truth, which is the origin of all temporal things, we behold by a perception of the mind [*visu mentis*] the pattern which governs our being and our activities, whether within ourselves or in regard to other things, according to the rule of truth and of right reason; and from it we derive a true knowledge of things which we possess, as it were, in the form of a word conceived by an interior utterance." Augustine, *The Trinity*, in *Nicene and Post-Nicene Fathers*, series I, vol. 3, ed. Phillip Schaff (New York: Cosimo Classics, 2007).

78. Wear and Dillon, *Pseudo-Dionysius*, 111, citing Pseudo-Dionysius, *Ecclesiastical Hierarchy*, 372AB.

79. Ibid.

80. For a delightful popular discussion of several such "languages," see Arika Okrent, *In the Land of Invented Languages: Esperanto Rock Stars, Klingon Poets, Loglan Lovers, and the Mad Dreamers Who Tried to Build a Perfect Language* (New York: Spiegel and Grau, 2009).

81. Baudrillard, *Seduction*, 177.

82. Ibid., 54.

83. "What calls me most radically into question? Not my relation to myself as finite or as the consciousness of being before death or for death, but my presence in the proximity of another who by dying removes himself definitively, to take upon myself another's death as the only death that concerns me, this is what puts me beside myself, this is the only separation that can open me, in its very impossibility, to the Openness of a community." Maurice Blanchot, *The Unavowable Community*, trans. Pierre Joris (Barrytown, N.Y.: Station Hill Press, 1988), 9.

84. See also "The Inoperative Community," trans. Christopher Fynsk, in Jean-Luc Nancy, *The Inoperative Community*, ed. Peter Connor (Minneapolis: University of Minnesota Press, 1991), 1–42.

85. Cf., of course, Merleau-Ponty, *The Visible and the Invisible*.

86. Rahner writes that: "The world is permeated by God's grace. To be sure, the sacraments are grace-events, but not in the sense of discrete discharges of grace into a profane world. The world is permanently graced at its root. It is borne up by God's self-communication even before free creatures decide whether to accept this proffered grace." Rahner, "How to Receive a Sacrament," 73.

87. See Gilles Deleuze, *The Fold: Leibniz and the Baroque*, trans. Tom Conley (Minneapolis: University of Minnesota Press, 1992), on the notion of inflection as an in-folding.

3. Because Being Here Is So Much: Ethics as the Artifice of Attention

1. This is so whether or not we include some sense of the transcendent in our ethical system. As Jeffrey Bloechl writes of Levinas, "Ethics, one must therefore conclude, has as much to do with *limiting* a desire beyond being as it does with keeping that desire in view." Jeffrey Bloechl, "Ethics as First Philosophy and Religion," in *The Face of the Other and the Trace of God: Essays on the Philosophy of Emmanuel Levinas*, ed. Jeffrey Bloechl (New York: Fordham University Press, 2000), 149.

2. Aristotle, *Nicomachean Ethics*, trans. Terence Irwin (Indianapolis: Hackett Publishing, 1999), bk. 2, §13; David Hume, *An Inquiry Concerning the Principles of Morals*, (Old Chelsea Station, N.Y.: Cosimo, Inc., 2006), 99.

3. For the classic statements of utilitarianism, see the essays of Jeremy Bentham and his student John Stuart Mill, e.g., as collected in Bentham, *Utilitarianism and Other Essays* (New York: Penguin Books, 1987), or Mill, *Utilitarianism and On Liberty: Including the "Essay on Bentham" and Selections from the Writings of Jeremy Bentham and John Austin*, ed. Mary Warnock (Malden, Mass.: Wiley-Blackwell, 2003).

4. Immanuel Kant, *Groundwork of the Metaphysics of Morals*, trans. Mary Gregor (Cambridge: Cambridge University Press, 1997). Gilles Deleuze takes up this concern with pleasure as central to his discussion of Kant's ethics, which he reads as ultimately aporetic; see his *Kant's Critical Philosophy: The Doctrine of the Faculties*, trans. Hugh Tomlinson and Barbara Habberjam (Minneapolis: University of Minnesota Press, 1985).

5. See esp. Augustine, *Confessions*, 10.30.41–35.54.

6. As Catherine Conybeare notes, "even if one wishes to move beyond sense-perception, one needs precisely to make a start with *sensibilia*." Conybeare, *The Irrational Augustine*, 95. Conybeare adds later: "Despite Augustine's intellectual bias, we see again that the mind is not sufficient for an approach to God; it is not even the most important aspect of such an approach. The mind is again firmly set—by implication—within a body; and it is how that body behaves in the *mundus sensibilis* that is in fact most important." Ibid., 134.

7. "From a more modern point of view, talking about 'moods' would seem to be mainly about feeling and experience.... it is clear that, instead of being concerned with authentic emotions, the monastic author focuses on the artificiality of a technical process in which emotions are being established and handled as part of performative exercises rather than as feelings that are present and accessible as such." M. B. Pranger, *The Artificiality of Christianity: Essays on the Poetics of Monasticism* (Stanford, Calif.: Stanford University Press, 2003), xiii. Cf.: "late medieval texts ... are designed to help the reader, through the very toughness of their imagery, to sharpen his mind and to arouse affectivity and devotion." Ibid., 10.

8. Sebastian Moore, O.S.B., "The Crisis of an Ethic Without Desire," in *Theology and Sexuality: Classic and Contemporary Readings*, ed. Eugene Rogers (Oxford: Wiley-Blackwell, 2002), 158.

9. The framing structure of the *Symposium* is impressively, and somewhat comically, complex. Thus when "Diotima" speaks, what we have is in fact the following: Socrates' story of her speech (a story, the text makes clear, that he has created or at least embellished on the spot), as retold by Aristodemus (a guest at the symposium, who admits he doesn't remember it perfectly) to Apollodorus

some fourteen years later, and retold by Apollodorus, from memory, to an un-named companion, in a repetition of a retelling he had given a few days earlier to Glaucon. We are also warned that Apollodorus may not be perfectly sane. Plato could hardly have done more to head off the treatment of the text as authorita-tively decisive. *Symposium*, trans. Alexander Nehamas and Paul Woodruff (India-napolis: Hackett Publishing, 1989), 172A–173E.

10. Plato is infamous for the association of *eros* with lack—we can only de-sire, says Diotima, what we do not have. There are at least two problems with assuming that this means that desire is a lack: first, it conflates desire with its object, a conflation for which Socrates has just witheringly mocked Agathon; second, desire in this story is only half impoverished—it is also half plentiful and resourceful, active, and motivating. It lacks the desired, but it does not lack energy or forcefulness.

11. The value of the reminder is a recurrent theme in Plato's dialogues; the beautiful as reminder is most thematic in the *Phaedrus.* The anti-sensual theme is present as well in the *Republic,* but there, perhaps even more than elsewhere, one must be alert for Plato's ironic wit.

12. Nancy, *Dis-Enclosure,* 49.

13. Cf. Plotinus: "This is the spirit that Beauty must ever induce, wonder-ment and a delicious trouble, longing and love and a trembling that is all de-light." *The Enneads,* trans. Stephen MacKenna (Burdett, N.Y.: Larson Publications, 2004), I.6.4.

14. For Augustine, a sign is, as Mark Jordan glosses it, "the kind of thing which starts a motion towards what it signifies and, mediately, towards whomever employs it as a sign." Mark Jordan, "Words and Word: Incarnation and Signifi-cation in Augustine's *De doctrina Christiana,*" *Augustinian Studies* II (1980): 186.

15. "When you see that you yourselves are beautiful within, what do you feel? What is this Dionysiac exultation that thrills through your being, this straining upwards of all your Soul, this longing to break away from the body and live sunken within the veritable self? These are no other than the emotions of Souls under the spell of love." Plotinus, *Enneads,* I.6.5.

16. It is, in fact, "An unclean thing . . . ; flickering hither and thither at the call of objects of sense, deeply infected with the taint of body, occupied always in Matter, and absorbing Matter into itself; in its commerce with the Ignoble it has trafficked away for an alien nature its own essential Idea." Ibid.

17. Porphyry, "The Life of Plotinus and the Arrangement of his Work," in Plotinus, *The Enneads,* cii–cxxv, §I. Porphyry's assessment seems to be based less on asceticism than on Plotinus's reluctance to provide biographical details or to sit for a portrait.

18. Margaret Miles, *Plotinus on Body and Beauty: Society, Philosophy and Religion in Third-Century Rome* (Oxford: Wiley-Blackwell, 1999).

19. "He that has the strength, let him arise and withdraw into himself, forgoing all that is known by the eyes, turning away for ever from the material beauty that once made his joy. When he perceives those shapes of grace that show in body, let him not pursue: he must know them for copies, vestiges, shadows, and hasten away towards That they tell of. . . . one that is held by material beauty and will not break free shall be precipitated, not in body but in Soul, down to the dark depths loathed of the Intellective-Being, where, blind even in the Lower-World, he shall have commerce only with shadows, there as here." Plotinus, *Enneads*, I.6.8.

20. "For not he that has failed of the joy that is in colour or in visible forms, not he that has failed of power or of honours or of kingdom has failed, but only he that has failed of only This, for Whose winning he should renounce kingdoms and command over earth and ocean and sky, if only, spurning the world of sense from beneath his feet, and straining to This, he may see." Ibid., I.6.7.

21. Miles, *Plotinus on Body and Beauty*, 50; Martha Nussbaum, *Love's Knowledge: Essays on Philosophy and Literature* (New York: Oxford University Press, 1990), 37.

22. Miles, *Plotinus on Body and Beauty*, 50–51.

23. Ibid., 51.

24. Ibid., 167. Cf. 165: "Although Plotinus's idea of the 'strange sympathy' shared by all living beings supports concern about ecology, and social and economic justice, he explicitly advocated a nonchalant attitude toward suffering."

25. Porphyry, "The Life of Plotinus," §8.

26. Ibid., §9.

27. Ibid., §§9, 8–9, 8, and 2 and 11, respectively.

28. Miles, *Plotinus on Body and Beauty*, 166.

29. Ibid., 124: "Indeed, his treatise 'On Virtue' (1.2) states that the point of virtue is to 'escape from here' by 'being made like god.' It does not provide an ethic that encourages generous caretaking of needy others." Miles adds in a footnote: "John M. Dillon characterizes Plotinus's ethical system as 'uncompromisingly self-centered and other-worldly': 'An Ethic for the Late Antique Sage,' in *The Cambridge Companion to Plotinus*, (Cambridge: Cambridge University Press, 1996), 331)."

30. There are exceptions, of course. An entirely deontological ethics has no place for our sensitivities; if we should alleviate suffering, it is because such alleviation is right, not because we suffer with. The Marquis de Sade, to take an especially obvious example, develops an ethical system in accordance with his understanding of nature, in which we are not only indifferent to the suffering of

others, but may even delight in it. See esp. "Yet Another Effort, Frenchmen, If You Would Become Republicans," in *Philosophy in the Bedroom*, trans. Joachim Neugroschel (New York: Penguin Books, 2006), 104–49.

31. Conybeare, *Irrational Augustine*, 159.

32. Carol Harrison, *Beauty and Revelation in the Thought of St. Augustine* (Oxford: Oxford University Press, 1992), 35. Later Harrison adds a more Platonic variant on this idea: "if all the best minds are urged to seek God, openly, as it were, by the outward appearance of the universe, which assuredly must be believed to emanate from some fountain of truest beauty, and privately, by some inward consciousness, there is no need to give up hope that God has constituted some authority, relying on which as on a sure ladder we may rise to him"; "No man can obtain the supreme and most certain good unless he fully and perfectly loves it." Ibid., 50, referring to *De utilitate credendi*, 34 and 33. Augustine's text appears in English as *On the Profit of Believing*, trans. C. L. Cornish, in *Nicene and Post-Nicene Fathers*, series I, vol. 3, ed. Philip Schaff (Buffalo, N.Y.: Christian Literature Publishing Co., 1887); online edition by Kevin Knight, 2009. Accessed at http://www.newadvent.org/fathers/1306.htm.

33. Harrison, *Beauty and Revelation*, 257.

34. Ibid., 257, citing Augustine, Sermon 159.6.

35. Ibid., 123.

36. "Augustine departs from the classical theory [of the passions], however, in treating the passions not as irruptions into the mind from the body or from the lower, irrational part of the soul, but precisely as forms of will. Desire and joy are the affective shapes of the will when it is in accord with what it anticipates or what it actually has on hand." William S. Babcock, "The Human and the Angelic Fall: Will and Moral Agency in Augustine's *City of God*," in *Augustine: From Rhetor to Theologian*, ed. Joanne McWilliam (Waterloo, Ontario: Wilfred Laurier Press, 1992), 137.

37. Cf Miles, *Plotinus on Body and Beauty*, 34: "to perceive beauty is to experience the universe as a gift."

38. "I am tempted to say, based on what I have learned from Augustine's confessional psychology, that this is what God would like to know. Why are human beings so intent on undoing an incarnation? On returning flesh to will? When Augustine claims as his own life only the life that he has willed—and then out of false piety calls this life sinful—his God turns his invention into a question. What is this life of yours like? If Augustine has a good answer to this question, it is only because he really cannot, any more than anyone else can, turn flesh into will and undo a birth. All human attempts to do so have been preempted. The only will that finally counts in the matter of sin has already chosen

knowledge of the flesh. If there is some original sin still to be reckoned with, it is in the human disposition to find in this choice a cause for ingratitude." James Wetzel, "Body Double: Saint Augustine and the Sexualized Will," in *Weakness of Will from Plato to the Present*, ed. Tobias Hoffmann (Washington, D.C.: Catholic University Press, 2008), 81.

39. Merleau-Ponty, *The Visible and the Invisible*, 132.

40. Ibid., 143.

41. Pranger links this gift relation to the puzzle of Augustinian predestination: "How do these reflections on delay and falling short relate to the immediacy implied in the divine calling on the one hand and a fitting response to that call on the other, both of them going all the way back to the integral moment of God's mercy? // If we do indeed succeed in drawing the attention away from the unsolved and insoluble problems of foreknowledge and predetermination and try to bring out the voices involved in the offering and the (non)-acceptance of gift, we face an even more formidable problem than the aporias of predestination, and that is the voice and shape of destiny. In other words, behind the problem of predestination *sec* looms another, more basic and, perhaps, more compelling one: how and when to accept or refuse a gift?" Pranger, *Eternity's Ennui*, 282.

42. Paul Celan, *Collected Prose*, trans. Rosmarie Waldrop (Riverdale-on-Hudson, N.Y.: Sheep Meadow Press, 1986), 8.

43. Peter Casarella, "Cusanus on Dionysius: The Turn to Speculative Theology," *Modern Theology* 23, no. 4 (October 2008): 671: "Cusanus begins the sermon [on the feast of Mary] with an invocation of the Dionysian etymology whereby the Greek term for beauty ('kalos') is closely related to the verb 'to call,' thereby linking the attractiveness of beauty to the pursuit of the good. Accordingly, the path opened by Dionysius is also one of discipleship to the call of beauty. This theme plays a decisive role in the later works."

44. Jean-Louis Chrétien, *The Call and the Response*, trans. Anne Davenport (New York: Fordham University Press, 2004), 8.

45. Ibid., 3.

46. Plato, *Cratylus*, trans. Benjamin Jowett (San Diego: Icon Classics, 2008), 120–30. I am grateful to Sean Kirkland for reminding me of this passage.

47. Chrétien, *The Call and the Response*, 35. Cf. ibid., 34: "The eye ceases to listen not when it returns to the allegedly normal exercise of sight construed as deaf and dumb, but when it finds nothing in the visible that calls it or responds to it—when the visible no longer has a voice. Wherever one can no longer listen, there is nothing left to see."

48. "What is beautiful is what calls out by manifesting itself and manifests itself by calling out. To draw us to itself as such, to put us in motion toward it,

to move us, to come and find us where we are so that we will seek it—such is beauty's call and such is our vocation." Ibid., 9.

49. Pranger, *Eternity's Ennui*, 49.

50. Pranger, *The Artificiality of Christianity*, 25, comments on an essay by Richard of St. Victor, "About the Four Degrees of Violent Love": "Violent love, then, should be reserved for an object proportionate to it, that is, an object without measure that really is insatiable—God."

51. "There are two main human sins from which all the others derive: impatience and indolence. It was because of impatience that they were expelled from Paradise; it is because of indolence that they do not return. Yet perhaps there is only one major sin: impatience. Because of impatience they were expelled, because of impatience, they do not return." Kafka, *The Blue Octavo Notebooks*, 15. Cited in Hawkins, *Reluctant Theologians*, 27.

52. Pranger, *The Artificiality of Christianity*, 21.

53. Chrétien, *The Call and the Response*, 1.

54. Ibid., 10. Cf. 25: "Our response can only repeat. It starts by repeating. Yet it does not repeat by restating. Repetition is not the mere reproduction of a first time or the retelling of what was said before. First because we only have access to the alleged first instance in the second instance, which is repetition."

55. Augustine, *Confessions*, 7.17.23.

56. "In the philosophy of Levinas, moments of supreme commitment—or if one prefers, events of grace—erupt from beneath individual freedom, taking possession of the soul long enough to carry it briefly beyond the range of actions oriented first to oneself." Bloechl, "Ethics as First Philosophy and Religion," 146. The connection between grace and beauty, Richard Viladesau argues, remains strong in Christian art if underemphasized in its theology. "The patristic and Thomistic notions of grace as divinization persisted especially in the theology of mysticism (the 'unitive way') and also as an undercurrent in the theology of grace (the Council of Trent's systematization of the Roman liturgy included this prayer at the mixture of water and wine for the Eucharist: 'Grant through this mystery of water and wine that we may be participants in the divinity of Jesus Christ your Son, who deigned to partake of our humanity'). The connection of grace with beauty, while little emphasized in theology, remained strongly implicit in Christian art." Richard Viladesau, "Theosis and Beauty," *Theology Today* 65, no. 2 (2008): 184.

57. Bloechl, "Ethics as First Philosophy," 140.

58. Chrétien, *The Call and the Response*, 20.

59. Gilles Deleuze clearly shows this tension at work in his study of Kant's ethics, in *Kant's Critical Philosophy*.

60. Dictionary.com. Based on *The Random House Dictionary of the English Language* (New York: Random House, 1971).

61. James Alison, "The Gay Thing," in *Queer Theology*, ed. Gerard Loughlin (Malden Mass.: Blackwell, 2002), 55.

62. See Burrus, "A Saint of One's Own," 15. Burrus cites Emmanuel Levinas, *Totality and Infinity: An Essay on Exteriority*, trans. Alphonso Lingis (Pittsburgh: Duquesne University Press, 1969), 34.

63. Cited in Harrison, *Beauty and Revelation*, 189–90.

64. Ibid., 190.

65. Ibid., 53, cites Augustine, *De Musica (On Music)* (*Patrologia latina*, ed. J. P. Migne [Paris: Garnier, 1844–1904], 32:1081–1100, 13.38): "delight orders the soul . . . we can only love beautiful things." Plotinus also argues that the perception of beauty is the experience of love. Margaret Miles, in *Plotinus on Body and Beauty*, 104, cites *Ennead* 2.9.16: "For how could there be a musician who sees the melody in the intelligible world and will not be stirred when he hears the melody in sensible sounds? Or how could there be anyone skilled in geometry and numbers who will not be pleased when he sees right relation and proportion, and order with his eyes? For indeed, even in pictures those who look at the works of art do not see the same things in the same way, but when they recognize an imitation on the level of sense of someone who has a place in their thought they feel a kind of disturbance and come to a recollection of the truth. This is the experience from which passionate love arises."

66. Paul Moyaert, "The Phenomenology of Eros: A Reading of *Totality and Infinity* IVB," in *The Face of the Other and the Trace of God*, ed. Jeffrey Bloechl (New York: Fordham University Press, 2000), 33.

67. Emmanuel Levinas, *Ethics and Infinity: Conversations with Philipe Nemo*, trans. Richard A. Cohen (Pittsburgh: Duquesne University Press, 1985), 85.

68. Rudolf Bernet, "The Encounter with the Stranger: Two Interpretations of the Vulnerability of the Skin," in *The Face of the Other and the Trace of God*, ed. Jeffrey Bloechl (New York: Fordham University Press, 2000), 51.

69. Levinas, *Ethics and Infinity*, 86.

70. Ibid., 87–88. Levinas adds: "In discourse I have always distinguished . . . between the *saying* and the *said*. . . . the *saying* is the fact that before the face I do not simply remain there contemplating it, I respond to it. The saying is a way of greeting the other, but to greet the Other is already to answer for him." Ibid., 88.

71. Ibid., 89.

72. See Elliot Wolfson, "Secrecy, Modesty, and the Feminine: Kabbalistic Traces in the Thought of Levinas," in *The Exorbitant: Levinas Between Jews and Chris-*

tians, ed. Kevin Hart and Michael A. Signer (New York: Fordham University Press, 2009), 59. Wolfson cites Levinas, *Otherwise than Being or Beyond Essence*, trans. Alphonso Lingis (Pittsburgh: Duquesne University Press, 1998), 44, 46; and Edith Wyschogrod, "Language and Alterity in the Thought of Levinas," in *The Cambridge Companion to Levinas*, ed. Simon Critchley and Robert Bernasconi (Cambridge: Cambridge University Press, 2002), 195–98.

73. See Wolfson, "Secrecy, Modesty, and the Feminine," 60, citing Levinas, *Totality and Infinity*, 254, 264, 257–58.

74. Chrétien, *The Call and the Response*, 23, citing Paul Claudel, *Paul Claudel interroge le Cantique des cantiques* (Paris: Egloff, 1948), 108.

75. Chrétien, *The Ark of Speech*, 93. He quotes Augustine's famous passage from the *Confessions*, beginning "You called and cried out loud and shattered my deafness" and goes on to add: "In this evocation of what theology would later call the spiritual senses, there is a fivefold wound, which is an essential part of the manifestation of God's beauty. God breaks in, he comes towards us and upon us as the Lord, by creating the conditions of possibility of his own manifestation. He alone can take the initiative . . . and he does not come to fulfill or satisfy as desire that is already ours, but he himself comes to rouse the flame within us. // What is being said here of the divine beauty? We do not so much speak of it as to it."

76. Even the generally problematic idea of creation ex nihilo can be reconceived as a call to what is not, so that it comes to be what is—a call to the possible, which is not the actual yet is never unimplicated in it. Eriugena writes, along these lines: "Whoever calls, often cries out. Most appropriately therefore is God said to be good and to be goodness, since he cries out to all things through an intelligible cry to come from non-being into essence." Cited in Chrétien, *The Call and the Response*, 17, from John Scotus Eriugena, *Periphyseon*, ed. I. P. Sheldon-Williams (Dublin: Dublin Institute for Advanced Studies, 1972), 2:124.

77. Cf. Rainer-Maria Rilke, First *Duino Elegy:* "For beauty is nothing but the beginning of terror, / which we are still just able to endure / And we are so awed because it so serenely disdains to annihilate us." In *The Selected Poetry of Rainer-Maria Rilke*, trans. Stephen Mitchell (New York: Vintage, 1989), 150–51.

78. Chrétien, *The Call and the Response*, 44.

79. Again, cf. Rainer Maria Rilke, First Duino Elegy, in *Duino Elegies and the Sonnets to Orpheus*, trans. Stephen Mitchell (New York: Vintage, 2009), 3.

80. Chrétien, *The Ark of Speech*, 78.

81. Levinas, *Ethics and Infinity*, 68 citing Emmanuel Levinas, *Time and the Other*, trans. Richard Cohen (Pittsburgh: Duquesne University Press, 1990).

82. "In *eros* an alterity between things is exalted which does not reduce to the logical or numerical difference which formally distinguishes any individual from any other. . . . In the erotic relation it is not a matter of another attribute in the Other, but of an attribute of alterity in the Other." Levinas, *Ethics and Infinity*, 65.

83. Hawkins, *Reluctant Theologians*, 212.

84. Chrétien, *The Call and the Response*, 14.

85. Cf. Hawkins, *Reluctant Theologians*, 213: "In the other, this look becomes dynamic rather than static, inspires becoming rather than being."

86. Jean-Luc Nancy, *The Birth to Presence*, trans. Brian Holmes et al. (Stanford, Calif.: Stanford University Press, 1993), 30. Later, Nancy provides a more overtly aesthetic version of this chiasmic transience: "Listening is musical when it is music that listens to itself. It returns to itself, it reminds itself of itself, and it feels itself as resonance itself: a relationship to self deprived, stripped of all egoism and all ipseity. Not 'itself,' or the other, or identity, or difference, but alteration and variation, the modulation of the present that changes it in expectation of its own eternity, always imminent and always deferred, since it is not in any time. Music is the art of making the outside of time return to every time, making return to every moment the beginning that listens to itself beginning and beginning again. In resonance the inexhaustible return of eternity is played—and listened to." Nancy, *Listening*, 67.

87. Levinas, *Ethics and Infinity*, 58. In this passage, Phillipe Nemo quotes Levinas, *Time and the Other*, 42.

88. Derrida quotes Angelus Silesius: "*One abyss calls the other* / The abyss of my spirit always invokes with cries / The abyss of God: say which may be deeper?" Derrida, "*Sauf le nom*," in *On the Name*, 77. Derrida quotes Angelus Silesius, *The Cherubinic Wanderer*, trans. Maria Shrady (Mahwah, N.J.: Paulist Press, 1986), 1:68.

89. Derrida, "*Sauf le nom*," 58.

90. Stephen H. Webb writes, "In Levinas, the accent in the revelation of an infinite otherness is on the finite other, who is a trace of the infinite." "The Rhetoric of Excess: A Christian Theological Response to Levinas," *Modern Theology* 15, no. 1 (1999): 8.

91. Cf. Catherine Keller: "spatiality of spirit, an articulate space that cannot be opposed to interior depth, has been little thematized in the western tradition." *Face of the Deep*, 167.

92. Robert Gibbs, "Suspicions of Suffering," in *Christianity in Jewish Terms*, ed. Tivka Frymer-Kensky, David Novak, Peter Ochs, David Fox Sandmel, and Michael A. Signer (Boulder, Colo.: Westview Press, 2000), 221.

93. Robert Gibbs, "The Disincarnation of the Word: The Trace of God in Reading Scripture," in *The Exorbitant: Emmanuel Levinas Between Jews and Christians*, ed. Kevin Hart and Michael A. Signer, (New York: Fordham University Press, 2010), 36.

94. Wolfson, "Secrecy, Modesty and the Feminine," 56. Wolfson cites esp. *Totality and Infinity*, 79–81. Regarding the moral stance, he refers to David G. Leahy, "Cuspidal Limits of Infinity: Secret of the Incarnate Self in Levinas," in *Rending the Veil: Concealment and Secrecy in the History of Religion*, ed. Elliot R. Wolfson (New York: Seven Bridges Press, 1999), 209–48. He also suggests Diane Perpich, "Sensible Subjects: Levinas and Irigaray on Incarnation and Ethics," in *Addressing Levinas*, ed. Eric Sean Nelson, Antje Kapust, and Kent Still (Evanston, Ill.: Northwestern University Press, 2005), 296–309.

95. Wolfson, "Secrecy, Modesty and the Feminine," 72.

96. For a more extensive discussion of constitution by wound and scar, see "Cut," in my *Word Made Skin*, 137–60. Cf. Keller: "I suspect . . . that the deep flesh, even in its resurrection, will carry the scars." *Face of the Deep*, 221.

97. Rubenstein, *Strange Wonder*, 62.

98. Bloechl, "Ethics as First Philosophy and Religion," 132.

99. To try to find God solely within ourselves becomes, as James Wetzel notes, a paradox: "As a way back to God, the path of introspection [probably taken from Plotinus] ends in paradox. Augustine finds God within himself, but he also finds himself far from God, in a strange place of interior exile (*in regione dissimilitudinis*); it is from there that he has his extraordinary vision of divinely created beauty." James Wetzel, "Snares of Truth: Augustine on Free Will and Predestination," in *Augustine and His Critics: Essays in Honour of Gerald Bonner*, ed. Robert Dodaro and George Lawless (London: Routledge, 2000), 135, citing Augustine, *Confessions* 7.10.16.

100. Bernet, "The Encounter with the Stranger," 51: "It is not my outer invisibility [to myself] but only the radical *passivity* of my exposure to an appeal that obliges me to respond which truly counts as a strangeness in me." Bernet adds in a footnote, "This passivity is then also a *susceptiveness*, even if also, as Levinas puts it, 'pre-originary.'"

101. Webb: "God is known, in fact, for Levinas, only through the infinitely other person, not in any direct contact." "The Rhetoric of Excess," 3.

102. Chrétien, *The Call and the Response*, 10.

103. Blanchot, *The Step Not Beyond*, trans. Lycette Nelson (Albany: State University of New York Press, 1992), 49.

104. Wetzel, "Body Double," 24. Wetzel cites Augustine, *Confessions* 7.17.23: *et pondus hoc consuetudo carnalis*, rendered by Chadwick "This weight was my sexual habit."

105. Augustine, *Confessions* 4.6–8.

106. Peter Brown, *The Body and Society: Men, Women, and Sexual Renunciation in Early Christianity* (New York: Columbia University Press, 1988), 405.

107. Emmanuel Levinas, "Reality and its Shadow," trans. Alphonso Lingis, in *Collected Philosophical Papers* (Pittsburgh: Duquesne University Press, 1998), 12; cited in Rubenstein, *Strange Wonder*, 77.

108. Anonymous, "The Gospel of Thomas," trans. Marvin Meyer, in *The Nag Hammadi Scriptures*, ed. Marvin Meyer (New York: Harper-Collins, 2007), 133–56, verse 5.

109. *Ennead* 4.4.37; cited and translated in Miles, *Plotinus on Body and Beauty*, 83.

110. Chrétien, *The Unforgettable and the Unhoped For*, 116.

111. Nancy, *The Birth to Presence*, 169.

112. Nancy, *Dis-enclosure*, 49: "God is first the giver. And it is as such that he is the 'Father of lights, with whom there is nor change nor a shadow of variation.' He gives as light and what he gives is first, essentially, his light. . . . He gives not so much some thing as the possibility of the clarity in which alone there can be things. If the logic of the gift is indeed, as the other James [*Jacques*] enjoys thinking, that the giver abandons him- or herself in his or her gift, then that is what is taking place here. In giving, in fulfilling the gift, God gives himself just as much as he remains in himself without shadows, since it is this dissipation of the shadow, this clearing of light that he gives, and since he 'gives to all, simply' (James 1:5)."

113. Rubenstein, *Strange Wonder*, 65.

114. Ibid., 76.

115. Chrétien, *The Call and the Response*, 32.

116. "Beauty that is seen requires that we speak in order to respond to it and requires that we answer for it with beauty." Ibid., 11.

117. Celan, *Collected Prose*, 49.

118. Wallace Stevens, "Large Red Man Reading," in *The Collected Poems of Wallace Stevens* (New York: Vintage Books, 1982), 423. I am indebted to Jennifer Glancy for drawing my attention to this lovely poem.

119. Rainer Maria Rilke, Ninth Duino Elegy, in *Selected Poetry*, 59.

120. Ibid., 57.

121. Levinas, *Ethics and Infinity*, 92.

122. William Franke, "Edmond Jabès or the Endless Self-Emptying of Language in the Name of God," *Literature and Theology* 22, no. 1 (March 2008): 102.

123. Franke points out that, for Jabès, the emptiness, the infinitely deferred meaning, of the name of God makes space for human speaking. See ibid., 103.

124. Celan, *Collected Prose*, 48.

125. Ibid., 52.

4. Prayer: Addressing the Name

1. Nancy, "Of Divine Places," 121.

2. Augustine, *Confessions*, 10.6.

3. Jill Robbins writes: "Solitary prayer does not have that opening function. The collectivity that opens the ultimate meaning of prayer is itself conceived as a keeping open or a holding open of the possibility of community. It is more of an interrogation than an assertion. . . . Collective prayer is a room with windows. This figure of opening is prolonged when Levinas states 'God is close to whomever invokes him [a virtual citation from Psalm 145], but the invocation presupposes an opening [*une ouverture*].'" "Who Prays? Levinas on Irremissible Responsibility," in *The Phenomenology of Prayer*, ed. Bruce Ellis Benson and Norman Wirzba (New York: Fordham University Press, 2005), 39. Robbins cites for the quotation Emmanuel Levinas, *Difficult Freedom: Essays on Judaism*, trans. Seán Hand (Baltimore: Johns Hopkins University Press, 1997), 270.

4. Nancy, "Of Divine Places," 117.

5. Ibid.

6. Hölderlin, "Heimkunft / Homecoming," in *Selected Poems and Fragments*, 164–65.

7. Nancy, "Of Divine Places," 118.

8. Ibid., 121.

9. Maurice Blanchot, *The Space of Literature*, trans. Ann Smock (Lincoln: University of Nebraska Press, 1989), 72. The exchange can be found in Gustav Janouch, *Conversations with Kafka*, trans. Goronwy Rees (New York: New Directions, 1971), 47. Interestingly, Kafka also sees prayer in human interaction: "the relationship to one's fellow man is the relationship of prayer." Kafka, *Blue Octavo Notebooks*, 51; cited in Hawkins, *Reluctant Theologians*, 102.

10. Celan, *Collected Prose*, 34–35.

11. Merold Westphal, "Prayer as the Posture of the Decentered Self," in *The Phenomenology of Prayer*, ed. Bruce Ellis Benson and Norman Wirzba (New York: Fordham University Press, 2005), 30.

12. Celan, *Collected Prose*, 49.

13. Pranger, *Eternity's Ennui*, 45.

14. "Late have I loved you, beauty so old and so new: late have I loved you." Augustine, *Confessions*, 10.27.38.

15. Blanchot, *The Infinite Conversation*, 20.

16. Ibid., 18.

17. "Speech affirms the abyss that there is between 'myself' and '*autrui*,' and it passes over the impassible, but without abolishing it or reducing it. Moreover, without this infinite distance, without this abysmal separation there would be no speech, so it is accurate to say that all veritable speech recalls the separation by which it speaks." Ibid., 63.

18. Ibid., 65.

19. Barthes, *The Pleasure of the Text*, 5.

20. Ibid., 6.

21. Nancy, *Dis-Enclosure*, 118.

22. Westphal, "Prayer as the Posture of the Decentered Self," 17.

23. More completely: "For the illocutionary act implicit in Samuel's prayerful speech act is the presentation of himself to God as a listener, and that is easier said than done. It is a performative, to be sure, but one that can scarcely be said to be performed more than to a certain degree." Ibid., 19.

24. Ibid., 17.

25. Pranger, *Eternity's Ennui*, 294.

26. Kevin Hart, "God and the Sublime," in *God Out of Place*, ed. Yves de Maeseneer (Utrecht: Ars Disputandi, 2005), 35–36.

27. Hölderlin, "Patmos," in *Selected Poems and Fragments*, 230–31.

28. Nancy, *The Birth to Presence*, 318.

29. Ann Smock, in conversation with Jean-Luc Nancy, in *The Birth to Presence*, 311.

30. Nancy, "Of Divine Places," 115, 119.

31. Nancy and Smock, in *Birth to Presence*, 315.

32. Ibid., 314.

33. James R. Mensch, "Prayer as Kenosis," in *The Phenomenology of Prayer*, ed. Bruce Ellis Benson and Norman Wirzba (New York: Fordham University Press, 2005), 63–72. On the other hand, Kevin Hart argues that "God opens a space wherein love can be ventured, and the first step is always his." "The Experience of the Kingdom of God," in *The Experience of God: A Postmodern Response*, ed. Kevin Hart and Barbara Wall (New York: Fordham University Press, 2005), 80. While enjoying the elegance of Hart's sentiment, I would be inclined to problematize agency, especially one-sided agency, somewhat more.

34. Nancy and Smock, in *The Birth to Presence*, 310.

35. Oliver Davies, "Soundings: Towards a Theological Poetics of Silence," in *Silence and the Word: Negative Theology and Incarnation*, ed. Oliver Davies and Denys Turner (Cambridge: Cambridge University Press, 2002), 211.

36. Virginia Burrus, "Praying Is Joying: Musings on Love in Evagrius Ponticus," in *Toward a Theology of Eros*, ed. Virginia Burrus and Catherine Keller (New York: Fordham University Press, 2006), 199.

37. Davies, "Soundings." 216. The quotation is from Jacques Derrida, "How to Avoid Speaking: Denials," in *Languages of the Unsayable: The Play of Negativity in Literature and Literary Theory*, ed. Sanford Budick and Wolfgang Iser (New York: Columbia University Press, 1989), 62.

38. My argument here is greatly influenced by Pranger's arguments about prayer and language in *Eternity's Ennui*.

39. Derrida, "*Sauf le nom*," 38.

40. Chrétien, *The Ark of Speech*, 93.

41. Blanchot, *The Infinite Conversation*, 25.

42. "The center allows finding and turning, but the center is not to be found." Ibid., 26.

43. Augustine, *Confessions*, 10.26.37.

44. Pranger, "The Unfathomability of Sincerity," 209: "we have to leave behind the autobiographical genre in its descriptive guise . . . and focus on the autobiographical promise, not as 'certitude' in the shape of 'reflex action'—never to be heard of again—but as performative. Inside the account of events or the story . . . the promise has really to be promised, it has to be sustained as such. // Let us assume then that in the *Confessions* the concept of conversion as promise holds the centre of the stage."

45. Ibid.: "the first thing that strikes us if we look at the conversion from the viewpoint of a promise is Augustine's self-confessed inability to keep it."

46. This is a point made at length by Nancy, in "Shattered Love," in *The Inoperative Community*, 82–109. I have previously taken it up in considering love and forgiveness in *Fragmentation and Memory*.

47. Kevin Hart, "Paul and the Reduction," interview with Lee Cole, *Journal of Philosophy and Scripture*, undated. Accessed at http://www.philosophyandscripture .org/Issue2-2/Hart/hart.html.

48. Pranger, "The Unfathomability of Sincerity," 213.

49. "All we can do to trace what really happened is to analyse the nature of the voices that have come together in the moment of conversion and to search for the way in which they are made to sound simultaneously." Ibid., 223.

50. Hart, "God and the Sublime," 35–36.

51. Pranger, "The Unfathomability of Sincerity," especially but not exclusively 218, 223–24.

52. Ibid., 227.

53. Blanchot, *The Infinite Conversation*, 65.

54. Pranger, "The Unfathomability of Sincerity", 224.

55. Westphal, "Prayer as the Posture of the Decentered Self," 20.

56. Mark Cauchi, "The Infinite Supplicant: On a Limit and a Prayer," in *The Phenomenology of Prayer*, ed. Bruce Ellis Benson and Norman Wirzba (New York: Fordham University Press, 2005), 227.

57. See Augustine, Sermon 30 on the New Testament (Matt. 17:19), trans. R. G. MacMullen, in *Nicene and Post-Nicene Fathers*, series I, vol. 6, ed. Philip Schaff (Buffalo, N.Y.: Christian Literature Publishing Co., 1888.) Online edition by Kevin Knight, 2009. Accessed at http://www.newadvent.org/fathers /160330.htm

58. Chrétien, *The Ark of Speech*, 75.

59. Nancy, *Listening*, 13.

60. Chrétien, *The Unforgettable and the Unhoped For*, 122.

61. Franke, "Edmond Jabès or the Endless Self-Emptying of Language in the Name of God," 115–16. Franke cites Edmond Jabès, *La mémoire des mots: Comment je lis Paul Celan* (Chitillon-sous-Bagneux: Fourbis, 1990), 9.

62. Franke, "Edmond Jabès or the Endless Self-Emptying of Language," 115–16. Franke adds in a footnote, "I explore the relationship between Jabès and Celan in 'The Singular and the Other at the Limits of Language in the Post-Holocaust Poetry of Edmond Jabès and Paul Celan,' *New Literary History* 36/4 (2005): 621–38."

63. Nancy, *Listening*, 30.

64. Ibid., 41.

65. Nancy and Smock, in *Birth to Presence*, 311.

66. "On this account, we should say . . . that music (or even sound in general) is not exactly a phenomenon; that is to say, it does not stem from a logic of manifestation. It stems from a different logic, which would have to be called evocation, but in this precise sense: while manifestation brings presence to light, evocation summons (convokes, invokes) presence to itself." Nancy, *Listening*, 20.

67. On the nondiscursive function of praise, particularly in relation to eternity, see Karmen MacKendrick, "The Temporality of Praise," in *Relocating Praise: Literary Modalities and Rhetorical Contexts*, ed. Alice den Otter (Toronto: Canadian Scholars Press, 2000), 19–32.

68. Augustine, Ennaratio in Psalmos, 86.1; cited in Chrétien, *The Ark of Speech*, 47.

69. Of Psalm 37:14, cited in Harrison, *Beauty and Revelation in the Thought of St. Augustine*, 259.

70. *Der cherubinische Wandersmann*, accessed at http://www.mscperu.org/deutsch /cherub/cheru401.htm

71. Derrida, *"Sauf le nom,"* 56.

72. Cf. Pierre Klossowski: "In giving itself over to God, the soul knows that God gives himself over to the soul." *Sade My Neighbor,* trans. Alphonso Lingis (Evanston, Ill.: Northwestern University Press, 1991), 115.

73. Denys Turner, "How Not to Pray," in *Faith Seeking,* 98.

74. Nancy, *Dis-Enclosure,* 137.

75. Ibid., 136.

76. Augustine, *Ad Simplicianum,* I.2.21, translated and cited in Pranger, *Eternity's Ennui,* 339. Available as "To Simplician: On Various Questions," in *Augustine: Earlier Writings,* ed. John H. S. Burleigh (Philadelphia: The Westminster Press, 1953), 370–406, and online at http://www.romancatholicism.org/jansenism/augustine-simplician.htm.

77. Michael Purcell, "When God Hides His Face: The Inexperience of God," in *The Experience of God: A Postmodern Response,* ed. Kevin Hart and Barbara Wall (New York: Fordham University Press, 2005), 113.

78. Ibid., 114, 120–21.

79. Ibid., 126–29.

80. Ibid., 115. In this claim, Purcell interestingly echoes the thought of Franz Rosenzweig on the possibility of false messiahs. Rosenzweig writes that: "The false Messiah . . . is the changing form of the enduring hope." In Barbara E. Galli, *Franz Rosenzweig and Juhuda Halevi: Translating, Translations, and Translators* (Montreal: McGill-Queen's University Press, 1995), 259; cited in Elliot R. Wolfson, *Open Secret: Postmessianic Messianism and the Mystical Revision of Menaḥem Mendel Schneerson* (New York: Columbia University Press, 2009), 266.

81. Matthew 27:46 and Mark 15:34; cited in Kevin L. Hughes, "Schools for Scandal: A Response to Michael Purcell," in *The Experience of God,* ed. Kevin Hart and Barbara Wall (New York: Fordham University Press, 2005), 132.

82. Hughes, "Schools for Scandal," 131.

83. Ibid., 133.

84. Ibid., 133–34.

85. Ibid., 135.

86. Rainer Maria Rilke, "The Olive Garden," in *New Poems [1907],* trans. Edward Snow (New York: North Point Press, 1984), 39. Ellipsis in original.

87. Ibid., 39–41.

88. Celan *Collected Prose,* 54–55. Ellipsis original.

89. Ibid., 50: " 'Attention,' if you allow me a quote from Malebranche via Walter Benjamin's essay on Kafka, 'attention is the natural prayer of the soul.' " I have not attempted to track down the nested references, which are not provided. Cf. Simone Weil: "Absolutely unmixed attention is prayer." *Gravity and*

Grace, trans. Emma Crawford and Mario van der Ruhr (New York: Routledge, 2007), 117.

90. Among Christian traditions, this aspect of prayer is perhaps most pronounced in hesychasm, with its sometimes elaborate prescriptions of breathing, posture, and words connected in meditative prayer. Hesychasm is particularly associated with Orthodox Christianity.

91. Nancy, *Listening*, 7.

92. Ibid., 65.

93. Ibid., 42.

94. Jean-Louis Chrétien, "The Wounded Word," in *Phenomenology and the "Theological Turn": The French Debate*, by Dominique Janicaud, Jean-François Courtine, Jean-Louis Chrétien, Michel Henry, Jean-Luc Marion, and Paul Ricoeur (New York: Fordham University Press, 2000), 149–50.

95. Chrétien, *The Unforgettable and the Unhoped For*, 127.

96. Chrétien, "The Wounded Word," 175.

97. Ibid., 174.

98. Nancy, *Dis-Enclosure*, 6.

99. Nancy, *Listening*, 67.

100. Chrétien, *The Call and the Response*, 69.

101. "To be listening is always to be on the edge of meaning, or in an edgy meaning of extremity, and as if the sound were precisely nothing else than this edge, this fringe, this margin." Nancy, *Listening*, 7.

102. Following, again, Pranger, "The Unfathomability of Sincerity."

103. I borrow the term "in-finition" from Anne O'Byrne, who has used it in relation to Nancy in "Body Singular Plural," delivered at the International Association for Philosophy and Literature, 2004.

104. Blanchot, *The Infinite Conversation*, 40.

105. Nancy, "Of Divine Places," 124.

106. Alexandre Kojève, *Introduction to the Reading of Hegel: Lectures on the Phenomenology of Spirit*, assembled by Raymond Queneau, ed. Alan Bloom, trans. James H. Nichols, Jr. (Ithaca: Cornell University Press, 1980), 3.

107. Muriel Barbery, *The Elegance of the Hedgehog*, trans. Alison Anderson (New York: Europa Editions, 2008), 44. I am grateful to David Macallum, S.J., for bringing this text to my attention.

108. Ibid., 44, 43.

109. Elliot R. Wolfson, "Assaulting the Border: Kabbalistic Traces in the Margins of Derrida," *Journal of the American Academy of Religion* 70, no. 3 (September 2002): 506.

110. Ibid.

III. Patricia Cox Miller, "'Words with an Alien Voice,'" 460, citing *Tripartite Tractate*, 65.39–66.5. Miller notes "This use of the Greek word *ichnos*, "trace," is closely paralleled by Plotinus' understanding of the term, precisely in the context of theological language."

112. Burrus, "Praying Is Joying," 200, citing Nancy, "Of Divine Places," 119.

113. Barbery, *The Elegance of the Hedgehog*, 43.

114. Nancy, *Dis-Enclosure*, 49.

115. Mackey, *Peregrinations of the Word*, 18–19.

5. Take and Read: Scripture and the Enticement of Meaning

I. Ellul, *Living Faith*, 100.

2. As James O'Donnell notes, "Many of [Augustine's] treatises on doctrinal or moral issues turn out to be extended meditations on scriptural passages." O'Donnell points out that these polemical and sometimes decontextualized readings are often "brilliant, even memorable," though they hardly fit contemporary norms for scholarly engagement. James O'Donnell, *Augustine, Confessions: Text and Commentary* (Oxford: Oxford University Press, 1992), 133.

3. Athanasius, *Life of Antony*, from *Athanasius: Select Works and Letters*, ed. Philip Schaff and Henry Wace, *Nicene and Post-Nicene Fathers*, series 2, vol. 4 (Peabody, Mass.: Hendrickson Publishers, 1994). Accessed at http://www.fordham.edu/halsall/basis/vita-antony.html, §2.

4. Ibid., §2. I cannot be alone in feeling anxious on his sister's behalf, but further details about her fate seem to be lacking.

5. See, e.g., Augustine, *Confessions*, 8.1.1: "Your words stuck fast in my heart and on all sides I was defended by you. Of your eternal life I was certain, although I saw it 'in an enigma and as if in a mirror' (I Cor. 13.12). All doubt had been taken from me that there is indestructible substance from which comes all substance. My desire was not to be more certain of you but to be more stable in you." The rest of Book 8 is full of similar instances.

6. Catherine Conybeare writes, "He has picked up on his mother's promptings to inclusivity. The result is a commitment to explain himself, and counter heretics, in simple language. But even as he teaches, it is also a theological commitment to consider himself, before God, one of the *paruuli* or the *imperitiores* from whom he would earlier have separated himself: one of those who is himself in need of the (apparently) simple language of the scriptures, because the 'language' of God is so impossibly far beyond his comprehension." *The Irrational Augustine*, 189.

7. R. D. Williams, "Language, Reality and Desire in Augustine's *De Doctrina*," *Literature and Theology* 3, no. 2–3 (1989): 142.

8. Elliot Wolfson elegantly traces a different, but equally seductive, circling without an origin in his consideration of Derridean and Kabbalistic readings: "To place the book at the beginning is not to lapse back into a logocentric positing of an origin or transcendental signified, for there is no book that is not composed by traces of another book, and so on in an endless chain of significations. The book is first, at the beginning, but the beginning, paradoxically, cannot begin and remain the beginning because to be the beginning it must have already begun. The beginning, then, must be conceived as a breaking-point, an interruption, interference, a rupture of the 'discontinuous series of instants and *attractions*'" Wolfson, "Assaulting the Border," 496; citing Jacques Derrida, "Point de folie—Maintenant l'architecture," trans. K. Linker, in *Architecture Theory since 1968*, ed. K. Michael Hays (Cambridge: MIT Press, 1998), 580.

9. That God writes two texts, or creates twice, first world and then scripture, is a thought widespread in both Jewish and Christian medieval theologies.

10. Catherine Brown, "Love Letters from Beatus of Liebana to Modern Philologists," *Modern Philology* 106, no. 4 (May 2009): 589.

11. James Wetzel makes this clear in "Snares of Truth," 124–41.

12. Nicholas Wolterstorff, *Divine Discourse: Philosophical Reflections on the Claim That God Speaks* (Cambridge: Cambridge University Press, 1995), 4.

13. Jacques Derrida, "Edmond Jabès and the Question of the Book," in *Writing and Difference*, trans. Alan Bass (London: Routledge, 1978), 66.

14. Cf. Derrida: "language is the *rupture* of totality with itself." Ibid., 71.

15. See Patricia Cox Miller, "'Words with an Alien Voice,'" esp. 459–61.

16. Augustine, *On Christian Doctrine*, 12.28.32: "After hearing and considering these views to the best of my weak capacity ... I see that two areas of disagreement can arise, when something is recorded by truthful reporters using signs. The first concerns the truth of the matter in question. The second concerns the intention of the writer. It is one thing to inquire into the truth about the origin of the creation. It is another to ask what understanding of the words on the part of a reader and hearer was intended by Moses. ... In the first category I will not be associated with all those who think they know things but are actually wrong. In the second category I will have nothing to do with all those who think Moses could have said anything untrue."

17. Marcia Colish notes that Augustine may have derived the principle indirectly from the exegetical tradition of Philo and Origen. *The Mirror of Language*, 43. See *Confessions* 12.25.35: "See how stupid it is, among so large a mass of entirely

correct interpretations which can be elicited from those words, rashly to assert that a particular one has the best claim to be Moses' view, and by destructive disputes to offend against charity itself, which is the principle of everything he said in the texts we are attempting to expound."

18. Markus, *Signs and Meanings*, 22. Markus cites *Confessions* 13.28.53 and, on semiotic anxiety, Martin Irvine, *The Making of Textual Culture: 'Grammatica' and Literary Theory 350–1100* (Cambridge: Cambridge University Press, 1994), 265–71.

19. Virginia Burrus, *Saving Shame: Saints, Martyrs, and Other Abject Subjects* (Philadelphia: University of Pennsylvania Press, 2008), 66. Burrus cites Patricia Cox Miller, *The Poetry of Thought in Late Antiquity*, 247–70.

20. Burrus, *Saving Shame*, 66.

21. Miller, " 'Words in an Alien Voice,' " 463.

22. Patricia Cox Miller, " 'Pleasure of the Text, Text of Pleasure': Eros and Language in Origen's Commentary on the *Song of Songs*," *Journal of the American Academy of Religion*, 54, no. 2 (1986): 247.

23. Mackey, *Peregrinations of the Word*, 54.

24. Conybeare, *The Irrational Augustine*, 188.

25. Augustine, *Confessions*, 11, esp. 11.14.17–31.41.

26. I consider the relationship between time, eternity, and language in the *Confessions* in my *Immemorial Silence*, chapter 4.

27. Elliot Wolfson writes, "We may conclude, therefore, that the Gospel of Truth preserves an alternative incarnational theologoumenon to the Prologue to John. Instead of the more familiar logocentric idea of the Word becoming flesh, the embodiment of Jesus is to be interpreted grammatologically as Christ's putting on the book of the living, a gesticulation that signifies the materialization of the imageless Father in the form of an image of the Son, the avowal of the nameless in the enunciation of the name, the etching of the book on the heart that beholds the form of the invisible in the utterance of the ineffable." "Inscribed in the Book of the Living," 266. Wolfson (256) warns against "dichotomizing the docetic and veridical perspectives" in this sign-obsessed text.

28. Augustine, *De catechizandis rudibus* 2.3, cited and translated in Markus, *Signs and Meanings*, 30. Available in English as "On the Catechising of the Uninstructed," accessed at http://www.newadvent.org/fathers/1303.htm.

29. For Socrates and for Plato (at least as they are usually understood) words, as objects of the senses, are only imperfect images of the perfect reality they endeavor to express. See Colish, *The Mirror of Language*, 9f.

30. Mackey, *Peregrinations of the Word*, 11.

31. P. C. Miller, " 'Words in an Alien Voice,' " 473.

32. Williams, "Language, Reality and Desire in Augustine's *De Doctrina*," 148.

33. For much more on desire and articulation, see "Fold," in my *Word Made Skin*, 91–114.

34. Mackey, *Peregrinations of the Word*, 9.

35. P. C. Miller, *The Poetry of Thought in Late Antiquity*, 248.

36. Mackey, *Peregrinations of the Word*, 53.

37. In the Nag Hammadi text "Trimorphic Protennoia," the redeemer declares, "I am a softly resounding voice. I exist from the first. I am in the silence that surrounds every one of them. It is the hidden voice that is in me." Anonymous, "Three Forms of First Thought," trans. John D. Turner, in *The Nag Hammadi Scriptures*, ed. Marvin Meyer (New York: Harper, 2007), 721.

38. D. Moody Smith, *Abingdon New Testament Commentary: John* (Nashville: Abingdon Press, 1999), 63.

39. Cf. Wolfson: "The first book that God writes is the world and the second the Torah. [Wolfson here cites the Hasidic master R. Zadoq.] This statement implies, in a quintessentially Jewish manner, that God's first book, the text of the cosmos, requires a commentary, Scripture, and that commentary, we can well imagine, engenders other commentaries that not God but human beings create in a seemingly endless effort to reveal the hidden depths concealed in the original tracts of God's writings that make up the universe. . . . In perfectly good Derridean fashion we may say that the way back leads not to an original truth but rather to an origin that is a text that needs to be interpreted by another text." Elliot R. Wolfson, "From Sealed Book to Open Text: Time, Memory, and Narrativity in Kabbalistic Hermeneutics," in *Interpreting Judaism in a Postmodern Age*, ed. Steven Kepnes (New York: New York University Press, 1996), 145; cited in Wolfson, "Assaulting the Border," 497–98.

40. Wolfson, "Inscribed in the Book of the Living," 251.

41. Elliot R. Wolfson, "The Body in the Text: A Kabbalistic Theory of Embodiment," *The Jewish Quarterly Review* 95, no. 3 (Summer 2005): 482. Wolfson notes that there is a fuller discussion of this point in his "Judaism and Incarnation."

42. Rist, *Augustine*, 34.

43. Ibid., 36.

44. Catherine Brown, "Love Letters," 583; citing Gertrude Stein, "Words That Are Coming Out," in *Lectures in America* (New York: Random House, 1935), 211.

45. P. C. Miller, *The Poetry of Thought in Late Antiquity*, 129. Miller cites Origen's commentary on the *Song of Songs*, 3.8, 3.6. Available in English as Origen, *The Song of Songs, Commentary and Homilies*, trans. R. P. Lawson (New York: The Newman Press, 1957).

46. P. C. Miller, "'Pleasure of the Text, Text of Pleasure,'" 241–42.

47. Giorgio Agamben connects this meta-meaning to language itself. He writes: "If the theological tradition has . . . understood revelation as something that human reason cannot know on its own, this can only mean the following: the content of revelation is not a truth that can be expressed in the form of linguistic propositions about a being (even about a supreme being), but is, instead, a truth that concerns language itself, the very fact that language (and therefore knowledge) exists." Giorgio Agamben, *Potentialities: Collected Essays in Philosophy*, ed. and trans. Daniel Heller-Roazen (Stanford, Calif.: Stanford University Press, 1999), 40. He adds, "there is a being whose nomination implies its existence, and that being is language" (41). Cf. Charles Sanders Peirce, as cited by Umberto Eco: "Now the Sign and the Explanation together make up another Sign, and since the explanation will be a Sign, it will probably require an additional explanation, which taken together with the already enlarged Sign will make a still larger Sign; and proceeding in the same way, we shall, or should, ultimately reach a Sign of itself, containing its own explanation and those of all its significant parts." Peirce, *Collected Papers*, 2:230. Eco remarks that Peirce fails to realize here that "the final Sign of which he speaks is not really a sign, but is the entire semantic field as the structure connecting and correlating signs with each other." Thus we read in structuralist terms a curious echo of ancient language mysticisms, whether in the image of the sign that is sign of itself or the image of a relation of all relations. Umberto Eco, *A Theory of Semiotics* (Bloomington: University of Indiana Press, 1976), 2.7.1.

48. Colish, *The Mirror of Language*, 26.

49. For Augustine, these are the spaces of silence in which meaning is gathered. Besides the discussion in *Confessions*, which goes along with the discussion of time in the second half of book 11, see his Tractate I on the gospel of John, par. 8: "What, then, is that in your heart, when you think of a certain substance, living, eternal, all-powerful, infinite, everywhere present, everywhere whole, nowhere shut in? When you think of these qualities, this is the word concerning God in your heart. But is this that sound which consists of four letters and two syllables? Therefore, whatever things are spoken and pass away are sounds, are letters, are syllables. His word which sounds passes away; but that which the sound signified, and was in the speaker as he thought of it, and in the hearer as he understood it, that remains while the sounds pass away." "Tractates on the Gospel of John," trans. John Gibb, in *Nicene and Post-Nicene Fathers*, series I, vol. 7, ed. Philip Schaff (Buffalo, N.Y.: Christian Literature Publishing Co., 1888). Online edition by Kevin Knight, 2008; accessed at http://www.newadvent.org/fathers/170101.htm.

Wolfson draws our attention to the graphic spaces of the "messianic Torah composed of the white spaces in which the letters are invisible." ("Assaulting the

Border," 492n27). In writing as well as in speaking, absence is needed for meaning to present itself.

50. Mackey, *Peregrinations of the Word*, 75.

51. The phrase is popularized by Roland Barthes in his essay "The Death of the Author," *Aspen* 5–6 (Fall-Winter 1967), accessed at http://www.ubu.com /aspen/aspen5and6/threeEssays.html#barthes. I have not been able to locate the page numbers for the original publication.

52. Ibid.

53. Mackey notes that, for Bonaventure (another Christian Neoplatonist): "We circumscribe God in tautologies, themselves figures of speech in this context. For what is affirmed in these tautologies is not the content intended by subject and predicate but just the form of perfect self-identity. God is beyond representation save in that Word that is himself and in which he represents himself to himself." Mackey, *Peregrinations*, 140. Chrétien also cites Bonaventure: "It is through the same Word by which the Father says himself that he says all that he can say and all that can be said in divinity." (Quaestiones disputatae de mysterio Trinitatis, IV, 2, 8). In English as *Disputed Questions on the Mystery of the Trinity*, trans. Zachary Hayes (St. Bonaventure, N.Y.: Franciscan Institute, 1979). Cited in Chrétien, *The Ark of Speech*, 141.

54. Nicholas Woltersdorff offers an intriguing possibility here, suggesting that we might understand scripture not as written by God but as divinely appropriated discourse: "Some of the discourse appropriated will be divine discourse; that will be true for those passages which are a record of prophetic utterance. Some or all of the rest, though not a record of utterances in the name of God, may nonetheless have been produced under a unique form of divine supervision—inspiration, let us say. But not even that need be true of a given part for it to belong to God's book. All that is necessary for the whole to be God's book is that the human discourse it contains have been appropriated by God, as one single book, for God's discourse." Woltersdorff, *Divine Discourse*, 54.

55. "For wherever one thing is said with the intention that another may be understood, we have a figurative expression. . . . And when an expression of this sort occurs where it is customary to find it, there is no trouble in understanding it; when it occurs, however, where it is not customary, it costs labor to understand it, from some more, from some less." Augustine, *On Christian Doctrine*, 3.37.56.

56. Augustine, Tractate I on the Gospel of John, para. I.

57. See, e.g., Wolfson, "The Body in the Text," esp. 481–82, where Wolfson also notes several intriguing transformations between flesh and word in both traditions. He writes, "If I were to translate my thinking into contemporary aca-

demic discourse, I would put it this way: Pitched in the heartland of Christian faith, one encounters the logocentric belief in the incarnation of the word in the flesh of the person Jesus, whereas in the textual panorama of medeval kabbalah, the site of the incarnational insight is the onto-graphic inscripting of flesh into word and the consequent conversion of the carnal into the ethereal, luminous body, finally transposed into the *literal* body that is the letter, hyper-literally, the name that is the Torah."

58. I would likely have missed at least some of these references in my own reading; they are gathered with a great many more references in Wolfson's *Circle in the Square*, 51f. Wolfson notes there, "The fascination with God's writing can be traced to the Bible itself."

59. In Deuteronomy, it seems possible that the people *could* hear God, but the prospect is too frightening, and so they have Moses act as intermediary (5:4–5).

60. Wolfson also notes references to a similar book at Psalm 139:16 and to a divine curse that becomes a flying scroll at Zech. 5:1–4. *Circle in the Square*, 51.

61. Augustine writes: "You have heard, . . . O teachers of the law, the guardian of the law, but have not yet understood Him as the Lawgiver. What else does He signify to you when He writes with His finger on the ground? For the law was written with the finger of God; but written on stone because of the hard-hearted. The Lord now wrote on the ground, because he was seeking fruit." Tractates on the Gospel of John, (John 7:40–8:11), Tractate 33, Par. 5. Accessed at http://www.newadvent.org/fathers/1701033.htm.

62. "The loose connection of chapter 8 with the preceding narrative is underscored by the fact that most manuscripts, but not the most ancient, insert at the beginning the story of the woman caught in an act of adultery. . . . There is no question that it was not a part of the original Gospel. In fact, a few manuscripts place it elsewhere, for example, at the end of the Gospel or after Luke 21:38." Smith, *John*, 179.

63. George Aichele, "Reading Jesus Writing." *Biblical Interpretation* 12, no. 4 (2004): 366.

64. Ibid., 354.

65. See, for valuable historical background, Wolfson, "Inscribed in the Book of the Living," 265: "The symbol of the 'book of life' derives from the ancient Near Eastern idea of heavenly tablets upon which the gods would inscribe the destinies of human beings, [see Wolfson, *Language, Eros, Being: Kabbalistic Hermeneutics and Poetic Imagination* (New York: Fordham University Press, 2004), 516n80] a notion whose reverberations are well attested in later Jewish and Christian sources." Wolfson's notes cite Dan. 12:1; 1QH 1:24; 1 Enoch 47:3, 108:3; Jubilees 6:29,

31, 35; 30:19–23; Joseph and Aseneth 15:4; Babylonian Talmud, Rosh ha-Shanah 16b; L. Ginzberg, *Legends of the Jews* (Philadelphia: Jewish Publication Society of America, 1968), 6:55n284; "several passages from the book of Revelation"; Luke 10:20; Phil. 4:3; Odes of Solomon 9:11; Testament of Jacob 7:27; and "the passage from the Hymn of the Pearl preserved in Acts of Thomas." Wolfson takes up but goes beyond the qualified suggestion of Hans Jonas (*Gnostic Religions* [Boston: Beacon Press, 2001], 75n28) that there are probably Jewish sources for this idea of the "living book of the living" and argues that "that the more precise background for this idea is a Jewish conception of Christ as the incarnation of Torah, which is designated the 'living book of the living.' ... New meaning is given to this tradition by the identification of the book with the Son." Wolfson, "Inscribed in the Book of the Living," 265.

66. Ibid., 234–39.

67. Anonymous, "The Gospel of Truth," trans. Einar Thomassen and Marvin Meyer, in *The Nag Hammadi Scriptures*, ed. Marvin Meyer (New York: HarperCollins, 2007), 38.

68. Augustine, *Homilies on the Gospel of John*, I.8.

69. Wolfson, "Inscribed in the Book of the Living," 243–44.

70. Cf. the book of Revelation, in which only the one who will be slain is suited to take up the book and break its seals. Rev; 5:9.

71. "The Gospel of Truth," 38.

72. "The Gospel of Truth," 38.

73. Wolfson, "Inscribed in the Book of the Living," 268.

74. "The Gospel of Truth," 39.

75. Jorge Luis Borges, "The Library of Babel," in *Labyrinths: Selected Stories and Other Writings*, trans. and ed. Donald A. Yates and James E. Irby (New York: New Directions Publishing, 2007), 51–58.

76. Williams, "Language, Reality and Desire," 148.

77. Ibid., 141.

78. Ibid., 141, citing *De Doctrina Christianae*, I.12.

79. "The Gospel of Truth," 41.

80. Ibid., 39.

81. Ibid., 45. Wolfson points out that "the doctrine of the Son bearing the name of the Father" is "an idea whose roots stretch back to Second Temple Jewish reflections on the Tetragrammaton and the theophanic figures enclothed thereby" and is also "a central motif in early Christology, attested in several books of the New Testament (John 17:11; Rev 19:12–13, 16; Heb 1:4; Rom 10:13; Phil 2:9; Eph 1:21)." Wolfson cites S. M. McDonough, *YHWH at Patmos:*

Rev. 1:4 in Its Hellenistic and Early Jewish Setting (Tübingen: Mohr Siebeck, 1999), 58–122, and C. A. Gieschen, "The Divine Name in Ante-Nicene Christology," *Vigiliae Christianae* 57 (2003): 121–127. Wolfson, "Inscribed in the Book of the Living," 249–50.

82. "The Gospel of Truth," 39.

83. "The Gospel of Truth," 18.25–30.

84. See Socrates' second speech in the *Phaedrus*.

85. On such dreams, see Umberto Eco, *The Search for the Perfect Language* (Oxford: Blackwell, 1995).

86. Cf. Pseudo-Dionysius: "a Source which tells us about itself in the holy words of Scripture. . . . To those who fall away it is the voice calling, 'Come back!' and it is the power which raises them up again." *Divine Names*, in *Pseudo-Dionysius: The Complete Works*, 589b.

87. Mark Vessey, "Theory, or the Dream of the Book (Mallarmé to Blanchot)," in *The Early Christian Book*, ed. William E. Klingshirn and Linda Safran (Washington, D.C.: Catholic University of America Press, 2007), 272–73. Vessey cites James J. O'Donnell, "Bible," in *Augustine Through the Ages: An Encyclopedia*, ed. Allan D. Fitzgerald (Grand Rapids, Mich: William B. Eerdmans, 1999), 99; and Jacques Derrida, "'This Strange Institution Called Literature': An Interview with Jacques Derrida," in *Acts of Literature*, ed. Derek Attridge (London: Routledge, 1992), 42.

88. Conybeare, *The Irrational Augustine*, 189.

89. See Augustine, *On Christian Doctrine*, 2.4.5: "But because words pass away as soon as they strike upon the air, and last no longer than their sound, men have by means of letters formed signs of words. Thus the sounds of the voice are made visible to the eye."

90. Mackey, *Peregrinations of the Word*, 35.

91. Derrida, "Edmond Jabès and the Question of the Book," in *Writing and Difference*, 67.

92. Mackey, *Peregrinations of the Word*, 42.

93. Derrida, "Edmond Jabès and the Question of the Book," in *Writing and Difference*, 72.

94. Derrida, "Ellipsis," in *Writing and Difference*, 295.

95. Williams, "Language, Reality and Desire," 143.

96. Wolfson, "Inscribed in the Book of the Living," 249. See also 264: "The secret, amongst other things, bears the characteristic of being a matter that is preserved, for it is precisely that which is preserved that is transmitted as secret, the withholding that offers a promise of something everlasting; hence, the placing of esoteric in proximity to soteric."

In Place of a Conclusion: Thoughts on a Prior Possible

1. Nietzsche, *Beyond Good and Evil*, §277.

2. Calvin O. Schrag refers to Kierkegaard's *Works of Love* as well as to Levinas and Derrida to note the difficulty of conceptualizing such a trace. Calvin O. Schrag, *God as Otherwise than Being* (Evanston, Ill.: Northwestern University Press, 2002), 114. Søren Kierkegaard, *Works of Love*, trans. Howard Hong (New York: Harper Perennial, 2009).

3. Keller, *On the Mystery*, x.

4. Meister Eckhart, Sermon on Acts 9:8, in *Wandering Joy: Meister Eckhart's Mystical Philosophy*, ed. and trans. Reiner Shürmann (Great Barrington, Mass.: Lindisfarne Books, 2001), 122.

5. Meister Eckhart, Sermon 83, *Renovamini Spiritu*, in *Meister Eckhart: The Essential Sermons*, 206. This is only one example out of dozens; divine namelessness— sometimes the unnameability of the soul, too—is a recurrent theme in Eckhart's sermons.

6. Barthes argues that the only modifier for the "holophrase" "I love you" is the name: "I resist making the other pass through a syntax, a predication, a language (the sole Assumption of *I-love-you* is to apostrophize it, to give it the expansion of a first name: *Ariadne, I love you*, Dionysus says)." *A Lover's Discourse*, 148.

7. Derrida, "*Sauf le nom*," in *On the Name*, 76.

8. Pierre Klossowski, *The Baphomet*, trans. Sophie Hawkes and Stephen Sartarelli (New York: Marsilio Publishers, 1998). Klossowski writes in his notes on the text: "in a general way *The Baphomet* reflects my affinities with the great heresiarchs of Gnosticism (Valentinus, Basilides, Carpocrates)" (164).

9. This theme is frequent in the French thinkers influenced by Nietzsche; see, most obviously, Gilles Deleuze, *Difference and Repetition*, trans. Paul Patton (New York: Columbia University Press, 1994).

10. Cited and translated in Tracy McNulty, "Hospitality after the Death of God," *Diacritics* 35, no. 1 (Spring 2005): 91. From Pierre Klossowski, "Protase et apodose," *L'arc* 43 (1970): 10.

11. This notion of the name thus echoes Eckhart's claim that God is distinct from all things by being that which is not distinct from any thing, while all things are distinct from one another.

12. Catherine Keller argues for the mutuality of creation in Nicholas of Cusa, pointing out that Nicholas's reading, which celebrates the potentiality of divine and world together, goes against not only Thomas Aquinas's firm insistence on a God of pure act (see, e.g., *Summa Contra Gentiles*, trans. Anton Charles Pegis [Notre Dame, Ind: Notre Dame Press, 1991], 1.16) but also the Derridean

valorizing of the impossible over the merely possible, seen as the predictable. Keller, *The Cloud of the Impossible: Theological Entanglements*, forthcoming, §6.

13. This discussion is hard to condense, being spread across a number of Aristotle's works and shifting in focus according to those works' divergent interests. For some important instances, however, see *Metaphysics* bk. Theta, *Prior Analytics*, *De Interpretatione*, and several sections of the *Physics*.

14. These two laws, ~(p & ~p) and (p or ~p), are foundational in Aristotelian logic.

15. Aristotle, *De Interpretatione*, in *Categories* and *De Interpretatione*, trans. J. L. Ackrill (New York: Oxford University Press, 1975), 9.

16. For the basics, the Stanford Encyclopedia of Philosophy entry on modal logic is quite good: http://plato.stanford.edu/entries/logic-modal/.

17. Richard Kearney, *The God Who May Be* (Bloomington: Indiana University Press, 2001), 3.

18. Ibid., 4. Kearney adds on the same page: "God will be God at the eschaton. This is what is promised. But precisely because this promise is just that . . . and not an already accomplished possession, there is a free space gaping at the very core of divinity: the space of the possible. It is this divine gap which renders all things possible which would be otherwise impossible to us."

19. Ibid., 22. Kearney opposes this God of the promised future to the pure stable actuality of the Scholastics' God (23). Others argue that at least Thomas Aquinas, among the subtlest thinkers of Scholasticism, is actually closer to apophasis than he might seem. Denys Turner, for example, quotes *Summa Theologiae* I Q3, prol: "since we cannot know of God what he is, but what he is not, we cannot inquire into the how of God['s existence], but only into how he is not." Turner argues that there are apophatic elements even in the five famous causal "proofs" of God's existence. Turner, "Apophaticism, Idolatry," 27. Herbert McCabe thus summarizes Thomas's argument: "God must be incomprehensible to us precisely because he is creator of all that is and, as Aquinas puts it: outside the order of all beings. God therefore cannot be classified as any kind of being." McCabe argues that Thomas thought "that to prove the existence of God was not to understand God but simply to prove the existence of a mystery. His arguments for the existence of God are arguments to show that there are real questions to which we do not and cannot know the answer." Herbert McCabe, "Aquinas on the Trinity", in *Silence and the Word: Negative Theology and Incarnation*, ed. Oliver Davies and Denys Turner (Cambridge: Cambridge University Press, 2008), 76.

20. In this, as she notes, Keller follows and develops the line of thought opened by Frans Maas, "Divine Omnipotence in the View of Nicholas of Cusa,"

in *Conflict and Reconciliation: Perspectives on Nicholas of Cusa*, ed. Inigo Bocken (Leiden: Brill, 2004), 177–87.

21. Nicholas of Cusa, *Trialogus de possest*, in *A Concise Introduction to the Philosophy of Nicholas of Cusa*, ed. and trans. Jasper Hopkins (Minneapolis: University of Minnesota Press, 1978), 71.

22. Ibid., 79.

23. Ibid., 69.

24. Ibid., 71.

25. This is the somewhat controversial axiom S5 in modal logic, stating both that if something is possible, then it is necessarily possible, and that if something is possibly necessary, then it is necessary. This is more theologically relevant than it might seem, being central to Alvin Plantinga's twentieth-century reconception of Anselm's ontological proof for God's existence. See Alvin Plantinga, *The Nature of Necessity* (Oxford: Oxford University Press, 1974), 198–202.

26. Keller, *Cloud of the Impossible*, chap. 3, §7.

27. In Nicholas of Cusa, *Selected Spiritual Writings*, 56–69.

28. Keller, *Cloud of the Impossible*, chap. 3, §7.

29. Catherine Keller, "Good Power," presented at Yale Divinity School, 2007. Accessed at http://users.drew.edu/ckeller/essays-download.html. Not everyone reads possibility in a delightful sense. Giorgio Agamben writes: "For everyone a moment comes in which she or he must utter this 'I can' which does not refer to any certainty or specific capacity but is, nevertheless, absolutely demanding. Beyond all faculties, this 'I can' does not mean anything—yet it marks what is, for each of us, perhaps the hardest and bitterest experience possible: the experience of potentiality." *Potentialities*, 178.

30. Moreover, he shows this familiarity in the context we are considering. See, e.g., the mention of categories in Nicholas of Cusa, *de possest*, 71.

31. Ibid., 77.

32. See Keller, "Good Power," 14.

33. Meister Eckhart, Sermon on Ecclesiasticus 25:30, trans. C. Field, accessed at http://www.global.org/Pub/Eckhart_4.asp. Keller argues for thinking the divine as the very relation of seeing and notes that Cusanus's *de visione dei*, the vision of God, is a reversible genitive, in keeping with Nicholas's sense that to see God is to be seen by God, and vice versa. *Cloud of the Impossible*, chap. 3, §3.

34. Nicholas of Cusa, *de possest*, 71.

35. Though this formulation is made famous by Heidegger's use of it in his discussions of Nietzsche, it comes from Nietzsche himself. As John Sallis points out, it appears as early as a sketch for *The Birth of Tragedy:* "My philosophy an *inverted Platonism*: the further removed from true being, the more beautiful,

the better it is." Cited and translated in John Sallis, "Nietzsche's Platonism," in *Nietzsche: Critical Assessments*, ed. Daniel W. Conway (London: Routledge, 1998), 293.

36. The physical explanation appears most concisely in Friedrich Nietzsche, *The Will to Power* (posthumous collection), trans. W. Kaufmann and R. J. Hollingdale (New York: Random House, 1968), §1066.

37. Arthur Schopenhauer, *The World as Will and Representation*, trans. E. F. J. Payne (Mineola, N.Y.: Dover, 1966).

38. See, e.g., Marcus Aurelius, *Meditations*, trans. G. M. A. Grube (Indianapolis: Hackett Publishing, 1983), Meditation 14, which presents the idea of return as something already widely thought. Marcus undoubtedly derives his version from earlier mentions by Empedocles and the influential teacher Zeno of Citium. See Empedocles, *The Proem of Empedocles' Peri Physios: Towards a New Edition of all the Fragments—Thirty-one Fragments*, trans. N. van der Ben (Amsterdam: B. R. Gruner, 1975). No writings from Zeno survive.

39. Pierre Klossowski, *Nietzsche and the Vicious Circle*, trans. Daniel W. Smith (Chicago: University of Chicago Press, 1998), 56: "the character of a revelation—as a *sudden unveiling*."

40. Cf. Deleuze: the eternal return "is repetition by excess which leaves intact nothing of the default or the becoming-equal. It is itself new, complete novelty." *Difference and Repetition*, 90.

41. Chrétien, *The Ark of Speech*, 145.

42. Pierre Klossowski, *Such a Deathly Desire*, trans. Russell Ford (Albany: State University of New York Press, 2007), 120.

43. Friedrich Nietzsche, Letter to Peter Gast, August 14, 1881. In *Selected Letters of Friedrich Nietzsche*, ed. Christopher Middleton (Indianapolis: Hackett Publishing, 1996), 178.

44. Pranger, *Eternity's Ennui*, 305.

45. Klossowski, *Nietzsche and the Vicious Circle*, 57.

46. Ibid.

47. Mark D. Jordan, "Liturgies of Repetition: A Preface to the Prologue of the *Baphomet*," *Studies in the Literary Imagination* 41, no. 2 (2009): 64.

48. Cited and translated in James, *Pierre Klossowski*, 25, from Klossowski, "Qui est mon prochain?" *Esprit*, December 1938, 410.

49. James, *Pierre Klossowski*, 25. From "Qui est mon prochain?" 410.

50. James, *Pierre Klossowski*, 1.

51. Friedrich Nietzsche, *The Anti-Christ*, trans. R. J. Hollingdale (New York: Penguin Books, 1977), § 33, my emphasis.

52. Klossowski, *Such a Deathly Desire*, 10.

53. Klossowski, *Nietzsche and the Vicious Circle*, 71.

54. Jordan, "Liturgies of Repetition," 74: "This heresy exactly matches Klossowski's description of the lived experience of eternal return in his book on Nietzsche (see *Nietzsche*, esp. 93–112)."

55. Teresa of Avila, *The Collected Works of St. Teresa of Avila*, trans. Kieran Kavanaugh and Otilio Rodríguez (Washington, D.C.: ICS Publications, 1976). Cited in Luis M. Girón-Negrón, "Dionysian Thought in Sixteenth-Century Spanish Mystical Theology," *Modern Theology* 24, no. 4 (October 2008): 697.

56. Keller, *Cloud of the Impossible*, chap. 3, §1.

57. Conybeare, *The Irrational Augustine*, 185.

58. Elliot Wolfson points out "the age-old assumption that matter in its essential materiality lacks any definitive characteristic of its own, comprising instead the potential of every being that is to come to be." *Open Secret*, 101.

59. Conybeare, *The Irrational Augustine*, 190.

60. James, *Pierre Klossowski*, 53, cites Klossowski, *Sade Mon Prochain* (Paris: Seuil, 1947), 47. In English as *Sade My Neighbor*, 140: "The self dies with God."

61. To continue: "Klossowski insists that God is the *sole* guarantor of the identity of the self and of its substantive base. . . . One cannot conserve the self without also holding onto God." Gilles Deleuze, *The Logic of Sense*, trans. M. Lester and C. Stivale (New York: Columbia University Press 1990), 294. Cf. Klossowski: "The emphasis must be placed on the loss of a given identity. The 'death of God' (the God who guarantees the identity of the responsible self) opens up the soul to all its possible identities." *Nietzsche and the Vicious Circle*, 57.

62. Pseudo-Dionysius, *The Complete Works*, 56. Cited in Keller, *Face of the Deep*, 213.

63. See, e.g., Friedrich Nietzsche, *Thus Spoke Zarathustra*, trans. Graham Parkes (Oxford: Oxford University Press, 2005), "The Second Dance-Song;" "The Drunken Song" §§ 9–12.

64. Klossowski, *Nietzsche and the Vicious Circle*, 72.

65. Keller likewise observes that certainty would be no cause for optimism. *Cloud of the Impossible*, chap. 3, §8.

66. Nietzsche, *The Gay Science*, §337. Also cited in Klossowski, *Such a Deathly Desire*, 7.

67. Cf. Agamben, *Potentialities*, 181. Following Aristotle, *Metaphysics*, bk. Theta, 418–19, Agamben writes: "if potentiality were, for example, only the potentiality for vision and if it existed only as such in the actuality of light, we could never experience darkness (nor hear silence, in the case of the potentiality to hear). But human beings can, instead, see shadows . . . they can experience darkness: they

have the *potential* not to see, the *possibility of privation*. . . . The greatness—also the abyss—of human potentiality is that it is first of all potential not to act, *potential for darkness*. . . . Radical evil is not this or that bad deed but the potentiality for darkness. And yet this potentiality is also the potentiality for light."

68. Wolfson, *Open Secret*, 95.

Bibliography

Agamben, Giorgio. *Potentialities: Collected Essays in Philosophy.* Edited and translated by Daniel Heller-Roazen. Stanford, Calif.: Stanford University Press, 1999.

Aichele, George. "Reading Jesus Writing." *Biblical Interpretation* 12, no. 4 (2004): 353–68.

Alighieri, Dante. *De vulgare eloquentia.* Edited by P. Rajna. Florence: Le Monnier, 1896.

Alison, James. "The Gay Thing." In *Queer Theology*, edited by Gerard Loughlin, 50–62. Malden, Mass.: Blackwell, 2002.

Alston, William. "Perceiving God." *The Journal of Philosophy* 83 (1986): 655–66.

Ambrose of Milan, *De mysteriis.* Accessed at http://www.crossroadsinitiative.com /library_article/657/On_the_Mysteries_St_Ambrose_on_the_Sacraments .html.

Angelus Silesius. *The Cherubinic Wanderer.* Translated by Maria Shrady. Mahwah, N.J.: Paulist Press, 1986. Original accessed at *Der cherubinische Wandersmann* at http://www.mscperu.org/deutsch/cherub/cheru401.htm.

Anonymous. "The Gospel of Thomas." Translated by Marvin Meyer. In *The Nag Hammadi Scriptures*, edited by Marvin Meyer, 138–53. New York: Harper-Collins, 2007.

———. "The Gospel of Truth." Translated by Einar Thomassen and Marvin Meyer. In *The Nag Hammadi Scriptures*, edited by Marvin Meyer, 31–48. New York: Harper-Collins, 2007.

———. "Three Forms of First Thought." Translated by John D. Turner. In *The Nag Hammadi Scriptures*, edited by Marvin Meyer, 715–35. New York: Harper-Collins, 2007.

Aristotle. *Categories* and *De interpretatione*. Translated by J. L. Ackrill. New York: Oxford University Press, 1975.

———. *Metaphysics*. Translated by Hugh Lawson-Tancred. New York: Penguin Books, 1998.

———. *Nicomachean Ethics*. Translated by Terence Irwin. Indianapolis: Hackett Publishing, 1999.

———. *Physics*. Translated with commentary by Daniel Graham. Oxford: Oxford University Press, 1999.

———. *Prior Analytics*. Translated by Robin Smith. Indianapolis: Hackett Publishing, 1989.

Athanasius. *Life of Antony*. In *Athanasius: Select Works and Letters*, edited by Philip Schaff and Henry Wace. *Nicene and Post-Nicene Fathers*, series 2, vol. 4. Peabody, Mass.: Hendrickson Publishers, 1994. Accessed at http://www.fordham.edu/halsall/basis/vita-antony.html.

———. "On the Incarnation of the Word." Translated by Archibald Robertson. In *Christology of the Late Fathers*, edited by E. R. Hardy. 3:55–110. Philadelphia: Westminster Press, 1954.

Augustine. *City of God*. Translated by Henry Bettenson. New York: Penguin Books, 2003.

———. *Confessions*. Translated by Henry Chadwick. Oxford: Oxford University Press, 1991.

———. *De musica*. In *Patrologia latina*, vol. 32, edited by J. P. Migne, 1081–1100. Paris: Garnier, 1844–1904.

———. *De ordine*. In *Corpus Christianorum Series Latina*, vol.29. edited by W. M. Green. Turnhout: Brepols, 1970.

———. *Expositions on the Psalms*. Translated by J. E. Tweed. In *Nicene and Post-Nicene Fathers*, series 1, vol. 8, edited by Philip Schaff. Buffalo, N.Y.: Christian Literature Publishing Co., 1888. Online edition by Kevin Knight, 2009. Accessed at http://www.newadvent.org/fathers/1801.htm.

———. *Homilies on the Gospel of John 1–40*. Translated by Edmund Hill, O.P. Hyde Park, N.Y.: New City Press, 2009.

———. "On the Catechising of the Uninstructed." Translated by S. D. F. Salmond. In *Nicene and Post-Nicene Fathers*, series 1, vol. 3, edited by Philip Schaff. Buffalo, N.Y.: Christian Literature Publishing Co., 1887. Online edition by Kevin Knight, 2009. Accessed at http://www.newadvent.org/fathers/1303.htm.

————. *On Christian Doctrine*. Translated by D. W. Robertson, Jr. New York: Prentice Hall, 1958.

————. "On the Catechising of the Uninstructed." Translated by S. D. F. Salmond. In *Nicene and Post-Nicene Fathers*, series I, vol. 3, edited by Philip Schaff. Buffalo, N.Y.: Christian Literature Publishing Co., 1887. Online edition by Kevin Knight, 2009. Accessed at http://www.newadvent.org/fathers/1303 .htm.

————. *On the Profit of Believing*. Translated by C. L. Cornish. In *Nicene and Post-Nicene Fathers*, series I, vol. 3, edited by Philip Schaff. Buffalo, N.Y.: Christian Literature Publishing Co., 1887. Online edition by Kevin Knight, 2009. Accessed at http://www.newadvent.org/fathers/1306.htm.

————. "The Predestination of the Saints." In *Four Anti-Pelagian Writings*, translated by John Arthur Mourant and William J. Collinge, 218–70. Washington, D.C.: Catholic University of America Press, 1992.

————. Sermon 30 on the New Testament (Matt. 17:19). Translated by R. G. MacMullen. In *Nicene and Post-Nicene Fathers*, series I, vol. 6, edited by Philip Schaff. Buffalo, N.Y.: Christian Literature Publishing Co., 1888. Online edition by Kevin Knight, 2009. Accessed at http://www.newadvent.org/fathers /160330.htm.

————. *The Teacher*. In *Against the Academicians and The Teacher*, translated by Peter King. Indianapolis: Hackett Publishing, 1995.

————. "To Simplician: On Various Questions." In *Augustine: Earlier Writings*, edited by John H. S. Burleigh, 370–406. Philadelphia: The Westminster Press, 1953. Online edition at http://www.romancatholicism.org/jansenism/ augustine-simplician.htm.

————. "Tractates on the Gospel of John." Translated by John Gibb. In *Nicene and Post-Nicene Fathers*, series I, vol. 7, edited by Philip Schaff. Buffalo, N.Y.: Christian Literature Publishing Co., 1888. Online edition by Kevin Knight, 2008. Accessed at http://www.newadvent.org/fathers/1701.htm.

————. *The Trinity*. In *Nicene and Post-Nicene Fathers*, series I, vol. 3, edited by Philip Schaff. New York: Cosimo Classics, 2007.

————. *De vera religione*. In *Corpus Christianorum Series Latina*, 32. Edited by K. D. Daur and J. Martin. Turnhout: Brepols, 1962.

Austin, J. L. *How to Do Things with Words*. Edited by J. O. Urmson and Marina Sbisà. Cambridge: Harvard University Press, 1975.

Babcock, William S. "The Human and the Angelic Fall: Will and Moral Agency in Augustine's *City of God*." In *Augustine: From Rhetor to Theologian*, edited by Joanne McWilliam, 133–50. Waterloo, Ontario: Wilfred Laurier Press, 1992.

Barbery, Muriel. *The Elegance of the Hedgehog.* Translated by Alison Anderson. New York: Europa Editions, 2008.

Barth, J. Robert, S.J. *Coleridge and Christian Doctrine.* New York: Fordham University Press, 1987.

Barth, Karl. *Dogmatics in Outline.* New York: Harper and Row, 1959.

Barthes, Roland. "The Death of the Author." *Aspen* 5–6 (Fall-Winter 1967). Accessed at http://www.ubu.com/aspen/aspen5and6/threeEssays.html#barthes.

———. *A Lover's Discourse: Fragments.* Translated by Richard Howard. New York: Hill and Wang, 1979.

———. *The Pleasure of the Text.* Translated by Richard Miller. New York: Hill and Wang, 1975.

Bataille, Georges. *Inner Experience.* Translated by Leslie Anne Boldt. Albany: State University of New York Press, 1988.

Baudrillard, Jean. *Seduction.* Translated by Brian Singer. New York: St. Martin's Press, 1991.

Benjamin, Walter. *Reflections: Essays, Aphorisms, Autobiographical Writings.* Edited by Peter Demetz. Translated by Edmund Jephcott. New York: Schocken Books, 1978.

Bentham, Jeremy. *Utilitarianism and Other Essays.* New York: Penguin Books, 1987.

Bergo, Bettina. "Ontology, Transcendence, and Immanence in Emmanuel Levinas's Philosophy." *Research in Phenomenology* 35 (2005): 141–77.

Bernet, Rudolf. "The Encounter with the Stranger: Two Interpretations of the Vulnerability of the Skin." In *The Face of the Other and the Trace of God: Essays on the Philosophy of Emmanuel Levinas,* edited by Jeffrey Bloechl, 43–61. New York: Fordham University Press, 2000.

Bernstein, Susan David. "Confessing Lacan." In *Seduction and Theory: Readings of Gender, Representation, and Rhetoric,* edited by Dianne Hunter, 195–213. Champaign: University of Illinois Press, 1989.

Bishop, John. *Believing by Faith: An Essay in the Epistemology and Ethics of Religious Belief.* Oxford: Oxford University Press, 2007.

Blanchot, Maurice. *The Blanchot Reader.* Edited by Michael Holland. Oxford: Blackwell, 1995.

———. *Friendship.* Translated by Elizabeth Rottenberg. Stanford, Calif.: Stanford University Press, 1997.

———. *The Infinite Conversation.* Translated by Susan Hanson. Minneapolis: University of Minnesota Press, 1993.

———. *Lautréamont and Sade.* Translated by Stuart Kendall and Michelle Kendall. Stanford, Calif.: Stanford University Press, 2004.

———. *The Space of Literature*. Translated by Ann Smock. Lincoln: University of Nebraska Press, 1989.

———. *The Step Not Beyond*. Translated by Lycette Nelson. Albany: State University of New York Press, 1992.

———. *The Unavowable Community*. Translated by Pierre Joris. Barrytown, N.Y.: Station Hill Press, 1988.

———. *The Writing of the Disaster*. Translated by Ann Smock. Lincoln: University of Nebraska Press, 1995.

Bloch, R. Howard. *Etymologies and Genealogies: A Literary Anthropology of the French Middle Ages*. Chicago: University of Chicago Press, 1983.

Bloechl, Jeffrey. "Ethics as First Philosophy and Religion." In *The Face of the Other and the Trace of God: Essays on the Philosophy of Emmanuel Levinas*, edited by Jeffrey Bloechl, 130–64. New York: Fordham University Press, 2000.

Boff, Leonardo, O.F.M. "The Sacrament of Marriage." In *The Sacraments: Readings in Contemporary Sacramental Theology*, edited by Michael J. Taylor, S.J., 193–203. Staten Island, N.Y.: Alba House, 1981.

Bonaventure. *Disputed Questions on the Mystery of the Trinity*. Translated by Zachary Hayes. St. Bonaventure, N.Y.: Franciscan Institute, 1979.

Borges, Jorge Luis. "The Library of Babel." In *Labyrinths: Selected Stories and Other Writings*, translated and edited by Donald A. Yates and James E. Irby, 51–58. New York: New Directions Publishing, 2007.

Bourke, David, ed. *St. Thomas Aquinas: Summa Theologiae, 3a.60–65*. Cambridge: Cambridge University Press, 2006.

Brown, Catherine. "Love Letters from Beatus of Liebana to Modern Philologists." *Modern Philology* 106, no. 4 (May 2009): 579–600.

Brown, Peter. *The Body and Society: Men, Women, and Sexual Renunciation in Early Christianity*. New York: Columbia University Press, 1988.

Burrus, Virginia. "Praying Is Joying: Musings on Love in Evagrius Ponticus." In *Toward a Theology of Eros*, edited by Virginia Burrus and Catherine Keller, 194–204. New York: Fordham University Press, 2006.

———. "A Saint of One's Own: Emmanuel Levinas, Eliezer ben Hyrcanus, and Eulalia of Mérida." *L'Esprit Créateur* 50, no. 1 (Spring 2010): 6–20.

———. *Saving Shame: Saints, Martyrs, and Other Abject Subjects*. Philadelphia: University of Pennsylvania Press, 2008.

Burrus, Virginia, Mark D. Jordan, and Karmen MacKendrick. *Seducing Augustine: Bodies, Desires, Confessions*. New York: Fordham University Press, 2010.

Calvin, John. *Institutes of the Christian Religion*. Translated by Henry Beveridge. Edinburgh: Calvin Translation Society, 1845.

Carse, James. "Religion Is Poetry." Interview in *Salon*, July 21, 2008. Accessed at http://www.salon.com/books/atoms_eden/2008/07/21/james_carse /index1.html.

Casarella, Peter. "Cusanus on Dionysius: The Turn to Speculative Theology." *Modern Theology* 23, no. 4 (October 2008): 667–78.

Cauchi, Mark. "The Infinite Supplicant." In *The Phenomenology of Prayer*, edited by Bruce Ellis Benson and Norman Wirzba, 217–31. New York: Fordham University Press, 2005.

Celan, Paul. *Collected Prose*. Translated by Rosmarie Waldrop. Riverdale-on-Hudson, N.Y.: Sheepmeadow Press, 1986.

Certeau, Michel de. *Heterologies: Discourse on the Other*. Translated by Brian Massumi. Minneapolis: University of Minnesota Press, 1986.

Chauvet, Louis Marie. *Symbol and Sacrament: A Sacramental Reinterpretation of Christian Existence*. Collegeville, Minn.: Liturgical Press, 1995.

Chrétien, Jean-Louis. *The Ark of Speech*. Translated by Andrew Brown. London: Routledge, 2003.

———. *The Call and the Response*. Translated by Anne Davenport. New York: Fordham University Press, 2004.

———. *The Unforgettable and the Unhoped For*. Translated by Jeffrey Bloechl. New York: Fordham University Press, 2002.

———. "The Wounded Word." In *Phenomenology and the "Theological Turn": The French Debate*, by Dominique Janicaud, Jean-François Courtine, Jean-Louis Chrétien, Michel Henry, Jean-Luc Marion, and Paul Ricoeur, 147–75. New York: Fordham University Press, 2000.

Cicero. *On the Best Style of Orators*. Translated by C. D. Yonge. Lawrence, Kans.: Digireads.com, 2009.

Claudel, Paul. *Paul Claudel interroge le Cantique des cantiques*. Paris: Egloff, 1948.

Cobb, John B., Jr. *Grace and Responsibility: A Wesleyan Theology for Today*. Nashville: Abingdon, 1995.

Colish, Marcia. *The Mirror of Language: A Study in the Medieval Theory of Knowledge*. Lincoln: University of Nebraska Press, 1983.

Conybeare, Catherine. *The Irrational Augustine*. Oxford: Oxford University Press, 2006.

Cowell, Andrew. *At Play in the Tavern: Signs, Coins, Bodies in the Middle Ages*. Ann Arbor: University of Michigan Press, 1999.

Cox, Harvey. *The Future of Faith*. New York: HarperCollins, 2009.

Crehan, Joseph. *Early Christian Baptism and the Creed: A Study in Ante-Nicene Theology*. London: Burnes Oates & Washbourne, 1950.

Davies, Oliver. "Soundings: Towards a Theological Poetics of Silence." In *Silence and the Word: Negative Theology and Incarnation*, edited by Oliver Davies and Denys Turner, 201–22. Cambridge: Cambridge University Press, 2002.

Deleuze, Gilles. *Difference and Repetition*. Translated by Paul Patton. New York: Columbia University Press, 1994.

———. *The Fold: Leibniz and the Baroque*. Translated by Tom Conley. Minneapolis: University of Minnesota Press, 1992.

———. *Kant's Critical Philosophy: The Doctrine of the Faculties*. Translated by Hugh Tomlinson and Barbara Habberjam. Minneapolis: University of Minnesota Press, 1985.

———. *The Logic of Sense*. Translated by M. Lester and C. Stivale. New York: Columbia University Press, 1990.

Derrida, Jacques. *Acts of Literature*. Edited by Derek Attridge. London: Routledge, 1992.

———. "How to Avoid Speaking:: Denials." In *Languages of the Unsayable: the Play of Negativity in Literature and Literary Theory*, edited by Sanford Budick and Wolfgang Iser, 3–70. New York: Columbia University Press, 1989.

———. *On the Name*. Edited by Thomas Dutoit. Translated by David Wood, John P. Leavey, Jr., and Ian McLeod. Stanford, Calif.: Stanford University Press, 1995.

———. "Point de folie—Maintenant l'architecture." Translated by K. Linker. In *Architecture Theory since 1968*, edited by K. Michael Hays, 566–81. Cambridge: MIT Press, 1998.

———. *The Truth in Painting*. Translated by Geoffrey Bennington and Ian McLeod. Chicago: University of Chicago Press, 1987.

———. *Writing and Difference*. Translated by Alan Bass. London: Routledge, 1978.

Dillon, John M. "An Ethic for the Late Antique Sage." In *The Cambridge Companion to Plotinus*, edited by Lloyd P. Gerson, 315–35. Cambridge: Cambridge University Press, 1996.

Dionysius the Areopagite. *Exaiphnès esti to par'elpida*. In *Patrologia grecque*, vol. 3. Paris: J. P. Migne, 1857–1866.

———. *Pseudo-Dionysius: The Complete Works*. Translated by Colm Luibheid. Mahwah, N.J.: Paulist Press, 1987.

duBois, Paige. *Torture and Truth*. New York: Routledge, 1991.

Eckhart, Johannes. *Meister Eckhart: The Essential Sermons, Commentaries, Treatises and Defense*. Translated by Edmund Colledge and Bernard McGinn. Mahwah, N.J.: Paulist Press, 1981.

————. Sermon on Acts 9:8. In *Wandering Joy: Meister Eckhart's Mystical Philosophy*, edited and translated by Reiner Shürmann, 119–28. Great Barrington, Mass: Lindisfarne Books, 2001.

————. Sermon on Ecclesiasticus 25:30. Translated by C. Field. Accessed at http://www.global.org/Pub/Eckhart_4.asp.

Eco, Umberto. *The Search for the Perfect Language*. Oxford: Blackwell, 1995.

————. *Semiotics and the Philosophy of Language*. Bloomington: Indiana University Press, 1984.

————. *A Theory of Semiotics*. Bloomington: Indiana University Press, 1976.

Ellul, Jacques. *Living Faith: Belief and Doubt in a Perilous World*. Translated by Peter Heinegg. San Francisco: Harper and Row, 1983.

Empedocles. *The Proem of Empedocles' Peri Physios: Towards a New Edition of All the Fragments—Thirty-one Fragments*. Translated by N. van der Ben. Amsterdam: B. R. Gruner, 1975.

Eriugena, John Scotus. *Periphyseon*. Edited by I. P. Sheldon-Williams. Dublin: Dublin Institute For Advanced Studies, 1972.

Foucault, Michel. *The Order of Things: An Archaeology of the Human Sciences*. New York: Vintage Books, 1994.

————. "The Prose of Actaeon." Introductory essay to Pierre Klossowski, *The Baphomet*, translated by Sophie Hawkes and Stephen Sartarelli, xix–xxxviii. New York: Marsilio Publishers, 1998.

Franke, William. "Edmond Jabès or the Endless Self-Emptying of Language in the Name of God." *Literature and Theology* 22, no. 1 (March 2008): 102–17.

————. "The Singular and the Other at the Limits of Language in the Post-Holocaust Poetry of Edmond Jabès and Paul Celan." *New Literary History* 36, no. 4 (2005): 621–38.

Galli, Barbara E. *Franz Rosenzweig and Juhuda Halevi: Translating, Translations, and Translators*. Montreal: McGill-Queen's University Press, 1995.

Gallop, Jane. *The Daughter's Seduction: Feminism and Psychoanalysis*. Ithaca, N.Y.: Cornell University Press, 1984.

Gellrich, Jesse M. *The Idea of the Book in the Middle Ages: Language Theory, Mythology, and Fiction*. Ithaca, N.Y.: Cornell University Press, 1985.

Gibbs, Robert. "The Disincarnation of the Word: The Trace of God in Reading Scripture." In *The Exorbitant: Emmanuel Levinas Between Jews and Christians*, edited by Kevin Hart and Michael A. Signer, 32–51. New York: Fordham University Press, 2010.

————. "Suspicions of Suffering." In *Christianity in Jewish Terms*, edited by Tivka Frymer-Kensky, David Novak, Peter Ochs, David Fox Sandmel, and Michael A. Signer, 221–29. Boulder, Colo.: Westview Press, 2000.

Gieschen, C. A. "The Divine Name in Ante-Nicene Christology." *Vigiliae Christianae* 57 (2003): 121–27.

Ginzberg, L. *Legends of the Jews*. Philadelphia: Jewish Publication Society of America, 1968.

Girón-Negrón, Luis M. "Dionysian Thought in Sixteenth-Century Spanish Mystical Theology." *Modern Theology* 24, no. 4 (October 2008): 693–706.

Haag, Pamela. *Consent: Sexual Rights and the Transformation of American Liberalism*. Ithaca, N.Y.: Cornell University Press, 1999.

Harl, Marguerite. "Origène et la sémantique du langue biblique." *Vigilae Christianae* 26 (1972): 161–88.

Harrison, Carol. *Beauty and Revelation in the Thought of St. Augustine*. Oxford: Oxford University Press, 1992.

Hart, Kevin. "The Experience of the Kingdom of God." In *The Experience of God: A Postmodern Response*, edited by Kevin Hart and Barbara Wall, 71–86. New York: Fordham University Press, 2005.

———. "God and the Sublime." In *God Out of Place*, edited by Yves de Maeseneer, 33–38. Utrecht: Ars Disputandi, 2005.

———. "Paul and the Reduction." Interview with Lee Cole, *Journal of Philosophy and Scripture*. Accessed at http://www.philosophyandscripture.org/Issue2-2/Hart/hart.html.

Hawkins, Beth. *Reluctant Theologians: Kafka, Celan, Jabès*. New York: Fordham University Press, 2003.

Hegel, Georg Wilhelm Friedrich. *Lectures on the History of Philosophy*, vol. I. Translated by E. S. Haldane. London: Kegan Paul, Trench, Tübner and Co., Ltd., 1892.

Heidegger, Martin. *Being and Time*. Translated by John Macquarrie and Edward Robinson. New York: Harper and Row, 1962.

———. "Plato's Doctrine of Truth." In *Philosophy in the Twentieth Century,*. edited by William Barrett and Henry D. Aiken, 251–70. New York: Random House, 1962.

Hölderlin, Friedrich. *Friedrich Hölderlin: Selected Poems and Fragments*. Translated by Michael Hamburger. New York: Penguin Books, 1994.

Horkheimer, Max, and Theodor W. Adorno. *Dialectic of Enlightenment: Philosophical Fragments*. Translated by Edmund Jephcott. Stanford, Calif.: Stanford University Press, 2002.

Hughes, Kevin L. "Schools for Scandal: A Response to Michael Purcell." In *The Experience of God: A Postmodern Response*, edited by Kevin Hart and Barbara Wall, 130–35. New York: Fordham University Press, 2005.

Hume, David. *An Enquiry Concerning Human Understanding*. Indianapolis: Hackett Publishing, 1993.

————. *An Inquiry Concerning the Principles of Morals.* Old Chelsea Station, N.Y.: Cosimo Inc., 2006.

Irenaeus of Lyons. *Against the Heresies.* In *Irenaeus of Lyons*, translated by Robert M. Grant, 55–187. London: Routledge, 1997.

Irigaray, Luce. *The Forgetting of Air in Martin Heidegger.* Translated by Mary Beth Mader. Austin: University of Texas Press, 1999.

Irvine, Martin. *The Making of Textual Culture: "Grammatica" and Literary Theory 350–1100.* Cambridge: Cambridge University Press, 1994.

Jabès, Edmond. *The Book of Questions.* Vol. 2, *The Book of Yukel.* Translated by Rosmarie Waldrop. Middletown, Conn.: Wesleyan University Press, 1991.

————. *The Book of Resemblances.* Vol. 3, *The Ineffaceable, the Unperceived.* Translated by Rosmarie Waldrop. Middletown, Conn.: Wesleyan University Press, 1992.

————. *La mémoire des mots: Comment je lis Paul Celan.* Chitillon-sous-Bagneux: Fourbis, 1990.

James, Ian. "Evaluating Klossowski's *Le Baphomet.*" *Diacritics* 35:1 (Spring 2005): 119–35.

————. *Pierre Klossowski: The Persistence of a Name.* Oxford: Legenda, 2000.

Janouch, Gustav. *Conversations with Kafka.* Translated by Goronwy Rees. New York: New Directions, 1971.

Jordan, Mark D. "Liturgies of Repetition: A Preface to the Prologue of the *Baphomet.*" *Studies in the Literary Imagination* 41, no. 2 (2009): 63–82.

————. "Words and Word: Incarnation and Signification in Augustine's *De doctrina Christiana.*" *Augustinian Studies* 11 (1980): 177–96.

Kafka, Franz. *The Blue Octavo Notebooks / Reflections on Sin, Suffering, Hope, and the True Way.* Edited by Max Brod. Translated by Ernst Kaiser and Eithne Wilkins. Cambridge, Mass.: Exact Change, 1991.

Kant, Immanuel. *Critique of Pure Reason.* Translated by Werner S. Pluhar. Indianapolis: Hackett Publishing, 1996.

————. *Groundwork of the Metaphysics of Morals.* Translated by Mary Gregor. Cambridge: Cambridge University Press, 1997.

Kearney, Richard. *The God Who May Be.* Bloomington: Indiana University Press, 2001.

Keller, Catherine. "The Cloud of the Impossible: Feminist Theology, Cosmology and Cusa." Presented at Harvard University, March 22, 2007. Accessed at http://users.drew.edu/ckeller/essays-download.html.

————. *The Cloud of the Impossible: Theological Entanglements.* Forthcoming.

————. *The Face of the Deep: A Theology of Becoming.* London: Routledge, 2003.

————. "Good Power." Presented at Yale Divinity School, 2007. Accessed at http://users.drew.edu/ckeller/essays-download.html.

———. *On the Mystery: Discerning Divinity in Process*. Minneapolis: Fortress Press, 2008.

Kelly, J. N. D. *Early Christian Creeds*. London: Longmans Green, 1950; 3rd ed., 1951.

———. *Early Christian Doctrines*. London: Adam and Charles Black, 1958.

Kennedy, Daniel. "Sacraments." In the *Catholic Encyclopedia*, vol. 13. New York: Robert Appleton Company, 1912. Online edition by Kevin Knight, 2009. Accessed at http://www.newadvent.org/cathen/13295a.htm.

Kierkegaard, Søren. *Works of Love*. Translated by Howard Hong. New York: Harper Perennial, 2009.

Kirkland, Sean. *The Ontology of Socratic Questioning in Plato's Early Dialogues*. Albany: State University of New York Press, 2012.

Klossowski, Pierre. *The Baphomet*. Translated by Sophie Hawkes and Stephen Sartarelli. New York: Marsilio Publishers, 1998.

———. *Nietzsche and the Vicious Circle*. Translated by Daniel W. Smith. Chicago: University of Chicago Press, 1998.

———. "Protase et apodose." *L'arc* 43 (1970): 8–20.

———. "Qui est mon prochain?" *Esprit* (December 1938): 402–23.

———. *Sade My Neighbor*. Translated by Alphonso Lingis. Evanston Ill.: Northwestern University Press, 1991.

———. *Such a Deathly Desire*. Translated by Russell Ford. Albany: State University of New York Press, 2007.

———. *La Vocation Suspendue*. Paris: Gallimard, 1950.

Kojève, Alexandre. *Introduction to the Reading of Hegel: Lectures on the Phenomenology of Spirit*. Assembled by Raymond Queneau. Edited by Alan Bloom. Translated by James H. Nichols, Jr. Ithaca, N.Y.: Cornell University Press, 1980.

Kripke, Saul. *Naming and Necessity*. Cambridge: Harvard University Pres, 1981.

Leahy, David G. "Cuspidal Limits of Infinity: Secret of the Incarnate Self in Levinas." In *Rending the Veil: Concealment and Secrecy in the History of Religion*, edited by Elliot R. Wolfson, 209–48. New York: Seven Bridges Press, 1999.

Levinas, Emmanuel. "Desacralization and Disenchantment." In *Nine Talmudic Readings*, translated by Annette Aronowicz, 136–60. Bloomington: Indiana University Press, 1990.

———. *Difficult Freedom: Essays on Judaism*. Translated by Seán Hand. Baltimore: Johns Hopkins University Press, 1997.

———. *Ethics and Infinity: Conversations with Philipe Nemo*. Translated by Richard A. Cohen. Pittsburgh: Duquesne University Press, 1985.

———. *Otherwise than Being, or Beyond Essence*. Translated by Alphonso Lingis. Pittsburgh: Duquesne University Press, 1998.

———. "Reality and Its Shadow." Translated by Alphonso Lingis. In *Collected Philosophical Papers*, 1–13. Pittsburgh: Duquesne University Press, 1998.

———. *Time and the Other*. Translated by Richard Cohen. Pittsburgh: Duquesne University Press, 1990.

———. *Totality and Infinity: An Essay on Exteriority*. Translated by Alphonso Lingis. Pittsburgh: Duquesne University Press, 1969.

Lombard, Peter. *The Sentences*. Book 4, *On the Doctrine of Signs*. Translated by Giulio Silano. Toronto: Pontifical Institute of Medieval Studies, 2010.

Lombardi, Elena. *The Syntax of Desire: Language and Love in Augustine, the Modistae, Dante*. Toronto: University of Toronto Press, 2007.

Lossky, Vladimir. "Elements of 'Negative Theology' in the Thought of St. Augustine." *St. Vladimir's Theological Quarterly* 21, no. 2 (1977): 67–85.

Luther, Martin. *Reformation Writings of Martin Luther*. Translated by B. L. Woolf. Cambridge: Lutterworth Press, 1952.

———. "A Treatise Concerning the Blessed Sacrament of the Holy and True Body of Christ and Concerning the Brotherhoods." In *Works of Martin Luther*, 2:5–33. Philadelphia: A.J. Holman Co., 1915.

Maas, Frans. "Divine Omnipotence in the View of Nicholas of Cusa." In *Conflict and Reconciliation: Perspectives on Nicholas of Cusa*, edited by Inigo Bocken, 177–87. Leiden: Brill, 2004.

MacKendrick, Karmen. "Carthage Didn't Burn Hot Enough: St. Augustine's Divine Seduction." In *Toward a Theology of Eros*, edited by Virginia Burrus and Catherine Keller, 205–17. New York: Fordham University Press, 2006.

———. *Counterpleasures*. Albany: State University of New York Press, 1999.

———. *Fragmentation and Memory: Meditations on Christian Doctrine*. New York: Fordham University Press, 2008.

———. *Immemorial Silence*. Albany: State University of New York Press, 2001.

———. "The Temporality of Praise." In *Relocating Praise: Literary Modalities and Rhetorical Contexts*, edited by Alice den Otter, 19–32. Toronto: Canadian Scholars Press, 2000.

———. *Word Made Skin: Figuring Language at the Surface of Flesh*. New York: Fordham University Press, 2004.

Mackey, Louis. *Peregrinations of the Word: Essays in Medieval Philosophy*. Ann Arbor: University of Michigan Press, 1997.

Malamud, Martha. "Writing Original Sin." *Journal of Early Christian Studies* 10, no. 3 (2002): 329–60.

Marcus Aurelius. *Meditations*. Translated by G. M. A. Grube. Indianapolis: Hackett Publishing, 1983.

Markus, Robert A. *Signs and Meanings: World and Text in Ancient Christianity.* Liverpool: Liverpool University Press, 1996.

Martin, James. "A Saint's Dark Night." *New York Times Magazine.* August 29, 2007. Accessed at http://www.nytimes.com/2007/08/29/opinion/29martin.html ?_r=1&em&ex=1188532800&en=9e59f11fbd412882&ei=5087%0A.

Martos, Joseph. *Doors to the Sacred: A Historical Introduction to Sacraments in the Catholic Church.* New York: Image Books, 1982.

McCabe, Herbert. "Aquinas on the Trinity." In *Silence and the Word: Negative Theology and Incarnation,* edited by Oliver Davies and Denys Turner, 76–93. Cambridge: Cambridge University Press, 2002.

McDonough, S. M. *YHWH at Patmos: Rev. 1:4 in Its Hellenistic and Early Jewish Setting.* Tübingen: Mohr Siebeck, 1999.

McIntosh, Mark A. "The Formation of Mind: Trinity and Understanding in Newman." In *Silence and the Word: Negative Theology and Incarnation,* edited by Oliver Davies and Denys Turner, 136–58. Cambridge: Cambridge University Press, 2002.

McNulty, Tracy. "Hospitality after the Death of God." *Diacritics* 35, no. 1 (Spring 2005): 75–98.

Mensch, James R. "Prayer as Kenosis." In *The Phenomenology of Prayer,* edited by Bruce Ellis Benson and Norman Wirzba, 63–72. New York: Fordham University Press, 2005.

Merleau-Ponty, Maurice. *The Visible and the Invisible.* Translated by Alphonso Lingis. Evanston, Ill: Northwestern University Press, 1969.

Miles, Margaret. *Plotinus on Body and Beauty: Society, Philosophy and Religion in Third-Century Rome.* Oxford: Wiley-Blackwell, 1999.

Mill, John Stuart. *Utilitarianism and On Liberty: Including the "Essay on Bentham" and Selections from the Writings of Jeremy Bentham and John Austin.* Edited by Mary Warnock. Malden, Mass.: Wiley-Blackwell, 2003.

Miller, David L. *Gods and Games: Toward a Theology of Play.* New York: Harper and Row, 1970.

———. "Theopoetry or Theopoetics?" *CrossCurrents* 60, no. 1 (March 2010): 6–23.

Miller, J. Hillis. "Ariadne's Thread: Repetition and the Narrative Line." *Critical Inquiry* 3 (1976): 57–77.

Miller, Patricia Cox. "'Pleasure of the Text, Text of Pleasure': Eros and Language in Origen's Commentary on the *Song of Songs.*" *Journal of the American Academy of Religion* 54, no. 2 (1986): 241–53.

———. *The Poetry of Thought in Late Antiquity.* Aldershot: Ashgate Publishing, 2001.

————. "'Words with an Alien Voice': Gnostics, Scripture, and Canon." *Journal of the American Academy of Religion* 57, no. 3 (1989): 459–83.

Moore, Sebastian, O.S.B. "The Crisis of an Ethic Without Desire." In *Theology and Sexuality: Classic and Contemporary Readings*, edited by Eugene Rogers, 157–69. Oxford: Wiley-Blackwell, 2002.

Moser, Paul K. *The Elusive God: Reorienting Religious Epistemology.* Cambridge: Cambridge University Press, 2008.

Moyaert, Paul. "The Phenomenology of Eros: A Reading of *Totality and Infinity* IVB." In *The Face of the Other and the Trace of God: Essays on the Philosophy of Emmanuel Levinas*, edited by Jeffrey Bloechl, 30–42. New York: Fordham, 2000.

Nancy, Jean-Luc. *The Birth to Presence.* Translated by Brian Holmes et al. Stanford, Calif.: Stanford University Press, 1993.

————. *Dis-Enclosure: The Deconstruction of Christianity.* Translated by Bettina Bergo, Gabriel Malenfant, and Michael B. Smith. New York: Fordham University Press, 2008.

————. "The Inoperative Community." Translated by Christopher Fynsk. In *The Inoperative Community*, edited by Peter Connor, 1–42. Minneapolis: University of Minnesota Press, 1991.

————. *Listening.* Translated by Charlotte Mandell. New York: Fordham University Press, 2007.

————. "Of Divine Places." Translated by Michael Holland. In *The Inoperative Community*, edited by Peter Connor, 110–50. Minneapolis: University of Minnesota Press, 1991.

Nicholas of Cusa. *A Concise Introduction to the Philosophy of Nicholas of Cusa.* Edited and translated by Jasper Hopkins. Minneapolis: University of Minnesota Press, 1978.

————. *Nicholas of Cusa: Selected Spiritual Writings.* Translated by H. Lawrence Bond. Mahwah, N.J.: Paulist Press, 1997.

Niebuhr, H. Richard. *The Responsible Self: An Essay in Christian Moral Philosophy.* New York: Harper and Row, 1963.

Nietzsche, Friedrich. *The Anti-Christ.* Translated by R. J. Hollingdale. New York: Penguin Books, 1977.

————. *Beyond Good and Evil.* Translated by Walter Kaufmann. New York: Vintage Books, 1966.

————. *The Gay Science.* Translated by Walter Kaufmann. New York: Vintage Books, 1974.

————. Letter to Peter Gast, August 14, 1881. In *Selected Letters of Friedrich Nietzsche*, edited by Christopher Middleton, 178–79. Indianapolis: Hackett Publishing, 1996.

————. *Thus Spoke Zarathustra*. Translated by Graham Parkes. Oxford: Oxford University Press, 2005.

————. *The Will to Power* (posthumous collection). Translated by Walter Kaufmann and R. J. Hollingdale. New York: Random House, 1968.

Nolan, Joseph T. "Do We Still Need the Sacraments?" In *The Sacraments: Readings in Contemporary Sacramental Theology*, edited by Michael J. Taylor, S.J., 3–17. Staten Island, N.Y.: Alba House, 1981.

Noth, Winfried. *Handbook of Semiotics*. Bloomington: Indiana University Press, 1990.

Nussbaum, Martha. *Love's Knowledge: Essays on Philosophy and Literature*. New York: Oxford University Press, 1990.

O'Byrne, Anne. "Body Singular Plural." Delivered at International Association for Philosophy and Literature, 2004.

O'Connor, Flannery. "Revelation." In *The Complete Stories*, 488–509. New York: Farrar, Strauss and Giroux, 1971.

O'Donnell, James J. *Augustine, Confessions: Text and Commentary*. Oxford: Oxford University Press, 1992.

————. "Bible." In *Augustine Through the Ages: An Encyclopedia*, edited by Allan D. Fitzgerald, 100--103. Grand Rapids, Mich.: William B. Eerdmans, 1999.

Okrent, Arika. *In the Land of Invented Languages: Esperanto Rock Stars, Klingon Poets, Loglan Lovers, and the Mad Dreamers Who Tried to Build a Perfect Language*. New York: Spiegel and Grau, 2009.

Online Etymology Dictionary. Accessed at http://www.etymonline.com/.

Origen. *Contra Celsum*. Accessed at http://www.ccel.org/fathers2/ANF-04/anf04 -55.htm#P7780_1841901.

————. *The Song of Songs: Commentary and Homilies*. Translated by R. P. Lawson. New York: The Newman Press, 1957.

Osborne, Kenan B., O.F.M. *Sacramental Theology: A General Introduction*. Mahwah, N.J.: Paulist Press, 1988.

Peirce, Charles Sanders. *Collected Papers*. Edited by Charles Hartshorne, Paul Weiss, and Arthur W. Burks. Cambridge: Harvard University Press, 1933.

Perpich, Diane. "Sensible Subjects: Levinas and Irigaray on Incarnation and Ethics." In *Addressing Levinas*, edited by Eric Sean Nelson, Antje Kapust, and Kent Still, 296–309. Evanston, Ill.: Northwestern University Press, 2005.

Pike, Nelson. "Divine Omniscience and Voluntary Action." *Philosophical Review* 74 (January 1965): 27–46.

————. *God and Timelessness*. New York: Schocken Books, 1970.

Plantinga, Alvin. "Intellectual Sophistication and Basic Belief in God." *Faith and Philosophy* 3 (1986): 306–12.

———. *The Nature of Necessity*. Oxford: Oxford University Press, 1974.

Plato. *Apology*. In *Plato: Euthyphro, Apology, Crito*. Translated by F. J. Church. New York: Prentice Hall, 1987.

———. *Cratylus*. Translated by Benjamin Jowett. San Diego: Icon Classics, 2008.

———. *Meno and Phaedo*. Edited by David Sedley. Translated by Alex Long. Cambridge: Cambridge University Press, 2011.

———. *Phaedrus*. Translated by Alexander Nehamas and Paul Woodruff. Indianapolis: Hackett Publishing, 1995.

———. *Republic*. Translated by G. M. A. Grube. Indianapolis: Hackett Publishing, 1992.

———. *Symposium*. Translated by Alexander Nehamas and Paul Woodruff. Indianapolis: Hackett Publishing, 1989.

Plotinus. *The Enneads*. Translated by Stephen MacKenna. Burdett, N.Y.: Larson Publications, 2004.

Porphyry. "The Life of Plotinus and the Arrangement of His Work." In Plotinus, *The Enneads*, translated by Stephen MacKenna, cii–cxxv. Burdett, N.Y.: Larson Publications, 2004.

Pourrat, P. *Theology of the Sacraments: A Study in Positive Theology*. St. Louis, Mo.: B. Herder, 1910.

Powers, Joseph M. "Eucharist, Mystery of Faith and Love." In *The Sacraments: Readings in Contemporary Sacramental Theology*, edited by Michael J. Taylor, S.J., 117–27. Staten Island, N.Y.: Alba House, 1981.

Pranger, M. B. *The Artificiality of Christianity: Essays on the Poetics of Monasticism*. Stanford, Calif.: Stanford University Press, 2003.

———. *Eternity's Ennui: Temporality, Perseverance and Voice in Augustine and Western Literature*. Leiden: Brill, 2010.

———. "The Unfathomability of Sincerity: On the Seriousness of Augustine's *Confessions*." In *Actas do Congresso International As Confissoes de santo Agostinho 1600 Anos Depois: Presenca e Actualidade*, 193–242. Lisbon: Universidade Catolica Editora, 2002.

Purcell, Michael. "When God Hides His Face: The Inexperience of God." In *The Experience of God: A Postmodern Response*, edited by Kevin Hart and Barbara Wall, 113–29. New York: Fordham University Press, 2005.

Rahner, Karl. "How to Receive a Sacrament and Mean It." In *The Sacraments: Readings in Contemporary Sacramental Theology*, edited by Michael J. Taylor, S.J., 71–80. Staten Island, N.Y.: Alba House, 1981.

Ravaisson, F. *La philosophie en France au XIXième siècle*. Edited by P. Millot. Paris: Fayard, 1984.

Rilke, Rainer-Maria. *Duino Elegies and the Sonnets to Orpheus.* Translated by Stephen Mitchell. New York: Vintage, 2009.

———. *New Poems [1907].* Translated by Edward Snow. New York: North Point Press, 1984.

———. *The Selected Poetry of Rainer-Maria Rilke.* Translated by Stephen Mitchell. New York: Vintage, 1989.

Rist, John M. *Augustine: Ancient Thought Baptized.* Cambridge: Cambridge University Press, 1996.

Robbins, Jill. "Who Prays? Levinas on Irremissible Responsibility." In *The Phenomenology of Prayer,* edited by Bruce Ellis Benson and Norman Wirzba, 32–49. New York: Fordham University Press, 2005.

Rubenstein, Mary-Jane. *Strange Wonder: The Closure of Metaphysics and the Opening of Awe.* New York: Columbia University Press, 2008.

Sade, D. A. F. *Philosophy in the Bedroom.* Translated by Joachim Neugroschel. New York: Penguin Books, 2006.

Sallis, John. "Nietzsche's Platonism." In *Nietzsche: Critical Assessments,* edited by Daniel W. Conway, 292–302. London: Routledge, 1998.

Saussure, Ferdinand de. *Course in General Linguistics.* Translated by Wade Baskin. New York: Columbia University Press, 2011.

Scholem, Gershom. *Judaica.* Frankfurt am Main: Suhrkamp, 1973.

Schopenhauer, Arthur. *The World as Will and Representation.* Translated by E. F. J. Payne. Mineola, N.Y.: Dover, 1966.

Schrag, Calvin O. *God as Otherwise than Being.* Evanston, Ill.: Northwestern University Press, 2002.

Smith, D. Moody. *Abingdon New Testament Commentary: John.* Nashville: Abingdon Press, 1999.

Smith, Wilfred Cantwell. *Faith and Belief.* Princeton, N.J.: Princeton University Press, 1979.

Spender, Stephen. "Remembering Eliot." In *T. S. Eliot: The Man and His Work,* edited by Allen Tate, 38–64. New York: Delacorte Press, 1966.

Stanford Encyclopedia of Philosophy. http://plato.stanford.edu.

Stevens, Wallace. "Large Red Man Reading." In *The Collected Poems of Wallace Stevens,* 423–24. New York: Vintage Books, 1982.

Stroumsa, G. G. "A Nameless God: Judaeo-Christian and Gnostic 'Theologies of the Name.'" In *The Image of the Judaeo-Christians in Ancient Jewish and Christian Literature,* edited by P. J. Tomson and D. Lambers-Petry, 230–43. Tübingen: Mohr-Siebeck, 2003.

Swinburne, Richard. *Faith and Reason.* Oxford: Oxford University Press, 2005.

Taylor, Michael J., S.J., ed. *The Sacraments: Readings in Contemporary Sacramental Theology*. Staten Island, N.Y.: Alba House, 1981.

Teresa of Avila. *The Collected Works of St. Teresa of Avila*. Translated by Kieran Kavanaugh and Otilio Rodríguez. Washington, D.C.: ICS Publications, 1976.

Thomas Aquinas. *Summa Contra Gentiles*. Translated by Anton Charles Pegis. Notre Dame, Ind: Notre Dame University Press, 1991.

———. *The Summa Theologica of St. Thomas Aquinas*. Second and Revised Edition. Translated by the Fathers of the English Dominican Province. Allen, Tex.: Christian Classics, 1981. Online Edition by Kevin Knight, 2008. Accessed at http://newadvent.org/summa/.

———. "Truth," Questions 21–29. Translated by Robert W. Schmidt, S.J. Chicago: Regnery Company, 1954. Online edition by Joseph Kennedy, O.P. Accessed at http://dhspriory.org/thomas/QDdeVer26.htm.

Tourage, Mahdi. "The Hermeneutics of Eroticism in the Poetry of Rumi." *Comparative Studies of South Asia, Africa and the Middle East* 25, no. 3 (2005): 600–16.

Turner, Denys. "Apophaticism, Idolatry and the Claims of Reason." In *Silence and the Word: Negative Theology and Incarnation*, edited by Oliver Davies and Denys Turner, 1–34. Cambridge: Cambridge University Press, 2002.

———. *Faith Seeking*. London: SCM Press, 2002.

Vance, Eugene. *Mervelous Signals: Poetics and Sign Theory in the Middle Ages*. Lincoln: University of Nebraska Press, 1986.

Vessey, Mark. "Theory, or the Dream of the Book (Mallarmé to Blanchot)." In *The Early Christian Book*, edited by William E. Klingshirn and Linda Safran, 241–73. Washington, D.C.: Catholic University of America Press, 2007.

Viefhues-Bailey, Ludger. "Displacing Bodies: The Eucharist, Ritualization, and Resistance." Delivered at Calvin College, 2008.

Viladesau, Richard. "Theosis and Beauty." *Theology Today* 65, no. 2 (July 2008): 180–90.

Ward, Graham. "In the Daylight Forever? Language and Silence." In *Silence and the Word: Negative Theology and Incarnation*, edited by Oliver Davies and Denys Turner, 159–84. Cambridge: Cambridge University Press, 2002.

Wear, Sarah Klitenic, and John M. Dillon. *Dionysius the Areopagite and the Neoplatonist Tradition: Despoiling the Hellenes*. Aldershot: Ashgate, 2007.

Webb, Stephen H. "The Rhetoric of Excess: A Christian Theological Response to Levinas." *Modern Theology* 15, no. 1 (1999): 1–16.

Weber, Max. *Essays in Sociology*. Translated and edited by H. H. Gerth and C. Wright Mills. New York: Oxford University Press, 1946.

Weil, Simone. *Gravity and Grace*. Translated by Emma Crawford and Mario van der Ruhr. New York: Routledge, 2007.

————. *Waiting for God*. Translated by Emma Crawford. New York: Harper Perennial, 1992.

Westphal, Merold. "Prayer as the Posture of the Decentered Self." In *The Phenomenology of Prayer*, edited by Bruce Ellis Benson and Norman Wirzba, 13–31. New York: Fordham University Press, 2005.

Wetzel, James. "Body Double: Saint Augustine and the Sexualized Will." In *Weakness of Will from Plato to the Present*, edited by Tobias Hoffmann, 58–81. Washington, D.C.: Catholic University Press, 2008.

————. "Snares of Truth: Augustine on Free Will and Predestination." In *Augustine and His Critics: Essays in Honour of Gerald Bonner*, edited by Robert Dodaro and George Lawless, 124–41. London: Routledge, 2000.

Wicks, Jared, S.J. "The Sacraments: A Catechism for Today." In *The Sacraments: Readings in Contemporary Sacramental Theology*, edited by Michael J. Taylor, S.J., 19–30. Staten Island, N.Y.: Alba House, 1981.

Williams, R. D. "Language, Reality and Desire in Augustine's *De Doctrina.*" *Literature and Theology* 3, no. 2–3 (1989): 138–50.

Wirzba, Norman. "Attention and Responsibility: The Work of Prayer." In *The Phenomenology of Prayer*, edited by Bruce Ellis Benson and Norman Wirzba, 88–100. New York: Fordham University Press, 2005.

Wittgenstein, Ludwig. *Philosophical Investigations*. Translated by G. E. M. Anscombe, P. M. S. Hacker, and Joachim Schulte. Oxford: Blackwell, 2009.

Wittgenstein, Ludwig, R. G. Bosanquet, and Cora Diamond. *Wittgenstein's Lectures on the Foundations of Mathematics, Cambridge, 1939: From the Notes of R. G. Bosanquet, Norman Malcolm, Rush Rhees, and Yorick Smythies*. Ithaca, N.Y.: Cornell University Press, 1976.

Wolfson, Elliot R. "Assaulting the Border: Kabbalistic Traces in the Margins of Derrida." *Journal of the American Academy of Religion* 70, no. 3 (Sept. 2002): 475–514.

————. "The Body in the Text: A Kabbalistic Theory of Embodiment." *The Jewish Quarterly Review* 95, no. 3 (Summer 2005): 479–500.

————. *Circle in the Square: Studies in the Use of Gender in Kabbalistic Symbolism*. Albany: State University of New York Press, 1995.

————. "Facing the Effaced: Mystical Eschatology and the Idealistic Orientation in the Thought of Franz Rosenzweig." *Journal for the History of Modern Theology* 4 (1997): 39–81.

————. "From Sealed Book to Open Text: Time, Memory and Narrativity in Kabbalistic Hermeneutics." In *Interpreting Judaism in a Postmodern Age*, edited by Steven Kepnes, 145–78. New York: New York University Press, 1996.

————. "Inscribed in the Book of the Living: *Gospel of Truth* and Jewish Christology." *Journal for the Study of Judaism* 38 (2007): 234–71.

————. "Judaism and Incarnation: The Imaginal Body of God." In *Christianity in Jewish Terms*, edited by Tivka Frymer-Kensky, David Novak, Peter Ochs, David Fox Sandmel, and Michael A. Signer, 239–54. Boulder, Colo.: Westview Press, 2000.

————. *Language, Eros, Being: Kabbalistic Hermeneutics and Poetic Imagination*. New York: Fordham University Press, 2004.

————. "Occultation of the Feminine and the Body of Secrecy in Medieval Kabbalah." In *Rending the Veil: Concealment and Revelation of Secrets in the History of Religions*, edited by Elliot R. Wolfson. New York: Seven Bridges Press, 1999: 112–54.

————. *Open Secret: Postmessianic Messianism and the Mystical Revision of Menaḥem Mendel Schneerson*. New York: Columbia University Press, 2009.

————. "Secrecy, Modesty, and the Feminine: Kabbalistic Traces in the Thought of Levinas." In *The Exorbitant: Emmanuel Levinas Between Jews and Christians*, edited by Kevin Hart and Michael A. Signer, 52–73. New York: Fordham University Press, 2010.

Woltersdorff, Nicholas. *Divine Discourse: Philosophical Reflections on the Claim That God Speaks*. Cambridge: Cambridge University Press, 1995.

Wyschogrod, Edith. "Language and Alterity in the Thought of Levinas." In *The Cambridge Companion to Levinas*, edited by Simon Critchley and Robert Bernasconi, 195–98. Cambridge: Cambridge University Press, 2002.

Zwingli, Ulrich. *Commentary on True and False Religion*. Jamestown, N.Y.: Labyrinth Press, 1981.

Index

Rist, John M., 11, 90, 96n76, 184, 184n42, 185n43
Robbins, Jill, 142n3
Romans (Biblical book), 174
Robert, William, 25n105
Rosenzweig, Franz, 158n80
Rubenstein, MaryJane, 55n72, 131, 135–36

"The Sacrament of Marriage" (Boff), 8n23
Sacramental Theology: A General Introduction (Osborne), 76n14, 77n17, 78n19
"The Sacraments: A Catechism for Today", 94n74
The Sacraments: Readings in Contemporary Sacramental Theology, 8n23, 78n20, 94n74
The Sentences (Lombard), 73, 81n34
The Space of Literature (Blanchot), 143n9
The Step Not Beyond (Blanchot), 133n103
Sade, D. A. F., 58n82, 108n30, 207, 214
Sade My Neighbor (Klossowski), 157n72, 207, 216n60
"A Saint's Dark Night" (Martin), 38n16
"A Saint of One's Own: Emmanuel Levinas, Eliezer ben Hyrcanus, and Eulalia of Mérida" (Burrus), 86n47, 119n62
Sallis, John, 211n35
"Sauf le Nom" (Derrida), 4n8, 9n27, 10n31, 19n78, 36n13, 129n88, 130n89, 149n39, 156, 157n71, 207n7
Saussure, Ferdinand de, 10, 30
Saving Shame: Saints, Martyrs, and Other Abject Subjects (Burrus), 178n19–20
Scholem, Gershom, 16n69
"Schools for Scandal: A Response to Michael Purcell" (Hughes), 159n81–85
Schopenhauer, Arthur, 211
Schrag, Calvin O., 206n2
The Search for the Perfect Language (Eco), 197n85
"Secrecy, Modesty, and the Feminine: Kabbalistic Traces in the Thought of Levinas" (Wolfson), 123n72–73, 130n94–95
Seduction (Baudrillard), 5n13, 87n48–50, 88n51, 89n54, 97n81, 98n82
Selected Poems and Fragments (Hölderlin), 24n102, 142n6, 147n27
The Selected Poetry of Rainer Maria Rilke, 125n77, 126n79, 138n119–20
Selected Spiritual Writings (Nicholas of Cusa), 53n67, 54n69, 209n27
Semiotics and the Philosophy of Language (Eco), 91n67
"Sensible Subjects: Levinas and Irigaray on Incarnation and Ethics" (Perpich), 130n94
Sermon 30 on the New Testament (Augustine), 153n57
Sermon on Acts 9:8 (Eckhart), 206, 206n4

Sermon on Ecclesiasticus 25:30 (Eckhart), 210n33
Signs and Meanings: World and Text in Ancient Christianity (Markus), 8n20, 10n36, 11n40, 13n53, 14n54–55, 17n72, 26n108, 26n110, 86n46, 89n57, 96n77, 177n18, 179n28
"The Singular and the Other at the Limits of Language in the Post–Holocaust Poetry of Edmond Jabès and Paul Celan" (Franke), 154n52
Smith, D. Moody, 183, 192n62
Smith, Wilfred Cantwell, 40–42, 40n26, 41n28, 46, 56, 62
Smock, Ann, 147n29, 147n31, 148, 154
"Snares of Truth: Augustine on Free Will and Predestination" (Wetzel), 132n99, 175n11
The Song of Songs: Commentary and Homilies (Origen), 185
"Soundings: Towards a Theological Poetics of Silence" (Davies), 148n35, 149n37
Spender, Stephen, 45n41
Stein, Gertrude, 12, 185
Stevens, Wallace, 137
Stories and Texts for Nothing (Beckett), 151
Strange Wonder: The Closure of Metaphysics and the Opening of Awe (Rubenstein), 55n72, 131n97, 136n113–14
Stroumsa, G. G., 25n106
Such a Deathly Desire (Klossowski), 212n42, 214n52, 217n66
Summa Contra Gentiles (Thomas Aquinas), 207n12
Summa Theologica (Thomas Aquinas), 34n2, 34n4–5, 46n44, 73n5, 81, 81n34, 82n35–36, 208n19. See also Summa Theologiae
Summa Theologiae, 81, 81n34, 108n19. See also Summa Theologica
"Suspicions of Suffering" (Gibbs), 130n92
Swinburne, Richard, 47n48
Symbol and Sacrament: A Sacramental Reinterpretation of Christian Existence (Chauvet), 76n16
Symposium (Plato), 104–5, 104n9–10
The Syntax of Desire: Language and Love in Augustine, the Modistae, Dante (Lombardi), 8n21, 10n33, 13n51, 14n56, 18n76, 20n84, 72n4

The Teacher (Augustine), 11, 11n41, 11n43–45, 12n46–47, 13, 13n50, 20, 91, 90n59, 91n66, 201
"The Temporality of Praise" (MacKendrick), 155n67
Teresa of Avila, 215–16
Thérèse of Lisieux, 38
Theron, Stephen, 50
Theology of the Sacraments: A Study in Positive Theology, 83n41